A Future for
REGIONAL
AUSTRALIA
Escaping Global Misfortune

This book interprets the predicament faced by regional Australians from their own perspective and proposes a means by which they can act together to find a secure future under globalisation. It argues that neoliberalism in combination with its 'real world' effects in economic policy are driving regional Australia further into social, environmental and economic decay. Gray and Lawrence advocate a new kind of regionalism with broad objectives for people to pursue. This takes discussion about rural and regional policies out of the contexts of trade and industry policies and into the realm of the social and political. Ideas developed throughout the book are drawn from rural sociology, community studies, rural geography, political economy and regional studies. The book will be of great interest to all concerned about the future of regional Australia, and will make a lively and relevant text for students studying the social sciences in the countryside or in the major cities.

Ian Gray is an Associate Professor at Charles Sturt University, where he is an Associate Director of its Centre for Rural Social Research. He is the author of *Politics in Place* (Cambridge University Press, 1992).

Geoffrey Lawrence is the Professor of Sociology and Executive Director of the Institute for Sustainable Development at Central Queensland University. Among his many publications are *Environment, Society and Natural Resource Management* (2001) and *Capitalism and the Countryside: The Rural Crisis in Australia* (1987).

A Future for
REGIONAL
AUSTRALIA

Escaping Global Misfortune

IAN GRAY AND GEOFFREY LAWRENCE

CAMBRIDGE
UNIVERSITY PRESS

CAMBRIDGE UNIVERSITY PRESS
Cambridge, New York, Melbourne, Madrid, Cape Town,
Singapore, São Paulo, Delhi, Mexico City

Cambridge University Press
The Edinburgh Building, Cambridge CB2 8RU, UK

Published in the United States of America by Cambridge University Press, New York

www.cambridge.org
Information on this title: www.cambridge.org/9780521002271

First published 2001

A catalogue record for this publication is available from the British Library

National Library of Australia Cataloguing in Publication Data
Gray, I. W., 1951–.
A future for regional Australia: escaping global misfortune.
Bibliography.
Includes index.
ISBN 0 521 80753 0
ISBN 0 521 00227 3 (pbk.).
1. Regionalism – Australia. 2. Globalization.
3. Australia – Economic conditions.
I. Lawrence, G. A. (Geoffrey A.). II. Title.
330.994

ISBN 978-0-521-80753-1 Hardback
ISBN 978-0-521-00227-1 Paperback

Contents

Acknowledgements   viii
Glossary   ix
Map: Australia's Population Distribution   x

1   The Global Misfortune of Regional Australia   1
Global Misfortune   4
The Challenges   12
The Structure and Argument of this Book   13
Further Reading   14

2   Understanding Globalisation   16
Competing Conceptions of Globalisation   17
Features of Globalisation   20
Causes and Contradictions of Globalisation   25
Consequences of Globalisation for Farming in the Advanced Nations   31
Conclusion   34
Further Reading   35

3   People versus Policy   36
Old Thinking   38
People Suffering Change   41
The Poverty of Rational Action Theory   42
Social Power Relations   43
New (Reflexive) Thinking   45
Perspectives on Farming and 'The Rural'   48
Rural–Urban Relativities   49
Conclusion   50
Further Reading   51

4   The Social Transformation of Australian Farming   52
Restructuring Farming in Australia and Overseas   53
Social Restructuring   64
Conclusion   69
Further Reading   70

5   Voices from the Farm   **71**
Rural Ideology and Culture   72
Ideology and Power   74
Ideology and Restructuring   75
Australian Research Findings   79
Perceived Impacts of Restructuring   80
Perceptions of Causes   84
Conclusion   91
Further Reading   93

6   Regional Decline: Division amid Disadvantage   **94**
The Changing Spatial Distribution of Regional Population   95
Spatial Variation   97
Some Case Studies   98
Regional Social Conditions   99
Neoliberalism and Regional Economics   103
Policy Impacts   104
Postmodernity   109
The Transformation of Regional Policy   112
Conclusion   114
Further Reading   115

7   People Confronting Dependency   **116**
Economic Individualism   117
Some Regional Histories   119
The Relationship between Metropolitan and Regional Australia   124
Power and Interests   127
Community Resistance   128
The Presentation and Interpretation of Development Issues   131
Conclusion   135
Further Reading   136

8   Beyond Productivism and Environmental Degradation?   **137**
Colonial Agriculture: Compromising the Australian Landscape   138
The Entrenchment of Productivist Agriculture   141
Environmental Degradation in Australia   143
Genetic Engineering: The Latest in Productivist Agriculture?   146
Greening and the Organic Option   149
The Prospects for Sustainable Agriculture in Australia   151
Conclusion   157
Further Reading   158

9   New Cultures for Old   **159**
Rural Tradition in the Context of Globalisation   160
The Nature of Tradition   162
Theories of Detraditionalisation   163
Farming Tradition   163
The Detraditionalisation of Farming   164
Newcomers   165
Farm Succession and Inheritance   166
Pluriactivity   168
Farmer Knowledge   170
Values   171
The Trajectory of Change   172
The Detraditionalisation of Rural Community   173
Structural Differentiation   176
Cultural Differentiation   177
The End of Rural Australia?   179
Further Reading   180

10   The New Millennium: Pathways and Policies   **181**
Neoliberal Hegemony   182
Neoliberal Inconsistencies   184
Reflexivity and Social Change   185
Developing Alternatives to Productivism and
    Neoliberal Countrymindedness   187
Sustainable Regional Development   188
Some Limitations of Sustainable Regional Development   193
The Weakness of a Communitarian Solution   195
Institutional Incapacity   196
Prospects for Regional Autonomy   199
A Regional Solution   199
Regional Social Capital   201
Regional Government   202
Institutional Change   203
Equity and Sustainability   205
Further Reading   208

Bibliography   209
Index   243

Acknowledgements

We would like to thank the many people who have helped us with the preparation of this book and with the research which preceded it. Colleagues and present and former post-graduate students at Charles Sturt University (CSU) and Central Queensland University (CQU) were a critical but constructive audience helping us to formulate many of the ideas developed here. We wish to make special mention of the support provided by Tony Dunn, Emily Phillips, Helen Swan, Judith Crockett, Margie Thomson and Rachael Williams at CSU, and of Lynda Herbert-Cheshire and Stewart Lockie at CQU. Hugh Campbell (University of Otago), Vaughan Higgins (Monash University-Gippsland), Phil McMichael (Cornell University), Toby Miller (New York University), David Rowe (University of Newcastle), Jim McKay (University of Queensland), Mark Shucksmith (University of Aberdeen), Reidar Almas (University of Trondheim), Murray Knuttila and Wendee Kubik (University of Regina) provided very different, but insightful and invaluable, perspectives on culture, the state and globalisation. Jim Cavaye (Queensland Department of Primary Industries) and Allan Dale (Queensland Department of Natural Resources and Mines) helped us to recognise the potential for, but present limits to, the extension of regional policy in Australia. David Burch and Kristen Lyons (Griffith University), Bill Pritchard and Frank Stilwell (University of Sydney), Peter Smailes (University of Adelaide), Roger Epps (University of New England) and other members of the Australian-based Agri-food Research Network and the Institute of Australian Geographers have helped to mould our ideas over the past decade. Members, and associates, of CSU's Centre for Rural Social Research and CQU's Institute for Sustainable Regional Development provided very useful comments on draft material. We also recognise the importance to our research of the financial support received from the Australian Research Council, Land and Water Australia, the Rural Industries Research and Development Corporation and the Queensland Department of State Development. We thank these bodies for their continuing faith in the discipline of sociology and in our ability to conduct rural-based studies. (The arguments we develop in our analysis are not necessarily those of these organisations.) Peter Debus and the anonymous readers for Cambridge University Press helped us to reformulate sections of the book. Dania and Kimberley Lawrence assisted in the construction of the reference list and the index. We pay a special tribute to our partners Noelene Milliken and Dimity Lawrence for their encouragement and perseverance. Finally, we thank the many rural and regional Australians who have given their time to be involved in focus groups, in face-to-face interviews, in answering questionnaires, in phone conversations and in a variety of other activities which provided the empirical bases for our writings. This book is dedicated to you.

Glossary

Detraditionalisation – decline in the belief in a pre-given or 'natural' order of things. Individuals are called upon to exercise authority in the face of disorder and contingency, without 'certainty' of knowledge or outcomes.

Economic Rationalism – those economic policies and instruments that follow from neo-liberalism: market liberalisation, restrictive monetary policy, reduction in tariff levels, removal of the welfare net, privatisation of government utilities, and outsourcing.

Globalisation – a process through which space and time are compressed by technology, information flows, trade and power relations allowing distant actions to have increased significance at the local (regional) level.

Liberalism – a belief that individual decision-making and action (to fulfil particular needs and desires) provides the most appropriate/beneficial basis for the socio-political and economic organisation of society.

Neoliberalism – not only the above, but also that given the state has previously intervened in social and economic relations and is perceived to have 'corrupted' market signals, the best outcomes for society will be realised when the state retreats from involvement in economic and social matters.

Pluriactivity – diversification of farming work and business into alternative fields including employment and business development off the farm and the diversification of farming into new endeavours like tourism.

Reflexivity – people's ability to reflect upon/act in pursuit of their own and their community's interests. To be reflexive is to monitor actions, assess outcomes and alter behaviour.

Rurality – the distinguishing features of rural life and the condition of possessing them, which make differences apparent between urban and rural situations.

Subsumption – the process through which farmers lose autonomy, often informally and imperceptibly, as they come under the control of large-scale business and industry.

Photography credits

Murray Darling Basin Commission (MDBC) (chapters 1, 4, 8); News Limited (chapters 2, 5, 6, 9); MAFF Rural Division (chapter 3); Bendigo Bank (chapter 7); and Tourism New South Wales (chapter 10).

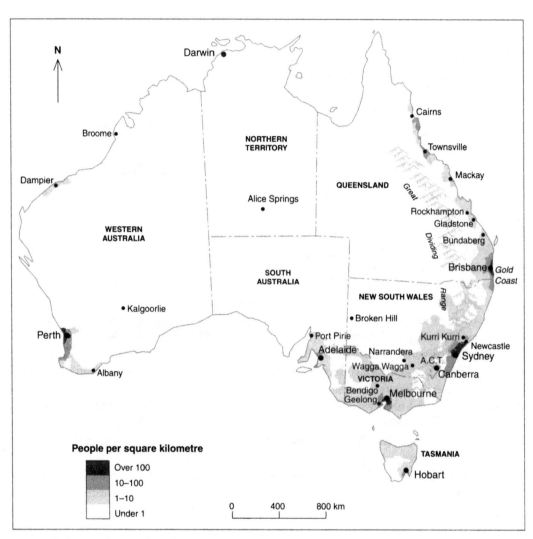

Australia's population distribution

To assess our nation's future in the new millennium, the *Australian* newspaper presented, in May 1999, a series of articles under the banner 'Australia Unlimited'. With some irony, the first feature was 'The Lost Cities of Our Hinterland'. The article contrasted the 'groaning infrastructure and social dysfunction' of the cities to the underdeveloped and 'lonely' towns of the inland. But the opportunity to establish a cause-effect relationship was lost, and there was no solution to either problem. Importantly, Australia could not afford the 'expansive vision' of large-scale national investment for its regions – something that would demand 'massive intervention'. That was not to suggest that the regions could be left alone. It was stressed that the regions would continue to falter unless governments did *something*! (*Weekend Australian*, 1–2 May 1999: 16).

What is being described here is both systems failure and the narrowing of choice. It highlights the present incapacity or unwillingness of journalists, planners, politicians and a host of social commentators to think beyond the limits imposed by current economic theory and the institutions of governance. It is symptomatic of the catatonic state of policy making at the opening of the new millennium. Article upon article has appeared since the depths of the rural 'crisis' of the mid-1980s reporting the impacts of the closure of banks, police stations, court houses and schools upon rural communities. Agencies as diverse as the Institute for Health and Welfare, the Ignatius Centre and the Productivity Commission have all acknowleged the problems of rural and regional Australia. The Deputy Prime Minister has hosted two 'regional summits' – one in Canberra in 1999 and one in Katherine in 2000. Headlines have dramatised the concerns and problems experienced by non-metropolitan Australians: 'Violence Worse In Rural Areas', 'Farming Families Take on Jobs Off the Land for Survival', 'Indigenous [health] Record Worst in Developed World', 'Great Dividing Rage', and so on. The sudden rise in the mid-1990s of the conservative fundamentalist One Nation Party and other right-wing populist groups, as an albeit occasionally significant political force in non-metropolitan Australia, obliges us to recognise the anger and despair felt by those whose economic opportunities have been seriously eroded. There is evidence of a feeling among rural and regional Australians that their voices have been ignored, and their demands for appropriate economic development have been treated with contempt. Moreover, it appears to them reasonable to conclude that nothing beyond tokenism is being done to address their problems.

We use the term 'regional' to refer to that part of Australia and its population which has a distinctive relationship, sometimes incompletely described as dependency, with metropolitan Australia. The metropoles are the State and Territory capital cities plus Canberra, in which the dominant activities of Australian political, social and economic life take place. We use the term 'rural' to describe those segments of Australia and its population whose economic and social lives are connected with, if not dependent upon, agriculture. This obviously covers farms and farmers but also includes villages, towns and cities which are socially, economically and culturally associated with agriculture. Under this definition, regional includes rural, in that the operation of Australia's agricultural system and the communities which sustain it is carried on within (in principle) the same metropolitan–regional relationship as that experienced by regional areas which are not so closely connected with agriculture, such as those with extensive extractive or manufacturing industries including cities like Newcastle, Wollongong, Geelong and Gladstone. We consider such cities, but our main focus is on those places which have a significant rural component in their economic and social constituencies. The situation of rural people, as those whose livelihood is related to farming whether they live on farms or in towns, will be discussed under the banner of 'regional issues' when the main factors for consideration stem from regionality. We use the term regional because we see the metropolitan–regional relationship as a fundamental issue for all non-metropolitan dwellers, whether or not they or their communities are associated with agriculture. We write for – and about – rural people but we see their regionality, which they have in common with all non-metropolitan dwellers, as the keystone of the system which substantially determines their lives and life-chances.

The state's continuing withdrawal from the support of family-farm based agriculture is leading to increased polarisation and to the intensification of the so-called 'farm problem' (income-poor but asset-rich producers who see no alternative to struggling on in agriculture) alongside deteriorating quality of life in country towns. In many places, government-employed service workers are being dismissed or being relocated, leaving those towns without an appropriate level of services, and without a secure middle-class base from which to draw leadership and direction. The aged and other disenfranchised groups in inland rural towns are especially disadvantaged by the removal of services. While governments and companies in the corporate sector are being targeted for having abandoned the needs of regional Australians there is no evidence that the policies which have led to regional disadvantage will be altered. Scapegoating has also emerged in some quarters. This might always have been present in countless conversations but now it exists in formal politics – with Indigenous groups and Asian migrants allegedly being responsible for Australia's economic problems.

This book identifies some of the ways in which people might come to terms with change and redirect it to serve their interests more effectively and equitably. It accepts that the interests of citizens are foremost and it maintains that their energies and initiative are ultimately the only possible sources of beneficial change. It also recognises that people cannot struggle against powerful forces alone. They must act collectively. And we believe that, if it is not the responsibility of government alone to carry out collective action, it is at least among government's responsibilities to create the conditions which make it possible for people to act together.

After carrying out a people-centred analysis of rural change, it is our objective to contribute to debate about the future direction of collective effort to achieve the conditions necessary for the development of a sustainable regional Australia. For this purpose, some radical changes in policy thinking are essential. We see great danger in the present economic and policy trajectory. If a change in direction is not achieved, we face the prospect of creating a small, culturally insignificant rural society which is prosperous and healthy for some but wretched, brutish and despairing for many others.

The latter society would be far from the idyll of community and rurality held so high for so long by urban as well as rural people. Rather, it would be a place which even those few people living there would want to hide from, like the residents of the walled neighbourhoods now appearing in most of our largest cities (see, for example, Hillier and McManus, 1994). Such change has happened with little recognition, at the same time as our cities have become increasingly divided – not in terms of 'racial ghettos' as some have supposed (Burnley et al., 1997) but, rather, attenuated along class lines (Badcock, 1997). Regional Australia is slipping towards a bifurcated society in which the wealthy focus their lives on the nation's cities and on the world. It is leaving its poor in isolation and deprivation, with any remaining opportunities for productive activity to be undertaken within a degraded bio-physical environment – one vulnerable to the demands and desires of global capital.

In such a scenario, tourist attractions are all that are left to remind us of rurality and its cultural tradition. Family farms as museums to the past will provide an income, of sorts. While exhibiting some of the attributes of a productive farming lifestyle, their new role will be to pro-duce entertainment for urban and overseas visitors. Sometimes this is both financially desir-able and part of a new 'postmodern' future. At other times it represents the antithesis of why the family went into farming. Meanwhile, many of those farmers denied the 'tourist option' cling to their farms, often dependent on meagre government services and low paid jobs, where work can be found. They form a rural underclass which is becoming socially, culturally and politically isolated from Australian society. We argue, against the 'flow' which views the pres-ent trajectory as inevitable, that it is not too late to challenge these undesirable trends.

Before seeking alternative options, we must consider the conditions in which rural and regional Australians find themselves. We must ask:
- How did rural and regional Australia come to be in the present state of social, economic and environmental degradation?
- What forces have combined to reduce opportunity, and to promote social malaise in Aus-tralia's non-metropolitan regions?
- Is there any hope of harnessing global forces to produce a stronger regional Australia?

Global Misfortune

Regional Australians experience global misfortune in two ways. They are subject to economic and political processes which have global origins – very distant from the influence of even the most powerful Australian institutions. In our current politico-economic framework they have little chance of altering this trajectory of disadvantage. Another misfortune is that impacts are not confined to economic well-being. Global impacts affect all aspects of their lives, including their family and community, and the bio-physical environment in which they live and work.

There are three elements which comprise what we term Australia's global misfortune. The first is our colonial legacy: the attempt to recreate the institutions of European agriculture and North American federalism within a colonial economic system in spatial locations which lacked the social, political and economic resources of an industrial base.

The second element is that of exploitative European farming practice undertaken within a fragile ecosystem. Today, our so-called 'advanced' agriculture cannot promise farmers a decent income. Rather, it places them on what is known as a 'productivist treadmill' which, at one and the same time, undermines farm viability as it ruins our natural resource base.

The third element, stemming from the first and exacerbated by the second, is the vul-nerability accompanying the peculiar kind of marginality of family-based farming systems. Their marginal position in the wider economy makes them easy victims to arguments for neoliberal approaches as the best means of addressing socio-economic and environmental problems.

While not of the making of rural and regional people, these three elements nevertheless continue to create the conditions for social, economic and environmental disadvantage.

The Legacy of Colonialism

British occupation of the Australian continent was undertaken from 1788 primarily to meet a particular need: the disposal of criminals. Criminals were 'made' in Britain largely through the process of the breakup of feudalism and, with it, the creation of dispossessed serfs. These people had limited opportunity to stay on the newly-enclosed lands, yet were unable to obtain work in the cities. For many of those caught in the acts of stealing food and poaching, punishment for their sins was a one-way ticket to the colonies. Political activists opposing colonisation in Ireland joined them. A stipulation of settlement was that the colonies must produce their own food and so reduce the economic burden on the home government. Although there was opposition from the Indigenous inhabitants, the Australian continent was to be viewed as an empty land, a *terra nullius*. This being the case, the colonists had no reason to negotiate the division of lands with the native inhabitants. They simply imposed a British system of political and economic organisation. Australia's misfortune included being colonised by a distant nation which neither understood, nor apparently was sensitive to, the environment or the peoples of the land it conquered.

Officers, 'free men' and new settlers recognised the economic potential of such vast territory. Built initially on the backs of the convicts, the settlements of Sydney, Hobart, Melbourne and other port cities developed as miniature British towns with the same legal systems, religions, bureaucracies and culture. The architecture was 'imported'. Parklands were created to represent the home country, and even wildlife was imported to provide the necessities of a good hunt. Separate colonies were established in what were to become the States of New South Wales, Tasmania, Western Australia, South Australia and Victoria. They were soon granted representative government, with roughly similar political institutions. Queensland followed. They all voted to federate in 1901, forming the Commonwealth of Australia. Since that time the Northern Territory and the Australian Capital Territory have been formed and granted self-government. Neither has achieved full statehood.

As Britain's export markets expanded and its prowess at sea grew during the eighteenth century it began to fashion its economy around the importation of cheap raw materials from its colonies, and the sale of its manufactured goods to other colonies – principally to those people who had prospered in the lands it had conquered. With its agricultural base unable to support its population, cheap food and fibre were secured from Australia in the nineteenth century (McMichael, 1984). When economic expansion within Australia became profitable to British investors and to an emerging colonial compradore bourgeoisie, there were demands for the formalisation of land tenure, and the spread of legal institutions which would protect newly acquired private property. The holdings of 'squatters' who had occupied land and grazed their stock without legal sanction as the colony grew were, from the 1860s, divided and made available to small-farm operators. These immensely significant political acts were justified and bolstered by the rhetoric of agrarianism – expressions of belief in the rightfulness of the creation of a class of landed workers ennobled by their vocation and their commitment to family, community and nation. Australia thereby avoided establishing itself as a nation populated extensively by peasants, and at the same time established a class of small proprietors. The system of governance created a dispossessed Indigenous population at the same time as it stimulated strong capital growth. It also produced the framework for the future liminality of the rural petty bourgeoisie: a group facing continued economic uncertainty and eventual political marginality.

Marginalisaton has occurred despite Australia having experienced major periods of economic prosperity and a high degree of upward social mobility. Although a gentry was founded on large estates and with an expectation of power, the rigidity of the agrarian social structure in Britain was not reproduced in Australia. Social inequality has nevertheless remained apparent, with a strong spatial dimension within and between urban and regional areas. A combination of espoused egalitarianism, the early development of trade unions and a labour party might indicate a collectivist society, but Australia has remained an individualistic society based on a pioneering and entrepreneurial ethic. It has also been urbanised. About one-third of the population lived in the State capitals at the time of Federation, a figure which has since increased to two-thirds. Australian agriculture, having been based on production for sale including export rather than subsistence, has not involved such large proportions of the population as in comparable countries, including the United States. Significantly, its productivity enabled the growth of commerce upon which urbanisation was based.

The creation of the States of Australia was a step towards producing a legacy of regional economic dependency. The capital cities became conduits for the inflow of money and the outflow of goods. The regions developed sufficient infrastructure to produce the desired economic outcomes for the investors, but they were never to be self-directing. Their own political power was circumscribed by the States. New State Movements, as they were called, came and went without producing any new states, or any novel forms of regional government. (The only two recent, yet seemingly improbable, calls have been made for a State of Far North Queensland, or for a State of Gondwanaland to be declared above the Tropic of Capricorn (*Weekend Australian* 28 October 2000: 8).) Partly as a consequence of the failure of such movements the existing States have become entrenched, producing a 'regionalism' of a misbegotten form. The regions have very little power as they have no effective institutional base. Their future development is subservient to the needs and demands of the States. In Australian federalism the States retain very significant powers. They effect most public spending, although they have lesser revenue-collection power with income and sales taxation being controlled by the Commonwealth Government. Much of that revenue is distributed back to the States using equalisation procedures which result in the smaller States receiving a higher proportion of revenue per capita than the larger and more wealthy States. Local government has been created under, and is controlled by, State legislation and government. The continued federation of the States is universally taken for granted in Australia and became the focus for much (white) celebration during the one-hundredth anniversary of Federation in January 2001.

The ability of the State capitals to provide the main ingredient to success within capitalism – employment – and the contrasting inability of the regions to create jobs are, together, the basis for continued city growth. Employers and employees alike have been seen to be reluctant to move to the regions (particularly inland) because of a perceived lack of cultural, educational, recreational and other opportunities, possibly including less opportunity to bene-fit from rising property values. A more narrow economic base limits the extent to which the regions can attract new investment and, in an era where public and private investment is con-tracting, many regions experience the downward spiral of economic contraction. The misfor-tune of regional settlement is that it has grown after, or at best alongside, an industrialisation that has been firmly metropolitan – a very different situation from that which occurred in the United States, for example.

However, regional settlement has also given Australia some distinctive aspects to its political history. For nearly all of the twentieth century Australian voters had to choose between a Labor (social democratic rather than socialist) and a Liberal (basically conserva-tive, but with renewed energy for economic individualism) party at State and Federal elec-tions. However, many rural-dwelling voters have been offered alternative conservative candidates, from the National (formerly Country or National Country) Party, which has formed governments in coalition with the Liberal Party. The National Party has developed since early in the twentieth century, based on belief among rural people that government poli-cies favoured the cities. Its substantial membership consists of farming people and town-dwellers. Not surprisingly, it has argued for special support for rural industries, and despite occasionally calling for regulation which might be labelled 'socialist', has been the loudest voice against anything that it terms 'socialism'. There have been frequent suggestions that it should merge with the Liberal Party, but despite finding it impossible either to extend itself across all States or establish itself in the cities, it has resisted such suggestions. The One Nation Party has been seen as a threat to the National Party in parts of regional Australia. It succeeded in obtaining seats in the Queensland parliament, but internal politics led to its par-liamentary members resigning to form the City-Country Alliance.

Farmer organisations have a longer, but in some ways equally troubled, history. Farmers and graziers formed separate organisations in the late nineteenth century, with the former organising themselves in order to combat what they saw as the latter's status as a privileged and powerful 'establishment'. This division remained manifest, though less passionately expressed, through to the establishment of comprehensive State-based groups and eventually the industry-based National Farmers' Federation (NFF) in 1979. Through the 1980s and 1990s the old conflicts reappeared as debate intensified over the national organisation's ten-dency to support government deregulation of agricultural industry and the elimination of mechanisms for protecting the interests of small farmers (Connors, 1996). The future of the NFF has been questioned just like that of the National Party. While the colonial governments' land reforms had saved Australia from a system of peasant agriculture, the remnants of elitism and the perpetuation of the economic and political dominance of the State capital cities have not prevented rural political volatility. In fact, they have fuelled it.

European Farming in a Fragile Environment
While it was once fashionable to argue that Indigenous Australians occupied an empty conti-nent and created very little environmental change, a more considered assessment suggests that they substantially modified the environment. Through the use of fire they actively managed

the native vegetation to increase food availability (Dovers, 1992). When the colonists arrived they engaged in what has been termed 'settler capitalism' – a family-farmer variant of British agriculture which destroyed the Indigenous system of land management. The colonisers ignored the food supply system that had been developed by Indigenous populations over some 50 000 years. There were few products 'grown' by the Aboriginal peoples, and there was no prospect of domestic or international demand for their staple plant and animal foods. Faced with limited rural labour but with vast lands readily available to those who moved beyond the Great Dividing Range, the settlers adopted a mix of farming (cropping the soil) and pastoralism (growing pastures for animals). Productivity was advanced dramatically, particularly with cropping technology from the 1840s, but the late nineteenth century saw productivity decline as areas planted increased rapidly. Hooved animals severely damaged shallow soils. Tree clearing, the introduction of foreign plant species, and the desire by pastoralists for maximum profits in minimum time ensured that the destruction would continue (Taylor, 1997). By the end of the nineteenth century rural Australia was facing severe drought on top of economic depression. Yet rural populations continued to grow well into the twentieth century. People 'battled on' then as they do now (though more recently in diminishing numbers) through cycles involving environmental and economic calamities. It has been estimated recently that the unsustainable use of Australia's land, water and vegetation costs the nation in the vicinity of $3.5 billion per annum (Standing Committee on Environment, Recreation and the Arts, 2001: 11).

A continued reliance on 'modern' scientific and technological applications in farming underlies a problem with long historical roots. Australia has developed a highly productive agricultural system since the 1860s, but early in that history, when its product was largely wool, Australia became heavily indebted by borrowing extensively to fuel development. As pastoralism and farming expanded into less productive areas, so investment and the risk associated with it increased, both at the level of the farm and of the national economy. The 'productivist agriculture' of the twentieth century refers to the growth and application throughout the world of the system of 'high-tech' farming developed in, and exported from, the United States (Altieri, 1998). It has been both a blessing and a curse. By using the inputs of corporate agribusiness firms, farmers achieve increasingly high levels of output. When markets have been buoyant (such as from the late 1940s to the mid-1970s) productivity has translated into profit. In such circumstances increased income can be used to purchase adjacent lands thus allowing, through economies of scale, ever-larger machinery to be applied. The productivist model, based on the use of synthetic fertilisers, agrichemicals, agricultural biotechnologies, and sophisticated machinery, encourages labour displacement. Farm labourers are retrenched, and those farmers who cannot compete are told to 'get big or get out'. Through price supports and production incentives, pro-agribusiness extension advice and other state interventions aimed at stimulating output, farmers have been able to improve their productivity and ensure that an ever-increasing volume of food and fibre has become available on domestic and international markets. In producing such large volumes for export and in adopting a model which requires ever-higher levels of inputs and specialisation, farmers are vulnerable to international market fluctuations and to the pricing policies of agribusiness firms. This model has promoted the 'corporatisation' of farming. It has led to the demise of certain sections of family farming, to the exodus of rural people and to increasing the environmental degradation.

Food abundance has come at a price – a price being paid by both the environment, and by farmers whose economic well-being, health and family lives are under constant pressure. For now, we must recognise that farmers and others suffer a predicament which, insofar as it is a product of external and structural conditions over a long history, is only partly of their own making. Moreover, with the increasing internationalisation of industrial and finance capital, Australian agriculture has become quite vulnerable to decisions made in distant locations. Finance capital has gained an ability to by-pass many of the strictures previously set in place by once-protectionist nation states. And many of those directing international capital flows do not share the interest which rural people might have in the protection of the environment (McMichael and Lawrence, 2001).

Vulnerability to Neoliberalism
Up until the mid-1970s agricultural production and distribution in Australia occurred under a mantle of protection, subsidisation and state regulation – support structures which have crumbled or disappeared in recent decades. Regional towns were, to a limited extent, 'planned' by Federal and State governments which supported railways, roads, schools, law courts, police stations and other facilities and services. Such state involvement was consistent with ideologies of decentralisation, state-assisted economic growth and egalitarianism. Commitment to such ideals has now been replaced by a more narrow focus on free markets, 'user pays' and 'self help' – as part of what is known as neoliberalism.

Following the collapse of the socialist state system in Europe and the emergence of a more interconnected world economy, neoliberalism – which acts, specifically, to foster global competition (Teeple, 1995; Lawrence, 2000; McMichael, 2000) – has emerged worldwide to challenge (and eventually to defeat) older conservative and socialist ideologies (Giddens, 1994). Giddens believes that while neoliberalism may retain a vestige of conservatism (attachment to the nation, religion and patriarchy) it has become the most radical approach to economic management and social arrangement, leaving conservatives to lament the passing of older forms of privilege and order, and socialists to defend – against the forces undermining it – the welfare state.

'New Right' ideologies which have taken hold in Australia since the 1980s have influenced both the Liberal/National Party Coalition and the Australian Labor Party. Importantly, the Federal bureaucracy is heavily populated with economists trained in neoliberalism (see Pusey, 1991) and the NFF has been dominated by groups whose products leave Australia's shores, and in whose interest it is to see freer world trade (NFF, 1993). For most Australian economists, or at least those who are heard most frequently and loudly, the move to a more globalised world in which freer trade prevails is viewed as essential if Australian agriculture is to prosper. It is currently seen *not* to prosper because of a combination of the trade in 'bulk' agricultural commodities, low commodity prices, unfair world competition, and the way assets are 'fixed' in farming (see Malcolm et al., 1996 for a discussion of this issue).

When we examine what is happening abroad, it is clear that the position often taken by our home-grown neoliberal economists is both essentialist and profoundly apolitical. In recognising no way forward other than permitting market forces to take their toll, such economists blindly endorse Adam Smith's hidden hand of the market without recognising the not-so-hidden agenda of nations which have chosen to shape agriculture in ways which match their commitment to new priorities like environmental improvement, countryside amenity and cultural diversity. In many of the developed overseas nations, especially in France and Britain, agriculture can no longer be considered as a stand-alone industry. Its direction is being shaped by a myriad of forces seemingly unconnected with food production. For example, in Britain farmers have been paid to keep their hedgerows, to restore dilapidated farm buildings, and to maintain public lanes and walkways through their properties. Why? Because international tourists want to stroll the hills photographing Constable-like scenes of fat sheep and village life, and domestic tourists want to see the 'real' (for 'real' read 'imagined') England.

In France, where there has been strong opposition to any reduction of price support to agriculture, farmers have convinced provincial leaders and urban-based governments to ensure that there is a French countryside retained for the national heritage. In the face of any logic which might suggest that the peasantry should be dismantled and all food imported from 'unsubsidised' nations like Australia, the farmers have lobbied very successfully for continued assistance (ultimately via a tax on the purchasers of farm products, that is, domestic consumers). The French appear quite happy to pay higher prices for their 'home-grown' food. They place a high but intangible social value on the maintenance of tradition, history and other benefits of rural community life and provincial food production. As in Britain, that value is not some simplistic calculation which puts the figures of international and domestic tourism alongside the profits foregone from not developing a more productive agriculture. The 'battle' over the meaning and eventual structure of the countryside is conducted in the political arena where the economics of farming is only one factor – alongside those of nationalism, history, culture and community – in decisions about any 'farm adjustment'. In Europe, the term 'multifunctionality' is used to describe the benefits of agriculture other than those of food and fibre production (Johansen et al., 1999). There are, literally, many functions performed by agriculture. Benefits might include rural development, cultural heritage, food security and the maintenance of communities. Because these are not well 'captured' in the models of economists, they are often ignored. Yet, as we now see in Europe, they form part of a strong case for supporting agriculture so that it can continue to deliver such benefits (Johansen et al., 1999). This is not to advocate European policies for Australian agriculture. But it does serve to indicate that there are possibilities other than those forming part of current public discourse in Australia.

Australian farmers and other rural dwellers have the misfortune to suffer under a narrowness of thinking among those who have heavily influenced the rural policy agenda. Australian neoliberal economists and policy makers believe that social arrangements flow logically considered to be from the market. It is inefficient to prop up producers who are not economically viable, nor is it desirable to seek to 'save' country towns whose economies are in decline. While there are some differences in the ways State and Federal governments react to this, they generally accept that changes are in line with economic realities. If market forces dictate that towns or regions must shrink, then so be it; that is the 'natural' outcome which will move resources into more appropriate endeavours. In some mechanical way, 'failures are part of a steering mechanism that directs an economy toward prosperity' (Gow, 1994: 11). The basis of this notion is both contradicted and supported by farmers' political representatives, rendering the advancement of debate in the interests of rural people very difficult.

Such then is the 'global misfortune' which Australia's rural and regional dwellers suffered at the end of the twentieth century. Their problem is not just a simple matter of declining terms of trade to be solved by finding more export markets for rural-based products. Certainly this is part of the dilemma. But the conditions which constrain their future run deeper, even into their own culture. Their tradition is based on a history of international economic relationships which, while sometimes appearing favourable to regional Australia, have left its people with:

- a terminally weakening economy and a nation state either unwilling or apparently unable to do much to change those circumstances;
- a limit to the productive capacity of the bio-physical environment on which they have come to depend;
- no apparent alternative to, and limited resources for critical reflection upon, the philosophy and policies of neoliberalism which are narrow and often self-contradictory.

It is paradoxical that under neoliberal thinking the actions of individuals are paramount, yet this same thinking either prevents or limits attempts to consider the constraints on individual action. These constraints are embedded in social structures or intangible features of societies like social inequality or cultural habits, which are constructed, without any necessary intention or awareness, by the people themselves. Social structures, however, can be enabling as well as constraining. They can provide people with resources and motivation. The assertions of neoliberal economists could be considered highly deterministic. In contrast, sociologists argue that change emanates *from* people who actively accept and actively resist the forces which impact upon their lives.

Structural and cultural constraints are important partly because rural people appear as tenacious as ever in defending their 'rights'. They seem unwilling to surrender to their misfortunes. The rate at which rural Australia is being depopulated appears out of proportion to the threat from the economic and environmental forces of change. It is of no use to suggest that adjustment should proceed in a clear-cut fashion in a way which frees up society's resources for better use elsewhere if the people who possess those resources choose to retain them. Farmers may, at times, see themselves as unfortunate pawns in the international chess game of commodity trade. But their actions are not those of people who will meekly submit to the inevitable forces of agricultural adjustment. They are integrated into local communities from which they derive their social status; they have an attachment to their land and to the farming lifestyle; and they are well aware that their skills are not valued highly outside agriculture. Many farmers will struggle to remain in agriculture under conditions of severe economic stress and personal and family deprivation (see Gray et al., 1993). This is, after all, economically rational at the level of the individual and family (see Vanclay and Lawrence, 1995). At the intersection of the economics of farming and of the cultural and social lifestyle choices of family farm members, farm people are changing their attitudes and behaviours. As a consequence, this is changing the cultural, social, political and economic basis of Australian agriculture. But it cannot be concluded that these changes are better equipping rural and regional people for the challenges of globalisation and environmental deterioration.

We argue that while economic and political structures have impacted, and continue to impact, negatively on regional people, these people have developed their own interpretations of their social conditions and have actively resisted the forces which oppose them. Because the causes of change and the depth of the structural conditions which constrain their actions and thinking have not always been apparent, people have not been able to identify readily a progressive way forward. But regional citizens *do* have their own culture, *do* have ways of seeing, and *do* desire to be part of the 'good' society. The tradition of 'the bush' has underpinned Australian values. The culture of regional people must be respected and maintained if we are to guarantee the long-term sustainability of regional life. But it should also be made open to the possibility of change for the better brought about by the people who construct it and are affected by it.

The danger of emphasising structural constraint could lead us to miss the enabling capacity of structure, like the capacity for collective action for which rural communities have a reputation. Our approach might be clarified by applying the analogy of a river, in a way similar to that adopted by Metcalfe (1988). Rural and regional people are moved as if by the current of a river – the stream of their own history – toward their present unfortunate circumstances. They are constrained by the banks of the river. However, rivers can and do change their course when their currents are strong enough. A change in the course of a river does not happen by coincidence. It occurs when the stream is able to move the banks which direct it. Here, however, the analogy ceases to be useful. The flow of a river has no capacity for reflection about its course. Rural people do have reflective capacity. The nature of their reflection and reflexivity assumes great significance to the future of rural Australia but remains as much a product of history as their structural misfortunes.

The Challenges

Three major challenges face regional Australia: to continue to be economically productive, to ensure social viability, and to produce in an ecologically sustainable manner. (Some would rightly argue that there is a fourth arising from all three: that of reforming institutional structures so that they are responsive to community needs.) The problem for regional Australia is that, in a globalising capitalist economy, pressures are being exerted which 'force' regions to exploit both their people and their natural resources. If productivity and efficiency gains are privileged over societal benefits and environmental security, the form of development which is likely to occur cannot provide a balanced or viable future. In a deregulated economy Australian governments have been unable or unwilling to intervene to challenge those forces. At best, they ameliorate them. Yet, Australia's future is viewed by our governments as being intimately tied to the global economy and its corporate players and they do not want to challenge such authority through increased interventions. We accept that processes behind globalisation are bound to continue unless deflected. We accept that people have the capacity to resist, organise, oppose and bring change. They do not have to be victims of global circumstances.

Post-1980s Australian governments (both Labor and Coalition) have not veered from a course of opening up the economy to increased international competition via deregulation, privatisation, and the lowering of protection (Wiseman, 1998; Lawrence, 2000; Pritchard and McManus, 2000). The promise is supposed to be greater exports – particularly of efficiently-produced agricultural products and minerals – more jobs, a more prosperous economy, new industries, and a more market-oriented (consumer-driven) production system. Importantly, the promise is that freer trade regimes allow local (regional) economies to capture trans-national investments in ways circumscribed by more tightly regulated national systems of production and control (see Lash and Urry, 1994). This accords with Naisbitt's (1994) paradox – the bigger the world economy, the more powerful are its smaller players. In this scenario, regional Australia has a lot to gain via globalisation.

We take the objective of policy making to be the creation of conditions in which regional Australia can achieve sustainable development. Definitions of sustainability are discussed in chapter 8. For now, it is sufficient to say that we give equal priority to maintaining the bio-physical enviroment along with the economic conditions and social relationships which are conducive to well-being and equity among all Australians – rural, regional, urban or metropolitan.

The Structure and Argument of this Book

In order to find a way ahead without the blinkers and contradictions of current endeavours, we seek ways people may identify and act upon the structures which constrain them in a glob-alised system. First, though, we must analyse the process of globalisation in order to isolate its most significant enabling as well as constraining features. Chapter 2 provides an analysis of globalisation in its economic, social and political manifestations. It becomes clear that some novel thinking is necessary if we are to cast aside the dubious assumptions of neoliberalism. Some re-thinking of policy principles is attempted in chapter 3, paying particular attention to theoretical issues related to reflexivity. We find it necessary to break from the paradigms of what is now considered orthodox policy analysis, and so set out a new framework, based on sociological concepts.

The next stage in the development of the basis for formulating new policy involves interpreting what is happening to regional people. From the theoretical basis in chapter 3 we are able to develop our understanding of the processes of change as they affect people. Here we move beyond the simple observations of economic and social change to the accompanying fundamental changes in social relationships which embody what is called 'rural restructuring'. Chapter 4 examines rural restructuring, focusing specifically on change in agriculture and its consequences for the human activities and social relations embraced in farming. Chapter 6 takes a parallel look at regional Australia – the experience of those who live, mostly, in country towns. It depicts social conditions and the impacts of policy against analysis of change in regional communities.

The chapters which analyse rural and regional restructuring are each followed by a chapter which analyses the 'reflexivity' of rural and regional people respectively. We seek to develop an understanding of the processes through which rural and regional dwellers may, or may not, see a way forward to change 'the course of their river'. Chapter 5, for example, presents and analyses the 'voices' of rural people, offering interpretations of their views based on acknowledgement and examination of their culture. It also explores the problematic nature of the interpretations of rural people – the 'blinkers' which they may inadvertently create for themselves or allow others to create for them. Chapter 7 carries out a parallel analysis of regional communities. It pays particular attention to the relationships of power which they have found themselves to be cast in, and the nature and consequences of their reflexivity.

The possibilities for action based on appreciation of the interests of rural and regional people are further explored in chapters 8 and 9. Chapter 8 presents the context and constraints posed by the bio-physical environment and the consequences of productivism. It begins to consider the prospects for sustainability. It provides a consideration of the environmental situation confronting Australian agriculture and some possible options in the face of the structural and cultural conditions confronting farming families. Action to achieve sustainability is considered at the levels of individual, community and the state. Chapter 9 introduces the sociological concept of 'detraditionalisation', as something which may or may not foster reflexivity in the context of structural and environmental constraint. It examines those features of culture which might reveal a pathway out of the structural constraints of 'global misfortune' before considering the possibility that rural Australia may, indeed, inevitably cease to exist as we know it. The final chapter looks at current policies and explores possibilities for the implementation of new vehicles for change which promise greater prospects for sustainability in rural and regional Australia.

It is argued throughout this book that there is a growing tension between the control of our future by global entities and the legitimate claim of rural and regional populations for a secure and healthy lifestyle and environment. The point is not to deny or to run from the influence of global forces, or merely to propose direct intervention by the nation state as the only pathway to sustainability, but rather to assess what people can do to improve their futures. This means identifying the processes, structures and actions which might combine to produce future opportunities for prosperity, harmony and security for Australia's rural and regional dwellers.

Further Reading

Bambrick, S. (1994) *The Cambridge Encyclopedia of Australia,* Cambridge: Cambridge University Press.
- provides historical introductions to the social, environmental, economic and political characteristics of Australia
Costar, B. and Woodward, D. (1985) *Country to National: Australian Rural Politics and Beyond,* Sydney: Allen & Unwin.
- offers extensive background on the National Party
Lawrence, G. (1987) *Capitalism and the Countryside: the Rural Crisis in Australia,* Sydney: Pluto Press.
- a political economy of Australian agriculture, focusing upon the structural constraints faced by rural producers during the 1980s rural crisis

Lockie, S. and Burke, L. (eds) (2001) *Rurality Bites: the Social and Environmental Transformation of Rural Australia*, Sydney: Pluto Press.
  – a broad-ranging and introductory examination of contemporary change in agriculture and rural society
Pritchard, B. and McManus, P. (eds) (2000) *Land of Discontent: The Dynamics of Change in Rural and Regional Australia*, Sydney: University of New South Wales Press.
  – a contemporary, critical overview of recent changes in non-metropolitan Australia

2
Understanding Globalisation

More than peoples from many other nations, Australians should be aware of the importance and impacts of global processes. White Australia's history is the story of the spread of colonial capitalist relations and of the 'logic' of interdependence between Australia and Britain, something which was later to be transformed, with relative ease, into dependent relations between Australia and the new 'centre' – Japan, Korea, the United States and other developed economies. The removal and marginalisation of the nation's Indigenous population, and the subordination of the nation to the demands of colonial capital – including the formation of the cities as conduits for the outflow of goods demanded by overseas nations – meant that Australia's economic future remained, and still remains, reliant upon the decisions of economic entities residing well beyond its shores. Australia's political structures, commerce and trade, and cultural predispositions are products of colonialism, part of the legacy of which is to have the nation firmly embedded into a grid of international production, exchange and consumption. We are part of a global economic system.

While this might be inevitable, the concept of globalisation remains somewhat elusive. It is hard to fathom just what it is and what real effects it is having. As a 'real world' process its history, causes, present-day contours and its effects are the subjects of much debate. The point is, if globalisation is to be more than a catch-all phrase for change in the modern world, its contours need to be traced, its causes identified and its impacts described. Any definition of the term will rest on particular assumptions about what underlies the processes of change in the modern world. This chapter explores the ways social scientists have sought to understand global processes. It seeks to establish how the regions, particularly those dependent on agriculture, are changing as a consequence of globalisation.

Competing Conceptions of Globalisation

Although globalisation might have become 'one of the cliché's of our times' (Held et al., 1999: 1) it is important to identify its common features and to consider how it has been defined. Albrow (1990: 9) has defined globalisation as 'all those processes by which the peoples of the world are incorporated into a single world society, global society'. For Held et al. (1999: 2) globalisation is viewed as 'the widening, deepening and speeding up of worldwide interconnectedness in all aspects of contemporary social life, from the cultural to the criminal, the financial to the spiritual'. One main insight is that space is being made less relevant. Waters (1995: 3) goes so far as to predict that 'territoriality will disappear as an organising principle for social and cultural life'. If we consider the world system to be a structure, globalisation might best be viewed as a set of processes within that structure (King, 1991; Held et al., 1999). For Pieterse (1996) there are many 'globalisations' which are noted for their fluidity, indeterminacy and 'open-endedness'.

Preferring the term 'global capitalism' to globalisation, Ross and Trachte (1990) suggest we are entering an era in which monopoly capital is giving way to a new variant of capital: global capital. That is, it is giving way to a system in which the 'core' (long industrialised) and 'periphery' ('developing') of national economies are blurred, where the spatial mobility of capital is enhanced, where unions are 'disciplined' and the strategic strength of labour is undermined, and where the power of the state is circumscribed by the ability of capital to move more easily across borders. The key issue for these authors is a fundamental shift in the bargaining and power relations between capital and labour. It is facilitated by what they suggest are revolutions in technology, specifically those relating to transportation and information technologies, and its contours and impacts can best be traced by investigating relations of power in society.

We now have genuinely global firms which view regions of the world as differentiated sites for potential investment (Held et al., 1999; Beck, 2000). A new policy environment has emerged in which businesses are able to move their capital around the world with minimal restriction, and where deregulation of the labour market is viewed as crucial by both these firms and by nation states as a basis for continued capital accumulation. If firms must now compete globally, they must adopt new sophisticated and productivity-generating technologies as well as minimise labour costs. In this climate, 'driving down costs becomes the single most important priority for business and the state' (Drache and Gertler, 1991: 4; and see McMichael, 2000).

The decolonisation of many nations has subsequently 'unlocked' their potential to provide relatively cheap labour. The spatially flexible corporations have then set about restructuring production on a global scale. Some common themes appear to be gaining hold. One is the pro-business view that the 'unmitigated rule' of corporate private property must be sacrosanct. Another is that the welfare state should be largely dismantled. As Teeple (1995: 6) suggests, 'the same changes wrought by globalisation are the rationale for neoliberalism'.

The rise of neoliberalism is one of the key features of globalisation. Neoliberalism is associated with notions of individual freedom, the sanctity of the marketplace, and minimal government involvement in economic matters (see Overbeek, 1990; Lawrence, 2000). While these ideals have been modified by a continuing consensus of sorts between labour, capital and the state, the rejection of corporatist or tripartite approaches to the solving of economic problems appears to be emerging. The voices of subordinate groups are given little credence; the state – on behalf of capital – is actively undermining the union movement through policies designed to 'liberate' labour from employment laws; and the Keynesian-style welfare 'net' which helped to redistribute funds to the working class is being dismantled. Neoliberalism is a set of beliefs which provide the basis for the unimpeded flow of capital across national boundaries – and with the least political interference. Such a change represents a massive attack on the rights of workers and their incomes and life chances (Martin and Schumann, 1997). Neoliberalism is also putting pressures on foreign governments in former Second (Soviet-inspired) and Third World nations to open their economies and to become more like the compliant states of the west (Beck, 2000). And, of course, in the developed nations where a commitment to Keynesian welfare policies allowed the working classes to obtain state benefits, neoliberalism challenges and removes such gains. For Hamilton (1996), the subordination of the interests and needs of citizens to international financial markets is an insult to democracy.

It is important to recognise that globalising processes are not necessarily making the world more uniform and standardised. There may be some synchronisation brought about by technological, economic and cultural flows, but the effect is hybridisation where cultural forms become separated from current practices and are recombined in new practices (see

Pieterse, 1996; Tomlinson, 1999) forming not a global whole but a global 'melange' of hybrid sites and spaces. Pieterse believes it is possible to replace an older 'homogenising' vocabulary with a new one. Instead of modernisation we have (many) modernisations; instead of westernisation as a unidirectional force we have global melange; instead of cultural synchronisation we are seeing 'creolisation' and crossover; and instead of a totalising world civilisation we can talk, instead, of a global ecumene (Pieterse, 1996: 62).

For McMichael (1996; 2000) – who wants to capture the dynamics of contemporary change – globalisation is viewed as a 'project' in which corporations, driven by imperatives of capital accumulation, create and foster financial and spatial interdependencies. In so doing, nationally organised economic growth has given way to globally organised economic growth (McMichael, 2000). The global project is contrasted to that of post-World War II 'developmentalism'. For McMichael the globalisation project is that of the creation of conditions where trade is organised and regulated on a world basis by a largely unaccountable political and economic elite. The latter become functionally parasitic 'virtual taxpayers' by escaping the state-based regulatory frameworks which constrain national capital (Beck, 2000). The globalisation project has its base in the neoliberal beliefs in the virtue of self-regulating markets, in the theory of comparative advantage, in the ability of entrepreneurialism to bring benefits to all economies, and the perceived desirability of extending the products of global industry to all peoples. Producers and consumers are integrated across space and through time by the actions of the global marketplace. As a result, they are intimately connected to the policies and practices of corporations, international law, financial capital flows, and to other manifestations of production and regulation occurring beyond the borders of any one nation state. As indicated above, this is not to suggest that the globalisation project has an homogenising effect throughout the world. It is a contradictory and uneven process. For McMichael (1997: 648) globalisation 'assigns communities, regions and nation-states new niches, or specialised roles (including marginalisation), in the global economy'.

From the above discussion the key ideas in any adequate conceptualisation of globalisation would include the following: the pre-eminence of transnational capital; altered conditions for nation states to control capital and information flows; pressures on the nation state to adopt neoliberalist policies which conform to the interests of transnational capital; the growth of supra-state bodies to monitor and regulate the new global system of production and exchange; differentiating impacts at the local level, in the face of the growth of the development of a global culture (or global consciousness); the interconnectedness of locations around the world in a manner which reduces the importance of space and time; increasing significance of the flows of people across national boundaries; and the combined effects of all resulting in the removal both of mechanisms designed to provide safety nets for workers (including farmers), and of protection to firms operating within national borders.

While these features provide an 'objective' assessment, we must also be conscious of policy-making not as some unproblematic, deterministic outcome but rather as a discursive and contingent formulation in which global processes can be contested (Alexander, 1998). Although globalisation may be responsible for large-scale restructuring of local, regional and national economies, the results of which are social dislocation, it is essential to recognise that political responses are negotiated, and that social action in the form of protest, opposition and resistance can shape political responses in a manner which can challenge any 'global hege-mony' (de Haan, 2000). One of the purposes of this book is to establish how non-metropolitan people might best act to enhance their own, and their community's, well-being by capturing the benefits from any global future.

Features of Globalisation

Global Production Systems
There have been numerous attempts to outline the changes that have occurred in the produc-tion and distribution of goods, services and knowledge since World War II. What concerns us here is to develop a coherent picture of what constitutes specifically *global* production. For Ross and Trachte (1990) contemporary capitalist development can be viewed as a movement from competitive capitalism to monopoly capitalism to global capitalism. Each period exhibits different features regarding relations between capital and labour. In global capitalism, trans-national corporations (TNCs) compete aggressively for market share. They are interested in multisourcing (disaggregation of production across national boundaries) so as to disperse investment and to ensure continuity of supply in the face of potential labour problems. In a global forum such companies can employ their economic power to discipline and/or cheapen labour. With their power to move beyond boundaries of the nation state, the TNCs have pro-duced a 'world factory' which links geographically diverse sites of production serviced by 'global' workers (see McMichael, 1996; McMichael and Lawrence, 2001) many of whom are employed in labour-intensive, assembly-line production of goods which are part of the 'third industrial revolution' – information-based technologies and electronic products. Central coor-dination by the TNCs allows a certain 'fluidity' of production with component manufacturing locations scattered throughout the world. Plant production can be accelerated, decreased, or halted at the behest of the TNC. It can ensure components from one site in one country arrive at another at a specific time and that, after assembly, the product can be readily dispatched – often back to those nations within which individual components were made.

Such production is skewed and uneven (Held et al., 1999). As McMichael (1995: 90) has noted, TNCs arrange production to suit their needs with, typically, high technology processes remaining in the First World as labour-intensive activity goes where labour is cheaper. While we are now familiar with the concept of the 'World Car', we should add to that list the world computer, camera, television, or – in agriculture – the 'world steer' (see Sander-son, 1986). Much has been achieved by what has been referred to as 'flexible specialisation' incorporating strategic management (to understand and plan for predicted, rather than cur-rent, demand); just-in-time delivery of components (to ensure surplus inventory is not held, unproductively, by the manufacturing firm); total quality management (to ensure products delivered to and leaving the factory are standardised for desired quality); devolved power within the organisational structure (reducing the rigidities of hierarchical organisations); flexibility in the employment of staff (achieved, largely, through part-time staffing, outwork-ing and subcontracting); and multiskilling (allowing both task rotation and involvement by manufacturing workers in managerial decisions) (see Waters, 1995).

The development of an international division of labour has been occurring throughout the history of capitalism. In its global form, however, it represents a change from older colonial arrangements where some nations in the periphery provided raw materials for manufacturing firms in the core. Even though they suffered a period of economic stagnation in the mid- to late 1990s, the growth of the showcased Asian 'tiger' nations has been based, for example, on the production of high value added goods. As Mittelman (1996a) suggests, manufacturing has been subdivided for a world market, alongside large-scale migration and the feminisation of labour. It is the feminisation of labour which Mittelman believes to be one of the crucial factors allowing capital to prosper. Low skill levels and low wages are characteristic of manufacturing employment associated with globalisation, and it is here that women in regions of the developing world provide the fuel for continued corporate profit making.

Global Regulation

Transborder migration of labour, information, technologies and products have been fostered by the nation state as a means of assisting business operations. At the same time, however, the velocity of such flows has undermined the nation state's ability to control them. Capital is now able to circumvent the so-called 'grand compromise' between labour and capital that existed as part of the Keynesian Welfare State (Teeple, 1995; Latham, 1998). Neoliberalist policies allow transnational capital literally to bypass the social and economic reforms which have been achieved by workers who have otherwise had the ability, within the framework of nation-state regulation, to organise, win concessions, and have political access. The effect of this is not only to weaken the working class and small capitalists, such as farmers, but also to increase structural and long-term unemployment, bring about lower standards of living, increase the rates of poverty, and degrade the environment. Importantly, it also undermines state regulatory policies which have hitherto provided a basis for capital accumulation. The three state-based tendencies toward deregulation, liberalisation and privatisation lead to pressures for structural adjustment which push the system toward global integration (see Cheru, 1996). In other words, the state is no longer able to control and regulate capital in the way it did in an earlier era. This does not mean, however, that the state has no regulatory functions: it clearly does. Nor does it mean that a regulatory framework is not in place at the global level. It clearly is. The issue is to identify what specific global regulatory forms have emerged and to understand their effects.

The General Agreement on Tariffs and Trade (GATT), the International Monetary Fund (IMF) and the World Bank predate the global era. Their combined role has been to create an appropriate economic and political climate for capital investment and to discipline nations which are not prepared to act in ways conducive to the fostering of international trade. In doing so, these organisations have promoted the actions and importance of TNCs as actors on the global stage. The role of GATT has been to have nations replace subsidies, quotas, concessions, and price underwriting by tariffs, and then seek to have those tariffs reduced or removed – something that has assisted in the movement of goods across national borders and has helped to facilitate global economic interdependence. It is also something that has contributed to the undermining of the economic basis for family-farm agriculture, and once-protected regional manufacturing, in nations such as Australia.

It appears that the purpose of these macro-regulatory organisations has changed from pre-1970 times (where state-regulated markets were required to enhance the 'development project'), to post-1970 times (where the growth of self-regulating markets is facilitated by the recently-formed World Trade Organisation (WTO) as part of the 'globalisation project') (see McMichael, 1996; 2000). The role of the WTO is to oversee global trade, including the planned removal of those barriers established by individual nation states to protect the local economy. Unlike earlier GATT decisions, which could be overruled by individual nation states, the WTO's 135 member nations are obliged to follow rulings of the WTO (Retallack, 2000). This is the first organisation to have powers of global governance. It can overrule state powers in areas of food safety and environmental protection – with current evidence suggesting that it is prepared to enforce lowest common denominator regulations in relation to these issues. It has, for example, weakened the United States Clean Air Act, the United States Endangered Species Act, and Japan's standards in relation to pesticide residues in food. It has overruled the European Union's (EU) ban on hormone-treated beef, and has removed the previous preferential treatment given to family-farm scale banana producers in the Caribbean (Retallack, 2000: 31). In every one of its decisions it has sided with corporate capital. In undermining national sovereignty and jurisdiction and in subordinating national policies to those developed at the global level for global economic players, are we viewing a direct attack on democracy? For example, the WTO is comprised of bureaucrats who are not elected (they are not answerable to any one country or people) and its deliberations are conducted behind closed doors.

The 'selling' of the supposed benefits of globalisation does not happen in a direct, or uncontested, manner. Resistance and protest within the nation state is one manifestation. Another is the gathering worldwide assault on globalisation. An interesting example of the latter concerned the efforts of over 40 000 demonstrators at the so-called 'Millennial Round' of the WTO held in Seattle in December 1999 and by 10 000 demonstrators at the gathering in Melbourne of the World Economic Forum in September 2000. At both, a variety of protesters highlighting the perceived negative outcomes of globalisation – from global warming, to exploitation of the seas, to corporate ownership of genetic material, to the anti-democratic nature of 'global governance' – joined in large street marches and other protest action. The extent and ferocity of protest led to the postponement of talks in Seattle, and to disrupted meetings in Melbourne (*Australian*, 12 September 2000: 1; Retallack, 2000).

Another element in global regulation is that of the Free Trade Agreements. The basis of these is the decision by nation states in a particular region of the world to agree to abide by rules developed and approved by that regional grouping. North American Free Trade Agreement (NAFTA), incorporating Canada, Mexico and the United States, the European Community (European nations) and Asia Pacific Economic Conference (APEC) (Asia-Pacific economies) are the best known. These 'mega regions' produce 77 per cent of world exports and act to foster economic reform amongst constituent members (see McMichael, 1996). While it might appear that such regional groupings are producing anti-global outcomes (by fostering trade within the bloc of nations), their real effect is to discipline and control at the supranational level. The development of these regional blocs represents both symbolically and economically the need for trade relations to exist beyond the level of the nation state.

Such trading blocs do not want trade wars or the limitation of trade to partners within the blocs. Suggestions of the development of Fortress Europe or Fortress North America, for example, overlook the intentions of the corporations that are the motor forces within such blocs. These firms seek to expand their operations globally (see Wilkinson, 1996). Groupings such as NAFTA, APEC and the EU either explicitly or tacitly endorse the move toward a freely-regulated global market. There is likely to be some reorganisation among the regulating bodies. The World Bank and IMF are likely to become responsible for using national funds to finance the development of global markets; the WTO is expected to replace the UN in terms of world economic governance; the UN will continue in its role of providing law and order – and disciplining nations not willing to join the new order; and the UN's functions associated with the Food and Agriculture Organisation (FAO), with *Codex Alimentarius* (a joint FAO and World Health Organisation agency which monitors food standards), and intellectual property functions, will move from the UN to the WTO to give that organisation much more power to control transnational trade (see Kneen, 1995).

This is not to suggest that the states are hapless victims of processes beyond their control. But to use Moreira's (2000: 6) apt phrase, there are 'diminishing degrees of freedom' for state-based activity. Globalisation is producing *altered* states – ones that are developing new forms of governance and which are regulating in a different manner from the past. With complex forms of governance the state is creating the conditions for globalisation while establishing 'state-led, quasi-official, voluntaristic, and institutional structures that anchor economic activities spatially' (Pritchard, 1999: 287) which offer appearances of devolution and freedom. We explore this further in chapter 10.

Global Culture and Ideology

Neoliberalist ideologies, the programs which they inspire, as well as the justifications for the emerging transnational culture they help promote, are essential to our understanding of globalisation. For Teeple (1995) current changes in public policy brought about by adherence to neoliberalism are responses to the needs of global commerce. This suggests the extension of a set of propositions about the ways society and economy should be ordered and understood, which override older formulations. That we all gain by the extension of free markets, that governments should reduce their activities in the sphere of welfare support, that those who 'use' should 'pay', that the unions have been too powerful, and so on, are put forward as being self-evident.

In our view, such ideas should be seen as social constructions which happen to accord nicely with the global ambitions of corporations. Importantly, where the global agenda is being threatened, corporations have been known to finance 'front groups' to represent their cause under a cloak of community concern. Their aim is to change public opinion, and to do so not by confrontation, but by positioning themselves as moderates who seek to oppose, from the middle ground, those whose views are more extreme (and anti-business). Beder (1997) has written an entire book on how the corporate sector puts its 'global spin' on public debate. Beck (2000) warns of the 'semantic hegemony' of globalisation, while Strange (1998) wants us to recognise that when we hear the overgeneralisations – 'the global village', the 'international superhighway', the 'borderless world' and so on – we should realise that much of this is boosterism, or 'globaloney'.

According to Waters (1995: 126) a totally globalised culture would be one in which value, taste and style preferences would be available 'without constraint for purposes either of self-expression or consumption'. While this state of affairs has hardly been reached, there is evidence that we are viewing the expansion of a 'continuous flow of ideas, information … values and tastes mediated through mobile individuals, symbolic tokens and electronic simulations'. This is not only the world of the Internet, but of television, fashion, and popular culture. Appadurai (1990) believes it is possible to understand the flows of cultural objects by viewing them as belonging to 'fields' that are perceived and organised by postmodern subjects. The fields or 'scapes' of particular significance to global culture are the mediascapes (pertaining to distribution of cultural images) and the ideoscapes (concerning political ideas and values). It is the mediascapes which have significance in terms of popular culture. As Appadurai (1990: 299) has explained:

> 'Mediascapes' … tend to be image-centred, narrative-based accounts of strips of reality and what they offer to those who experience and transform them is a series of elements (such as characters, plots and textual forms) out of which scripts can be formed of imagined lives … These scripts can and do get disaggregated into complex sets of metaphors by which people live … as they help to constitute narratives of the 'other' and proto-narratives of possible lives …

Rather than suggesting that this is a recipe for cultural domination, however, Appadurai notes the possibilities for complex and confusing images and messages, depending on one's location with the flows of information in the global mediascape and ideoscape. Similarly, Lash and Urry (1994) raise the important question of whether these scapes generate and promulgate mass culture for a mass global audience. They argue that media-based technologies have created opportunities for multiple siting of niche-marketed products for diverse communities. There can be no 'dominant ideology' flowing in a single direction to uncritical viewers. Instead, there is a multiplicity of forms and meanings which audiences will give to the messages received. People's 'imagined worlds' respond in various ways to global cultural flows (Appadurai, 1990; Miller, 1993; Tomlinson, 1999). Moreover, there is the possibility for new kinds of social interaction – some of which will be unintended and oppositional.

Despite unexpected outcomes, it is still possible to suggest that consumerism is one of the driving forces for global incorporation leading, according to Appadurai (1990: 305), to a 'craving … for new commodities and spectacles'. Via commodity flows, and especially through advertising, consumers are positioned as having independence of thought and having wide choices, whereas they are constrained financially within the money economy and are, at best, able to make quite limited choices. These consumers are not, as Appadurai (1990: 307) emphasises, homogenised. As we stressed earlier, the globalisation of culture is not the homogenisation of culture. In fact, at the level of the nation state there is the 'repatriation of difference' in terms of goods sold, and the slogans, signs and styles which help to distinguish one national (or subnational) group from another.

Communities of interaction (though not necessarily communities of common interest) can be formed via mass mediation and electronic interaction, in relation to a diversity of ideas and issues. These communities are very different from communities where interaction is *situated* (face to face and local). The former communities are *simulated*, and they comprise people who are separated by geography and time. The Internet, for instance, acts to compress time and renders space unimportant for interaction. It puts people in touch with others with similar interests and concerns and allows them to interact in a way that the telephone was never able, and television is not yet able, to provide.

As we have pointed out, cultural processes have not been moving in some inexorable way toward standardisation. There may be cultural synchronisation but this is not the same as cultural homogeneity. Non-western cultures are having major impacts on the west and they are taking the cultural products of the west and reinterpreting them to suit local conditions. We have 'creolisation' – hybrid cultures, interculturalism rather than a simple multiculturalism. We have, as mentioned earlier, a 'global melange' (Pieterse, 1996: 53). Such a formulation helps to overcome a major concern raised by Scrase (1995) who has criticised cultural theorists' tendency to privilege culture over political economy for leading to a denial, or playing down, of the iniquitous effects of globalisation (see also Shucksmith, 2000). When culture is presented epiphenomenally it is divorced from concrete historical and social processes, thereby ignoring local struggles and outcomes. This is of particular importance for regional Australians who often resort to 'country' stereotypes as a means of displaying and celebrating an anti-metropolitan 'difference'.

For Lash and Urry (1994) the global world is one defined by economies of space and signs where reflexive accumulation (the production of knowledge) combines with flexible specialisation in the workplace to challenge orthodox notions of space and time. Whether regional Australia likes it or not, mobile citizens emerge out of globalisation. They are part of information flows, flows from which they derive, and in which they create, meaning. In rendering problematic both space and time, globalisation processes confuse identity. One effect of this is to undermine nationalism (this is happening at the same time that global economic and political forces are reducing the importance of the nation state). Another is to undermine 'tradition' as an organising principle of social life in the regions. Regional people may see their own, and their nation's, future wrapped up in the globalisation project. Further consequences of this are explored in chapter 9.

Causes and Contradictions of Globalisation

The processes creating the conditions for globalisation are wedded firmly to capital accumulation. Capitalism is an economic system that requires the creation of surplus value (the basis of profits) which can be reinvested to create greater wealth in subsequent production periods. Firms are in competition and must seek, wherever possible, to reduce costs and/or innovate in ways of increasing productivity and efficiency. Yet, in a situation in which the immediate interest of each individual firm is to reduce wage levels, while seeking to sell goods and services to consumers whose wages are kept at a reduced level, a contradiction emerges. The conditions which may advantage each individual producer – low wage levels and displacement of labour – result in reduced demand and unemployment within the system as a whole. These are the very things which will prevent capital realising value, inducing – at specific times – a 'realisation crisis', the results of which are a recession or depression. Capitalism is a system riddled with various crises, and proceeds in waves of 'creative destruction' (Shumpeter, 1975).

Importantly, while the theory of monopoly capital saw that form as the 'highest stage', something new appears to have come along. The 'restructuring' occurring today is an attempt by capital to resolve crisis tendencies which were apparent in the monopoly capital era (dominant in the mid-1960s) (see Ross and Trachte, 1990: 222). With an expanding world market we now have very strong competition between large-scale organisations that do not behave (and cannot behave) as if they are part of monopoly capitalism (see O'Connor, 1974; Ross and Trachte, 1990). As Moreira (2000: 2) has suggested, the number of globalising firms has grown very quickly. While, some twenty years ago there were about 7000 such firms, today there are approximately 53 000. There is a new and vigorous competition at the global level replacing what was seen as price fixing, market manipulation and uncompetitive practices of monopoly firms at the national and international levels. Therein lies the new dynamic for the extension of capitalist relations of production on a world scale.

The issue of debt is also important to the story. The development regime of the postwar period (1950–70) was financed by a banking system which understood that, with the extension of credit to the First World (of which Australia is part), workers would have increased purchasing power. This would fuel the fires of capital accumulation enhancing profit making (especially for those lending capital). Similarly, economic growth in the Third World would result in the repayment of loans. The banks (and their shareholders) would win in both ways. However, the move to monetarism – which stressed the need for 'inflation first' policies, and hence the need to contain lending – heralded the reduction of credit provision to First World consumers as well as to Third World development projects. McMichael (1995) considers that the move from a development regime (1950–70) to a debt regime (1980–) has significantly reduced the ability of the state to manage the economy in an independent manner. He considers the debt regime was the 'dress rehearsal' for the globalisation project that has become prominent in the 1990s (see McMichael, 1999: 10). Thus:

> The fundamental shift was from state to capital as the organizing principle of international political economy ... Banks and financial institutions have emerged as the leading fraction of capital, with a global reach allowing them to uncouple from national regulation as well as from productive capital. As Keynesianism disappeared and metropolitan economies slowed, declining consumption produced excess liquidity, elevating the power of the financiers ... In turn, an unregulated global banking proliferated, the multilateral financial institutions (the World Bank and the IMF) have assumed a central banking role for the world. From being the handmaidens of national development under Bretton Woods, they have become the henchmen of transnational investors (McMichael, 1995: 41).

Capitalists, however, have not been slow to recognise that capitalism is vulnerable. The development of the Keynesian welfare state was a distinct compromise by capital in the face of a number of postwar 'realities'. What it allowed, within economically advanced nations like Australia, was the development of a relatively prosperous working class – the new customers for the goods of capitalism – together with a safety net for those who suffered unemployment or sickness. In Australian agriculture, for example, it provided assistance in the forms of price underwriting, fertiliser bounties, taxation concessions for land clearing and machinery purchase, and tariff protection. At the macro level the capitalist state (particularly the United States) fulfilled its role as protector of trade relations by ensuring local conditions for enhanced accumulation through military interventions and/or containment of socialism.

Following World War II the overall stability of these arrangements provided a basis for capitalist growth both nationally and internationally. With the United States as world peacekeeper, the corporate sector was able to invest in overseas operations, seeking taxation advantages, better state support, lower wages, or a less-regulated environment for production – all of which enhanced profit making. In going beyond national boundaries capital was in a position to argue for conditions to be set in place for its continued expansion, something which host governments would ignore at their peril. What capital desired was more flexible credit systems, taxation relief, favourable exchange and interest rates, and conditions under which firms could trade among their own international branches without having to encounter hold-ups in transactions or component supply (see Teeple, 1995; McMichael, 1999). Supranational government and non-government bodies grew as a necessary consequence of the demands of transnational capital.

It is impossible to mark any specific date at which this 'capitalist world economy' became the globally-oriented 'world capitalist economy'. However, by the mid-1970s four 'events' suggest that this new creature had emerged. The first was the significant reduction in barriers to world production and exchange which occurred as a consequence of the combined efforts of the TNCs and of the IMF, World Bank and other financial institutions. The second was the rise of corporations from nations outside the United States, which viewed their progress as tied to international laws and processes, not to United States hegemony in economic policy-making. The third was the collapse of colonial regimes throughout the world and the opening up of new markets – not for former colonisers, but for those who could negotiate deals with the new political/military elites or quasi-democratic governments. Finally, the extension of the microelectronics 'revolution' to all facets of capital accumulation: to production (primary and secondary industry), distribution (transportation and communication), and circulation (finance, administration and state activities) was essential in providing the mechanism for time-space contraction as well as flexibility in firm interaction.

The combination of these factors resulted in the movement to postmodern options in production and distribution (see Ross and Trachte, 1990; Mittelman, 1996a). Technology, in combination with the conditions that favoured its application and geographical expansion, fuelled productivity and flexibility: the two key elements in providing the basis for enhanced profit making in the global era. Conceivably, without the necessary technological break-throughs, globalisation processes would have been limited (Mittelman, 1996b).

The creation of a global labour market enabled companies to pay less in wages and so placed downward pressure on incomes in established regions of production. As unions in those regions responded through strikes and demands for higher pay, the state reacted by tightening labour legislation and promises of taming the unions and by enticing capital to locate via taxation and other concessions. Yet, the jobs being created in new, technologically-sophisticated industries – the sort which governments wanted to 'capture' as a basis for future prosperity – did not compensate for jobs being lost from declining manufacturing and other industry. With investments beginning to drain from some regions, and wage levels stagnating, the call was made by workers for taxation relief. Importantly, the way the state chose to support such moves was by reducing the social wage, one of the cornerstones of Keynesian welfare state policy. With both production and financial markets 'beyond' the control of any one nation state, and with an international labour force from which to choose, corporations were free to play on a global stage. Born of the nation state they were now more powerful than their progenitor, and would demand conformity to new norms pertaining to investment and regulation before they would agree to situate their branch plants or headquarters. Here were the conditions for the disciplining of labour, the withdrawal of the state from many areas which it had previously supported, the extension of neoliberalist ideologies, and the development of institutions, such as the WTO, to regulate capital accumulation globally. By the beginning of the 1980s Keynesianism had given way to monetarism, and at the start of the new century monetarism had become the backbone of economic policy throughout the developed world.

Monetarists seek to depoliticise economic policy by arguing against attempts by workers to achieve improved wage levels, or businesses to obtain protection, or attempts by the state to regulate the environment, or use the central bank to control financial flows. They argue that it is the marketplace which should sort out what is bought and sold and at what price, and market distortions will only lead to lack of efficiency in the allocation of scarce resources. Labour and capital are viewed as actors on an international stage and there are 'rules' that must be obeyed. Federal Treasurer Peter Costello's remark that the most appropriate way to create jobs in regional Australia was to lower the wage rates of regional workers (*Courier Mail*, 14 December 1999: 4) is entirely consistent with the neoliberalist view that 'fixed' wage rates are an impediment to investment and that our labour must be 'flexible' to be globally competitive. Much state activity is viewed as being a hindrance to economic integration at both the state and global levels. There is seen to be no place for a large public sector in an economy which is supposedly self-regulating (see Wiseman, 1998). Monetarism does not desire state mechanisms: it demands that central banking in the nation state responds to global forces. It wants the state to create independence for central banking agencies, not be bothered with programs to appease labour or to assist local industry. The direct outcome of such demands can be seen in the extent of current capital flow. According to McMichael (1999: 3) the total value of funds exchanged on a world basis annually is more than double the total value of world production, with 97.5 per cent of foreign exchange transactions being of a speculative nature.

Contradictions

Contradictions are mounting as the globalisation project proceeds. A primary one is that as globalisation ensures wealth generation on the global scale it leaves in its wake poverty, falling real incomes and the need for state support in those nation states which have, for whatever reason, lost corporate favour (McMurtry, 1998). As de Haan (2000: 342) reminds us:

> In 1960 the richest 20% of the world had 30 times the income of the poorest 20%, but this gap had increased to 82 times by 1995 ... If we put the poverty line, for the sake of convenience and not without cynicism, at a monetary income equal to $1 purchasing power per day, then 20% of the 6 billion people in the world would live in poverty. If we put the line at $2, then we are talking about as much as half the world population. Thus, we have to conclude that, despite the progress made, between 20% and 50% of the world population is excluded from progress.

Globalisation is not measuring up to its economic promise. It is creating many more losers than winners. While Australia is not in the league of poor nations, growth and decline have had uneven spatial outcomes – something of not inconsiderable significance for regional Australia. Jobs have been reduced and wage levels have generally stagnated. New technologies appear to have exacerbated the problem of long-term unemployment. Although the Australian state might be pressured by political forces to intervene to retrain workers and/or provide them with poor relief, its ability to raise taxes to do so is circumscribed – as suggested throughout this chapter – by neoliberalist ideologies about the negative impact of government 'interference' and by the reality that any attempt to tax wealth or corporate profits would result in capital flight. Limited by the inability to tax corporate wealth, the two remaining options for the Australian state are to reduce assistance to those disadvantaged by the processes of change, or to increase the taxes on wage workers to help pay for assistance for their displaced counterparts. The difficulties with the latter are obvious: in taking increasing amounts of purchasing power from the working class, the national economy is likely to be propelled further into a realisation crisis, the outcome of which would be a spiral of recessionary downturn leading, ultimately, to large-scale unemployment, wage declines and economic depression. This is a distinct possibility in an era where few states have the ability to enclose themselves in a protective mantle of union/company/state agreements (so-called 'corporatist' policy).

A second contradiction relates to regulation. At the very time the nation state is being called upon by its citizens to provide the framework for individual and family well-being, global corporations are demanding new opportunities for profitable investment. The capacity of the state to do both is limited by its reduced status within the global economy (see Cox, 1996). In choosing, moreover, to *attempt* to do the latter rather than the former, it faces the likelihood of a legitimation crisis (see O'Connor, 1973). That is, in being seen to be directly supporting industry – in the face of the growing needs of its citizens – its credibility is likely to be tested and found wanting. Normally, the 'challenge' would have come through the trade union movement. However, given its relative demise in a number of key nations, protest may be driven by 'green' or other parties or alliances. For example, there is already growing evidence that people are not prepared to tolerate environmental pollution. The present solution is really no solution at all: those with strength (such as in the United States) are having their toxic waste problems literally exported to other nations, which in turn receive payment for doing so (see discussion in Mittelman, 1996b). It is unlikely that this sort of trade will be tolerated without protest from those who may gain short-term benefits while ultimately suffering its consequences.

Another contradiction relates to citizenship and democracy. It seems that the more neoliberalist ideas about freedom to choose, freedom to locate, freedom to invest and so on are mouthed, the more restrictions are placed on those whom the message is designed to impress. Ideas of freedom and democracy are matched by a reality of constraint, political alienation and exclusion (Latham, 1998; McMurtry, 1998). One consequence of this appears to be not the creation of the global citizen but fragmentation of societies into often spiteful and resentful groupings which find more meaning in their ethnicity or religion than in shared citizenship (see Cox, 1996; Lawrence et al., 1999). While Australia has not been Balkanised, and has no equivalent of a Kosovo, we do experience the rantings of those who believe that Australia is suffering because of Asian migration. The political processes that have resulted in the triumph of neoliberalism have severely reduced opportunities for democratic participation by workers in a large number of nations. In some countries, such as Australia and New Zealand, there is very little to choose from in the way of political opposition parties: all more or less agree that the future for those nations is to increase participation in the global economy. All are driven by monetarist economic doctrine. Without forming new parties (which is also being done, but which is unlikely to provide a real challenge in the short term) and in the context of a working class which is becoming differentiated and politically emasculated, the opportunity for real opposition is greatly limited.

If democracy rests on accountability, and leaders become more accountable to global bankers and investors than their own citizens, one must ask what sort of 'democracy' is being practised. International organisations such as WTO, the IMF and World Bank are diminishing the opportunities for nations to control standards, enact laws and embark on alternative regulations which may better reflect the needs of citizens. These large organisations are able to enforce global rulings on member nations. As Teeple (1995: 123) indicates they 'continually diminish even the right to curtail certain kinds of exploitation of resources or to encourage economic development in certain directions'.

Democracy should be about fairness and distributive justice, yet an unfettered free market increases economic polarisation (Latham, 1998; McMurtry, 1998; Wiseman, 1998). Democracy's claim is that all are equal under the law, and that equality of social opportunity will prevail, something which the market appears increasingly unable to deliver. Challenges to the system which prevents real democracy from occurring are a likely outcome, but so are neo-fascist attempts to control protest and dissidence while holding the existing order in place (see Overbeek, 1990).

A final contradiction relates to the environment. A truism to date has been that as capitalism has expanded, so has environmental degradation. The contradiction for capitalism is that the more successful it becomes in producing and distributing commodities, the more environmental damage it causes. Can capitalism's growth be sustained without completely ruining the foundation upon which that growth is built? The problem with such a simple formulation is that it does not account for the dynamics of other systems. As the Soviet state expanded so did environmental degradation. What has linked both systems has been the belief in – and use of – advanced technologies. So, the question must be asked, is advanced technology at the heart of the problem? If so, is it all advanced technologies or only some? The unravelling of the question of how to allow economic growth to proceed in an ecologically sustainable manner will be key to the future of global capitalism.

The role of transnational corporations in promoting unsustainable production systems is undeniable. As will be suggested in chapter 8, the pursuit of productivist goals within agriculture has created and/or exacerbated many of the environmental problems facing the world today – erosion of soils, water pollution, salinisation, species decline, and wilderness and habitat destruction. And yet, the productivist model is the one that is at the heart of the global agricultural economy (Lawrence, 1987; Altieri, 1998). One of the greatest problems facing today's globalising world is the extent to which this model can be replaced by another, before it is extended throughout the world as the basis for continued accumulation in agriculture. Capital accumulation in modern agriculture is equivalent to natural resources destruction. Rather than having localised effects, this time ecological destruction will follow capitalism on to the global stage. Importantly, while viewed in a global form (see Beck, 1992), it has the potential to induce protest action at that level (see Chew, 1995).

Consequences of Globalisation for Farming in the Advanced Nations

One of the most important contributions to debates about change in post-World War II agriculture has been made by Harriet Friedmann (1993). According to Friedmann, a division of labour in the production and distribution of foods and fibres has developed alongside two specialisations: food grain exports by the United States to the rest of the world, and United States' oilseed exports to Western Europe to provide a basis for that region's increased production in the intensive livestock industries. This so-called 'second food regime' (the first was colonial) was one based on productivity and efficiency increases – on lands that had already been settled and cultivated – through the use of agro-chemicals, new hybrid seed varieties, genetically-improved livestock, new management regimes (displacing much labour) and more sophisticated machinery and equipment. The output gains from intensive production created food surpluses that could not be sold domestically. The aim of the United States was to derive external income from its agricultural surplus or, where its interests in securing political stability were served, to provide food aid (see McMichael, 2000).

According to Friedmann (1993), despite the second food regime's unquestioned ability to generate increases in production and labour efficiencies, by the 1970s it was in crisis. The reasons given are twofold. First, that the overproduction generated through agro-industrialisation was creating huge and unmanageable 'disposal' problems for the United States. Indeed, European nations subsidised by mechanisms within the Common Agricultural Policy (CAP) were, *at the same time* as United States producers, generating massive surpluses. The second reason for the crisis was that the relative stability that the United States had achieved in selling soybeans and other grains to Europe's burgeoning intensive livestock industry was being threatened by cheaper sources from countries such as Brazil and Argentina. Writing in 1993, Friedmann was not completely clear about what might emerge from the 'crisis' but she believed it might be one of two forms of regulation – private global regulation linked directly to the interests and needs of the transnational corporations in the food industry, or a form of public democratic regulation which would arise as people became increasingly concerned about issues of food security and safety.

Despite the growth in the public's concerns about food safety, it is private global regulation which appears to be emerging as part of the 'globalisation project' (McMichael, 1996). It is based on global sourcing by TNCs, minimal interference in the activities of corporations by nation states which are anxious to secure capital investment by these firms, and a deterioration in legislation to protect the environment and the wages of workers involved in agricultural work or food industry employment. America's agricultural history has been summed up by one group of authors as being a progression from 'Columbus to ConAgra' (see Bonanno et al., 1994).

There have been a number of concerns raised about the food regimes approach, particularly its insistence that globalisation has won an historic victory when evidence suggests major 'instabilities' and 'active and passive resistance' are replete within the system of international agricultural production and trade; and its supposed 'misreading' of the importance to free market liberalisation of the Uruguay round of GATT (see Goodman and Watts, 1994: 21). However, what it captures is the essence of change within the system of agricultural production. TNCs operating globally are capable, through contractual relations, to decide what products farmers will produce, when, and with what inputs.

According to Friedmann and McMichael (1989), Le Heron (1993) and Burch et al. (1996; 1998; 1999) the integration of world capital has blurred any previous distinction between 'agriculture' and 'industry' and in order to grasp the changes occurring in farming and in farm-dominated rural regions it is necessary to conceive of an 'agrifood sector' run by transnational corporations which links various elements of rural production to manufacturing and service industries. The agrifood sector has become an intermediary between agricultural producers and food consumers, creating industrial inputs rather than food for the kitchen (Friedmann, 1991). The creation of a 'mass diet' via industrial food production processes has been one of the outcomes of the development of a global agrifood sector, a sector whose profits were able to grow enormously by convincing consumers that the purchase of takeaway, prepackaged and convenience foods was a necessary and desirable part of modern living. With the durable food industry capable of disguising the ingredients of a final product it was a short step to replacing the costly or unreliably supplied or inferior natural substances with what Friedmann (1991) has labelled 'generic ingredients', like sweeteners in preference to sugar or protein rather than beef.

This so-called 'substitutionism' (Goodman et al., 1987) allows a higher degree of control by corporate capital over agriculture because it can, through increased interchangeability of components, by-pass entire products and regions in 'sourcing' its industrial requirements. While there is some evidence of consumer concern over the processing of foods, and in some countries a move back to traditional preparation and consumption of meals (the so-called 'slow food' movement – see Miele and Murdoch, 2000) the industrial processing of foods remains one of the largest global industries.

The Elements of Rural Global Misfortune
In the analysis above there are two important elements to the continuing global misfortune of Australia's rural people. First, it is anticipated that the earlier comparative advantage enjoyed

by 'settler states' such as Australia and New Zealand has virtually disappeared with the emergence of a global food system. Whether or not these two countries can help to determine which agricultural practices are adopted in sourcing the transnational food system is of great importance. If TNCs decide Australia will provide bulk undifferentiated products for mass markets, possibilities for value adding and for capturing higher priced niche markets will be greatly diminished. Producers will be required to conform to demands of companies that want the separation of livestock and crop growing (the continued movement towards specialised systems of production). There are growing pressures for farmers to conform to both the upstream and downstream components of transnational capital by utilising the modern inputs and producing corporate-required outputs. Becoming increasingly subordinated to finance capital, producers have little room to alter production regimes.

The second important element in this analysis is that, given the continuation of the influence of corporations in supplying existing and new (especially Asian) markets with durable foods, it is likely that there will be increasing pressures on the environment. Ecological problems will invariably increase with any intensification of existing practices (see Redclift and Woodgate, 1997; Altieri, 1998; Lawrence et al., 2001; Lockie and Pritchard, 2001, and chapter 8). There will be demands from consumers for cleaner agricultural practices, many of which will translate to higher costs of production that may mark the demise of Fordist agricultural practices in those countries. It also may result, however (under conditions where the nation state is reluctant to impose tighter regulations for fear of capital flight) in continued (although unacceptable) abuse of natural resources.

Family-farm agriculture in the developed world is becoming both 'subsumed' by global corporations and abandoned by governments which once provided the underwriting of prices and inputs. These allowed many producers to continue in farming with a reasonable income and lifestyle. Agriculture must satisfy the wishes of its customers. But who are the customers? For many rural producers they have become agrifood corporations, many of which use the foods and fibres produced on-farm as generic ingredients in the production of durable foods. Here, value is added at the stage of industrial manufacture and is captured by the food firm. And, with global sourcing, it is the agrifood companies that know which locations of the world will feed others. The actual producer of food and the eventual consumer are, literally, worlds apart and are only brought together by profit making opportunities identified by the corporate food industry.

Regional Misfortune

And what of regional Australia? An argument has been advanced by writers such as Waters (1995) that territoriality is largely devoid of meaning when everyone can be connected to the Internet. Instantaneous telecommunication, and greatly improved transportation, are the keys to the future incorporation of formerly 'backward' areas into the global economy. The collapse of time and space allows participation in a global culture from anywhere in the world. The optimistic 'reading' of such a prophecy is that in a world where knowledge industries will be paramount, geographical location is not crucial to lifestyle or life-chances.

There are problems with such a formulation. Gill (1996), Cox (1996) and Stilwell (1998) argue that sites of knowledge production and consumption in the world's major cities are becoming increasingly important, not less important, as headquarters for global capital.

The main financial centres of New York, London and Tokyo, and the 'lower order' world cities including Paris, Los Angeles, Toronto, Sydney, Singapore and Hong Kong, are gaining in prominence as globalisation proceeds. Some are now appearing in other parts of the world – Kuala Lumpur, Bangkok, Shanghai, and Mexico City. They are the homes for the privileged workers who are key to the success of the transnational corporations. And they are the sites of research and other knowledge-linked production (see Mittelman, 1996a: 14) In this world, there is little flowing to the non-urban regions in terms of capital, knowledge and people. Indeed, the lure of the city would seem to be as great as it ever has been, 'pulling' those who – particularly in areas where agricultural restructuring is forcing increasing scale in farming and where there are no new jobs in regional areas to compensate those forced off farms (see McMichael, 1996) – would otherwise choose to remain in non-metropolitan regions. And moreover, regional Australians are firmly implicated in this process.

A sobering analysis is provided by O'Hearn (1995) in relation to Ireland. The lesson is one which should be heeded by those believing that the 'TNC-ing' of the regions is the solution to their problems of stagnation. For O'Hearn (1995: 85):

> Irish industry, which was destroyed after EC accession in 1973, was only partly replaced by FDI (Foreign Direct Investment). However, TNCs were unreliable engines of growth because of their short life span and their failure to expand, and also because they created a dependence on ever-increasing flows of FDI for economic expansion, which were not forthcoming. After investment in basic manufactures dried up, the Irish turned to electronics, then to pharmaceuticals and, most recently, to international services. The result – between indigenous closures, TNC cutbacks and restructures, and the difficulty in attracting new investment – was a steady decrease in manufacturing employment and a rising rate of unemployment. Increasing numbers of Irish people were marginalized in the periphery of the EU during the 1980s. Seventy per cent of the unemployed are now long-term unemployed – and essentially unemployable.

According to O'Hearn, the EU's 'restructuring' regime has produced a 'semiperipheral reserve army' which must accept lower wages, reduced the policy choices for local areas (the EU demands continuing privatisation or the threat of 'Cuban-type isolation'), has increased competition between peripheral regions and has increased the 'disparity between the profitable high-tech, but still delinked, foreign sectors and the low profit, unstable, indigenous ones' (O'Hearn, 1995: 86). As McMichael (1995: 48) points out, neoliberalist ideologies accompanied by free market policies appear to be providing most benefit to the metropolitan states and their core classes rather than spreading any advantage in a socially just manner.

Conclusion

Regional areas within 'peripheral' states like Australia would appear to be doubly affected by state-based policies which accord with the new rules of globalisation. Such policies lead to the reduction of state investment but fail, at the same time, to create alternative options for economic growth. It is essential therefore to think of uneven development as occurring not only between nation states but also between and within regions at the level of the nation state.

With rural and regional communities within nation states becoming increasingly vulnerable, there is likely to emerge a scramble to secure their piece of the global world order. This might mean local governments using scarce resources to provide cheap land or inputs (such as gas, electricity or water) for those corporations agreeing to site their plants in those areas. It might also mean providing the sort of anti-union climate which the corporations believe is essential to stable production. With many regions competing with others we may see, as Brecher and Costello (1994) have argued, a 'race to the bottom' as localities employ whatever combination of resources they can in an attempt to lure corporate investment. It is this particular aspect of the 'global future' which could further disadvantage Australia's currently depressed regional spaces. The challenge is to identify viable, alternative, options without denying the 'reality' of globalism. It is the choice as Latham (1998) has reminded us, of potentially becoming a victim of, or acting instead to civilise, global capitalism. The trajectory of current debate seems certain to ensure that regional people become unfortunate victims, with the nation state rendering itself unable to intervene.

The concept of globalisation points toward the range of phenomena which we must consider. It highlights the potential breadth of change and the interactions among the economic, social, cultural and political factors which drive restructuring. At one and the same time it points to important origins of change affecting regional Australia, identifies the ideologies and policies which are facilitating and accelerating change and indicates the impossibility of those ideologies and policies adequately serving the interests of regional people. Before analysing the processes of change at the human level it is wise to consider a framework for such analysis which will account for the interests of regional people and provide a basis for reasoned and realistic policy development.

Further Reading

Latham, M. (1998) *Civilising Global Capital: New Thinking for Australian Labor*, Sydney: Allen & Unwin.
  – identifies globalisation as a social issue for Australia and proposes some accommodating rather than radical policy responses
McMichael, P. (2000) *Development and Social Change: A Global Perspective*, 2nd edn, California: Pine Forge Press.
  – analyses the process of globalisation, its causes and effects
McMurtry, J. (1998) *Unequal Freedoms: the Global Market as an Ethical System*,
Toronto: Garamond Press.
  – discusses the ethical issues surrounding globalisation and neoliberalism
Tomlinson, J. (1999) *Globalization and Culture*, Cambridge: Polity Press.
  – traces accounts of the relationship between economic globalisation and culture
Wiseman, J. (1998) *Global Nation? Australia and the Politics of Globalisation*, Cambridge: Cambridge University Press.
  – considers globalisation in the Australian context with an eye to politics and possible political and other actions in response

3
People versus Policy

As both a process of economic and social change and a vehicle for a political ideology, globalisation offers no glimpse of anything beyond its own formula. It looms as a juggernaut: a systemic force for change imposing new social relationships and, importantly, providing a simple belief system to explain what is happening, justify it and advocate more of it. A different way of thinking is essential to prevent the establishment of an oppressive orthodoxy. In this chapter we take a closer look at neoliberal economics and the basis it has lain for policy. We then look for the tools necessary to move toward developing a new kind of policy. But we also consider some dangers in using those tools in an uncritical way, among which we confront the notion of rurality itself.

The key to a new understanding comes through the related sociological concepts of 'reflexivity' and 'postmodernisation', when used with an awareness of power relations among interest groups in society. Reflexivity is really about people's reflection and consequent action. To be reflexive is to monitor the actions of oneself and of others, to assess the outcomes, and to alter behaviour as a consequence. We argue that all people – but for our purposes, regional people – are actively engaged in creating their worlds, and world visions, through such a process. Social activity is constantly informed by knowledge from social interaction, from the media, from educational institutions, and from a host of other influences. Society is reproduced according to the ways such knowledge is interpreted and acted upon. We need to understand the process of reflexivity, including the constraints on people's understanding and action imposed by systematic relations of power in which all people are engaged.

Postmodernity is an historical period, said to have started in the late twentieth century, during which fundamental changes are occurring in society and social relations. Postmodernisation refers to the current process of change within capitalism in which new 'postindustrial' options (for example, the growth of tourism, recreation, and the knowledge industries) combine with postmodern culture (represented by new symbols, social arrangements and 'flows' of ideas and values) to create a highly 'disorganised' and differentiated form of social and economic system. By eroding the boundaries of social life, postmodernity is creating the conditions for confusion, disillusionment, resentment and resistance as rural and regional people seek to live in meaningful and purposeful ways. At the same time as it undermines older styles of work, politics and culture, it also presents new opportunities for economic enterprise and social interaction. This is the dialectic of postmodernity (Crook et al., 1992) – the tearing away of older symbols, values and ways of economic life, while creating alternative modes. The essential thing to remember is that the process of postmodernisation, like that of globalisation, is not 'neutral' in its effects: there are those whose power is enhanced, and there are those who lose power. In its present trajectory, postmodernisation is creating circumstances in which regional Australians are losing power.

We also need to be aware of a new way of looking at the world, known as postmodernism. It has counterparts in the arts and architecture, but for our purposes it refers to a highly controversial but nevertheless significant way of analysing society. Postmodernism is independent of theories of postmodernity and postmodernisation, except insofar as it might be thought of as a product of a postmodern age. Acceptance of a theory of postmodernity does not necessarily involve accepting postmodernism as a perspective on society, but nevertheless lessons may be drawn from it.

Postmodernism is sceptical: questioning commonly accepted principles of the social sci-ences. This has happened, with productive outcomes, throughout the history of sociology. Postmodernism, however, when attacking the notion that there is a real society which is open to analysis, has been criticised reasonably for being unproductive. All it seems able to tell us is that everything about society is relative to everything else. Nevertheless, it is necessary to look closely at definitions when analysing the comprehensive and rapid processes of change into postmodernity. This means opening our perspective to frameworks which extend to the defi-nition and interpretation of reality and what it means to be a regional or rural person. Post-modernism prompts us to do this much at least. It could be seen as a polar opposite to the stark and unquestioning empiricism and positivism of that form of economics which underpins neoliberalism and hence the juggernaut of globalisation.

Old Thinking

We must be prepared to accept that many Australians, for productive reasons, will want to live, or have little choice but to live, outside the metropolitan cities. We must also acknowledge that many of those people are socially disadvantaged (Cheers, 1998; Stehlik and Lawrence, 1999). If economic forces are left alone to dictate population location, many regional dwellers will find themselves in poorer, ageing, communities. They will not be able to leave, and probably many would not want to. The basic policy question currently is: to what extent should market forces (alone) determine population distribution and, indirectly, provision for that population, in Australia? In other words, should policy be supportive of (complement) current trends towards the centralisation of economic activity in the cities and larger regional service centres, or should it challenge those trends? The neoliberal response is likely to be negative for regional interests, but regional people will neither 'go away' nor surrender to globalisation.

The question is particularly confronting to governments due to an apparent need for greater provision for the people in the regions at the same time as the state faces demands from metropolitan centres for infrastructure provision and from voters for taxation reductions, something to which neoliberal thinking allocates high priority. As a result of policies which are based on notions of an homogeneous regional Australia, entrenched problems among cer-tain sections of the population are unlikely to be addressed (Stehlik and Lawrence, 1999). Yet, to treat the regional as something different will often raise the spectre of 'pork barrelling' or bias in government policy. Why should the regions be treated any differently from the main cities? If Australia is to retain any notions of social justice and equity, they must be applied spatially across the metropolitan areas and the regions. There is an additional answer: funda-mentalism is likely to thrive among resistance to metropolitan dominance, emanating from the creation of an increasingly disaffected, economically marginalised, and politically volatile rural community which is itself suffering internal social division and exclusion. These con-cerns are not new, but they must be maintained and respected.

Rural policy-making has come to be dominated by the academic discipline of economics, particularly what is known as neoclassical economics which, while not denying need for equity and justice, would tend to assume that they will be taken care of. It has been practised and advocated in universities, various research institutions, 'think-tanks' and government bureaucracies with substantial if varying influence throughout the western democracies. In their comparative research, Coleman and Skogstad (1995) found that Australia rather more than Canada has possessed an 'epistemic community': a network of like-minded and influential people stretching from research organisations through government departments to farmer organisations which has fostered the development of policy based on neoliberal beliefs. Such is the source of the main thrust of what is now old policy thinking.

The neoliberal perspective accepts and implicitly praises the inevitability of globalisation, thereby endorsing and justifying all the negative effects which accompany it. Take, for example, the position of Australia's leading rural economic forecaster, the Australian Bureau of Agricultural and Resource Economics (ABARE). Following closely on the news that some 40 000 farms had disappeared over the past two decades (*Weekend Australian* 19–20 September 1998: 14) and that the prospects for rural commodities were bleak, the Executive Director of ABARE delivered a speech to the Annual Outlook Conference explaining that even more farmers must abandon agriculture. Under the heading 'Battling Graziers Told to Quit Land', the Executive Director was quoted as saying that those in need should get welfare and counselling to assist them in their decision: they had simply run out of any other options (*Courier Mail*, 18 March 1999: 6). Under this view, the best that people can do is to obtain 'welfare' and 'counselling' and to leave agriculture so that, through farm amalgamation, their neighbours can improve farm viability. If country towns disappear and regional centres stagnate, that too must be seen as a consequence of the laws of supply and demand acting in a logical fashion. The global market *will* prevail, and people need to adjust to that reality; such are the exhortations of neoliberalism.

As has now been demonstrated by many scholars (see Rees et al., 1993; Stewart, 1994; Kelsey, 1995) the neoliberal economistic approach overlooks a number of factors: that the 'free market' is a myth (and that for most nations economic decisions which influence industry are greatly tempered by political and social considerations); that the attempts of governments further to expose Australia's industries to international competition are – in a world of continuing protection abroad – disadvantaging, rather than enhancing prospects for growth of those industries; that the 'level playing field' is a 'lie' promulgated to justify industry restructuring, but which results in deindustrialisation; and that economic 'signals' are only one set which producers take into consideration when making decisions about location and resource use (see Rees et al., 1993; Stewart, 1994; Vanclay and Lawrence, 1995; Barr and Cary, 2000).

This blinkered outlook stems from a textbook approach which focuses on the inevitable 'pressure' that continued economic growth – viewed as essential for Australia's well-being – puts on the farm sector. 'The problem' arises because, even as prices fall and consumer incomes rise, the demand for farm products fails to rise (because people do not spend more on food) and technology enables increases in productivity which only lead to further price falls (see Malcolm et al., 1996: 57). Farmers have little choice but to remain trapped within this cycle, due to difficulty in obtaining fulfilling and well-remunerated full-time off-farm employment in situations of declining work options. The cultural tradition of farming has placed value on perseverance

and attachment to land and community at the same time as it has not placed value on education, especially education of a kind which could lead toward alternative careers. Under this
analysis it appears inevitable that there will either be ever fewer farmers or ever poorer farmers.
There is a third possibility, extensively adopted in the United States and Europe, which
involves subsidisation of farmers by taxpayers and consumers (Malcolm et al., 1996: 58). For
neoliberalists only the first two scenarios are to be countenanced: the third is anathema because
it involves the supposedly distorting impacts of state intervention (see Gow, 1994).

Proponents of globalisation talk of the negative impacts of anything which would limit
free trade. They lambast tariffs and protection, view as futile organised labour's attempts to
'protect' wage levels, see an inevitability in the spread of the technologies and products of
TNCs, and believe that government actions which counter global processes will damage Australia's trading future. For those who see globalisation as an inevitable process in the progressive development of capitalism, anything blocking such progress is considered to place limits
on competition, job creation and economic development (see Kanter, 1995: 353–4).

We have seen arguments advocating isolationism (older thinking) emerge in Australia
from the Conservative Right (see Carroll and Manne, 1992; Santamaria, 1997) and from the
Radical Left (see Rees et al., 1993). They are driven largely by the realisation that Australia is
being deindustrialised and that manufacturing industry (the backbone of many regional cities
as well as suburbs in the capital cities) has suffered immeasurable damage. The general argument from both sides is to expose the extent of inequality in Australia (where the top 5 per
cent of people own half the nation's total wealth) (see Rees et al., 1993: 307), to suggest this
mirrors overseas trends (in the United States the top one per cent of society controls 40 per
cent of the nation's wealth – see Santamaria, 1997: 22) and to indicate that such polarisation,
which is viewed as neither socially desirable nor economically sensible, is a direct outcome of
the government's blind obedience to international capital. Both call for a more socially just
policy mix. For the Conservative Right the aim is to return to a Menzies/McEwen style 1960s
Australia where the nation state protects local capital and controls the finance sector. For the
Radical Left the aim is to restore a sort of benign corporatism where the state intervenes to
reskill workers through higher levels of investment in education and training, and to restore
community services through public sector expenditure. The Left would restrict imports, limit
the activities of TNCs, create a wealth tax, and stipulate that superannuation funds are
invested in Australian-based companies (Rees et al., 1993; Stilwell, 1993). Both Left and
Right combine elements of import substitution industrialisation with export oriented industrialisation. Both 'put the market in its place' by reasserting the importance of interventionist
policies by the nation state (see Santamaria, 1997: 22). Both, unfortunately, are devoid of
means to deal with the wider processes of postmodernisation and globalisation, and both are
currently rejected by the Coalition and Labor opposition. Yet, what we have from the major
political parties is an exclusively pro-globalisation stance denying the spatial inequalities
which are emerging from global restructuring.

The determinism of neoliberal thinking hints at a starting point for seeking a way out of
this impasse. Structural economic modelling cannot readily accommodate people, despite the
actions of people being central to the market mechanism on which its logic relies. People do

not just make market choices. As reflexive citizens they create economies, and can act to change them when they do not deliver personal or social benefits.

People Suffering Change

Many of Australia's regional people are confronting – and are confronted by – a period of fundamental change. There seems little they can do to direct it. They are seeing members of their families pursuing work and careers of kinds they had not anticipated. They are finding their communities depleted and their social relationships disrupted by the departures of friends and relatives and sometimes the arrival of new residents. They are finding the businesses which they had relied on for purchase of their products, provision of supplies and maintenance of services disappearing as their local economy deteriorates. They are feeling increasingly insecure as the health and community services they had come to rely on dwindle. Many are struggling to maintain a basic, healthy standard of living while they see a few others acquiring great wealth. They feel that the rest of Australia has turned against them. And yet they hang on to their land, their community, and their tradition. This situation would seem ready for a direct challenge to the system rather than the reordering of choices made within it.

At the same time they are hearing that they have new opportunities to obtain prosperity. They are told that the world is opening to them, but they are also told that they should change the ways they operate their farms and their businesses to participate in a new technically and culturally sophisticated international economy with which very few have had direct contact. They can see the 'ground rules' changing. The institutions they relied on for financial and material support, over which they felt they at least should have had some control and which they could previously expect to stand behind them and provide some security which they themselves could not, are being dismantled. And behind all this they can see the world changing, with institutions from overseas countries appearing to have a growing representation in Australian society and a great deal of material and ideological influence. A globalising system is unlikely to stand still in order to be challenged.

People do respond to these changes. They are changing their own lives in ways which can be either private (such as within their families) or public (such as within their communities and the nation). They organise and act politically. They operate farms differently. All these actions may individually and collectively alter the course of regional social change in large and small ways. It is these processes which we need to understand in order to find a basis for a new policy, one in which people can make a globalising system work for them. Accepting, and operating within, the neoliberal/neoclassical economics paradigm will not help them to achieve that goal. It will, instead, exacerbate their already tenuous position.

Much policy-making is carried out with little regard to those who are likely to feel the brunt of that policy. This is 'top down' planning at its best – or in this case, worst. Such is the dominance of the economic paradigm that writers on rural policy feel able to title their work as though it were the only source of wisdom which rural policy-makers would need. Readers of the opening pages of Godden's (1997) *Agricultural and Resource Policy* are introduced to a book which advocates asking why and how governments make decisions, an admirable suggestion, but it offers a relatively narrow view of government and relevant social processes.

The Poverty of Rational Action Theory

The point that much economic analysis ignores the problem of power relations has been made many times. Not even the most ardent neoliberal economist can ignore the fact that decisions are made in the context of power relations and that their own prescriptions help to create those relations. It would be quite easy to ignore relations between people if one were a member of the neoliberal 'epistemic community' of like-minded thinkers who share a number of assumptions about how the world works. Regional people are generally remote from such a community, including members of the farmer organisations representing their rural constituents (see chapter 5).

What is now popularly termed the 'economic rationalist' approach to policy-making is usually based on what is referred to as rational action theory in sociology. This is particularly alarming because the globalisation/neoliberal agenda places much importance on the actions of individuals, but its conceptualisation of that action is severely limited. When we can be confident that people have a clear perception of their aims, that they are acting consciously and intentionally and that they can predict with some certainty the results of their actions, then a rational action model can usefully be applied to develop predictions of outcomes. It is so only if we can be confident that we too have a clear perception of their aims. When people's aims and the outcomes of their actions can be reduced to economic variables, an economic rational action model might be applied.

However, there are many situations which do not meet these criteria. For example, as Hindess (1988) points out, much behaviour is either habitual, unconscious or both. How often can people be sufficiently confident of the outcomes of their action to be able to say that their decision to act was purely rational? What are we to make of unintended consequences which may arise? Rational action theory offers little to address these questions. Moreover, its acceptance at the expense of other approaches, which help us to understand why people do what they do, leaves a huge gap in our analysis of Australia's rural economy and society.

Rural society offers an example of behaviour which is economic but obviously not always determined entirely by purely rational consideration of economic factors alone. Decisions of farmers offer illustrations, as they work valuable properties for little return against a tide of financial pressure, trust their self-reliance and perseverance, 'tighten their belts' and impoverish themselves while remaining trapped in cycles of increasing productivity for diminishing returns at great potential cost to their families (see Gray et al., 1993; 1996). In making decisions to remain on their land, at times attracting the press to sites of conflict as banks attempt to evict them, they are expressing values constructed over time and amid specific social relations. It may be possible to develop a predictive model which quantifies those values – one based upon rational action precepts – but it would be impossible and pointless to do so without understanding the process through which the relevant values were formed and maintained.

We recall hearing a Commonwealth finance minister, when asked to justify his 'economic rationalist' approach to policy, asking if he should be expected to be 'economically irrationalist'. But it is possible to be 'rationalistic' in ways, which are not economically driven. He was wrong if assuming that economic motivation offers the only credible form of rationality. Being economically rational may be socially irrational and vice versa: economic irrationality may be socially rational. To some extent the questioner was also misguided: the problem lies in the impossibility of the economics paradigm alone illuminating the major social processes through which the negative aspects of purely economically-driven policy thinking arise. This is not to say that all economists fail to account for non-economic, non-market behaviour. The problem for policy is that the only prescriptions arising from economics which are being heeded in a neoliberal climate are those which have purely economic outcomes.

The policy prescriptions of the economic paradigm rely heavily on an extension of the rational action model in the form of public choice theory. This approach has been extensively criticised elsewhere on grounds which parallel arguments against rational action theory. Public choice theory is founded on the assumption that political behaviour is driven by a simple logic, such that voters will always seek only to maximise their political benefit in a predictable way. However, it is apparent that political, like economic motivation is diverse and changeable and the causes of social action are too complex to be reduced to a simple model (Stretton and Orchard, 1994).

None of this implies that the economics paradigm does not offer insight into social factors or that it is not concerned with social outcomes. Godden (1997: 11) indicates a concern for welfare, as it can be threatened by politicians after their 'capture' by interest groups. 'Welfare', however, is often assumed to arise from maximisation of the efficiency of the economic system, with the opposition of the objectives of efficiency and distribution being one of the policy-maker's problems. Although basing their models on assumptions about rationally acting agents, some writers treat the economic system as an object (committing the logical sin of reification, or thinking of it as a 'thing' when it basically consists of what people do) which when adequately groomed will maximise the well-being of all who are subject to it. The problem for such an approach is that the economic system is not simply an object. It is operated by agents under the constraints it imposes, but those agents are capable of action in response to those constraints within their own social relations. That action may not be just economic: people act outside the market, even though it may be possible for the realms of social life to be redefined so that they conceptually resemble a market.

Social Power Relations

The point that political action is relevant to economics is widely accepted. The economics paradigm, however, only admits a narrow conceptualisation of political action. When viewed in the context of social power relations a much wider view of the significant factors emerges. Economists frequently discuss relevant political actors and action, referring to 'political constraints' on policy proposals and apparently powerful 'rent-seekers' who obtain arguably unjustifiable benefits. These suffer from narrowness of perspective rather than necessarily being simply wrong. Broader approaches to power are available.

Lukes' (1974) formulation of a 'three-dimensional view' offers insights. Power has manifestations beyond what can be seen happening in politics. As a starting point, he accepts that power relations are readily evident in struggles between people or organisations. This is what we see when we look at the actions of politicians and interest groups as they are carried on in the public eye. If we are privy to the behind-the-scenes activities of interest groups and the machinations within political parties, we might see a lot more. What we see there is debate or argument: struggles to assert the interests of some individual or group over those of others. Sometimes we might see one individual or group succeed in having their view prevail. We could conclude that the winner is more powerful than the loser. That would be a reasonable conclusion, but it would not necessarily tell us all that we might want to know about power relations in that context. What if the concerns of some groups were not fought over, argued or discussed at all? Might there not be some people whose interests are simply ignored, or just not acknowledged by politicians, political parties, lobby groups, etc? Those people are never likely to enter a struggle, or in some other way have their interests represented in the political arena. Australian history contains many examples of such people, most notably Indigenous people and migrants of non-English speaking background. Regional people might, hypothetically at least, be in a parallel situation at the beginning of the twenty-first century, despite earlier histories of political prominence among both conservative and Labor parties. As we will see later, decline in prominence is not just a product of population, or voter, movement.

Lukes (1974) proposes that we should consider the possibility that agendas are being set, not necessarily intentionally by any identifiable group, but with the effect that the interests of other groups are ignored. Looking for power relations where no overt conflict or debate is apparent is what he would call using a two-dimensional view. It has been used effectively to examine the social conditions experienced by sub-populations within towns and cities (see Bachrach and Baratz, 1970; Gray, 1991) but it can be applied in principle more widely. The two-dimensional view is extended, though not with such theoretical clarity, into an equally useful three-dimensional view. Under this perspective, agenda setting is also important, but those subject to power are unconsciously complicit in agenda setting, contrary to their own interests, by adhering to values and beliefs which deny any need to place their interests on the agenda. This has also been applied in power studies (see Gray, 1991) and has underpinned much radical sociology, notably but by no means only, feminist thinking. It is compatible with a 'governmentality' perspective (see Dean, 1999). The three-dimensional view, like 'governmentality', guides our analysis towards the processes which determine the values and beliefs of people and make people complicit in their own governance. Such people-focused approaches are crucial to analysis of post-modernisation but appear impossible within orthodox economics, the foundation stone of which is simply aggregate supply and demand. What is missing from the latter is a capacity to examine the processes through which people perceive their own interests and act upon them.

Economics might accommodate the two-dimensional view. For example, Godden (1997: 10) stresses the importance of the media on the grounds that 'information is a key commodity in the political market place'. However, by regarding power relations as a marketplace he is only able to observe what is in the market. This is disappointing because he notes that media proprietors may have political interests and stresses the dominance of the Australian media by a small number of firms, which are capable of influencing what is offered in the 'market place'. He also points to attempts by politicians to control the agenda of the media, and by implication to set the agenda of politics. This does not go as far as indicating the possibility that the agenda is being set by the media, and potentially other members of what he might call 'business', by way of influencing the values and beliefs of people. This is not to say that economists are blind to this possibility. Gow (1997) for example, notes that media depictions of farm families suffering under drought conditions and the public response helped to persuade the government that it should (as Gow saw it) reverse its 'economic rationalist' policy and provide welfare relief. Godden (1997) offers some analysis of the ideology underpinning the National and former Country Parties, but Lukes' three-dimensional view takes us further with the prospect of explaining how that ideology is embedded in social relations. The choices of individuals, and the ways in which those choices become constrained by the consequences of those choices, cannot be made apparent without analysis of power relations from a broader perspective. Here the application of the concepts of reflexivity and postmodernity, with an eye to power relations, becomes crucial.

The three-dimensional view, like 'governmentality', indicates the importance of reflexivity. People may come to question their values and beliefs related to their own identity and status, and the ways in which they are governed. 'Does the identity I develop and express for myself make sense given the status I have been accorded by the economic and social system?' Reflexivity is ultimately about examination of the social relations in which one's life is embedded. 'Do my social relationships really reflect the kinds of values which I would attach to them?' 'What are those values, as I perceive them?' 'Is my community working towards the values-based mutual goals of its members?' Or at the level of the social system: 'Is it wise to trust the system of governance which I expect to maintain my democratic rights and a reasonable economic status for myself and my family?' Such reflection can question the kind of power relations which become apparent using the three-dimensional view. However, not all reflection would necessarily be of this kind. Institutions like family, community and government would not necessarily come under such questioning. Hence, the processes of reflection, the structures within which it arises and the social interaction though which it develops, all become very important to our analysis. They underpin the prospects for people perceiving and acting on the interests which will serve them best.

The potential questioning of governance leads to another problem for those writing in the economics paradigm, at least as far as they aim their policy prescriptions at national government. The context in which people make decisions, provided by the nation-state, is being changed by forces beyond it. There have certainly been instances of the Commonwealth Government widening its powers. Acquisition of responsibility for Indigenous affairs is perhaps the most prominent example. But ironically, it is matters of economics where governments are most vulnerable to the power of 'global' agents like transnational corporations and financial institutions. However, the nation state does not bound reflexivity.

New (Reflexive) Thinking

The development of a new approach to policy must be one which accounts for social relations. This involves relations among rural people, between regional and urban people and between all Australians and their governments. It must account for impersonal global forces and the reflexivity and capacity of communities and individual people. As a first step towards new policy, we address the ways in which we can look upon regional Australia and its society. We must do a little theoretical thinking so that we ask the right questions and look for answers in the right places.

In order to develop 'new policy', we must set out to answer some questions which will help us to plot the trajectory of Australian rural society. What are the changes which are affecting people? How do people look upon these changes? How should we interpret their views and actions? How can we ensure that we view the entire scene: both change inflicted and change created? How might they look for and develop alternative futures? In order to begin the substantial task of answering such questions, it is first necessary to find ways of looking at change and the people it affects from outside and above. Our aim is to see the relationships among the many events, which are occurring in families, towns and corporations and interpret, in an informed and reasoned manner, the attitudes adopted and the actions taken. This calls for application of some abstract concepts.

Theoretical concepts enable us to 'see the big picture': to generalise from specific events and experiences, understand what caused those events and experiences and predict what might emanate from them. They can offer a means to ensure that we ask the appropriate questions and answer them in ways which are, if not free of bias, at least making clear the ways in which bias, or simply a breadth of different perspectives, might be accounted for. They also offer opportunities to develop solutions to the problems which will be encountered in this process.

It is important that we work out what we need to look for in order to develop our understanding of farmers' and other rural and regional people's views and actions. We must be alert to the range of possibly relevant factors which might lie behind, or in some way be associated with, change. Here we can take a lesson from postmodernism, insofar as it draws us to more basic questions of definition and relativity. Farming is usually taken to be a fundamental feature of rural life. But rural life is often described in ways which extend beyond farming. Surely people with other occupations who live in rural areas are also part of rural society? But our images of rurality universally present farming as a central feature. The fundamental questions can still be asked: what is rurality and how should we regard rural society and the place of farming within it? As globalisation threatens our concept of rurality both structurally and culturally, we must be certain of what we understand by rurality to begin with.

Our interpretations of change in farming are closely related to broader theories of rural change which are based on definitions of rurality. Those definitions lead towards the deeper questions about rural society, its people (including farmers) and the way it is changing. Simply defining rural implies acceptance of its existence. But if we believe that the rural or regional exists as a feature of modern or postmodernising society, might it embody a particular perspective on society? That is, could being a member of a rural or regional society mean adopting a unique view of society? Might we be adopting that particular perspective or at least accounting for it in our analysis? How would we know if the perspective which we adopt were unique? And, would it necessarily lead toward different conclusions from those to be developed from another, presumably metropolitan, perspective, which ignores the views developed by farming and other regional people?

These questions highlight a problem with reflexivity. We encounter reflexivity in society and in research itself. In interpreting the society we live in we try to grasp a particularly slippery object. This is because the object is also the subject. That is, what we interpret also creates our own interpretations. While we can see what is happening, the ways in which we observe are being made by us and for us. And what is happening now becomes available for interpretation once it has happened. In order to illustrate the problem, the German sociologist Klaus Lichtblau (1995) quotes Loewith (1960: 163): 'attempting to orient oneself to history while it is happening would be like trying to hold on to the waves during a shipwreck'. But how far can we step out of reality in order to grasp what is changing it? Is there a danger that we will find ourselves denying reality altogether? While the latter question can be answered affirmatively, it remains possible to adopt an alternative, or realist, approach to social science (see Keat and Urry, 1975) and avoid the plunge into futile relativism which postmodernism might lead us toward. Some would see no danger in relativism while others seek to apply postmodernism in critical ways and attract loud criticism in doing so (see the debate between Yapa (1996 and 1997) and Shrestha (1997) As Stone (1996) argues, there is still a path between realism and postmodernism which takes account of both.

For our purposes, reflexivity can be seen to have two elements which are related to each other like Russian dolls: the larger containing the smaller but both being independently identifiable. The larger doll is analogous to the reflexivity of society. In a 'post-traditional' society (Giddens, 1994) all individuals and institutions operate reflexively, able to perceive and react to each other in ways which had previously been constrained. For example, after obtaining legitimacy over tradition through the period of the Enlightenment, science had enjoyed insulation from society, but it 'is no longer regarded by the majority as sacrosanct ... In a reflexive social universe, where the essentially skeptical nature of scientific method becomes revealed to view, lay individuals have a much more dialogic involvement with science and technology' (Giddens, 1996: 220). This may become apparent in the political processes of research funding, but also when scientific debates appear to be won or lost according to the extent of popular support which the protagonists are able to obtain. As Giddens argues, the number of people convinced by the global warming thesis affects the veracity bestowed upon it (1996: 11).

The smaller doll is analogous to the immediate social environment of the observer: the social space in which research is carried out and reacted to. This doll draws our attention to the relationship between the researcher and those people who are studied. It is important to the practice of research in particular rather than social activity in general. The importance of the reflexivity of the research relationship is argued by Pierre Bourdieu, the best-known, but by no means the only, advocate for reflexive research. To Bourdieu, reflexivity is 'the inclusion of a theory of intellectual practice as an integral component and necessary condition of a critical theory of society' (Wacquant, 1992: 36). Bourdieu uses reflexivity to strengthen rather than weaken the knowledge base of sociology by directing attention to assumptions made in social research in general, not just the work of individual researchers. This approach also puts us 'at loggerheads' (Wacquant, 1992: 37) with postmodernism's versions of reflexivity but offers an important principle to address in both theorising and empirical analysis. We now address some important theoretical issues, namely defining rurality and its relation to farming and developing an approach to research and analysis with an eye to reflexivity.

Perspectives on Farming and 'The Rural'

There have been many debates about the value of 'the rural' as a concept to help us understand modern society. They follow the broader changes and developments which sociology has passed through and continues to negotiate. Among the 'classical' writers of sociology, Marx, Weber and Toennies perceived a distinctively rural society based on agriculture – but with each looking upon it quite differently. Marx depicted rural people as being left behind in the development of industrial capitalism. Weber took the view that in modern industrial society, such as the United States, there would no distinctively rural element, but recognised that the farming tradition which he observed and analysed may linger in some circumstances in Europe. However, if farmers became capitalists there would be nothing distinctively socially rural (Bonner, 1998).

Toennies observed the loss of the basis for traditional social relations as capitalism and rationality rose to become dominant social forces. He contrasted two types of society: the former 'Gemeinschaft' based on family and community and the modern and contrastingly impersonal, associational 'Gesellschaft'. This contrast has since been reified into the notion of the 'rural–urban continuum' by equating the former with rural society and the latter with urban. The rural was seen as socially different from the urban and value was implicitly placed on its characteristics including relatively sparse settlement, intimacy with the environment and a distinctive social identity fostered amid less impersonal social relations (Cloke and Thrift, 1994). All these characteristics were associated with farming and the characteristic features of life in small settlements. They might also be applied to regional lifestyles which are not based economically or socially on farming, as they are not dependent on social relations based on agriculture.

By the 1960s the heuristic value of the rural–urban contrast was seriously questioned, most notably by Pahl (1968), at the same time as the macro forces of advanced capitalism seemed to be providing many writers with explanations for all social phenomena in question. However, a functionalist, holistic approach to rural studies, most notably demonstrated in studies of local communities (see Bell and Newby, 1971) received few challenges until the 1980s when, in the wake of the demolition of the rural–urban continuum model, the question raised by Marx was resurrected. A political economy of agriculture steered rural sociology back to the analysis of world capitalism, including the growth of global agrifood systems (see Buttel, 2000). In such analyses the primary focus on rural–urban distinctions lost significance.

However, the significance of the anti-urban 'Gemeinschaft' features attributed to rural society and to rural living has remained. The popular value placed on these characteristics is one of the forces said to be pushing rural society beyond the 'modern' form arising with capitalism which was explored by Marx, Weber and Toennies. At the same time as those seeking to identify the structures which underpin social life moved their attention to the broader features of capitalism, those focusing on the cultures of modern society, led by Williams (1975) have identified the rural–urban distinction as central to those cultures. Note that what is significant is the distinction which is drawn rather than essential differences in terms of social structure, culture and way of life. The drawing of the rural–urban distinction since classical sociology has created an 'other', but in doing so created a problem for reflexivity (Bonner, 1998). If there are two societies, rural and urban, premodern and modern, or two different kinds of modernity, is it possible to regard one from a viewpoint offered by the other and maintain both elements of reflexivity discussed above?

Rural–Urban Relativities

This question raises problems for research which attempts to compare regional and urban places. When the work of Kelly (1987) was reported in the press as saying that rural people were more conservative in their attitudes to family life, it attracted rejoinders from rural dwellers proclaiming their pride in conservatism. Why would they wish to investigate it, or see it investigated? Why should the researcher's agenda be given priority? Why should the researcher's interpretations be given sole legitimacy? Many studies appear to have ignored such questions. Work such as Beggs et al. (1996), Grunseit et al. (1995), Hampel et al. (1995), Marotz-Baden and Colvin (1986) all risk attack from those demanding reflexivity. In addition, they may be criticised for ignoring differences among rural populations which a unidimensional rural–urban comparison would obscure, although some such as Beggs et al. (1996) do consider this point. Freudenberg (1991) and Bell (1992) take a more constructionist view. Bell in particular points out that rural–urban differences remain an important source of identity for rural people. Although in Portugal, where agriculture is practised extensively and with 34 per cent of all families having a farm, urban culture shares important attributes with the rural (Reis et al., 1990).

Some recent comparative studies appear to remain easy targets for postmodernist attack. Sarantakos (1998) undertook comparative quantitative analysis of responses to questions forming scales indicating perceived quality of life. Data were collected from urban and rural samples. The same questions were put to both samples. But if differences were hypothesised, so too might the possibility that the accepted concept of quality of life would differ between urban and rural dwellers. Adherents to postmodernism may argue that the research is inconclusive, at least without explication of the source of the concept of quality of life and its significance to both urban and rural dwellers. This all suggests an imperative to ascertain whether rural culture differs from urban. But none suggests that important social similarities and differences cannot occur between rural and urban places. Sarantakos (1998), for example, indicates that in response to some questions, rural dwellers offered many similar and some different responses when compared with urban dwellers. He attributes this result to a different tradition among rural people when compared to urban. It indicates that the reality of those similarities and differences is likely to be elusive and their significance more so. If we accept that there is a rural society we must accept its own reflexivity and, moreover, the necessity for the researcher to work reflexively within it.

This point is implicit in theoretical developments in rural studies, which have taken some note of postmodernist formulations. Rurality itself has come to be seen as socially constructed (Cloke and Thrift, 1994). This tells us that there may be more than one 'rural', more than one 'other'. Rurality may be built from the ideas of real estate developers, the media or academics in addition to whomever may be defined as rural dwellers. The rodeo held in a city may be just as rural as 'the back paddock'. From this perspective, the ways in which the meanings of rurality are constructed, and particularly the social relationships which provide context to their construction, attract paramount attention. Some research has adopted, at least implicitly, the constructionist approach. Perkins (1989) and Till (1993), for example, discuss the production and application of symbols of rurality by urban developers. Palmer and Quinn (1997) have identified at least four distinct types of farming discourses prominent within the media (they describe these as traditional farming; self-sufficiency; permaculture;

and an 'agronomic discourse' which combines notions of agro-science with markets to justify the current economic rationalist approach to farming). How many others might exist, and what might be their current and future symbolic and political potency? Who is to say that 'the back paddock' or the 'country town' are now, or might continue to be, the 'real' rurality?

Cloke and Thrift (1994) identify this thinking as a fourth phase in the defining of the rural. It takes us further into reflexivity as it brings forth the thoughts and actions of all who participate in the construction of rurality, including farmers, city dwellers and researchers who strive to define rural. The processes through which that participation does or does not occur are also open to examination. They constitute a discourse through which 'otherness' is created and in which the identity associated with rurality/regionality is developed and its boundaries are negotiated and fixed (Share, 1995). Power relations are inherent in this discourse, making it sociologically vital.

The reality of rurality diminishes in significance when we discuss the power which some people have to define it and have their definition popularly accepted. Kapferer (1990) sees a mythology of rurality as more important than any reality which might be attributed to it. The power to invoke images of rurality and obtain identity from them, the power to create the 'other' and to occupy it is the power to make what becomes accepted as knowledge available for consumption (Share, 1995). It is vastly important, then, that these processes be understood and that the voices of all concerned be heard. Lawrence (1997) adds a warning to what would seem to be a simple exhortation to conduct reflexive research: beware that those lay voices which appear neglected are not just heard, for that would risk missing their relationship to those who are powerful. (The more powerful might influence interpretation of the position of the marginalised to the latter's advantage.) As Gray et al. (1997) argue, attention should focus on all aspects of the processes through which the interests of some are pursued while the interests of others are neglected. The basic theoretical question is no longer 'what is rural', but rather: 'whose definition of rurality prevails'? The cultural process of definition should not be allowed to distract attention from its social associations and consequences, a point made by Cloke (1997). Later we extend our argument that rural Australia is becoming as important as an image to be deployed as it is as a reality of life. And the image, always only loosely tethered, is no longer tied to the reality which confronts farming people. Moreover, their power to define rurality and to exemplify its practice in ways which serve their own interests has become increasingly questionable. Rural dwellers have been marginalised and denied access to their own image. This makes it important to consider the reflexive processes through which rural people seek to defend their identity.

Conclusion

In the ways described above we explore rural/regional change, illuminating the underlying cultural and structural forces moving rural/regional society into 'postmodernisation'. We must also explore the ways those forces interact with each other in the everyday lives of people. This will direct our policy thinking towards mechanisms with which regional people can perceive and pursue their interests in a global system. We are obliged to examine the power relations which are obscured by neoliberalism and effectively ignored by the associated textbook economics. With the lens provided by Lukes' three-dimensional view we should be able to examine the depth of those power relations. We also note, however, that they are not necessarily immutable, being subject to reflexivity. The structural conditions in which reflexivity might arise, and the cultural conditions in which reflexivity is carried on, emerge as important themes. They lead us to consider the ways in which regional people come to identify and interpret their interests.

Our later explorations will enter the cultural landscape of rural/regional society and thereby encounter the dangers of cultural relativities. This is an inevitable hazard when regarding cultural change, as culture becomes a variable, which is constantly changing. The culture itself can be manipulated by powerful forces which also act on our means of perceiving and defining it. Hence, we respect the necessity for two-dimensional reflexivity: that which is carried out by the individuals and institutions we study and our own as we hold our findings against a range of culturally-dependent interpretations.

By rejecting economic essentialism and the assumptions of rational action theory, but not ignoring their contributions when appropriate, we seek to specify the social relations of which policy must be cognisant and respectful. Lack of respect for power relations, and perceptions of them, can render policy-making futile, as power struggles at least change or even threaten to unravel the institutions upon which policy depends. The (albeit uneven and problematic) entry of One Nation and of other fringe right-wing parties into Australian politics and the defeat of the 'right-wing' Kennett government of the late 1990s, highlight the uncertainty of politics. There is an ever-present possibility of the destabilisation of orthodoxy by popular movements, which threaten, perhaps quite unintentionally, the entire process by which policy is made. The political volatility occurring within rural and regional Australia – driven largely by global restructuring – is an issue which is crucial to the future, not only of non-metropolitan Australia, but also of the entire nation.

Further Reading

Beck, U., Giddens, A. and Lash, S. (eds) (1994) *Reflexive Modernization: Politics, Tradition and Aesthetics in the Modern Social Order*, Oxford: Blackwell.
  – perspectives on social and cultural change by three leading European sociologists
Cloke, P., Doel, M., Matless, D., Phillips, M. and Thrift, N. (1994) *Writing the Rural: Five Cultural Geographies*, London: Paul Chapman Publishing.
  – cultural analysis of rurality and change
Crook, S., Pakulski, J. and Waters, M. (1992) *Postmodernization: Change in Advanced Society*, London: Sage.
  – Australian analysis of the changes said to be moving society into a postmodern period
Lukes, S. (1974) *Power: A Radical View*, London: Macmillan.
  – a short, relatively easy to read (and now classic) text on theories of power
Pritchard, B. and McManus, P. (eds) (2000) *Land of Discontent: the Dynamics of Change in Rural and Regional Australia*, Sydney: University of New South Wales Press.
  – a contemporary critical overview of recent changes in non-metropolitan Australia

The Social Transformation of Australian Farming

The process of change in rural Australia is, to a substantial degree, propelled by the restructuring of farming. The social as well as economic bases of farming are changing fundamentally. Such restructuring is seen by neoliberal economists as a cleansing process, often referred to as 'structural adjustment'. This consists of elimination of inefficient farmers from the agricultural system (see Gow, 1994). From a sociological perspective we see people and their communities being forced to make fundamental changes which are likely to affect them detrimentally and severely, potentially affecting their livelihoods, state of health and general quality of life. The difference between these two perspectives involves the element of choice: while the orthodox economist sees farmers making autonomous decisions and reacting to market forces, the sociologist's 'restructuring' view questions the possibility of autonomy. Farmers can either resist the forces of change or acquiesce, but they have constrained influence on the system which is determining their very narrow range of options. Nevertheless, they can undeniably influence the system in some ways, for while it affects their well-being and their entire cultural and structural condition, it enables as well as constrains them. Some analysis of rural restructuring will permit us later to examine the condition of the reflexivity of rural people, highlighting their urgency to determine their interests and find voices in the struggle to deal with 'global misfortune'.

Restructuring Farming in Australia and Overseas

Farming in Australia has been seen as something done by families and valued as such. Family farms have been held up as icons of the Australian way of struggling to succeed through hardship and adversity, though not to the extent that they have been in the United States. In Australia, it has been the farm worker rather than the entrepreneur who has contributed to legend-building (Lees, 1997). Family farms are still very much dominant numerically, but they are only part of the system which produces the food and fibre purchased by consumers.

   Changes to the other parts of the system, including politics, are having enormous impacts on farm families. Farming is now becoming a more risky undertaking, but increasing risk is only serving to increase dependency on the family as supplier of labour (Wright and Kaine, 1997). The institution of the family remains central, with all its complexity of values, ideology and relationships, to analysis of economic impacts on farming (Barlett, 1993; Gasson et al., 1988; Lloyd and Malcolm, 1997; Stayner, 1997a). Their family lives are also tied to the lives of their local communities. What follows is an analysis of what farmers see happening around them and affecting them, their families and communities.

Farm Ownership and Size
The traditional family farm still dominates Australian agriculture, but corporate farming is growing. Among broadacre and dairy farms, which together constitute three-quarters of Australian farms, 99.6 per cent are operated by families and 0.4 per cent by corporations, or dependent somewhat on definitions, 2 per cent are owned by companies (Garnaut and Lim-Applegate, 1998). However, corporate farms contribute 6.5 per cent of broadacre and dairy production, and for some industries, notably beef and cotton, corporate involvement is much

greater (Martin, 1996). In some situations it approaches totality. Eighty per cent of the area planted to hops in Tasmania is owned by one company (Miller, 1996: 72).

As the number of farms in Australia has declined, so the possibility of a 'disappearing middle', leaving only relatively large and relatively small farms, has been discussed. With the number of farms having declined by 25 per cent in twenty-five years (Gleeson and Topp, 1997), there has certainly been room for speculation about change in the distribution of farm sizes. Rates of change have varied. It has, for example, been more rapid in the dairy industry than in broadacre agriculture. Coastal and north central New South Wales and parts of Western Victoria have experienced the most rapid decline in farm numbers (more than 2 per cent per annum between 1985–86 and 1994–95) while an area near Darwin and the East Kimberley Wyndham region has seen small increases (Lindsay and Gleeson, 1997). Moreover, Lindsay and Gleeson (1997) find that it is the small farms which are disappearing rather than those of middle size. This tallies with the findings of research conducted in Europe and the United States (Albrecht, 1997; Munton and Marsden, 1991). Davidson and Schwarzweller (1995) offer a warning, lest someone think that such restructuring is making for a more efficient farming sector throughout. Albrecht noted that his finding related particularly to those areas where agriculture is strongest. Davidson and Schwarzweller look at marginal dairy farming areas and find that farm operations are remaining small, barely viable and with little prospect for change. Davidson (1997) comes to a similar conclusion from a study of a dairy farming area in New South Wales, finding small operations may hang on, and expansion for the middle and larger sized operations was difficult. Deregulation has since forced closures. Nevertheless, larger farms were growing beyond the size which could be run by a family. These changes indicate that under such pressures many farm families are having to change their practices and expectations. The rate of restructuring varies from place to place and among industries, but overall, there is growing differentiation between wealthy and poor farm families.

Coping

Farm families under financial threat have long been devising means of avoiding loss of their farms. We frequently hear that one in five farms is liable to financial failure (Stehlik et al., 1998). Many farmers face this prospect, and almost universally the family is their first line of defence. A range of 'coping strategies' becomes available. Gray et al. (1993) find that at the farm level, these include reducing expenditure on household needs as well as farm inputs and equipment, debt restructuring, working harder and increasing production, seeking alternative sources of income either on or off the farm, retraining for an alternative occupation and seeking government assistance either to retain the farm or dispose of it and establish elsewhere. The last-mentioned strategy is usually seen as a last resort. Reducing expenditure is very frequently used, but so is seeking off-farm income, with debt restructuring and attempts at diversification occurring significantly but less frequently. Government assistance is obtained infrequently. At a personal level, farm people try to improve their management as they reduce their personal expenditure. People also report talking it through with family and friends and sometimes just hoping.

In a sense, coping is a process which is changing while remaining the same. There have always been farm families who had sufficient capital either on or off the farm that enabled them not to suffer from periodic crises associated with production loss due to weather, rapid price falls or cost increases, or all three at once. There have been periods of consistent income growth for some industries, such as the wool boom of the 1950s. (The sheep industry recorded the lowest farm cash incomes in broadacre agriculture throughout the 1990s and they are likely to continue to fall (Fisher, 1999).) But there have always been many farm families who face a struggle to keep going. The present period of change differs because the pressures on farming are now much greater; so great as to leave doubt that the family-based system can persist in a way which maintains Australia's rural pattern of settlement and our post-1788 relationship between rurality and agriculture.

Pluriactivity

Contrary to the view of farming as a pleasant, peaceful form of work, it is inherently stressful. The general frustrations of farm work, like failing equipment and ailing animals which have always occurred and can occur at any time, cause stress. So, too, does off-farm work (Gray and Lawrence, 1996). More than any other factor in rural restructuring, off-farm work, along with other forms of pluriactivity, is directly affecting the social basis of farming which underpins the entire agricultural system (see, for example, De Vries, 1990; Lawrence and Gray, 1997). Thirty per cent of the total income of Australian broadacre farm families was derived from sources off the farm in 1994–95, with about one in three spouses of operators having off-farm employment (Garnaut, 1998). This is broadly similar to European experience (Mackinnon et al., 1991; Fuller, 1990; Blekesaune, 1991).

Work may be taken off the farm with the ultimate aim of developing the farm. It can result from an intersection of circumstances including financial stringency, but also personal values including the desire of women and men to seek careers beyond the farm and the presence, or lack, of opportunities for them to do so (Fairweather, 1995; Hermann and Uttitz, 1990). Motivation for off-farm work may also come from a desire to retain the farm and lifestyle for the next generation. Moreover, it is only an option in areas where employment or business opportunities are available. Employment on nearby farms is less likely to be available as the demand for it has diminished with mechanisation, and rural towns are suffering from unemployment. Local labour markets then become crucial to change in farm activity (Efstratoglou-Todoulou, 1990; Fuller, 1990).

Many Australian farmers have changed their on-farm 'enterprise mix' by moving into new agricultural products. This can mean a change in balance between products for mixed farmers or establishment of new crops like oilseeds. For those farms which are traditionally more specialised it can mean substantial change, such as that encountered by sugarcane growers establishing a wine industry among other new types of production (Hungerford, 1996). A glance at the research program and publications catalogue of the Rural Industries Research and Development Corporation reveals the breadth of alternative agricultural activities being investigated and attempted. It includes niche products native to Australia and more extensive activities like farm forestry.

Less research interest has been shown in farm tourism and accommodation despite it becoming more apparent to anyone travelling in rural Australia and no doubt very important to those who undertake it as an adjunct to, or as a substitute for, their traditional means of income generation. European research has shown alternative farm enterprises (AFEs) being undertaken as well as off-farm work (Evans and Ilbery, 1993; Johansen et al., 1999), but while the latter may be a coping strategy for small operations it may be a growth strategy for larger ones (Campagne et al., 1990; Evans and Ilbery, 1992) in 'postproductivist' European agriculture (Bowler et al., 1996). Anosike and Coughenour (1990) found that in the United States larger farms were more diversified on-farm, while smaller farms tended to rely more on off-farm income and keep their farming specialised. Jones (1999: 26), apparently using industry sources, reports that 1300 farms in Australia offer 'farm stay' accommodation, with each making between 20 and 40 per cent of total on-farm income. Total international agritourism, of which farm stays constitute 30 per cent, has grown by 300 per cent since 1990. However, this growth is likely to be relatively concentrated. It seems that, in Australia, change to farming for tourist consumption rather than for production is likely to be much more rapid in areas where tourism is already significant. As this tends to be coastal areas (see Woolhouse, 1997) and possibly some inland areas of high scenic and amenity value, this 'postmodernisation' of farming is likely to lead to further bifurcation of rural society, this time with a clear spatial dimension. Jones (1999) also implies that a particular, outgoing, personality type is a prerequisite to success in farm tourism. Some farmers might find this notion quite challenging.

Gender Relations

Pluriactivity is bringing fundamental social change at the level of farm operation. But it does not appear to herald fundamental change to the patriarchal structure of farming. Farm women are known to be subordinated in farm decision-making and segregated in their farm work. Garnaut et al. (1999) report that farm men and women work a similar number of hours (about 60) per week. For women, work includes domestic duties, childcare, community work, off-farm work, and on-farm work. They averaged 19 hours per week in on-farm work and remained responsible for most domestic duties and childcare (estimated together at 36 hours per week compared to men's five). Women's 19 hours of on-farm work were less than half that of men's 51 hours per week. Some 33 per cent of women undertook off-farm employment, as did 23 per cent of men (Garnaut et al., 1999: 2).

Further, women's contribution to farm operation remains substantially hidden and their interests ignored by farmer organisations (Alston, 1995). Pluriactivity might be expected to threaten this system. It has been shown to be an increasingly individualistic activity in Europe (de Vries, 1990). As farms become pluriactive, men and women obtain incomes and careers independent of their farms and hence each other. Alternative farm enterprises may be established by women as separate businesses. Blanc and Mackinnon (1990) note that on-farm accommodation professionalises the domestic domain for women. While the effects of these changes are as yet unknown, research on off-farm work has not revealed any substantial change in patriarchal relations in terms of on-farm work tasks and decision-making (see, for example, Gray et al., 1993). This is consistent with the findings of Lyson (1985) and Wilson et al. (1994) from the United States. Alston (1997) notes that partnership arrangements have had no effect on decision-making. These changes may result merely in the addition of responsibilities to work in the home and on the farm (Blanc and Mackinnon, 1990). From a British study, Evans and Ilbery (1996: 90) conclude that despite female pluriactivity, 'archaic patterns of gender relations seem to be persisting in farming'. At an ideological level, farm women can be seen to be locked into a double bind: the solidity of patriarchal culture and an anti-feminist ideological culture (Teather, 1999).

However, women are appearing more frequently on committees and in management positions in farm organisations and government authorities as they become more organisationally and politically active (Leipins, 1998). State-sponsored networks of rural women are gaining prominence in Victoria, Western Australia, South Australia, Queensland, Tasmania and New South Wales. The former Commonwealth Department of Primary Industries and Energy established a policy unit for rural women. A National Plan for Women in agriculture and resource management has been developed. Australian women were very prominent at the International Farm Women's Conference held in Washington DC in 1998, one of their number having initiated the conference. Despite the emergence of a male backlash, Alston (1996) can claim the existence of a rural women's movement with a capacity to achieve change on the farm as well as in broader political circles. The fact that government-funded social research on farming is being carried out from a feminist perspective is very encouraging. Yet problems remain. Alston (1998) shows how official statistics and government research still obscure the work of farm women. Moreover, Pini (1999) argues that the agendas of rural feminism have been appropriated by the state. Pini is cautious, however, lest the valuable work of rural women and the institutions they have established be devalued. It would seem that change is happening more rapidly, or at least the seeds of change are being sown, in activity outside farming rather than in family relations on the farm.

Subsumption

Are Australian farms being 'subsumed' by agents of large-scale capital? The evidence for subsumption is mixed. Among industries where farming is closely tied to processing and marketing by way of ownership or contracts, the argument is strong (see Burch et al., 1992; Miller, 1996). Farmers are obliged to heed the requirements of those they supply, thereby consciously surrendering much autonomy. They forsake the authority to manage their farm as sustainably as they might wish. Contracts can create conditions in which farmers suffer financial penalties if they choose not to exploit their land as the contract indirectly requires. This is not to say that all contracts create such problems, but the potential exists. Farms that are owned by vertically-integrated agribusiness may have long-term plans which are determined solely by business considerations, rather than including the traditional farmer's desire to pass a farm to offspring with the promise of long-term viability. Certainly there is evidence from the United States that 'dominant firms can be expected to influence outcomes for agricultural producers regarding product price and selling opportunities' (Welsh, 1997: 493). Subsumption at a more personal level in terms of subservience to off-farm employers or in the realm of non-agricultural farm enterprises has not been examined in Australia. Evans and Ilbery (1992), however, suggest that farm tourism and accommodation ventures are highly dependent on promotion and travel agents.

The process of subsumption is not so apparent in less integrated industries, but the consequences of more subtle forms may be just as significant in the long term. Lockie (1997) applies the concept of subsumption to broadacre farming. Farmers may relinquish control to financial institutions through indebtedness, or to agribusiness through marketing contracts, but the farmers of Lockie's sample do not 'suffer' from subsumption. Lockie does, however, point to technological dependence as a form of subsumption. This is most blatant in the form of plant breeding rights which under 1994 legislation can be owned, traded and hence controlled by agribusiness, thereby denying farmers ready access to seed – including the seed they might normally have retained for planting during the subsequent season.

There are also more subtle forms of technological subsumption. The farm production 'treadmill' has two parts. One is economic: production has to increase to cover price reductions arising from increases in product supply. The other part is technological: in order to maintain production increases, and hence farm income, farmers are obliged to use farming methods which require more sophisticated technology. This includes farm chemicals as well as inputs like seed, and new equipment with associated techniques. The 'technological treadmill' provides agribusiness with substantial but subtle means of influencing farming. While it is harder to describe farmers on this treadmill as subsumed in the way that contracted farmers might be, there is no doubt that, when viewed as part of a power relationship, the 'technological treadmill' does diminish farmers' autonomy.

In order to perceive this relationship it is necessary to take a broad view of power, one which allows us to see power being exerted unintentionally and possibly unconsciously by agents who influence the values and ideas of farmers in a way that is ultimately detrimental to their interests. This raises some theoretical problems (discussed in Gray et al., 1997) emanating from the problem of unambiguously identifying the interests of farmers, but as Lockie (1998) shows, such a view can illuminate a subtle form of subsumption. Lockie argues that the degree of control which agribusiness exerts should be considered in terms of the ways it participates in the construction of good farming practice through its promotion and advertising activities. He found that agribusiness advertising portrays chemical use as a normal part of farming practice, and that the rural media tend to downplay or avoid controversies surrounding chemicals and their application.

Lockie (1998) further claims that the media represent farmers to themselves as the kinds of people they see themselves to be, suggesting that farmers are complicit. If so, this suggests an hegemonic relationship. This is consistent with the overall view of farmers as failing to perceive the forces which are subsuming them (Lawrence, 1987). Nevertheless, while subsumption may be proceeding in more or less subtle ways, it is unsafe to assume that it is not resisted. Their resistance is likely to be problematic, however, as their perceptions of subsumption are fraught with tension and contradiction.

Deregulation

From the 1940s to the 1980s the liberal-democratic states developed and applied 'corporatist' models in their relations with farmers. That is, they adopted policies and programs which treated farmers and their organisations as partners in a development project for agriculture (Lowe et al., 1994). Moreover, governments saw their role in that partnership as involving market intervention to create optimal conditions for the development of agricultural production. They created schemes to stabilise and improve the prices received by producers. Prior to World War II, Australian farmers faced markets in which they were dependent on a few local buyers, making them vulnerable to price discrimination. From 1948 to 1988 the Commonwealth established and maintained the Australian Wheat Board through Acts of Parliament with the aim of developing markets and maximising prices. The Board's membership consisted primarily of farmers. After the wool price boom of the 1950s had abated, and with the optimism of the 1960s, the Commonwealth established a stabilisation scheme to cushion the effects of dramatic price falls (Godden, 1997). Again the governing bodies were dominated by producer representatives.

Government intervention in the sugar industry goes back to the turn of the century and influences more than marketing. Production has been regulated by control over land used for cane growing, the processes of harvesting and milling and the prices paid for cane. This system arose in order to develop cane growing as a small farming system in which development could proceed without farmers being subservient to the local mills to which, due to the perishable nature of the product, they had to sell, and without threatening the established millers. As Queensland produces 95 per cent of Australia's sugar, its government's legislation has effectively determined the relationship between itself, the growers and the millers. However, actual control has been delegated by government to the mill companies, some of which are co-operatives, and grower organisations. Contrary to the 'socialism' metaphor, government had little direct involvement. The production system undoubtedly benefited from a stable family farming structure with its capacities for exploitation of family members and consequent survival through periods of low prices and drought (Drummond, 1996; Drummond and Marsden, 1999). Shaw (1985: 25) explains that governments saw fit to provide the more expensive infrastructure, favourable financial arrangements and facilitated market protection but left provision of the less expensive facilities to farmers.

Neoliberalism, however, paints such partnerships as unnecessarily restrictive. Where intervention was seen as supportive, it is now seen as constraining. The objective of policy-making has become one of 'releasing' farmers so that they have the 'freedom' to develop their industries. Banks and Marsden (1997: 382) quote a British government policy statement on its relationship to the British dairy industry: 'our aim is to help the industry do its job better, to liberate it from the shackles of the past and to realise its potential'. In this instance, liberation has involved replacing regulation of marketing with competition among farmers.

Operation of marketing schemes has been conducted by authorities, like the Australian Wheat Board, which until 1989 held a monopoly position in the Australian wheat market. Underwritten by the Commonwealth, the Board purchased all wheat and provided growers with a substantial part of their payment soon after they delivered their wheat to it. Growers were provided with a simple marketing arrangement in which they entrusted the Board with the task of obtaining an optimum price for their product. Since 1989 the Wheat Board has been deprived of its monopoly buying and selling position as the domestic market has been opened. Farmers can sell wheat to whichever domestic buyer they wish, determining a price with that buyer (Pritchard, 1998). They must thereby accept much more responsibility for marketing their product. The stated aim of increasing the efficiency of the industry has replaced earlier desire for stability and security for farmers and families. The price stabilisation (reserve price) scheme for the wool industry took such arrangements a step further with a corporation buying wool when prices were low and selling it when prices were high. This scheme was abandoned in

1991. An embargo on the importation of sugar was lifted in 1989 and replaced by a tariff which has subsequently been halved, but change has been slower in that industry (Godden, 1997). The effects have nevertheless flowed on to many aspects of farmers' lives (Passfield et al., 1996). Marketing arrangements in other industries, initially designed to ensure supply, control prices and maintain quality standards, have been altered along similar lines, with the deregulation of egg marketing and particularly the dairy industry being recent examples.

Australian corporatism has involved two policy streams: those which have sought to regulate the operation of markets by providing a single buyer of farm products (and through the other measures discussed above), and those which have offered direct support in order to maintain agriculture at times of common difficulty like drought or where the process of farm 'adjustment' is seen to require assistance. The themes of responsibility and efficiency have also echoed through changes to drought and adjustment policies. Once seen popularly and politically as a natural disaster, drought has been redefined as a human construction for which farmers must take responsibility – if not entirely for its creation then certainly for the amelioration or avoidance of its effects. Drought is now seen by the state as a normal event which must be planned for rather than an unforeseen disaster. Drought thereby becomes a 'challenge' to be handled with 'better climate forecasting, pasture and stock monitoring, and decision support systems to manage stocking rates', as well as the use of 'financial buffers' (Land Management Task Force, 1995).

Prior to redefinition in the early 1990s drought policies offered relief to farmers based on equity arguments: public monies should be used to support producers whose livelihood was affected by drought since they had restricted entitlement to such provisions as unemployment benefit (Simmons, 1993). They may also have been influenced by media depictions of drought as disasters and farmers as victims (West and Smith, 1996). Proponents of change away from financial support expressed concerns about the distortion of costs leading farmers to over-crop and over-graze in such ways that long-term financial and environmental problems were exacerbated. The significant policy change followed a government report which argued that farmers should become more self-reliant and incorporate risk management practices and that support should only be available under 'exceptional circumstances' and in the context of 'adjustment' assistance (Drought Policy Review Task Force, 1990). Again, it is the efficiency of industries rather than the situation of farms and families which has become the objective of policy.

The process of change has not always been smooth. Gow (1997) identifies an interruption occurring when, in 1994, Prime Minister Keating announced special drought assistance measures (the 'Drought Relief Payment') justified on equity grounds. Farmer organisations had successfully brought the condition of many rural families to the attention of the national media and the difficulties which farm people have in accessing the social security system were highlighted. Gow feels that this represents a divergence from the aim, as he sees it, of maximising the welfare of a (reified) 'whole society' after the successful politicisation of drought. He sees this as interference with a long-term planning process but only a 'partial fall from power of "economic rationalist" views' (Gow, 1997: 282).

Redefining 'Adjustment'

The long-term abandonment of equity considerations is also apparent in the context of 'adjustment' policies. The Rural Adjustment Scheme, having developed from earlier Rural

Reconstruction Schemes, operated for twenty years from 1977. Its initial objectives had a redistributional tone: to ensure that those farms which were becoming marginalised, but which had strong potential for long-term viability, were assisted to become larger, more efficient, to restructure their debt or a combination of these strategies. Change loomed in 1988 after a review considered the scheme in terms of its contribution to industry efficiency, leaving the situation of farmers out of recommended objectives (Higgins, 1998). After another review, the Minister for Primary Industries stated in 1992 that the government would 'ensure that the operating environment within which farmers' work is conducted is conducive to sound business decision-making, and that the messages farmers are receiving from us are consistent with an emphasis on self-reliance and risk management' (cited in Higgins, 1998: 12). The aims of the scheme had changed from attempting to ensure that farmers had adequate opportunity to become viable, towards creating conditions which would require those with good prospects to make *themselves* viable, which – from the government's perspective – was essential for the future growth of Australian agriculture.

By 1996 opinion about the scheme appeared to have polarised. Some claimed it was promoting industry efficiency. Others thought it was not (see Burdon, 1996). In 1997 the Rural Adjustment Scheme was replaced by 'Agriculture Advancing Australia', a scheme which offered fewer means of financial assistance, replacing them with financial risk management tools and education schemes. The emphasis has moved from what Australia can do to assist the always euphemistically-labelled farm 'adjustment' process to what agriculture can be made to do for Australia. Associated with this change, it is possible to see an element of reversal in a trend since 1994 of separating structural adjustment from welfare objectives. This is despite rhetoric about the importance of separating welfare from business management issues. The 'Farm Family Restart Scheme' ties assistance to the 'structural adjustment' objectives of government (Botterill, 1999). Along with deregulation, the changes in drought and 'adjustment' support are pushing farmers into a process of re-regulation, in which they must find new approaches to operating their farms, and are confronting them with notions of welfare. The contradictions inherent in sustaining the image of farmer as simultaneously business manager and welfare recipient in public discussion, combined with the difficulty which farm families encounter as asset-rich and income-poor applicants to the social security system, highlights the marginality of many during restructuring.

Water

The supply of water to agriculture and horticulture has attracted the attention of economic policy-makers since around 1990. Irrigation has provided a basis for the establishment of many industries and communities in Australia, and its supply has been controlled and operated by government agencies virtually since the initial private supply arrangements were found to suffer 'market failure'. But with about 80 per cent of all water used in Australia going to irrigation and being provided without an expectation that prices charged for it would cover costs (Watson and Johnson, 1993) there was room for economic analysis to point towards potential inefficiencies in allocation. A barrage of reports in the early 1990s led to consideration of applying 'user pays' principles. Full cost recovery in this way would have the potential to raise costs very significantly, pushing producers out of irrigation and off their land, bringing the prospect of depopulation of what have become thriving communities (Watson and Johnson,

1993). Governments are stepping back from direct involvement in irrigation systems, in some situations establishing corporations owned by farmers to provide and maintain infrastructure. Allowing rights to irrigation water to be bought and sold is one economic measure under discussion. Water rights have previously been tied to land title, as a system through which control of farm size has also been executed with the effect of enabling the development and maintenance of a system dominated by relatively small farms. The possibility of trading water rights, however, could also give rise to the prospect of community decline as industries with more intensive water needs offer higher prices (Alexandra and Eyre, 1993), but Bjornlund and McKay (1999) found social polarisation rather than overall decline.

Environmental considerations are also lending weight to the push for change. Irrigation has been found to create massive salinity problems and to leave rivers with insufficient water to maintain valued features of their ecology. In the early 2000s the New South Wales Government is imposing a cap on water supply for irrigation and proposals have been accepted to redirect water away from inland irrigation and return it to the Snowy River, which flows through non-agricultural land. Such 'environmental flow' considerations were recommended by an inquiry, with concern subsequently being expressed by irrigators who would, as a consequence, lose water. The same issue confronts Central Queensland producers where the Water Allocation Management Plan (or WAMP) is apportioning water to the environment. These issues remain under debate in many contexts, the Snowy issue having been important to the 1999 Victorian election, but still hold the possibility of strong downward pressure on the economies of irrigation areas.

Services

Farm families have been directly affected by application of neoliberal thinking to the provision of a wide range of government services. Of most direct effect on farmers, advice services which have been provided by State government agencies have been run down. Many farmers now depend far more heavily on commercial sources of advice and government services are now moving into 'purchaser-provider' models to put their management on business terms (Marsh and Pannell, 1998). Along with other rural dwellers, farmers have seen education, health and other services like language teaching for migrants move towards 'user pays'. In the hope of more efficient management of their systems when judged across the State, governments have reduced services and closed facilities where sparse target populations do not meet a critical mass judged to provide sufficient demand.

Government deregulation and application of the 'user pays' principle has extended well beyond the activities of governments themselves, with profound effects on farmers. Most notable has been the deregulation of the banking system. This had extensive unintended impacts in the late 1980s when banks set out on a lending spree in order to increase their market shares. Farmers who had known their bank managers as very conservative lenders were, in some notorious cases, said to be offered large loans. Acceptance of the loans later proved disastrous when interest rates rose rapidly and remained high. Similar problems arose for farmers who, with what they took to be the blessing of their very reputable banks, borrowed money in foreign currencies. At present, the main banks are in the spotlight again for closing rural branches in the name of efficiency and the interests of shareholders. The Commonwealth

Bank, once entirely government-owned and consequently thought of as the institutional example of security, reliability and availability, is among those closing branches, even in urban areas.

Perspectives on Restructuring

The declining numbers of farms and the changing distribution of farm sizes, the coping strategies which farmers have adopted, their increasing pluriactivity, the persistence of patriarchal relations, their subsumption to capital and their re-regulation of farm operation and everyday life associated with government deregulation and change in support mechanisms, have all brought a process of re-regulation in farm families' ways of organising and conducting their everyday lives. But this is not occurring evenly and its effects are also uneven, socially and spatially. That the well-being of regional Australia's population varies spatially has been established (see Sorensen and Weinand, 1991). Restructuring has had differential effects in different places. For example, the Wimmera of Victoria has attracted attention as an area of rapid decline in the past, but attention is now being drawn to the upland grazing areas of New South Wales which rely heavily on the wool industry and increasingly suffer land degradation problems. Interpretation of change and its effects can also vary spatially. Few would deny that the downturn in the wool industry has been detrimental to those areas most dependent on it, but other areas have undergone possibly beneficial change.

The Riverland region of South Australia provides a case of restructuring with, by some criteria, very promising outcomes. Kerby and Parish (1997) describe a horticultural area which was established in the 1880s with small irrigated farms applying communal ownership and management principles. It was further developed under soldier settlement schemes and independently, notably by large numbers of European migrants. Producer co-operatives carried much of the product marketing and offered pooled returns. By the 1980s however, fruit growers were suffering under deteriorating terms of trade and problems were arising with ageing irrigation infrastructure. Some of the co-operatives encountered financial problems. But the expansion of the wine industry in the 1990s opened new markets with high prices on offer. Kerby and Parish see the significant change in terms of secure and lucrative contracts being offered to farmers.

Also significant is what Kerby and Parish (1997: 134) describe as 'community spirit', which they curiously associate with both community action in planning for change and a popular belief that the government would assist people during hard times. Nevertheless, the people of the Riverland were found to be extensively involved in planning and plan implementation. Such actions are not, however, strengthening what Kerby and Parish see as a long-serving institutional base for community participation. A small number of very large firms are now buying and processing horticultural products. Kerby and Parish see this as desirable so products can obtain the necessary level of national and international marketing. But it also involves a degree of subsumption, under which the local community has forgone some degree of control over its resources at the same time as many of the social underpinnings of the 'community' have been lost. Kerby and Parish (1997: 137) conclude by noting large increases in production during the 1990s, the need to retain domestic and international competitiveness and, placing the onus on the community, expressing confidence that 'the Riverland community has the necessary skills, resolve and attitudes to achieve these improvements'. This last comment is, from a restructuring perspective, a little ironic, since 'the Riverland community' appears to have lost much of what had historically made it a community and possibly some of its capacity to influence its own destiny.

Some writers see changes increasing efficiency (Gow, 1994) and placing downward pressure on prices paid by consumers (Godden, 1997). Sorensen (1991) fears that too much attention to bad news will convey an incorrect impression and distract governments from their task of proceeding with 'reform'. Some even see farmers as villains, alleging complicity in the maintenance of inefficiency for their own advantage. Sorensen and Epps (1993) note a view of farmer participation in the management of wool marketing as not only an impediment to efficiency but the reason for the scheme's collapse. They see elements of rorting in marketing schemes which benefited farmers at the expense of taxpayers and consumers (Sorensen and Epps, 1993: 19).

Such views might be thought of as the basis for attempts to establish scenarios which would, in theory, maximise the welfare of all members of Australian society. This is a noble undertaking which is seriously hampered theoretically by its reification of the system which it sees as something to be manipulated by economic policy. It ignores significant features of the process of change as it obscures the impacts of change and the power relations involved in it. Importantly, seeing the economy as a system consisting only of consciously-acting individuals fails to explain the ways in which people respond to change in their economy and society and the political acts they may choose to take. It also obscures the power of its own rhetoric at the same time as it fails to perceive the significance of ideology, including nationalism and entrepreneurialism as well as agrarianism. The 'restructuring' view, on the other hand, opens a window on reflexivity.

Social Restructuring

Change in agriculture is transforming rural society. We will consider this transformation in terms of ageing, poverty, coping and stress, health and morale.

Ageing
While Australia's population ages, that of its rural areas ages more rapidly. This is particularly so among the farming population as fewer young people enter farming. In some areas the average age has been found to advance by five years during a ten-year period (Barr et al., 1999). Younger, more educated members of farm families are more likely to try to establish careers away from the farm (Stayner, 1994). Just as importantly, older farmers find they cannot afford to retire, perhaps being unable to sell their farms and finding their (often adult) children unwilling to take on the farm (or possibly for some, in present economic conditions, not wishing them to do so). They have to continue working as they have little or no superannuation and encounter difficulty accessing pensions (Warburton et al., 1997). The advancing age of farmers often attracts comment. A national survey found the average age of longer-term farmers to be 55 years, but it also found that the average age of those who had entered farming during the ten years prior to 1995 was 42 years (Garnaut and Lim-Applegate, 1997: 23).

Warburton et al. (1997: 29) quote Australian Bureau of Statistics (ABS) figures indicating that agriculture is the most common occupation among men aged over 65 and still in the labour force. Such statistics should be treated with a little caution because the definition of farmer used for statistical collections can be problematic, in that there may be adults of two or even three generations present on farms. But it is clear that in some areas, notably including the upland wool growing areas along the Great Dividing Range, there are many people who are staying on their farms until later in their lives than they would have done prior to the current restructuring process (Barr, 1999).

Declining farm numbers leave elderly people increasingly isolated – creating problems for those family and professional services seeking to care for them. As local opportunities and services dwindle in farming areas, young people, potential carers as well as contributors to the local economy and community, leave to seek education and careers in the larger centres. Entire families relocate as their farms, businesses and employment cease to offer a satisfactory livelihood. This creates increasingly serious problems for service provision to older people as communities which might offer services decline and government regulation prohibits the offering of services where populations are below a specified threshold (Cheers, 1998). People of non-English speaking background and others with particular problems face increasing difficulty as services are withdrawn.

Poverty

The number of people suffering poverty in rural Australia can be expected to grow. They will find access to services, which might assist them to escape their predicament, more difficult if not impossible to obtain (Lawrence, 1996; Cheers, 1998). The Productivity Commission (1999) has acknowledged that the relatively slow growth of total farm income (without acknowledging the variation among farms within that total) is having an impact on rural and regional Australia in general.

A substantial proportion of farm people have incomes below the Australian average (Garnaut and Lim-Applegate, 1998). Average income figures for farms can disguise a great deal, partly because of variation in farm incomes but also due to family members obtaining income off the farm. Martin (1997: 3) estimates that the average farm cash income (which takes no account of either stocks, depreciation or family labour costs) for all broadacre farms to have been $47 100 in 1996–97, having fallen $3400 during that year. However, sheep and beef properties indicated averages of $10 700 and $10 800 at the same time. Moreover, the proportion of farms reporting negative farm incomes was 26 per cent. This may be obscured by the relatively high overall average, which is itself influenced by the one-fifth of farms with cash incomes exceeding $100 000.

Farm incomes are widely distributed, providing a stronger indicator of a bifurcated farm society. The contrasts in farming are illustrated by the growth in very large operations. The annual 'barons of the bush' survey conducted for *Australian Farm Journal* (Jones, 1998) reports a doubling of the number of 'barons' in one year, applying unchanged criteria. While 32 of those described in detail by Jones are 'corporate', 68 are 'private'. Between them, the top 10 'barons' own 7.6 per cent of Australia's land mass, with the first (the Stanbroke Pastoral Company owned by the AMP) being the world's largest landholder. Welsh (1998) found that in the United States, where there were more farms owned by public corporations, farm cash incomes tended to be higher, but there was also a higher proportion of farms with low or negative incomes.

Spatial differentiation is also substantial. Farm incomes are affected by drought as well as the economic conditions facing particular industries. The areas which have suffered drought for long periods are particularly poor, as are those dependent on waning industries of which wool currently has the spotlight. Off-farm income sources are less dependent on, but by no means independent of, climate and industry problems and are used increasingly. However, they make only a small difference to the image of farm poverty. Garnaut (1997: 33) reports that 14 per cent of farm households stated incomes lower than $5000 in 1993–94, compared with a figure of 2 per cent of Australian households obtained from the 1991 Census of Population and Housing. Garnaut also found that 20 per cent of surveyed households had incomes below $10 000 and most of them would have been eligible for some form of government support (Garnaut, 1997: 2).

Very roughly, the proportion with very low incomes is the same as that often suggested as the proportion of farms which lack viability. Such figures have a tendency to be stable. For some years we seem to have been hearing of expectations that one in five farms will be surrendered. Yet the decline in numbers remains slow. One might expect that if so many are not viable there would be an exodus. Apart from the problems of selling properties on a flooded market, the explanation for the trickle of 'exits' lies partly in the farm family's capacity for persistence and to some extent, subsistence. It is also sometimes noted that the distinction between business costs and living costs becomes blurred on a farm, but this should not obscure a capacity to endure hardship.

Farm families are well able to 'tighten their belts' in hard times but in doing so they indicate their further descent into poverty. Gray et al. (1993: 47) found that all 106 farms of a sample containing a broad range of financial situations had reduced their costs due to an ongoing financial squeeze. This often included reducing living costs. Forty-two per cent reported that at some time they had had insufficient money to buy clothes and 18 per cent had had insufficient money to buy food (Gray et al., 1993: 42). Garnaut (1997: 3) obtained similar findings: '21 per cent of households had cut back on basic food during the previous two years and slightly more than a quarter were concerned about making ends meet "all the time" or "often"'.

The problem of farm poverty is exacerbated by two factors: the increasing age of the farm population creating a situation in which many people are unlikely to be able to work their way out of poverty either on or off the farm, and the difficulties which assistance programs encounter in obtaining acceptance of services. Governments have had difficulty establishing programs which can be effectively planned and delivered. They have been criticised for being 'urbocentric': planning to suit the needs of urban people and neglecting the different circumstances of rural people (Collingridge, 1989; Cheers, 1998). The problems of applying income and assets tests to farm families who may be 'asset-rich and income-poor' is well known, as are the difficulties of delivering services to spatially and possibly socially isolated people. The best known problem is encountered when assets testing renders parents ineligible for a pension even after they have handed the farm over as an inheritance.

Obtaining acceptance of services has been problematic at two levels. There has been some reluctance among rural local government to involve itself in social service or welfare programs. Gray (1991) analyses a political process in a rural shire through which local organisations, whose membership was predominantly female, struggled to establish local community services. American evidence shows similar resistance to 'welfare' in rural areas (Jacob et al., 1996). Reluctance has also been found among potential recipients. Garnaut et al.'s Australian survey (1999: 5) reveals widespread failure by farmers to apply for benefits which they may have been eligible to receive: 'For households with a member of eligible age, an additional 35 per cent might have qualified for the Age Pension, 24 per cent might have qualified for Austudy, and 27 per cent may have qualified for the Basic Family Payment'. They attribute this to a lack of information, the problem of valuing farm assets for testing and a perception among some that help was not needed. Need appeared to be as great among unaware non-applicants as it was among those who were aware and had applied. There are situations in which families become heavily dependent on assistance. This frequently occurs during drought when the income of many isolated families who cannot obtain off-farm work ceases altogether (see Stehlik et al., 1998).

Coping and Stress

The spectre of poverty and the coping strategies adopted in response to it lead to stressful situations and affect family relationships. Australian studies of farm stress have related the problem to economic conditions. Weston and Cary (1979) found such an association, but when they repeated their survey after an improvement in economic conditions, stress levels remained unexpectedly high. Slee's (1988) 'phone-in' attracted 266 callers of whom 48 per cent phoned due to experience of stress. She found that stress was related to the particular nature of economic life in non-metropolitan regions of Australia. Much United States research, including Belyea and Lobao (1990), Olson and Schellenberg (1986), Rosenblatt and Keller (1983) and Van Hook (1987) also reveal – not unexpectedly – that stress is part of farming during hard economic times.

Farm life differs from other occupations because it intimately connects home and workplace. Work relationships are also family relationships and despite off-farm work there is great interdependence among family members. There are many features of farm life which are inherently stress-producing, including 'shocks' from the rural economy, drought and flood. There is always risk of unpredictable events such as stock disease, machinery breakdown and family illness. Such frustrations can be just as stressful as family breakdown and illness and the more common stressful life events such as marriage and bereavement (Kenkel, 1986). Problematic family relations have also arisen with stress in times of financial hardship, as suggested by Bell et al. (1992).

Men and women tend to experience different stressors. Bell et al. (1992) suggest that women who tend not to participate in decision-making may be less stressed than their husbands. However, this assumes that what could amount to being excluded from decision-making and being kept ignorant of it, would not have stress effects. Women may also be affected by increased family and work responsibilities. However, women would become aware of their farm's financial problems as many regularly do the bookkeeping, closely watching the realities of farm income and expenditure (Duncan, Volk and Lewis, 1988).

The intersection of farm financial difficulty, off-farm work and stress creates a complex situation for farm families. Gray and Lawrence (1996) found that alongside financial matters and the general frustrations of farm life and work, perceptions of what is at stake and factors related to family relations are important predictors of stress. Farm women suffer self-questioning and personal conflict about their multiple roles as mothers and farmers, while farm men suffer expectations of themselves as farmers in very difficult circumstances. Taking off-farm work, among these other factors, is found to precipitate many personal conflicts which can destabilise family relationships.

Health

The health condition of rural Australians is relatively poor and health professionals have documented growing problems in rural areas (Kerby, 1992). Rural residents display an above average incidence of endocrine, nutritional, metabolic diseases and immunity disorders, respiratory, musculoskeletal and genitourinary diseases, and diseases of the skin and subcutaneous tissues (Rolley and Humphreys, 1993: 249). The issue has been set out by the National Rural Health Alliance (1997: 4). It reports that rural Australians generally have a worse health record than metropolitan dwellers. Death rates are much higher (32 per cent for women and 22 per cent for men) in remote areas than in the metropolitan centres. Even in the large regional centres, death rates are 8 per cent higher among men and 6 per cent higher among women. These statistics may differ from place to place and be affected by such demographic factors as the presence of large proportions of elderly and/or Aboriginal people with special problems, but the overall indication is one of substantial spatial differentiation in health experience. The National Rural Health Alliance points to coronary heart disease, injury, road accidents, asthma and diabetes as significantly more frequent causes of death in rural areas. Not all of these can be tied to Aboriginality or old age. The National Rural Health Alliance also points to male suicide being particularly worrying, with the suicide rate of the 15 to 24 years age group being more than double that of their metropolitan counterparts (National Rural Health Alliance, 1997: 6; see also Ruzicka and Choi, 1999). The Productivity Commission (1999) acknowledges that suicide is a particularly serious problem for rural Australia. There is some uncertainty, however, about the spatial characteristics of this problem, with inconsistent evidence from the States (Stokes and Wyn, 1998).

The difficulties which rural communities have in attracting doctors receive much publicity, as does the closure of health services which occurs from time to time in smaller centres. Not so well understood is the impact of stress associated with restructuring on farm populations. The health and social impacts of such stress could be inferred from Gray and Lawrence (1996) through the potential for marriage break-up, as well as directly through accidents and illness. They have, however, attracted some research attention. Walker and Battye (1996) found that the economic problems and drought were causing stress which was associated with excessive medication and alcohol abuse, insomnia, lower immune response and an increase in violent and aggressive behaviour. The rise in violence was publicised when western areas were said to have had the biggest increase in Apprehended Violence Orders in New South Wales: from 542 per 100 000 residents in 1996 to 831 in 1997 (Garcia, 1998). Long-term experience of hardship was found by Walker and Battye (1996) to reduce the capacity of farm people to cope, bringing anxiety, interpersonal problems and grief among people who were otherwise usually emotionally and physically healthy.

Morale

The early 1990s left much of rural Australia in a state of considerable flux in which many people could see their financial prospects in farming either diminished or virtually destroyed, the prospects for government support to be disappearing, and the state of health of themselves, their families, and their communities, deteriorating. In these conditions it would not be surprising to find that the morale of rural people was falling. When Smailes (1997) conducted a large survey of rural people's experience of change, he offered an opportunity for respondents to add comments and analysed their responses qualitatively. From that part of his sample which covered the main non-irrigated farming zone of South Australia, he concluded: 'The spontaneous comments from the wheat-sheep and marginal zones, and even the high rainfall pastoral and Riverland irrigation areas, produced a large and harrowing range of insights into the severe problems being faced by family farms and the deteriorating fabric of rural society ...' (Smailes, 1997: 33). A picture of depression and pessimism emerges from Smailes' analysis, yet he also found that people remained persistent and retained their faith in farming and rural living.

Conclusion

Rural restructuring is forcing change among farming people – something which is frequently affecting them detrimentally. Their misfortune is much broader than simple economic and environmental indicators would show. It reaches all aspects of their lives. But despite their deteriorating standard of living, state of health and morale, it is only reasonable to expect farming people to respond by coping on their farms, but also by seeking means of addressing the sources of restructuring which they perceive, quite reasonably, to be beyond their farms. One must expect them to attempt to understand restructuring with all the tools and evidence available to them. Fortified with their own interpretations – those made by farm people themselves but not in isolation from each other and the institutions of government and business – they will act, perhaps in the same ways they have for generations, but possibly also in new ways.

The conditions of their reflexivity are complex. This complexity demonstrates the incapacity of the kind of economics underpinning the neoliberal agenda and substantially driving restructuring through globalisation, to base its analysis and predictions on assessment of what people actually think and do. There is some irony in the point that despite this incapacity, neoliberal thinking forges ahead assuming that there is no such problem: assuming that individuals acting in pursuit of their interests will collectively maximise benefit to everyone. The unreliability of this assumption is more than suggested by the many ways restructuring is affecting people and the many ways in which they respond to it. We have developed a base from which to carry out some analysis of rural people's views in an attempt to understand their reflexivity, and hence their capacity and propensity to act for a common good under the constraints which neoliberalism has applied, often in the name of individual liberty. Are they discovering a way forward, or are they merely placed in a position in which all they can do is to suffer their global misfortune?

Further Reading

Alston, M. (1995) *Women on the Land: The Hidden Heart of Rural Australia,* Sydney: University of New South Wales Press.
  – a study of farm women, bringing to light their experiences of and responses to change
Burch, D., Goss, J. and Lawrence, G. (eds) (1999) *Restructuring Global and Regional Agricultures: Transformations in Australasian Agri-food Economies and Spaces,* Aldershot: Ashgate.
  – a collection of papers analysing changes in agriculture in the context of globalisation
Cheers, B. (1998) *Welfare Bushed: Social Care in Rural Australia,* Aldershot: Ashgate.
  – discusses the problems and issues surrounding the provision of welfare in rural areas
Gray, I., Lawrence, G. and Dunn, A. (1993) *Coping with Change: Australian Farmers in the 1990s,* Wagga Wagga: Centre for Rural Social Research, Charles Sturt University.
  – a study of change in agriculture across three States highlighting the effects on people and the responses they make

Globalisation and rural restructuring contribute to rapid and often damaging change for agricultural communities. But how do farm people interpret their experiences? To what do they attribute their predicament? What farm people are thinking and saying in response to restructuring has an important impact on its course. This is most bluntly apparent from the simple point that farmers have ownership and control of Australia's agricultural land resource. What they do with their land tomorrow will affect what is done with it for generations. But there is also the matter of reflexivity and power. Despite their misfortunes, and the powerful global forces behind restructuring and the government and business juggernauts pursuing it, farmers themselves can potentially exert influence. They may do so as individuals or through collective action. Whether they do so or not, and how they might go about it, will basically depend on their reflexivity amid restructuring under postmodernisation and globalisation. This chapter starts to look at their reflexivity by identifying and discussing the role of ideology and analysing qualitative data which cast light on the farmers' 'voice'.

Rural Ideology and Culture

Farmers' actions continue to be guided by a set of values and beliefs which enables them to persevere. Individual farmers' decisions and actions, alongside the policies and decisions of their political representatives and even governments, can only be understood against a background provided by the ideological climate in which farmers are socialised and their culture is formed and maintained. Rural ideology helps to explain farmers' reflection on their circumstances and their consequent actions as it lays the basis for a model of their reflexivity. Incorporation of ideological factors in such a model of farmer action can also introduce the process through which their reflexivity could be opened to other interests. The possibility arises that farmers may find themselves ignoring their own interests, supporting interests which differ from their own and, moreover, being influenced by those who would seek to create conditions which bring a radically altered rural society. Analysis of the place of ideology in the farming system opens windows on such problems.

It should be noted that rural ideology is a more encompassing concept than the social values attached to farming but remains one aspect of rural culture. Interest in farmers' values has been shown among economists perhaps as frequently as among sociologists. This is because economists have also been aware that farmers tend to behave seemingly irrationally, even today. Many farmers would be able to earn greater income and accrue more wealth by investing their money in something other than their land and other farm assets. Economically rational behaviour has not fully explained the persistence of farming. Hence much research has explored farmers' values (see, for example, Kerridge, 1978; Holmes and Day, 1995; Barr and Cary, 2000). This research has achieved considerable refinement, with different kinds of values and goals being described and associated with particular types of rationalisation for decision-making. Examples include value placed on lifestyle, community participation and independence being associated with a less entrepreneurial style of management than those which place greater value on income maximisation and business expansion. This research tends to be based on cross-sectional surveys with neither theoretical nor empirical accommo-dation for change. Ethnographic research analyses the cultural dynamics of farming communi-ties and their relationship with social values and contains a comparative element, but does not have a specific focus on ideology (Phillips and Gray, 1995; Phillips, 1998).

Some aspects of rural ideology are recognised in the old policy-making framework (dis-cussed in chapter 3). Godden (1997), for example, devotes about one and a half pages to 'countrymindedness', noting its importance to conservative political parties in rural situations but indicating that it may be in decline. Countrymindedness is only one element of rural ideology and Godden offers no analysis of the ways it has been used by farmers and others in reflection and action through the highly problematic process of determining 'a more or less considered view about how society should be organised ...' (Godden, 1997: 94). It is easy to overlook the inconsistencies and conflicts within rural ideology and struggles over its inter-pretation and application.

The term 'rural ideology' covers several concepts. Agrarianism is a belief that farming is an ennobling vocation which commands respect, not just for the necessities of life which it provides, but because it involves hard work, perseverance and family life. All of these are expected to contribute to building good character and citizenship. Craig and Phillips (1983) see agrarianism as a product of the history and political economy of settler capitalism rather than emanating from ecological and environmental factors. They also suggest that it contin-ues because of its capacity to help rationalise the otherwise degrading situation confronted by the many farmers who suffer insecurity and poverty.

The 'rural idyll' is a closely related concept. Williams (1975) found the image of an idyl-lic rural lifestyle to be fundamental to the culture of anglophone peoples, perpetuated by the urban-rural cultural contrast discussed above. Australian writers have also used the term. Poiner (1990) discusses the importance of the image of farming as a superior and honourable occupation to local social relations, particularly gender relations. Something similar has also been found to be significant to national political relations: countrymindedness. Countrymind-edness, although based on perceptions of farming, goes further by contrasting country and city. It envelops town as well as farming populations since it counterposes rural and metropolitan Australia as interest groups in conflict. Share (1995) views it as creating a focus for opposition by rural-based political forces at the same time as, according to some writers, it reflects the interests of those who subjugate rural populations.

Rural ideology is available for people to draw upon and apply. Some people may use it to justify their perseverance (or self-exploitation) or the perseverance of others. Some people may refer to it to proclaim the value of farming or some or all of its cultural and material attrib-utes. Some may call upon it to convince others that their interests are paramount, as farmers are often said to do. Some may use it to set an agenda, so that attention is drawn to an issue confronting farmers which would otherwise go unnoticed. And some may apply the rhetoric of belief in farming to bind a community and use it to act politically in defence of what comes to be seen as a common interest (see Gray (1991) for analysis of this phenomenon in an Aus-tralian locality and Naples (1994) for a similar discussion about the ways agrarianism is used in community relations in a United States situation).

Ideology and Power

Seeing rural ideology as the scene of struggle over political legitimacy raises its significance far higher than if it were seen as part of the ideological underpinnings of one or two political parties. The Australian agricultural system was to a large extent founded on an ideological platform of agrarianism and maintained by countrymindedness. The strength of that platform will substantially affect its future. With a rural society undergoing rapid cultural change there is contest over definition of the 'agriculture' behind agrarianism, of the 'rural' behind the idyll, and of the 'country' behind countrymindedness. This additional dimension of change will be discussed later. For now, we consider the elements of rural ideology which are disturbing it from within.

Where farming values affect individual decision-making, rural ideology affects policy-making and interpretations of policy-making. As characteristics of individuals, values are relatively easy to study. They are readily operationalised and can reasonably be expected to be consistently and unambiguously expressed by farmers. However, ideology, being contested and used in formal and informal political situations, is not necessarily consistent. Rural ideology is notoriously inconsistent and even contradictory. For example, the rural idyll, in its portrayal of women as mothers and community workers, is highly gendered and it remains a prop to patriarchal relations in farming (Little and Austin, 1996). The powerful image farming presents has always been denied by the reality of farming, even if it is still implicitly supported by official statistics (Alston, 1998).

There have been many statements of the contradictions, which can also be seen as sites of struggle, in political positions resulting from rural ideology. These often rhetorical points are made easily, given the history of Australia's rural development. A family farm-based system of agriculture arose largely because governments intervened to ensure that land was made available to families wanting to farm, rather than remaining in the hands of, or being acquired by, an elite of landholders. Such was the intention of the proponents of 'free selection', even though they may have been serving the interests of urban-based commerce rather better than the interests of the farm families who took advantage of the process (Gammage, 1986). The 'soldier settlement' schemes also aimed to place as many families on farms as was economically acceptable – that is, allowing families to derive a reasonable living from the land available to them. Irrigation areas were established in such a way that the land was occupied, and moreover water was used, in small portions, thereby enabling the growth of relatively densely populated and prosperous communities. The marketing schemes and support mechanisms discussed in the previous chapter were also the products of government intervention as it tried to maintain the family farm system. This has been described frequently as 'agrarian socialism' because of the historically high degree of government intervention when agriculture is compared with other sectors of the economy. This is misleading, however, as Australian farmers remain almost entirely property owners, capitalists in their own right, albeit mostly small ones. Extensive corporatism would be a more accurate description. But all these developments have been brought to effect with appeals to agrarianism. They are being dismantled, but rural ideology and expressions of it remain a feature of the struggles over restructuring.

Ideology and Restructuring

Research has universally shown farmers to adhere to agrarian ideals and share the rural idyll (see for example, Craig and Phillips, 1983, Gray, 1991; Halpin and Martin, 1996). However beliefs, like values, are subjected to contest and may change. Beus and Dunlap (1994), for example, hint at such change when they find in the United States that 'alternative' farmers do not see their farms and lives in such fundamentalist agrarian terms as others, believing rather in pursuit of a better social and natural environment. Lyons and Lawrence (1999) discovered that there were major differences in thinking among 'traditional' producers and organic producers, with genetic engineering being of major concern to the latter group.

Restructuring may bring a demand for corporatism and direct government intervention as people cling to agrarian ideals but see their future in farming being threatened. Such a proposition was tested by Lobao and Thomas (1992). Restructuring was found to have an effect, but only indirectly via subjective interpretations. Farmers who favoured intervention in trade and agriculture were also more likely to express support for broader policies which redistribute from richer to poorer. In addition to the research mentioned earlier, that of Clark and Little (1997), among others, points to contrasts and conflicts mediated through property exchange and associated rights as former urban dwellers obtain and settle land in rural areas with consequent changes in land use. Such drastic change could bring fundamental ideological tensions among local populations with unpredictable results.

There may still be important structural factors underlying variation and consequent tensions. Ideology at the societal level has often been said to reflect class position. Class has, however, been notoriously difficult to define in modern Australia's farming system. Historically, Waterson (1968) argues that small farmers, including the 'free selectors' of urban working class or gold-seeking background, came to adhere to the values and beliefs of the high status large landholding pastoralists, thereby eliminating a source of tension. However, class analysis has proceeded little further than identifying the problem of locating farmers in a class position when they are capitalists who are also subservient to capital. Australian community studies which might have regarded class relations in farming environments have neglected to do so. The class position of farmers remains problematic, as they are neither purely capitalist (in their subservience to larger capital) nor purely petty bourgeoisie (in that they may have substantial capital) nor proletariat (in that they enter the market with more than their labour).

Nevertheless, class does point towards an important feature of farming society which offers a dynamic element. While farming is often imagined as the antithesis of alienation (people working with their own family members for their families in a natural environment, and so forth), farming is 'liminal' in class terms. Farming has no clear class position. This is apparent from an economic perspective when farmers' business, unlike small service-industry family business, is seen to be capital intensive, large-scale commodity production, owned and operated by families. In sociological terms, farming is neither modern nor traditional but is rather seen to be in a state of transition. We might liken this situation to that of a young person moving through a stage in their socialisation when they are marginalised: neither child nor adolescent, neither adolescent nor adult. In structural terms, farmers face a duality in their social lives which creates an ideological tug-of-war (Share, 1987). This is often implied by identification of such dichotomies as farmers being both capitalists and victims of capital, accepting assistance while opposing government intervention and claiming self-reliance, the farm being both home and place of work, the farm as a resource to be exploited and essential to family tradition, and children being family members and employees at the same time.

Gender also provides a significant underlying dimension containing an inherent tension. As mentioned above, the rural idyll has long denied the reality of farm life and work for women, but has remained an important source of their identity (Little and Austin, 1996). Australian women's rural ideology has generally been held up as conservative, based on commitment to family and community and tacitly consenting to male dominance (Teather, 1992). It is notable that the experience of restructuring differs between men and women (Gray et al., 1993; Gray and Lawrence, 1996, Stehlik et al., 1998). It has also been established that, although possibly related to age and levels of education, women and men differ in their approaches to farm management (Geno, 1998). There is also more than ample evidence that the power structures of rural industries and communities have exhibited a patriarchal structure which women are working to change, but are finding such change to be very slow (Elix and Lambert, 1998). Even new 'sustainable' farming movements may lack awareness of their construction of gender and retain gender-specific goals and activities (Meares, 1997).

Nevertheless, such movements have succeeded in raising many social and environmental issues which have been ignored by male-dominated farmer organisations (Alston, 1996). The situation of women in farm families provides them with a different window on restructuring, and the highly gendered nature of their community participation (see Dempsey, 1992) also suggests potential for differing perspectives from those of men. The directions which women's collective agency will take, and its effect on restructuring, are hard to predict. Shortall (1994) describes the Canadian Farm Women's Network as distinctive in its possession of a broad agenda, but still emphasised such aspects as community work, rather than radical influence on policy. This is not to say that community work will not prove critical to radical change and resistance to the forces of restructuring, but rather that it offers little indication of its wider impacts. Similarly, Liepins' (1998: 152) review describes the impact of Australian farm women's organisation in terms of 'enhanced visibility and voice, as well as their networks of influence'. But the directions in which that influence may push for change are not so clear as are the continued occupation which farm women's organisations have with obtaining positions of influence, and fighting governments' and others' appropriation and reconstruction of their agendas – the latter leading to the maintenance of male dominance in policy-making.

The term 'agrarian socialism' highlights the inconsistency between the image of independent, self-reliant farmers and the historical extent of government intervention in, and guidance of, their industries. (It does not say anything about the subsumption of farmers to large-scale capital, which in some industries is a more significant denial of agrarian ideals.) At a political level, this contradiction gives the National Party the problem of having to claim to support all farmers as it praises the market system, which when set free, threatens the existence of the very system the National Party might seek to support. Among individual farmers, an inconsistency has been observed between those farmers' legitimate attempts to claim government support for such things as drought relief and their tendency to refer to unemployed urban dwellers as 'dole bludgers' (see, for example, Alston, 1997). Instead of the 'kings in grass castles' as Mary Durack named them, their latest label is 'kings of the welfare state' (*Australian Magazine*, 9 September 2000: 32) or in Taylor's (1997) more explicit terms 'bludgers in grass castles'. They appear to be caught in a contradictory structural relationship, proclaiming their independence at the same time as justifying their dependence on various state support schemes. Ideology is one tool which farmers can use to come to grips with their structural position and negotiate the tensions in these dichotomies through the course of restructuring. At the same time, this process of negotiation can lead to new interpretations and action both on and off the farm.

Farmers are also subjected to the interpretations of others. Analysis of the rural media shows expressions of ideology in what Palmer and Quinn (1997) describe as four discourses. This work loosely parallels research on farming values in which Walter (1997) describes four farming types and the implication of four contrasting and potentially contested types of values which farm people might adhere to and express. Palmer and Quinn (1997: 106) make brief reference to contest and strain within one discourse: their 'agronomic discourse' described as 'a combination of economic rationalism, scientific agriculture and a trend toward market-driven primary production'. This was revealed by opposing views of these forces expressed in letters to the editor of a rural newspaper. Some favoured the 'agronomic' view while others opposed it.

The tension is also readily apparent in other print media. In an article in the *Australian Farm Journal*, Connors (1998) quotes the use of rural ideology (first apparent in the title of the article) by a former head of ABARE, to criticise what appears to be seen as attributes of the culture of which it is a part. 'Farmers', he said, 'should rid themselves of the attitude that the middleman (sic) is ripping them off and they are always getting a rough deal, as that approach stifles innovation'. The bureaucrat was quoted as believing that 'the farmers who do best are the ones who just get on with the job' (Connors, 1998: 16), citing the wine industry as the shining light for its value adding, lack of regulation and apparently outstanding export successes. (He did not mention that the industry is dominated by just four very large corporations.) This article implicitly used rural ideology as it sought to change rural culture into one more amenable to the interests of capital. Farmers were also reminded of the disparities in capital among them, as in Jones (1998), and material focused specifically on restructuring, such as Paterson (1998) which indicates social bifurcation. The latter told farmers of the great disparity in the wool industry, where the most profitable 25 per cent of graziers were reported (by the ABARE) to have had an average annual profit of $27 700 while the least profitable had an average loss of twice that figure. The former group was also younger, had larger properties and was better educated. The article was headed 'bigger is better …'.

These tensions, among others, are apparent in farmer organisations. The National Farmers' Federation (NFF) has become a strong proponent of deregulation and freedom for market forces (Lawrence, 1987, Halpin and Martin, 1996) alongside its formally political counterpart, the National Party. It has endorsed the approach which places responsibility on individual farmers through drought and 'adjustment policies' and has supported trade liberalisation and deregulation. Rather like the National Farmers' Union in Britain, it has been effectively rendered an 'active and willing partner of the state' (Murdoch, 1995: 199). However, Halpin and Martin (1996) find some evidence that only the more active members of the New South Wales Farmers' Association support this approach. Furthermore, there was evidence that many farmers, particularly many who were not members of the Association, foresaw the extension of corporate farming and were concerned about it. Conflict arose when the New South Wales Farmers' Association withdrew from the Pork Council of Australia after the latter had campaigned against the National Party at the 1998 Federal Election due to the latter's support for free trade. Unfortunately, a gender dimension to this differentiation remains uninvestigated. Tension over policy has erupted among farmer organisations, but class and gender dimensions which relate to that tension have not yet been confirmed. Class liminality and heterogeneity of interests (often in terms of bifurcation along lines of wealth) is behind the argument of Halpin and Martin (1996) that the NFF is becoming increasingly irrelevant to a wide range of rural issues. They have observed both the New South Wales Farmers' Association and the NFF changing from an organisation pursuing collective and direct action among farmers to one which promotes solutions by way of support for farming as business. Farmer organisations, as Halpin and Martin (1999) propose, thereby risk loss of the capacity to define the interests of farmers from the broad palette offered by farm and regional issues and promote the formation of collective identity.

The 1998 industrial dispute on Australia's waterfront also brought some of these tensions to the surface. The leadership of the NFF established a company and hired non-union workers who were intended, with the support of the stevedoring company, to replace members of the Maritime Union. This action raised questions about the ways in which farmers define their enemies and their leaders. Farmer organisation leaders were seen as 'remote' from their constituents. Importantly, while farmers saw unions as defying the ideal of hard work and in doing so causing farmers' costs to rise, they also recognised the shared situation of relative powerlessness. Both unions and farmers could see themselves as facing corporate and government 'enemies', even if the farm leaders sought to place all the blame on the unions.

The extent of farmer support for the NFF was almost as big an issue, judging by comment in the rural press, as the waterfront dispute and its resolution. The columns of *The Land* frequently focused on farmer support. Page 3 of the 5 February 1998 issue contained three headlines: 'Why We Took on the Waterfront' by the president of the NFF, 'Playing Politics Says a Yass Grower' and 'Dispute a Worry for Grains Industry', an industry which had good industrial relations on the waterfront working for it. Page 5 announced 'near consensus', but the front page of the same issue promised to publish the results of a telephone poll on the NFF action the next week. Page 1 of that issue ran a single large headline proclaiming that growers had said 'yes' in that poll. Ninety per cent had said 'yes' to the question 'do you support the move by NFF President Don McGauchie to set up a waterfront stevedoring operation?' There was no question to indicate the extent of support for the dismissal of the Maritime Union members.

The significant point is that *The Land* felt it necessary to poll support for the NFF President. Page 5 of this issue (12 February 1998) proclaimed 'blanket backing for taking on wharf union'. However, the 2 April 1998 issue contained an item which described the Pastoralists and Graziers' Association of Western Australia as 'wimps' for supporting the union and publicly demonstrating that support by sharing a barbecue with them. Farmers' loyalties remained controversial, illustrating the tensions inherent in their relations with each other, their leaders, corporate capital and worker organisations. It is this kind of situation, combined with both the conservative parties' pursuit of free-market policies, which enabled Smailes (1997: 40) to argue that farmers had been left 'without a political home'. It is unclear to many people just whose interests are being pursued by farmer organisations, despite their continued espousal of aspects of rural ideology. Halpin and Martin (1996) argue that the NFF provides no avenue toward a collective reflexivity which will respond to the range of rural problems, as issues are effectively translated at the private rather than the collective level. The impotence of farmer organisations was illustrated prior to a referendum on deregulation to be conducted by the Victorian Government among dairy farmers. The Presidents of each other State's dairy farmer organisations were all broadcast on national radio (Australian Broadcasting Corporation, 1999) stating that deregulation of their industry must be pursued, simply because it was viewed as inevitable.

As part of farmers' everyday lives, rural ideology provides frames of reference which farmers use to interpret what is happening around them. It is subject to change from within and without. Some interests may be served better by change in those frames of reference, as they affect people's beliefs and allegiances. This is not to say that ideology is deliberately manipulated nor that ideology provides a smokescreen which obscures change, rendering it invisible. Australian research (Gray, 1994; Gray et al., 1995) has argued that farmers are aware of the forces of restructuring and the position it is leaving them in. It remains, however, to interpret the ways in which farmers understand the process of restructuring and the social relations which are pertinent to it in terms of both cause and effect. This can best be accomplished through ethnographic research which begins with perceptions of change and its impacts and goes on to explore interpretations and their consequences. We have seen the circumstances of change, become acquainted with the ideology of those participating in change and been introduced to some of the forces creating tension with that ideology. Let us now look at how farmers see what is happening, how they interpret change and deal with the ideological tensions with which it is associated.

Australian Research Findings

We offer analysis of some survey data and focus groups in order to develop an understanding of the ways in which farm people negotiate the impacts of restructuring and attempt to come to grips with what is happening around them and the demands made on them. The data were collected in the course of a survey conducted by the Centre for Rural Social Research at Charles Sturt University during 1992, supplemented by another data set collected for a study conducted jointly by the Rural Social and Economic Research Centre at Central Queensland University and the Centre for Rural Social Research at Charles Sturt University during 1996. Both projects sought to listen to and analyse the views of people affected by restructuring. The first was funded by both the Rural Industries Research and Development Corporation and the second by the Rural Industries Research and Development Corporation and the Land and Water Resources Research and Development Corporation. A third project conducted eight focus groups during 1994 in order ascertain farmers' perceptions of change and its impacts on environmental sustainability. It was funded by the Land and Water Resources Research and Development Corporation.

The first project involved interviews with 245 farm people on 106 farms in the dairy industry in Northern Victoria (60 respondents), mixed farming and horticulture in the New South Wales Riverina (61 respondents in each) and sugarcane growing in Central Queensland (63 respondents). The survey sought information on experience of restructuring, views of the process including its effects and the future for farming. It was carried out during a period of financial difficulty for many farmers brought about by, among other things, a high interest rate regime and increased competition in the global marketplace. Drought was adding another dimension to hardship in the sugar industry of Central Queensland. The sample was constructed to cover the breadth of experience among farms at the time by including those which were in a sound financial condition for comparison with those which were struggling. The circumstances prevailing at the time allowed investigation of the conditions in which restructuring was having substantial impacts. It followed a period of high interest rates, deterioration in terms of trade for many industries and the beginning of deregulation. The second project focused on farm management and family coping during drought but also looked at responses to aspects of restructuring.

Interviews for the first project were conducted on farms, with adult family members interviewed separately. Together, the interviews lasted between two and three hours. Topics covered farm outputs and size of operation, perceived recent climatic conditions and output levels, farm financial position, farm management and personal coping strategies, plans for the future of the farm, levels of personal stress and a range of open questions designed to prompt discussion about restructuring and the effects it was having. Some (mostly quantitative) findings of the project related to coping and stress have been reported in Gray et al. (1993), Gray (1994), Gray and Lawrence (1996) and Lawrence and Gray (1997).

The second (1996) survey was conducted among 103 adults on fifty-six farms in the western Riverina of New South Wales and inland Central Queensland. Both areas had been suffering severe drought, the latter for a rather longer period than the former. Questions covered some similar matters to those asked in the 1992 survey, except that more attention was paid to farm management and change in farm lifestyle and practices during drought, and less quantitative detail on family coping and stress was obtained. This project has been reported in Stehlik et al. (1998).

The questions on change and its effects used in the 1992 survey included:
- In general, how has the economic situation affected your life? (For those with children) How do you feel the economic situation has affected your children?
- What do you think has caused the economic problems that farmers are facing?
- How are changes to the marketing of farm products affecting you?
- Do you feel that you, personally, can have some influence on the problems of the rural economy?
- Do you think that farmers and their organisations are doing enough?
- What else should they do?

Perceived Impacts of Restructuring

Combinations of high interest rates with high input costs and low product prices, and drought for some, made the period of the first survey one of those recurrent economic crises of Australian farming. It was more critical for some than others, but all family members interviewed had been affected in some ways. Among the 245 people interviewed, just six offered anything which could be interpreted as a positive response to the question about effects of the economic situation on them. One related his experience to what might have happened had he and his wife not become farmers, which they had done relatively recently. No doubt their capacity to buy their farm outright had helped. Others had found an opportunity to battle on and build character, and could therefore look positively on their experience which otherwise would be seen as unpleasant. Some responses follow. (In some cases, the equity held in the farm by respondents is indicated where it may be particularly relevant. As high interest rates were problematic at the time, equity offers a very useful indicator of farm financial position.)

> Well I think it's made us better people ... I think that has made us stronger people. I think the kids benefited from that, losses – I'm just trying to think what we felt – apart from the monetary loss – I don't think we have lost out in any personal way or emotional way. Ummh, I think we were strong enough to get through that. (Female farmer aged 32 with primary education and 57 per cent equity)

Another producer offered a parallel response with emphasis on farm management:

> It has had its positives too, I think the fact that we have managed to put together a package and we look as though it is going to work for us. Yeah that is a positive point and it gives you a good feeling to go through it or getting through it. (Male producer aged 50 with agricultural secondary education)

One male farmer offered a rather ambiguous response which implicitly drew on an aspect of agrarianism: the ennoblement to be gained from hard work. Another drew on the ideal of self-reliance.

> Made us work a lot harder. [Big pause] Does that answer your question?
> *(Male farmer aged 57 with primary education)*

> I think it has made me fairly independent and self-reliant.
> *(Male aged 33 with secondary agricultural education)*

Some indicated that enforced rethinking was seen positively, after they had questioned their approach to farming. But again there is some ambiguity about the result.

> Well in the last six months, it has taught me to become much more philosophical about everything, and perhaps there is no need to succeed just to get rid of the overdraft, and get rid of the farm payments as such.
> *Interviewer:* So you have re-assessed your priorities?
> I think so. I've tried to – and I'm still in the process, I would think.
> *(Male aged 45 with primary education)*

Unambiguously negative responses were frequent. Many mentioned financial stringency, social isolation and personal stress, but others emphasised family considerations. Interpretations of what was happening to them showed bitterness and feelings of entrapment among some farm people. One respondent reported that his family's taxable income had been reduced from $150000 to $50000 but stressed his awareness that many people were suffering more than his family was. Others revealed quite difficult circumstances. They reported major lifestyle change. For some this meant that they could do little but work, but were unable to wind down towards retirement. For others it involved struggling to keep their farm operating at all. Others, notably as expressed below by women, could not maintain their household's standard of living and some were entirely dependent on social security payments for food.

> Penny pinching. I hate it, I find it degrading sometimes, but it is a matter of survival.
>
> *(Female aged 51 with primary education)*

> And that's a bit mean, like I need a new fridge because it defrosts every second day and I open the fridge and the water just pours out the bottom. A new stove – I haven't got a grill and only two hot plates left now.
>
> *(Female aged 57 with primary education)*

Stress had taken a toll.

> Oh emotionally, shocking actually. I just about was a nervous wreck there, I think. Sleepless nights and …
>
> *(Male aged 45 with secondary education and 43 per cent equity)*

> More stress … More uncertainty. I think it's probably had an effect on my self-confidence in a sense.
>
> *(Female aged 44 with tertiary education and 69 per cent equity)*

> All my kids have all grown up. In the last six years I haven't really seen them, not even for Sunday lunch – seven days' work.
>
> *(Male aged 42 with secondary education)*

Concern about disappointment among children who wanted to continue farming also emerged, as did feelings for their friends who had been forced to leave their farm. Through all this ran a seldom-spoken doubt about the quality of parenting being provided. This was most evident when respondents mentioned their lack of patience or bad moods affecting family relations after excessive work amid depressing circumstances. An image emerges of extensive self-exploitation which extends to family and friends, and while a degree of camaraderie may remain and even grow, families, friendships and community relations are all strained. In accord with other research, including the 1996 study (see Stehlik et al., 1998), isolation has particular significance to women:

my husband has to go away to supplement our finances, and therefore I'm coping
on my own for a good six months of the year.

(Female aged 34 with secondary education)

The 1996 study inquired about effects of drought and found similar patterns. Farm family members were asked about the biggest problem arising from the drought which the district had faced. Apart from lack of rain and depletion, or disappearance, of water supplies, answers included poverty, diminished social contact, stress, increased work demands and uncertainty. The point that loss of animals caused much anxiety and distress was made strongly. So, too, was the decline in morale, particularly as young people and whole families had to leave their communities. There are also indications in the 1992 study that morale was deteriorating as people were finding themselves working harder for little gain and few prospects for future betterment of their living conditions. Moreover, powerlessness emerged as a theme, but rather by implication from answers to the question about effects.

Well I mean, I myself – I have got to the stage where I ... it's just not worth doing
anything any more.

(Female farmer aged 38 with secondary education)

A sense of entrapment is suggested by people indicating that they feel they are on a treadmill. They have no choice but to work harder for less reward, only to see their hopes for their children further threatened. And they cannot afford to take risks and develop their farms innovatively in ways they once did.

I was one of the first to grow canola – but now we just don't do that sort of thing –
you can't afford to take that sort of risk.

(Male farmer aged 42 with agricultural tertiary education)

The treadmill theme emerges clearly.

Yeah, we've, um, been for a long time, going back to the last ten years, production
getting bigger ... we have been going with less and less every year, even though
production has been coming up. But things are just going backwards.

(Male farmer aged 27 with agricultural secondary education)

The 1994 focus groups made the environmental implications, and perceptions of them, very apparent. As reported in Gray et al. (1995), farmers were aware of long-term effects on the sustainability of their farming. They could see, and were making, valuable innovations in land management like conservation farming, but they were also aware of inadequacies and impossibilities in these changes. They could see little choice but to continue with current practices. They knew that current practices resulted in exploitation of the farm's resources (Gray et al., 1995: 60). A male farmer reported:

I can see a bit of a pattern. I have just got a couple of things written down here like cost of production. It's the first thing that is rising and the profitability is dropping and then secondly, that causes debt as costs go up and then I see thirdly, people start as they get into debt, to run more stock and put more land into crop and then they start getting on to the phase of mining the farm (quoted in Gray et al., 1995: 60).

My objective would be to stay where we are, and I think that can be done but the risk is that it will be done by more inputs, so that next year we have now got to put more lime on and then more gypsum and next year we have got to put more chemicals on and that is not sustainability. That is running faster to stay on the same spot (quoted in Gray et al., 1995: 61).

Some farmers, it would seem, feel pressured to destroy their own futures.

Perceptions of Causes

Widespread and continuing awareness of a difficult situation for farmers is quite apparent. There was evidence of people struggling to come to grips with change, appreciating that they were being left behind. Their interpretation of change has two important elements in addition to its effects. One is perception of its occurrence and the other is understanding of its cause. Both these can be problematic. Rapid change can be hard to 'keep up with' while change can also be too slow to be readily apparent unless an indicator of long-term movement is available.

The ways in which farmers use ideology to 'frame' their interpretations of change became apparent as they were asked to identify the cause of their economic problems. Ideology provides a systematic means by which farmers can make sense of complex processes in straightforward ways. It offers a means of identifying something which can readily be interpreted as central to the issue. It provides codes which are acknowledged and shared among farm community members. Mooney and Hunt (1996) identify three 'frames' for rural ideology which they apply historically to farmer political movements in the United States. Framing the perceptions of individual farmers might distil a small number of frames, but it offers insights regardless of numbers. This is because, as Mooney and Hunt (1996) explain, frames identify problems and attribute cause, encourage adoption of strategies and provide reasons for action.

Faith in hard work is a frame revealed by responses to the question about the cause of the economic problems facing farmers.

I think it is just too easy to take the soft option. I think if we were all prepared to all work and go without a bit.

(Male aged 44 with primary education)

Opportunities for contrast with agrarian ideals occurred, in particular, with reference to the unions. Sometimes individual union leaders were mentioned, at other times groups of employees, such as the 'wharfies'.

The view of hard work as both problem and solution can be related to work for farmer and community organisations as well as work on the farm:

> well probably the average cockie, and I'd be one of them, don't do enough our-selves because we don't go to enough meetings etc. ... We might just be lazy. Leave it to others.
>
> *(Male farmer aged 54 with primary education)*

Self-reliance and independence present another frame.

> They've got to – how would you say that – well really I think if the politicians kept their nose out and let the sugar industry – the powers-that-be run their own busi-ness – their own industry – we would probably be a lot better off.
>
> *(Male farmer aged 55 with secondary education)*

The perceived importance of farming is another frame, which obtains greater meaning when applied with rural–urban differentiation.

> Well the weather to start with, I suppose – the tariff cut-backs, and the Government sort of not worrying about – they tend to be more worried about people in the cities than people out in the country, which is the lifeblood of the country really.
> (Woman aged 36 with technical education)

Some respondents indicated strong feelings about governments being controlled by 'acad-emics', people with no practical experience of farming, who, furthermore, were urban dwellers. Bureaucrats also provided personification which facilitated application of this frame. The urban–rural differentiation frame covers ignorance as well as lack of interest among urban people:

> *Interviewer:* That was government mismanagement was it?
> Yeh, and probably lack of understanding of the rural – of the rural sector. I don't think anyone from the city can come within an inch of understanding it.

The 1996 (drought) study asked people if they felt neglected by government. Responses indicated that the sentiment was widespread among respondents and thought to be general. This is not surprising given recent changes in policy approaches to drought and extensive dependence on government income support in both areas studied, but particularly in Queensland.

> Country people as a whole do ... I think most country people do feel neglected by the government ... I don't think the government could care if we were here or not.
>
> *(Female beef producer)*

Not all responses used ideological frames, but nevertheless demonstrated a rural perspective on change. Identification of threats continues to be prominent among the 1992 survey responses.

A notion of malevolent interests extends overseas. Responses mentioned the European Economic Community (EEC) subsidies and the Closer Economic Relations agreement with New Zealand as threats, sometimes blaming government for allowing dumping and not creating a genuine level 'playing field'. There was also some tendency to see these issues in more conspiratorial terms.

> Well, I think the dairy farm is, because of the rural price, the prices of the milk products have fallen, and GATT is the organisation who sets the whole price and GATT is part of the United Nations.
>
> *(Male aged 45 with secondary education)*

Perception of a power relationship between farmers and the agents blamed for their problems indicated awareness of restructuring with a sense of powerlessness.

> Well I think, to be quite honest, we have been manipulated by politics, or the money market, one or the other.
>
> *(Male farmer aged 40 with technical education)*

People's views sometimes indicated a perception of the bifurcation process, acknowledging forces in both government and the private sector which were making survival increasingly difficult for smaller farms.

> Yeh, and the banks are actually loading – loading the farmer up with about anywhere between 2 and 4 per cent extra interest over the prime rate ... And yet big business can command prime rate and we can't.
>
> *(Male aged 49 with primary school education)*

> I reckon they are out to help the big person and not the little ones.
>
> *(Male farmer aged 42 with secondary education)*

Regulation, or rather deregulation was seen as bringing unfavourable change.

> I wouldn't mind a deregulated market if we could see a few more dollars in our pocket, but we're not – it's gone the other way.
>
> *(Male farmer aged 57 with secondary education)*

Some men and women expressed incomprehension while others pointed to government inadequacies.

> We can't understand why they're deregulating everything, it just does not make sense ... Well perhaps there most probably could be some changes, but I mean if we were the most efficient industry, why have they got to radically change it?
>
> *(Female farmer aged 47 with secondary education)*

Some responses to the question 'How are changes to the marketing of farm products affecting you?' were positive. Reasoning behind these answers referred to the opportunity for choice in marketing. One mentioned the possibility of the establishment of co-operatives. Some saw it as a stimulus to diversification.

> I think we will be producing more – even a greater diversity of products in the next few years. I can see myself just producing more and more different types of crops. Next year I am looking at possibly linseed and chick pea production here ...
>> *(Male farmer aged 35 with tertiary non-agricultural education)*

But qualifications were added. Changes to marketing, particularly the end of the Wheat Board's domestic monopoly, offered opportunities, but only to those farmers who had the time and, moreover, the skill to take advantage of them.

Others were negative.

> Well naturally (the changes) bloody affect you, I mean take, for example, the drop in the reserve price of wool, I'm sure it's affecting us. It's effectively cut about a third of our income or more.
>> *(Male farmer aged 48 years with secondary agricultural education)*

Sheep/wheat farmers had seen the wool floor price eliminated at the same time as wheat prices were descending.

> It's been devastating.
>> *(Male farmer aged 47 with secondary education)*

Lack of time to acquire the necessary skills and then to carry out the marketing work were common themes among those respondents who could only speak negatively. They expected the change to be difficult and expensive. Some saw the influence of forces working against the interests of farmers, sometimes applying familiar ideological frames and expressing a feeling of loss of control. In contrast to those who saw opportunity to exercise choice, some ultimately saw farmers further removed from the marketing process.

> Well I am not happy with it by any means. I don't know that farmers have been beneficiaries out of the deregulation. And I still resent the fact that the demise of the floor price scheme for wool was engineered by bureaucrats and politicians ... I think the deregulation of the financial system of the economy was a disaster and, you know, what are governments for ... like if you are going to deregulate every-thing why do you need governments?
>> *(Male farmer aged 54 with secondary education)*

> Well it seems as though we are supposed to do our own marketing but I really think it's just a waste of time because the big corporations have taken over ...

> There's really no competitive markets to sell your stuff. And it's just a ploy to divert our attention and think that we've got some control over our destiny which we really haven't.
>
> *(Female farmer aged 44 with secondary education)*

> See, it [the Wheat Board] has been around for a long time and it's getting all cut up and pulled apart, and I would like to see the growers being in control of it.
>
> *(Female farmer aged 52 with tertiary education)*

> I think the producer is being removed more and more from the marketing end of things.
>
> *(Female farmer aged 44 years with tertiary education)*

Those in the sugar industry also offered diverse interpretations, but they ultimately pointed to lack of grower control over grower interests. Pointing to the existing system rather than changes to it, some blamed the large milling corporations. Others attacked the marketing system as 'socialist':

> the mill's percentage is greater than the grower's percentage, and I think it's about time it was split up a little bit more evenly if they are going to keep growers on the land, you know. Because all the mills – they all get done up – they got money to do what they want to. All cane inspectors, mill managers and everything, all drive around in good cars, you know.
>
> *(Male farmer aged 40 with technical education)*

> As it is now, [a large agribusiness corporation] is our sole marketing agent.
>
> *(Male farmer aged 33 with technical education)*

> I don't know how the changes to the marketing of sugar is affecting me. All I see on that situation is that the bloody sugar industry is such a socialist bloody ... social- ist-run industry that we get paid for our bloody product when somebody feels like paying us.
>
> *(Male farmer aged 44 with tertiary education)*

When asked if they felt that they had any influence on the problems of the rural economy, some farmers said that by working better or more innovatively they could contribute. Many more, however, interpreted the question as seeking their view on what they could achieve outside the farm in the political environment. Some, notably the women, simply said nothing because they expected that nobody would listen. But the most common theme was positive: men and women felt that they could make a difference but only by acting with other farmers through their organisations and, as raised by one woman, through locally-based education programs. They saw organisation as problematic, however, because nobody had the time needed to attend meetings and, sometimes, the people failed to unite in their organisations. Some respondents raised points reminiscent of the ideological frames. Others pointed to the spread of larger corporate farms, indicating a feeling of diminishing significance.

> No, I don't suppose a lot ... well probably not, without guarantees, like ... so it's only a kind of a drop in the ocean really ... Especially now that there's kind of big (you know) bigger ummh corporate-owned farms and they have kind of got a lot more power because they are buying and selling a lot more.
> *(Male farmer aged 18 with secondary education)*

Some saw the production treadmill problem as an underlying and controlling factor, when asked about the cause of the economic situation.

> You know it would be awful to see some farmers go out of business, of course, but it's over-supply ... and when you get too much, the price goes down.
> *(Female farmer aged 32 with primary education)*

Farmers and their organisations received some blame. Lack of support was identified as a problem, with one farmer likening his organisation to a union in its need for unity and others looking at internal conflict.

> If you get three farmers together you have always got four different opinions on what we should do about it ... [During a dispute] we spent more time fighting amongst ourselves, than we did fighting the Government, which was the cause of the problem.
> *(Male farmer aged 43, education not stated)*

Opinions were divided on whether farm organisations were doing enough for their members. Some felt they were performing well in difficult circumstances while other farmers said that their organisations were quite inadequate. This theme was repeated in the 1996 (drought) study, with regard to a marketing organisation, when a respondent suggested that the government should 'sack the Australian Meat and Livestock Corporation'.

Responses to the 1992 question about what farmer organisations should do, which was put to those who felt farmer organisations were not doing enough, illustrated some of the tensions which afflict farmers as a 'collective agency'. This is partly indicated by contrasting opinions about their relationship with politics and the desirability of militancy. Some felt that their organisations should be apolitical, in the sense of not being associated with a political party, but should act as a lobby group. Others were not fearful of politics and a few advocated militancy, but stopped short of endorsing the actions of French farmers and their blockades. The familiar 'countrymindedness' frame was drawn upon with reference to the need to educate city people to the importance of agriculture. Much concern was expressed that farmers did not participate frequently enough. But the underlying tensions became apparent in discussion about leadership and its relations with membership:

> Well, they are disorganised, there is no unity. It is almost impossible to get a protest with farmers because they won't unite. Even though I'm anti-union I'm still for strength in, yeah, people in like situations, dairying must be the only industry where when the price goes down we increase production. What sort of idiots are we?
>
> *(Female farmer aged 48 with tertiary agricultural education)*

Some saw the problem as one of elitist leadership that was out of touch with 'real' farmers and obtaining advice from the wrong sources:

> No, because the people who run the [organisation] for example are all very wealthy comfortable people and I think they have lost contact with ordinary farmers.
>
> *(Female farmer aged 42 with tertiary education)*

> [The organisations should] become more realistic for a start. And get a cross-section view of the industry instead of just the – oh we call them silver-spoon farmers but ummh ...
>
> *(Male farmer aged 40 with technical education)*

> A lot of these organisations seem to be run by silvertails which is a term farmers probably use for the aristocracy because they are the ones that can afford the time off-farm to be agro-politicians. (Male farmer aged 45 with technical education)

Yet the implicitly opposite view was also held: praise for economic policies of the kind which had brought deregulation and the support given to those policies by farmer organisations.

> Never enough, but the reality is: I believe that the farmers' organisations are doing a damn good job, much better – a much better job than what the general public believes ... what they do for agriculture has to be good for Australia, that's what I'm really saying.
>
> *(Female farmer aged 56 with tertiary education)*

A critique of the organisations, however, brings a fundamental question which raises the tension between policy for agriculture and policy for farmers.

> They have got to get out of the red tape and just get back to the basics of what's needed ... Our farming organisations are more interested in what future there is for agriculture, and not what the future of the present lot of farmers is.
>
> *(Male farmer aged 47 with secondary education)*

Some were grappling with the likeness of their organisations to trade unions, as suggested by responses discussed earlier.

[They should] make it that all farmers have to be in it, because you can't – I don't really – I'm not a real unionist person, but a union works only if you've got full membership, otherwise you don't have ... And I mean we have to work with unions, as far as tanker drivers, etc. etc.

(Female, aged not stated, with primary education)

Conclusion

The 'voice' of farmers is divided. It does say that many farmers are struggling to survive in farming and they and their families are suffering. Farmers have no difficulty making their situation apparent to all Australians. However, explaining that situation and formulating an effective response to it are more difficult. Farmers are feeling angry, ignored and trapped, believing that they are suffering because of the greed, ignorance or ineptitude of others, leaving them locked in a system which is bound to perpetuate their exploitation. They can use agrarian ideology and countrymindedness to legitimate interpretations of their situation and identify others who are responsible. However, another 'voice' of farmers can also identify them as the culprits. The same rural ideology can be used, and is used, to identify farmers themselves as those responsible and to interpret change as opportunity for individuals rather than disaster for the collectivity. Their own organisation does so for them.

The 'voice' of farmers is better seen as a site of contest between competing interests – including perceptions of those interests – of those who seek to influence the agricultural political agenda in order either to hasten or to retard change. Ideology is available to make sense of what is happening but it is used by different groups for different purposes with contrasting interpretations. This duality is based in the liminality of farming and the ultimate subservience of family farms to larger-scale capital.

Ideology offers a means of managing the tensions inherent in this condition. It has often been said that agrarianism has facilitated the exploitation of farming families by capital. Considering farmers' reflexivity, however, allows us to see how it also enables farmers to justify their own self-exploitation to themselves. Farmers depend on differentiation, such as that between country and city, unionists and farmers, bureaucrats and farmers, in order to maintain their own identity. Agrarianism and countrymindedness provide frames through which interpretation of differentiation can be developed and brought to bear on the inconsistencies in the everyday conditions of farming. Perseverance should not be seen as merely value attached to a lifestyle or other aspects of tradition. It is also enabled by the maintenance of ideological differentiation between farmers and others. Like all groups in society, farmers readily employ their ideology to legitimate their existence to themselves.

Thus, sense can be made of global misfortune in terms of falling prices and rising costs (the work of foreign nations and their organisations and lazy unionists with excessive power who do not share the value which farmers place on hard work) and deregulation (the work of city-based bureaucrats who know nothing of farming). But sense can also be made of deregulation as creating opportunities for farmers to exercise their self-reliance and capacity for hard work. Falling prices and rising costs may be interpreted as a challenge which can be met in the same way. The political ingenuity with which farmer organisations and the National Party have appropriated ideology in such ways has resulted in a farming population which is having great difficulty finding a voice and, therefore, developing a capacity for reflection and effective collective action. Their struggle is not a simple product of declining wealth and loss of voting power. Forming the means to perceive and express their interests is highly problematic.

While women have been excluded from official leadership among farmers, there is no evidence, nor is there any *a priori* reason to expect, that they are out of touch with the issues arising from restructuring. Indeed, their growing political activism indicates that the opposite can be said of many farm women. However, the data presented above indicate that while many women have a different experience of restructuring from that of men, the range of their interpretations may well parallel, without necessarily being the same as, that of men as they draw on the same ideology. This remains despite farming women's evidently different experience, the significance they attribute to aspects of restructuring and in some ways their interpretations of change. It would also seem that women's activism may express the same tensions and conflicts. However, their reflexivity as women is growing and changing rapidly. As their resistance to the male domination of farming grows, so will their capacity to develop their own perspective free from that of men.

Their resistance will be facilitated as the structures, including those of small local organisations, are changed by women into systems which are more participatory and supportive (Claridge, 1999). The extensive participation of women in Landcare hints at such a trend (Lockie, 1997). It may also change trajectory within the farm organisation. As Kubik and Stirling (1998) put it, farm women are confronted with a dilemma. They can either resist the degradation of work associated with servicing the needs of agribusiness, or they can resist patriarchy within that system. Kubik and Sterling (1998: 20) observe that some Canadian farm women are 'struggling with the patriarchal view that if only farm income would increase, everything on the farm would be fine'.

Such evidence has suggested that there may be some interactive processes between the rising consciousness of women, the growth of alternative agricultures and the questioning of the interests of capital versus those of farming people in the productivist paradigm. As the previous chapter argued, the public strength of women is increasing, possibly more rapidly than their participation in the management of many farms. Perhaps the gendered structure of policy-making will be reflected upon by male and female farmers along with their gendered relationships on farm.

Farmers are vocal but have no effective voice. The liminality of farming makes it difficult for them to find a means of expression and their ideology, upon which they depend to make sense of liminality, can easily be turned to undermine the historical basis for their existence as small family-based operators. Many are aware that the voices which are heard from farmers are those which, as one respondent above put it, are representing 'industry' rather than farmers. In these circumstances, it is difficult to expect governments of any kind to listen and respond to the situation of farming families, rendering those smaller operators whose interests are not so easily identifiable with those of 'the industry', by their own perception, trapped and powerless. Their vulnerability to neoliberalism is such that it deepens their economic and social plight as it frames their reflexivity in a way which denies the structural basis of change.

Their reflexivity is complicit, quite unintentionally and non-consciously on their part, in the maintenance of barriers to the expression of their interests in political arenas at all levels.

Further Reading

Connors, T. (1996) *To Speak with One Voice: The Quest by Australian Farmers for Federal Unity*, Canberra: NFF.
  – a history of the NFF illustrating the continuing historical tensions experienced by farmers attempting to organise
Gray, I., Lawrence, G. and Dunn, A. (1993) *Coping with Change: Australian Farmers in the 1990s,* Wagga Wagga: Centre for Rural Social Research, Charles Sturt University.
  – presents and analyses the experiences of farm families during the difficult economic period of the early 1990s
Mules, W. and Miller, H. (1997) *Mapping Regional Cultures*, Rockhampton: Rural Social and Economic Research Centre, Central Queensland University.
  – analysis of Australian regional cultures and their significance
Share, P. (ed.) (1995) *Communication and Culture in Rural Areas*, Wagga Wagga: Centre for Rural Social Research, Charles Sturt University.
  – a collection of papers looking at the relationships between culture, ideology and power in rural situations

We have not intended to give the impression that regional Australia does nothing other than farm. Farming is only one activity of regional people and restructuring is threatening its significance. Farmers represent only a small proportion of the population of rural Australia – around 13 per cent (Garnaut and Lim-Applegate, 1998). The reasons that farmers remain so significant in economic, social and political terms lie in their contribution to regional income and their management of much of our natural resource base. And they are vocal. But there are villages, towns and cities which are very much a part of regional Australia, many of which do not have a strong relationship to agriculture.

When we look at regional Australia we see townspeople alongside farming people, but we also see communities which depend heavily on extractive industries and tourism, rather than agriculture. This creates an enormous variety among local economies and economic and social conditions. However, the issues facing many people living in regional settlements are like those confronting farmers. They face questions about their futures: are they destined to live in poverty; will they have to move elsewhere to try to make a living; will the services they need in their towns remain there, or in many cases, ever be restored to former levels; will their friends and relatives be able to stay in the community to which they have all contributed, perhaps over generations; will the community survive at all in a globalised world? In agricultural areas, these questions are especially significant for farmers. For some towns and rural hinterlands, the questions have been, and in some cases still are, quite different. Those areas which have experienced rapid growth are also facing questions about the adequacy of services, threats to quality of life and loss of community as the social composition of towns changes along with their economic bases. Regional Australia is changing in ways which are beginning to display the bifurcation process identified among farmers, and farming communities.

Among the global misfortunes described in chapter 1, regional Australia suffers in particular from the historical constraint of the colonial legacy and a lack of resources in its relationship with metropolitan Australia. This misfortune was obscured, at least from the metropolitan perspective, over many generations in the apparent reciprocity of metropolitan–regional dependency in an economy based heavily on agriculture and extractive industry. The rise of manufacturing, and more recently service industries in metropolitan centres, accompanying change in technology and other factors, has made the situation of regional economy and society more obvious. This chapter examines the processes of demographic and social change in regional Australia before considering the impact of globalisation and the push towards a radically different regional economy and society.

The Changing Spatial Distribution of Regional Population

The extent and pace of economic and social change can be seen in terms of population distribution and movement. Population decline is, at one and the same time, a symptom, a cause and an effect of economic and social ill-health. It also accelerates restructuring, with many rural communities finding themselves in a downward demographic-economic-social spiral. The process of urbanisation, whereby rural areas lost population to towns and cities, has been well known in Australia. In 1933 more than one in three Australians lived in rural areas, but by 1976 the proportion had fallen to one in seven, under the growing pull of opportunity amid urban expansion and the relative decline of rural employment (Hugo, 1996). It was suggested that the process of urbanisation might have been reversed during the 1970s, but it has become apparent that rural depopulation was continuing and happening much faster than had been anticipated. For many places, decline threatened to become terminal.

Interest in rural demography has been stimulated by press reports such as those of Cribb (1994) who showed that regional Australia was losing its population base. With the aid of a classification based on distance from cities for metropolitan, remote and rural areas (with sub-categories for town populations), Salt (1992) was the first to analyse the movement of regional population in detail. He concluded from analysis of data for the period between 1976 and 1989 that many rural and remote areas, including towns but excluding some larger centres and coastal areas, had more people who had permanently left than had arrived to settle. Also worrying was Salt's finding that while people of all ages were leaving rural and remote areas, young adults were notably over-represented. This is confirmed by Bell (1995: 102) for the 1986–91 inter-censal period. Forty-four of forty-eight non-metropolitan statistical divisions suffered net losses of 15- to 24-year-olds during this period, leaving rapidly ageing populations.

A 'rural–urban turnaround' in population distribution, through a process known as 'counterurbanisation', occurred in Australia during the 1970s and has continued. Analyses of census data in the 1980s revealed that the metropolitan areas' share of Australia's population was decreasing. This does not mean that all of the non-metropolitan areas were growing. Differences were emerging among them. Prior to the release of data from the 1991 Census, Hugo and Smailes (1992) concluded, on the basis of survey data collected in South Australia, that non-metropolitan Australia should really be divided into three areas: a sparsely settled interior, an agricultural zone suffering a downward population spiral, and a metropolitan hinterland which is experiencing growth through counterurbanisation. By looking at population change in regional New South Wales, Sant and Simons (1993) extend the notion: a stark contrast was emerging between the demographies of coastal and inland New South Wales in an unanticipated demographic change. By 1986 population projections calculated in 1976 were found to have underestimated coastal growth by 42 per cent and overestimated inland growth by 20 per cent (Weinand and Lea, 1990: 61). The 1991 Census revealed that counterurbanisation was happening, but not to the extent that it had occurred during the late 1970s, and in ways which continued the process of regional depopulation in most areas (Hugo, 1994). Hugo (1996) confirms the expectation that such patterns of counterurbanisation would continue.

The process was uneven, but the 1980s had brought substantial regional depopulation, reflecting relative opportunity, despite counterurbanisation. As Paris (1994) observed, people were deserting rural Australia. While the Australian Capital Territory and some parts of inland Victoria gained population, all other inland non-metropolitan regions suffered net losses (Bell, 1995). McKenzie (1994: 5) reported that while rural depopulation continued between 1986 and 1991, it was 'somewhat patchy'. Bell (1995) summed it up as centralisation on the capital cities with some dispersal from them. This process is giving rise to growth, which from a national perspective is concentrated 'at the metropolitan fringe and a few coastal areas with environmental amenity [which] are attracting the great bulk of population increase and redistribution' (Maher and Stimson, 1994: 27). Nevertheless, some inland regional areas have been identified as places of growth. Maher and Stimson (1994) found that areas around the largest regional cities, some mining centres and areas of increasingly intensive agriculture did experience growth.

Spatial Variation

The demographic literature suggests that it is possible to draw only two general conclusions about regional population decline: one, it is happening, and two, it is occurring in a spatially uneven manner. In contrast to smaller settlements and farming/grazing areas, most regional cities have experienced consistent growth. Beer et al. (1994) looked at the demography of the seventy-nine cities which were neither capitals nor adjacent to capitals but had populations greater than 10000 in 1991. Only 3 per cent had declined consistently between 1976 and 1991 while 19 per cent had fallen from growth to decline. Beer et al. listed eight cities as consistently declining, but all of them were heavily dependent on either extractive or manufacturing industry. They agreed with Salt (1992) that the regional cities can gain population from both their own regions and the capital cities. The regional cities which draw population from rural areas have been labelled 'sponge cities' (Productivity Commission, 1999). The rapidly growing coastal centres are similar but draw much higher proportions of their migrants from the capitals. Beer et al. (1994) wrote optimistically about the prospects for many of these cities, showing that they had been able to attract industry from the capitals. Some – especially those in areas attractive to tourists and retirees – may be relatively independent of agriculture. The Productivity Commission (1999) concurs with this image.

Those moving from rural areas to regional cities and the coast include relatively large proportions of elderly people. As Walmsley et al. (1995) showed, some rapidly growing coastal towns have a disproportionate number of elderly people. Migration of the elderly to inland cities is also significant, though it tends to be motivated by proximity to kin rather than lifestyle and environmental attractions (Drysdale, 1991). As confirmed by the Productivity Commission for inland towns, movement of elderly people from farms exacerbates the ageing of settlements brought about by the departure of young school-leaving seekers of further education and employment.

Beer et al.'s positive scenario, describing the living places of two million people or 12 per cent of Australia's population, can also hide significant localised variation and change which favours the largest rural towns and cities. Gray (1991) showed that, in the Shire of Cowra in New South Wales, the population of the rural part of the shire had exceeded that of the township of Cowra until 1933, but from the 1947 Census its share of the population was found to diminish. By 1986 the rural and village population of Cowra Shire was less than half that of the town. McKenzie (1996) pointed out that the New South Wales Statistical Local Area of Leeton, containing a substantial town, declined between 1986 and 1991 while its neighbour, the City of Griffith, grew. Such contrasts can be very strong. While the City of Mildura grew by 30 per cent between 1981 and 1991, the rural Shire of Wycheproof in the same statistical division declined by 21 per cent. In a different situation, the rural hinterland of Perth showed substantial growth, but when two towns which are only one hour's travel time from Perth are withdrawn, the statistical subdivision showed a population decline of 12 per cent between 1961 and 1996 (Haslam-McKenzie, 1998).

The process of bifurcation can be seen among what might appear to be otherwise similar towns. Geno (1997) indicated that those small towns with fewer than 500 people were largely unable to provide for themselves, although some that were able to attract tourists may be more prosperous than others. Sorensen (1990) saw towns locked into either vicious or virtuous circles of decline or growth. The smaller the town the more likely it was to be locked into decline, although the 'fulcrum of viability' declined westward (Sorensen, 1990: 42). Smaller, more remote, settlements can remain viable because they do not suffer such competition from larger towns and cities to the east, as do the small towns nearer to larger ones. Sorensen and Epps (1997) analysed the relative economic strengths of four inland Central Queensland shires and concluded that, while the available indicators were not consistent, one was emerging as a regional centre while another was very much lagging behind. The explanations offered were tentative but the town whose prospects are weakest was more remote and less diversified. Tonts and Jones (1996) also found some places growing while others were declining. They attributed growth to employment in manufacturing and the presence of local government in the Western Australian towns they studied. Stimson et al. (1999) saw polarisation among towns and cities with populations of 10 000 or more. While population size was not found to be significant on its own, the authors were able to distinguish clearly between what they termed 'communities of opportunity' and 'communities of vulnerability'.

More recent information confirms continuation of the trends. Salt (1997) pointed to decline in some single industry cities, noting that Whyalla and Broken Hill had lost one-quarter and one-fifth of their populations respectively since 1976, but some inland cities continued to grow and the coast remained attractive. The populations of towns in the wheat-sheep belt were changing slowly with some growth, but their hinterlands were declining rapidly. Except in coastal areas and the largest towns and cities, rural depopulation and ageing seem likely to continue. Even communities with economies based on resources like minerals and including some based on irrigated agriculture also have uncertain futures.

Uncertainty and rapid change are not new to rural communities. Buxton (1985) related how, in south-eastern Australia, towns which had grown rapidly with a rush of farmer settlement during the 1870s declined as the frontier moved on. A similar phenomenon followed initial railway development. The most voluminous changes, however, occurred around gold mining, with some smaller towns disappearing altogether as the gold ran out. The points which remain pertinent are that towns can disappear; they can 'age' rapidly; and small numerical population changes can be large in proportional terms and large in their effects on communities.

Some Case Studies

The experience of decline in country towns is best illustrated by case studies, like that conducted by Townsend et al. (2000) using interviews and focus groups in two small towns in western Victoria. The systemic nature of economic and social deterioration is illustrated by the interconnections between elements of change. The experience of change is basically the same in both towns. Reduction of government assistance and price supports, combined with worsening markets, has pushed farmers off their land and into the towns but left less money for local investment. Those who remain on their land seek off-farm income and tend to shop and do business where they work, which is unlikely to be in a small town. The increasing demands of farm and other work leave little time for supporting local community organisations. This is not unlike O'Toole's (1999) findings for south-west Victoria.

Local government services have been centralised with council amalgamations depleting jobs in the small towns. In addition, the requirement of State government that local council work be put to tender has meant that more jobs have moved to larger centres. In one of the small towns studied, a bank closed soon after the council amalgamation. Where bank branches have remained open, their management has been downgraded such that only more junior staff are available. More job losses were incurred in both towns after State government departments moved their offices to larger towns. Some services, such as the library, were reduced to a mobile or visiting basis. 'Rationalisation' of health care has brought the merger of three local hospitals into one regional facility. This was a gain for one town but a loss for the others. Other changes have meant the loss of staff with local knowledge. Population decline has also brought downgrading of education facilities. Under these circumstances it is not surprising that Townsend et al. (2000) reported a range of views among local people about their town from optimism (a minority) through apathy, to belief that the towns were doomed.

Regional Social Conditions

What is happening to those people who remain in declining communities? Their society is being divided economically and socially, they are suffering from continuing public and private disinvestment in the services they rely on, their prospects for secure employment are diminishing and their capacity to escape from these conditions is being eroded rapidly. All this can and does happen independently of the restructuring of agriculture, although that process affects town as well as farm people. Even where the economic status of the farm sector improves, there may be no complementary bonus to the towns which can be bypassed following improvements in transport and communications – populations continue to decline and services are further centralised. Smailes (2000) showed how this increasing prominence of larger centres at the expense of the smaller encompassed social as well as economic activity.

Much of rural Australia is dotted with the remnants of villages which have disappeared, with one or two buildings being the only remaining evidence of a once-thriving settlement. These places have been superseded, an unintended consequence of otherwise unrelated processes of change, and during these processes the conditions of community life have become very difficult. As the New South Wales Council for Social Services has argued, the processes of restructuring internationally and locally have particular effects on rural people in general. It nominates 'life chances, material and social deprivation, poverty, low income levels, high prices, and the effect of some taxes (eg. fuel) and charges for some public services such as telephones as especially problematic' (New South Wales Council of Social Service and Office of Social Justice and Youth Policy, 1995: 2). Davidson and Lees (1993) found a prevalence of poverty between 5 and 12 per cent less frequent in the capital cities than in the regions. Reports of a 40 per cent city–rural gap have appeared (*Morning Bulletin*, 2001).

Unemployment

Unemployment is a frequently used indicator of social conditions, but when applied to rural towns and cities it helps to draw the links between population and social change. The Productivity Commission (1999) found unemployment rates consistently higher in regional than in metropolitan Australia. Cheers (1998) suggested that unemployment is also more prolonged. Sidoti (1999) used ABS figures to reinforce the point that job losses are both cause and effect of service withdrawal. While extractive and manufacturing industries have seen the greatest job loss, telecommunications and particularly banking have seen large numbers of jobs disappear. As a consequence, the economies of smaller communities no longer offer a large enough base to support other activities, hence more services are 'rationalised' and the communities continue on a downward spiral. But the loss of services which prompts decline need not arise from prior decline. As Argent and Rolley (2000) argued, bank closures have largely been a product of mergers and management practice which would have occurred regardless of demographic change.

Beer et al. (1994) found that the overall unemployment rate of regional cities is significantly higher than that of the metropolitan cities. Very high rates occur in two types of city: those, mostly on the east coast, which also have high rates of employment (and often population) growth, and those which have experienced rapid and significant economic restructuring but which are too far from more attractive labour markets to permit ready access to them. Even among those with low labour force growth rates (less than 10 per cent), Beer et al. (1994) found situations of unemployment below the national average while others had unemployment rates double those of the more fortunate cities. Across regional Australia unemployment rates varied between 2 and 24 per cent (Commonwealth Department of Housing and Regional Development, 1994: 160).

At the local level, agricultural areas often have very low unemployment rates while nearby towns have high rates. Farm unemployment may be hidden, especially where struggling farm family members try to maintain a farm but are effectively unproductive, due to environmental factors as well as the farm economy. From an urban perspective they may as well be considered unemployed. Moreover, people on farms, while seldom formally 'employed', would almost always consider themselves to be engaged in farming and therefore in employment. Those who are not family members and lack paid employment may choose to move into the nearest town, raising its unemployment rate. Dawson (1994) found situations where town rates were double that of their rural hinterlands. This is another instance of population growth accompanying high unemployment rates.

The finding, also noted by Murphy and Watson (1995), that rapidly growing coastal cities – as well as some growing inland towns – are sites of high unemployment is especially worrying because it indicates that not all is well, even in those places which are 'performing' in basic demographic terms. This view was supported by Vinson (1999). There is some indication, without sufficient statistics to confirm the point, that high unemployment rates in these situations are at least partly due to the migration of already-unemployed people. Beer et al.

(1994) offered cautious support for this argument, but apparently did not wish be a party to a widely-held view without offering adequate evidence. They felt that immigration of unemployed people was probably a more significant problem for smaller towns than it was for regional cities, a scenario which gains plausibility from the long-term disintegration of on-farm employment in Australia. Experience in the United States has shown that substantial negative impacts can be wrought upon already impoverished communities when urban poor, unemployed and low-skilled people migrate (see Fitchen, 1995). There may be an inflated view of the capacity of some rural areas and some coastal cities to supply jobs, regardless of the fast pace of their economic and population growth.

The second type of regional city exhibiting high unemployment is of equal or greater concern. Many appear likely to suffer permanently high unemployment. They illustrate the disadvantage of remoteness from Australia's dominant metropolitan cities, especially Sydney and Melbourne. Cities like Goulburn and Lithgow in New South Wales and Colac in Victoria can effectively export their unemployment to Sydney and Melbourne respectively, but Burnie-Somerset in Tasmania cannot be relieved of its unemployment problem by Launceston or Hobart which suffer similarly. Some of the most remote towns and cities, on the other hand, being based on mining, have mobile workforces who would see no prospects if they remained there unemployed, may not own their homes in those places and may – in many cases – have had no expectation of staying indefinitely. In such situations unemployment is not likely to be a problem. The implications of Beer et al.'s (1994) work are that we should not 'read off' social conditions from demographic statistics alone and that the situation of regional towns and cities in relation to the metropolitan centres remains very important – more important than remoteness *per se*.

Regional Social Disparities
These findings are based on data collected up to the 1991 Census. However, a similar – though less detailed – picture emerges from more recent data. The National Institute of Economic and Industry Research (NIEIR) (1998) has divided Australia into regions, including parts of the metropolitan cities, according to function. This provides a categorisation of fifty-five regions into six types: core metropolitan, dispersed metropolitan (adjacent to metropolitan cities), producer zones (close to metropolitan plus Hunter, Illawarra and Westernport), resource-based (extractive industries), rural-based (agricultural) and lifestyle-based (tourism and retirement). The problems of rural Australia are illustrated by the finding that between 1991 and 1998 of the ten best-performing regional labour markets in terms of employment growth, six were metropolitan, one was a 'producer', one was 'resource' and two were rural. Of the ten worst, two were 'resource', two were 'producer' and six were rural. None was metropolitan. This same research also showed that in 1998, while only one metropolitan region had double-figure unemployment, five resource and rural regions had levels of unemployment at 10 per cent or higher. In a more recent report NIEIR divided the nation into fifty-eight regions, discovering that twenty were 'accelerating away' from the others. Of the twenty, thirteen were metropolitan, the others being strongly linked to mining, tourism or defense. No agricultural region appeared in the top twenty (NIEIR, 2001: 13). Evidence in the form of social indicators, derived largely from the work of the ABS, also support an image

of relative economic and social decay in regional Australia (see O'Connor et al., 1998; Productivity Commission, 1999; Vinson,1999).

According to the 2000 'State of the Regions' report (see National Economics 2000) the non-metropolitan regions of Australia are being denied most of the benefits of a more open, globally-linked economy. Parts of Sydney and Melbourne are now much more like their counterparts in Paris, London or New York than they are to other Australian suburbs or cities. We now have spatial locations which can be called 'global Sydney' and 'global Melbourne' – rich inner suburbs where there is full employment, well-paid workers, and which thrive because of the presence of knowledge-based economic activities. By contrast, many of Australia's rural-based regions are experiencing 'a vicious cycle of low or declining population growth, low investment, low incomes and high unemployment' (National Economics 2000: i). The authors of this report attempted to measure the strength of industry supply chains in various regions. They did this by calculating inter-industry linkages (including e-commerce), the level of skill of the workforce, and the facilities and opportunities for lifelong learning (that is, for improving the skill base of the population). They concluded that under current policy settings existing disparities between the regions would inevitably widen. Regional Australians – those living long distances from capital cities, and out of tourist pathways – can expect to be increasingly disadvantaged as globalisation continues.

This uneven distribution of employment and unemployment is largely responsible for increasing inequality among the regions. By applying eight statistical indicators to 176 regions, Walmsley and Weinand (1997) were able to map the well-being of Australia's population and change which occurred between 1976 and 1991. The indicators of well-being include population age structure, frequency of single-parenthood, education levels, proportion of population of non-English speaking background, rental rather than purchased/mortgaged housing as well as unemployment. Walmsley and Weinand concluded that no single particular type of region was faring either particularly well or badly. Rather, they saw a pattern of increasing differentiation among regions which was associated with agriculture and resource extraction, and industrial change in and near the cities compared with the wealthier suburbs and hinterlands of the big cities. Of the sixteen regions which deteriorated consistently during the period, only two were in capital cities. NIEIR (1998; 2001) has carried out research on income distribution which broadly supports these findings, and while conceptually narrower, they do suggest continuation of these trends. The Institute finds that long-term high levels of poverty in rural Australia are continuing. While regions near the big cities are experiencing declining income levels, the core metropolitan areas are having large upward shifts. Amid their discussion about economic gains made during the 1990s, Parham et al. (2000) note substantial variation in income and employment, with greater variation for income in particular among non-metropolitan regions than within the metropolitan areas.

Although clearly not applying to all of regional Australia, the process of regional economic restructuring can be described as bringing 'massive social dislocation' (Taylor, 1991). It will affect some people before others. Musgrave (1983) cites a 1981 report of the Australian Rural Adjustment Unit which identified children (due to declining opportunity), job-seekers, small business proprietors, the aged (due to diminishing services) and ratepayers (for whom local government services will become more expensive or of lesser quality) as making up most of the casualty list. Wulff and Newton (1996) pointed out that all residents of declining areas could easily be trapped by low market prices for housing and businesses. For them, moving to more prosperous areas where jobs and services were available could result in them living in significantly worse conditions and/or being impoverished by mortgage payments. It is also worth considering the ramifications of regional disadvantage for Australia's at-risk populations, such as Aboriginal and Torres Strait Islander people, single parents and homeless youth (Cheers, 1998). Such people are often poorly served with crisis accommodation (Beer et al., 1994) and other services.

Neoliberalism and Regional Economics

Why is regional Australia suffering? There is a simple but misleading answer. It is provided by the observation that small towns have been declining for many decades – alongside the economics of agriculture and the rise and fall of resource-based industries. In other words they have 'obeyed' the market pattern and should be allowed to 'adjust' as the market dictates. That is correct to a point but it is really no answer at all. It is based on the view that economic processes are inevitable and inexorable. The history of rural Australia is full of examples where seemingly powerful economic forces have been modified and turned aside so that the interests of people might be better served. It also tacitly assumes that economic forces should prevail and that they will somehow inevitably produce a good outcome, based on a blind worship of markets. (This expectation is no more valid than faith in the capacity of policy-makers to plan successful intervention which will serve everybody's interests every time.) It is a view that denies the power of social agency – the capacity of people to map their own futures.

The obeying of market forces offers an important, but ultimately incomplete, explanation for the economic and social decline and polarisation of regional Australia. Neoliberalism has contributed and is continuing to contribute to the deepening of the economic and social problems identified above. It is doing so in two ways: by directly and indirectly reducing employment through economic 'reform', and through the parallel destruction of many of the services which make country towns attractive to people and businesses. As Thorns (1992) observed, national development is becoming more uneven at the same time as government intervention aimed at reducing social inequality is decreasing. The Bureau of Industry Economics (1994) acknowledged that uneven development is inevitable under a market-oriented approach to policy. Similarly, the Industry Commission expects contraction where towns have failed to compete, seeing no alternative. With regard to infrastructure development, O'Neill (1999) acknowledged that regional Australia was missing out. This is all particularly worrisome for regional people as the largely prosperous and egalitarian, if not equal, society which they have enjoyed is itself a product of government intervention.

Such is the current manifestation of the global misfortune of regional dwellers. It provides a useful approach to the economic problems of regional Australia as they developed from the early 1990s. The late 1990s also saw the early impacts of National Competition Policy, an extension of the last of the four processes identified by Taylor, and vigorously condemned by community-based participants at the federal-government sponsored Northern Summit held in

Katherine in October 2000. We will set out the more direct impacts of neoliberal government policy, including competition policy, before reconsidering globalisation.

Policy Impacts

Taylor (1991) offered the examples of downsizing in railway and in telecommunication industries eliminating tens of thousands of jobs under the banner of micro-economic 'reform'. Reduction in industry protection has led to job losses in manufacturing which has provided work for vulnerable groups including women and non-English speaking migrants. While it is accepted that these industries may be inefficient, it is argued that their efficiency need not be pursued in ways which deliver such disastrous consequences.

Service closure and employment loss have continued through the 1990s across regional Australia, creating 'a domino effect of collapsing services which has brought many small communities to the brink of extinction' (Cribb, 1994: 13). The domino effect – described at an earlier time as the 'dynamics of decline' (see Lawrence and Williams, 1990) – accelerates as the most basic services disappear and the towns suffer the tyranny of centralised bureaucratic decision-making. Basically, 'critical mass' formulations comes into effect. Services are removed when governments deem the level of demand is below that for 'efficient' delivery (see Gray et al., 1991; Lippert, 1993; Cheers, 1998). This is particularly so for health, as hospitals are turned into aged care facilities and doctors leave, not to be replaced. Governments are considering the desperation of some country towns to be sufficient to justify the placement of doctors who are not yet deemed by the medical assessment system to be adequately qualified, implying that rural Australia is being provided with a health system inferior in relation to the skills of its workers as well as the facilities available to them. There is also evidence of relative under-funding of services. Barber (1998) revealed that, even without considering the higher cost of service delivery in regional areas, regional South Australia received proportionally less funding for Home and Community Care per instance of need than did the Adelaide metropolitan area.

Health
The Australian Institute of Health and Welfare (1998: 14) found that, between 1992 and 1996, mortality (death rates) were higher in rural and remote areas than in the capital cities. The health status of 'remote' populations is significantly affected by high proportions of Indigenous people, but this cannot be said of 'rural' – the less isolated part of regional Australia. Sidoti (1999) describes ill-health and high mortality as intractable problems among Indigenous people, many of whom live far from medical facilities which they sometimes need to sustain life. For some Indigenous people, health problems can be attributed to something as basic as an inadequate water supply. Indigenous Australians are also reported to suffer from culturally inappropriate practices among white health professionals and difficulties with communication. Care for the aged is an increasing problem in many smaller rural communities as their population ages with nil immigration and significant net loss of younger people. But perhaps the most telling problem is that of young people committing suicide, with a fast rising

rate among the white population and an even worse problem among Indigenous young people (see Cheers, 1998; Ruzicka and Choi, 1999).

Education
Regional populations have traditionally had less formal education, with training for farm work often being provided on the farm and in the family. High school retention rates have generally been lower outside the metropolitan areas. Now we are seeing a rapid decline in proportions of country children entering tertiary education (Sidoti, 1999). While some argue that telecommunications provide greater opportunities for distance education, the standard of telecommunication service to many regional areas is either inadequate, expensive or both, and it can be difficult for people to access services and get them working properly (Easdown, 1999). Many Indigenous people in particular suffer from deprivation of what most urban people would take as a normal standard of education service.

Social Injustice
Regional people are in effect being told that they are no longer entitled to services of reasonable quality, if any services at all, in their communities. The isolation of farm families often makes this issue even more pressing (for an example see Alexander and Jones, 1997). It is arguably tantamount to a denial of regional citizenship (see Fitzgerald, 1996) and is at best a denial of social justice under the weight of economic efficiency considerations (see Gain, 1996; McGinness, 1996). Sidoti (1999) takes a human rights perspective, arguing that people are being denied their basic rights to the best attainable standard of physical and mental health. These issues confront minority populations, notably Indigenous people but also migrant people of non-English speaking background (see Gray et al., 1991).

Loss of services had raised sufficient concern in the early 1990s for the Municipal Association of Victoria to conduct two surveys of non-metropolitan councils (Municipal Association of Victoria, 1994). Ninety-two of the then 155 non-metropolitan councils in Victoria responded to the first survey, conducted in 1991. Seventy-seven per cent of those respondents reported a recent loss of a government service. The most frequently mentioned were courts and transport services. When repeated in 1993, the survey revealed that 47 per cent of responding councils had lost one or more services since 1991. The most common were transport and utilities offices (electricity, gas and fuel). Slightly more reported services, particularly in education, being wound back. Henshall Hansen Associates (1988) argued that both government and community needed to understand the effects of the withdrawal of services on small towns. Whatever understanding the government may have acquired appears to have made no difference. Indeed, while the regional universities are being identified as the catalysts for future economic development of the regions (Kemp, 1999) their infrastructures are eroding, their postgraduate student numbers are being reduced, and their research budgets are stressed, all as direct outcomes of Federal government policy.

McKenzie (1996) has argued there can be no doubt that it is more efficient to operate services in larger centres. The problem is, how can services be provided to people in sparsely-settled areas so that there is some semblance of social equity? Network infrastructure, like transport and communication facilities, is also problematic because, rather than using it to equalise service and hence provide equal opportunities for communities to foster their own development, neoliberal thinking favours those regions which are likely to be more productive. It views such facilities as investments and seeks maximum returns, regardless of the effect on people and their life-chances and the economic and social prospects for their communities. It also constrains their prospects for participating in national economic, social and political life.

Alongside the loss of doctors, the effects of bank deregulation have been particularly prominent in the smaller and most vulnerable country towns. Beal and Ralston (1998) reported that one in three branches of the four major banks in Australia closed during the three years preceding their research. The statistics they used distinguish metropolitan from non-metropolitan situations but do not permit analysis of what is happening in the areas where population decline is most common. The rate of closure there is likely to be much higher. Hence, they undertook a study of the impacts of bank closure on seven inland towns. Their conclusions leave no doubt that, while individuals might make different arrangements for their banking and thereby cope reasonably well despite inconvenience, the communities do suffer substantial losses. Business proprietors expressed concern about the security implications of retaining cash and their difficulty obtaining change, but their main problem was a direct threat to their livelihood.

Injustice by Stealth

There are less visible processes through which government commitment to competition in all aspects of economic life is eroding the well-being of regional populations. The neoliberalisation of Australian economic policy followed the observation, made most notably by Treasurer Paul Keating in 1986, that Australia's economy had to be made more efficient to enable it to keep up with its international competitors. The development of a National Competition Policy from 1993 represents the main attempt to make Australia's economy more efficient. Economic efficiency has become the over-riding principle driving government and it is to be extended to 'all areas of national life' (Beeson and Firth, 1998: 224).

By opening – or potentially opening – local government work to tenders from outside the local community, and from city-based firms, the National Competition Policy poses a threat to local rural businesses. 'There is no doubt that some contracts are under threat from bigger players in the market place and the potential for further loss of local employment is very real' (South Gippsland Shire Council, 1998: 3). Some argue that the effects will differ spatially. The Wheatbelt Area Consultative Committee (1998) argued that the Western Australian wheatbelt would suffer more heavily than other regions. Loss of service quality has also been observed. The Murrumbidgee River Management Board (1998) reported a deterioration in service from providers who had chosen to concentrate on the larger cities.

Regional businesses, including substantial corporations, find themselves relatively disadvantaged as their operating costs rise with deregulation (Corby et al., 1998). While Bolam (1994) could be optimistic about the prospects for the maintenance and development of globalised manufacturing industry in regional cities, based on experience including tariff reduction up to 1991 and due to the availability of cheap land, transport, and cheap and compliant labour, it remains to be seen whether these will be so attractive after a decade of continued deregulation and privatisation. When combined with privatisation of such services as telecommunication, competition will provide more pressure for reducing community service obligations (an accounting concept adopted to set apart the cross-subsidisation component of services so that it could be extracted from their business losses) (Walmsley and Weinand, 1997).

The restructuring of public services involves many changes other than simple cut-backs. Those services which remain in public ownership are under increasing pressure to become more 'efficient'. Regional workers, residing in areas where unemployment is higher and their capacity to move is limited, are likely to be weaker in the enterprise bargaining process than those in more fortunate situations. The deregulation of labour markets has led to further marginalisation of workers and their representatives who are often left out of community affairs through the domination of voluntary and formal organisations by farmers. Regional industry has been the scene of notorious industrial disputes which have produced victories for management, aided by use of language which is compatible with agrarian rhetoric (Francis, 1993). Pressure, facilitated by the National Competition Policy (or compulsion as occurred in Victoria) for local government to put many of its services to competitive tendering risks the viability and even the existence of local organisations and businesses who do not have economies of scale enjoyed by those in the cities and hence cannot offer lower prices. Participants in the 2000 Northern Summit indicated recognition of this point. It is a recipe for further depletion of regional employment opportunities.

The proliferation of gambling (associated with its deregulation) can have harmful community effects, and while there may be some economic benefits, few of them may be available to regional communities (Marshall, 1998). Changes in organisation structures and management practices, such as increasing part-time employment at the expense of full-time, centralisation of decision-making alongside reduced career opportunities under flatter management hierarchies, intensification of work demands and contracting or sub-contracting of services, all have indirect effects on regional communities. As Pinch (1989) concluded from analysis of British health services, such decisions place more power in the hands of management. 'Management' does not tend to be located regionally. Rather, it is itself increasingly centralised in the major cities – thereby ensuring that government decision-making is 'distant' both in a literal and metaphorical sense.

Globalisation has thrown regional Australia into the maelstrom of world economic competition leaving it vulnerable and increasingly divided. The neoliberal quest for economic efficiency in our globalised economy has accelerated the rate of change and the proliferating inequities in Australian rural society. This is occurring through a system of economic relationships between industries and communities, be they agricultural or extractive, towns or cities. While not having the cataclysmic effects which the NAFTA has had on manufacturing in rural Canada (see Leach and Winston, 1995; Winston, 2000), globalisation and its accompaniments have changed the course of Australian regional development.

Interdependencies

On the surface it would seem obvious that towns and cities would prosper or decline depending on the performance of the industries associated with them and the attractiveness and accessibility of alternative places for both buyers and sellers. However, the nature of such associations is complex, partly because regional towns and cities are related economically to each other and the metropolitan cities. It is also subject to rapid change. Moreover, these economic relationships are embedded in social relationships and conditions. The following discussion outlines some analyses of the relationships between industry, mostly agricultural, and community before discussing the future trajectories of those relationships.

Changes in transport and communication are often said to be detrimentally affecting the smaller towns as larger centres become more accessible. It makes sense that people would shop in bigger towns which offer a greater range of goods when access to those towns becomes easier. Generalisation of this argument is dangerous. Smailes (1996) argues that as journey time from them to Adelaide has been reduced, many towns have lost their share of South Australia's retail trade to a core area surrounding, but not including, the centre of Adelaide city. However, some larger towns have gained. Smaller towns close to larger regional centres might gain a population of commuters as travel becomes faster. But evidence from the United States suggests that commuters tend not to do as much shopping as others in their town of residence (Pinkerton et al., 1995). A look at the main streets of some small towns surrounding the large regional cities in New South Wales would suggest confirmation of this point. Perhaps the extreme case is offered by mining companies which have begun flying in their workers, rather than establish or develop a town. Cowell and Green (1994), also analysing United States data, find that small town residents are generally less likely to spend locally but this appears to be related to proximity to what in Australian would be very large cities. Stabler and Olfert (1996) found that residents of small towns on the Canadian Plains were making fewer, longer shopping trips to the larger centres at the expense of smaller ones. Smailes' (1996) Australian analysis shows that a town's capacity to retain its share of retail business is not related to its size, but rather to the density of the population in its hinterland. In other words, those towns which have a demographically and spatially concentrated farming hinterland are economically more secure.

The effects of farm structure on town economies have been researched extensively overseas. It would seem likely that when farm incomes are declining, the businesses patronised by farm families are likely to suffer, but if incomes rise or remain stable while the number of farms diminishes, the issue becomes more complex. While there has been extensive debate, the evidence overall indicates that town economies fare better where their business hinterlands consist of small family-operated farms than where larger corporate farms dominate (the so-called 'Goldschmidt hypothesis', after its first proponent). Even if this result can be questioned, there is evidence of significant relationships between farm systems and local economies (Harrison, 1993). From an empirical test in Chile, Young (1994) concluded that the relationship holds for quality-of-life factors as well as economic effects. Government adjustment policies may not help if they assist people to leave their communities altogether rather than establish new businesses within them (Goetz and Debertin, 1996). Overall, the relationship is unlikely to have a major impact while Australia's farms continue to be so heavily dominated by family operations, but in some industries in some locations, the effect on nearby towns could be significant. Smailes' (1991) survey of town business people found concern that their businesses would suffer if there were fewer larger farms, preferring poorer small farms to fewer wealthier ones.

Postmodernity

Concern about the effects on towns of the restructuring of agriculture need not arise if towns are becoming free of their traditional dependence on agriculture. Some writers believe that this is occurring and Australian research has prompted a debate about its significance. More broadly, there is a theory which suggests that through the process of globalisation, changes in industrial systems, the rise of tourism and developments in communications, the spatial structure of industry is fundamentally changing. This has given rise to some optimistic views of the prospects for rural communities. We will first consider the hypothesised process of the 'uncoupling' of towns from their local agricultural economies.

Changing Relationships

It has been said that the ups and downs of agriculture decreasingly affect country towns (see Sorensen, 1991) and that the economic viability of towns is decreasingly determined by agriculture (Olfert, 1997). Some towns, such as 'railway towns' like Werris Creek (see Stayner, 1990a) have never really been 'coupled' to local agriculture. Powell (1998), however, argues that there is no longer a necessary connection between agriculture and regional development. The discussion above hints at this change. Many of the coastal areas of rapid population growth now have much larger economies in which the proportion of activity closely related to agriculture has diminished. Some areas which had supported intensive agriculture have been developed for retirement migrants and others and now resemble the suburbs of cities. Mining-based towns have been developed in remote areas which once supported only very extensive grazing. In these situations the decline in the relationship between the town and agriculture is clear. In others it is not. Some writers see the relationship changing alongside much broader change in industry associated with agricultural restructuring and globalisation.

There have been attempts to confirm the existence of 'uncoupling' with regard to towns which have not seen change, like retirement migration and mining, and which are not among the larger centres. The bifurcation of agriculture into a small-farm, large-farm system combined with the tendency, noted by supporters of the Goldschmidt hypothesis, for larger farms to bypass local suppliers and deal with larger centrally-located firms would at least partly 'uncouple' local businesses from farmers (see also Powell, 1998). So, too, would the centralisation of industries which had formerly processed farm products locally. Having analysed town population and agricultural economic data for 109 local areas in New South Wales, Stayner and Reeve (1990) claimed to have found uncoupling. Very many towns were either growing or declining while their agricultural economies were moving in the opposite direction. Stayner (1990b) adds a case study which offers further evidence of 'uncoupling'. However, Campbell and Phillips (1993) point out that the study covered many places, like coastal and mining areas, which are unlikely to be strongly 'coupled'. Further doubt is cast by Tonts (1996) who finds that while some Western Australian wheatbelt towns had turned around their population decline, such places still remained largely dependent on agriculture. Once again the conclusion which must be reached is that whether towns are 'uncoupling' or remain 'coupled', there is great variation in their experience.

The 'uncoupling' debate can mask the most significant processes. As Musgrave (1983) noted, the decline of towns losing business to larger centres or in other ways affected by economic restructuring, such as with the decline of small local industry amid global competition, will continue regardless of agriculture. Moreover, it has been shown overseas (Everitt and Annis, 1992) that farms have become dependent on towns. This issue was investigated in Australia by Stayner (1998), particularly with regard to the importance of towns as suppliers of off-farm work upon which farm families are becoming increasingly dependent. This suggests a change in the nature of the relationship – rather than confirmation of 'uncoupling'. It would seem that the postmodern scenario is one in which the remaining 'coupled' communities decline with agriculture but are required to support farms at the same time. Benedyka (1998) sees dependence on agriculture as indicating a fundamental weakness in a local economy, but Albrecht (1998) indicates that in the United States communities which remained dependent on agriculture had retained higher rates of employment, less poverty and higher incomes than those which depended on non-agricultural industries, especially (but not only) service industries. It may be that communities that 'couple' themselves to alternative industries will not necessarily be well served by them. At least the spirit of this argument is sustained by a report from a small South Australian town. The town claims to be turning the tide of decline with a railway push-cart race which attracts thousands of people and some new investments. 'To a certain extent we have learnt to realise what the town's here for ... that's primarily agriculture. People now generally shop locally and use the town where they can' (Hodge, 1999: 10).

Decentralisation

Some recent interpretations of long-term international processes of change have suggested brighter prospects for rural industries, and hence communities assuming that the consequent 'uncoupling' would be beneficial. This in part stems from theories of 'postmodernisation' which claim that industry is leaving an era of centralised mass-production ('Fordism') and becoming more flexible in its employment, production and organisation. This decentralisation of industry has brought sudden changes in standards of living (European Association of Development Agencies, 1995) – but only some areas are benefiting. This highlights, yet again, the great potential for uneven spatial development. With greater flexibility may come decentralisation in the form of organisational devolution to regional centres (Crook et al., 1992; Stilwell, 1992) but how this might become manifest in favour of agricultural areas is not clear. Examples of rapid development can be found, like the high-tech industries of 'Silicon Glen' in Scotland (see Boucher et al., 1991; Richardson and Gillespie, 1996).

This theory has suffered extensive criticism; it is not clear whether post-Fordism represents a new and stable system or just another manifest crisis of capitalism (Tickell and Peck, 1995). In some ways the restructuring of agriculture is moving farming into a Fordist model of industrialisation of production in large-scale enterprises (as described by Kerby and Parish, 1997). In a period of industrial globalisation and after the demise of the protective structures for agriculture of the Fordist era of regulation, it seems certain that communities will largely be left to their own devices as they strive to obtain development capital, often internationally. Some might attract development; many will not. It does seem certain, however, that local connections with globalising industries will develop. We are seeing plans being made in rural Australia for direct transport links with Asian markets, bypassing the traditional transport nodes of the metropolitan centres. One should also inquire as to the social impacts on local populations, especially in the light of the findings of Albrecht (1998). One of the likely attractions of rural areas, as has been identified in the past, is labour flexibility (see Bolam, 1994), suggesting – as was noted in chapter 2 – downward pressure on wages and working conditions.

Tourism

Another future sometimes posited for rural Australia is the 'postmodern' world of a consumption-oriented society in which the production of goods for a mass market is superseded by cultural or 'postindustrial' products, most notably tourism. This may not be a short-term 'fad'. As Lash and Urry (1994) argue, it is part of the development of a global society in which people obtain their personal identity from their consumption practices rather than from their class position. Tourism is one of those means of 'uncoupling'. The related process of retirement migration has had such effects (see Neyland and Kendig, 1996). Tourism could also form new relationships between agriculture and towns as they both offer 'attractions'.

Tourism has been seen to offer the potential to sustain regional economies. Hundloe (1997) makes such a claim with regard to Australia's wet tropics. However, this road to sustainability can be a very difficult one to traverse. When applied to agricultural areas, the change in culture from agricultural productivism is very substantial and it can be demanding of institutions which are not suited to change (Reed and Gill, 1997). Tourism may offer an escape from production and technology treadmills, the latter most notably when old technologies become part of the tourism experience. There is, however, an inherent tension for the farmer who remains under pressure to adopt the most efficient farm practices. This suggests a contrast with European farmers who are urged to retain old practices for the sake of tourism.

The point about opportunities for farm tourism made in the previous chapter can be applied from the regional development perspective: there is evidence that tourism development can be spatially uneven (Opperman, 1994). Some communities may be able to attract tourists by vaunting their heritage or scenery, but others may only be able to offer a degraded or otherwise unattractive or uncomfortable environment. Those areas which are suffering most from degradation resulting from agricultural productivism, and hence most in need of an economic boost, may be least able to generate one. Clearly, those areas which have landscape or other attractive features have a natural advantage. Moreover, the benefits of tourism do not necessarily accrue to all members of communities equally. Experience has shown justifiable scepticism among established residents (see Mansfield and Ginosar, 1994) and has indicated that upheaval of people's lifestyle might not be compensated by improvement in opportunity (Phillips and Campbell, 1993). Tourism cannot be assumed to be the major ingredient for 'postmodern' rural development – it is too site-specific, and cannot be generalised across the entire nation. One might rejoice in the prospect of a rural economy liberated from agriculture and given access to the international tourism economy as the world is swept into a unified postmodern culture. This future is uncertain, however. Not only is the existence of a 'postmodern' culture frequently questioned, but its offerings for rural communities are dubious.

Information

The 'postmodern' world might also bring a social revolution based on access to information and its technological media. Information becomes a key determinant of social inequality, replacing the 'old' structures like class (Lash and Urry, 1994). Communications technologies could foster the growth of rural employment as information-based industry is locationally unconstrained – employees can work at locations remote from their employers' offices. There is evidence of potential for development of small enterprises and facilities to assist others (Horner and Reeve, 1991; Hudson, 1992; Clark et al., 1995). Both Horner and Reeve (1991) and Hudson (1992) emphasise that such development depends very heavily on the provision of infrastructure – something with which regional Australia is not well equipped. It has been said that 'the impact of the information age is beginning to be felt in the major capital cities, yet, with some few exceptions, little of the benefits are available to people in rural Australia' (Moffatt, 1996: 166). Rural Australia suffers from relatively expensive access or the unavailability of access to telecommunications networks and has been slower to adopt computer networking services (St Clair, 1997).

It has been acknowledged that regional telecommunications users are disadvantaged. Service providers are reluctant to invest outside the more profitable metropolitan markets and government policies to redress these problems are not working. Service standards remain inferior (Standing Committee on Primary Industries and Regional Services, 2000). While this can be said of regional Australia in general terms, it is more applicable in some communities, notably those which are more remote or do not offer economies of scale, than among communities which are closer to the metropolitan cities and are better provided. Political leaders are apparently aware of these problems and tacitly acknowledge their significance with large statements containing extensive promises (see Anderson, 1998). Some rightly see such developments as opportunities, or at least potential opportunities, but also recognise that cultural change is required to ensure that the opportunity is taken (Hoy, 1998).

The Transformation of Regional Policy

There have been, and still are, government policies which are said by their proponents to support the regions. Regional development as a distinct policy objective has suffered an on-again off-again history under the vagaries of State and Federal politics (see Beer, 1998; 2000). It reached its zenith in the early 1970s under the Whitlam government as it attempted to redirect growth away from the burgeoning metropolitan areas towards inland growth centres. Small remnants survived the Fraser and Hawke governments, but regionalism was effectively kept alive by regional organisations of local government councils (Marshall, 1997). Regional development returned to the agenda in the 1990s following demographic observations like those of Salt (1992) and recognition of rapid development in some coastal areas (Hurley, 1994). The words 'regional development' again appeared in the name of a Commonwealth Government department (Industry, Technology and Regional Development).

Under the new regional development strategies, the regions were to make their best possible contribution to national development. This turned on its head the idea of the nation setting out to ensure that all its regions were equitably provided for and able to access the common wealth. The Department of Industry, Technology and Regional Development (1992) hinted at a fundamentally new approach when it identified attitudes of individual people as a retardant on regional development. But the Taskforce on Regional Development

(1993), led by Australian Council of Trade Unions Secretary Kelty, indicated some concern for regional inequalities. However, the regions are not seen as necessarily requiring assistance but rather as being sources of their own development. Financial assistance is proposed, but is aimed at helping regions and regional agencies to invest in themselves and enter partnerships with private enterprise.

The 'Working Nation' program remains quite consistent with the 1995 report of the Industry Task Force on Leadership and Management Skills and 'Lead Local Compete Global: Unlocking the Growth Potential of Australia's Regions' (McKinsey and Company, 1994) which identified leadership as one of those potentials to be unlocked. It is also consistent with the Bureau of Industry Economics (1994) which recommends self-help. It also resigns itself to persistent uneven development which it sees as inevitable under a market-friendly model. The Working Group on Development in Rural Areas (1993: 23) acknowledged deficiencies in rural infrastructure but announced that 'the major thrust of policy is towards attitude change in agricultural communities so that individuals and groups become more self-reliant with minimal involvement of governments'.

The regional development agenda is no longer development for the sake of the non-metropolitan regions, but rather one of ensuring that the regions do not adversely affect the nation's economic condition by ensuring that they get on with their own development. Optimism does not always prevail. The program intended to rehabilitate the degraded economy and environment of New South Wales' Western Division, which is a policy for a region rather than a regional policy, has more of the tone of a rescue package and does allow for some assistance in 'partnership' arrangements in which self-reliance remains the dominant theme. The 'Working Nation' program did not survive the first Howard Government budget, although the Financial Assistance Grants which provide direct and indirect (via the States) support respectively in the regions, have narrowly survived the tax changes of which a Goods and Services Tax is the keystone.

By 1997 the only Federal policies supporting regions (other than rural policies) funded some environmental projects, roads, the reorganisation of forest industries, some telecommunications infrastructure, cutting 'red-tape' for small businesses, assistance to local credit unions and the creation of the 'Supermarket to Asia Council' (Jones, 1997). The government sees itself supporting regional Australia by – as former Deputy Prime Minister Fischer (1998) indicated – reducing the current account deficit and keeping interest rates in check. Is this, with self-help schemes, all the 'vision' regional Australians need, one might ask?

The Federal Government's first Regional Australia Summit held in Canberra in 1999 revealed philanthropy as the cornerstone of its new regional development policy. Rather than remaining the principal source of funding for development, the Federal Government is to support those charitable organisations which might provide substantial amounts of money. (The philanthropy model is discussed in Timmons, 1999.) The Foundation for Rural and Regional Renewal, which is administering the policy, is encouraging the formation of local foundations which seek to channel local resources into development trust funds. This contains strong overtones of neoconservatism. It calls on a tradition of class-based charity. A capacity to keep local resources local is admirable, but, given the substantial extent to which it expects local foundations to raise their resources locally, it maintains the self-help ethos – one which ignores the structural nature of disadvantage. The States retain an expressed support for regional development, mostly offering assistance with facilitation and information plus some grants (Senate Employment, Workplace Relations, Small Business and Education References Committee, 1999), the administration of which indicates varying degrees of centralisation. Nothing remains of regional structuralism from a national perspective, certainly nothing of the kind which could potentially address regional dependency.

The Federal Government has shown itself to be unwilling to redress the inequitable effects on regions which have been seen to emanate from National Competition Policy. The Productivity Commission carried out an inquiry in response to pressure of popular demand (Productivity Commission, 1998). Its terms of reference acknowledge that the policy could create problems for regional Australia, but it leaves the regions to justify any curtailment. It is the opposite to a policy which would set out to support the regions, and be constrained by any apparent damage to wider interests which could not be justified by benefits. The Commission's report (Productivity Commission, 1999) acknowledges that there are uncertainties about the effects of the policy, but concludes that its ultimate economic impact will be positive.

Voices calling for support of regions might still be heard by government, however. For example, Huggonnier (1999) argues that state investment has an important place when it supports the more entrepreneurial local firms. How they will be supported is suggested by a parliamentary inquiry. Its chairperson writes in a foreword to the report that individuals' capacities can be harnessed to development where necessary to retain populations (Standing Committee on Primary Industries and Regional Services, 2000: x). The Committee's recommendations suggest that, while seeking to encourage investment in infrastructure, government intervention is very unlikely to deviate from the self-help ethos and the Productivity Commission's approach is implicitly supported. There are plenty of grassroots advocates for self-help (see, for example, Kenyon, 1996) who give a local 'spin' to the government's neoliberal agenda.

In contrast, Disney (1990) seeks support for infrastructure projects. The 2000 Northern Summit heard calls for increased infrastructural expenditure on roads and telecommunications, for large increases in tax concessions and zone allowances, for expenditure on tertiary education and health, and for a change to National Competition Policy. Like Jensen (1998), delegates at the Northern Summit raised equity issues about the 'north' and 'south' of Australia and argued for strong government leadership in creating conditions for economic prosperity in the north. Stilwell (1993, 1994) claimed that decentralisation policies remain necessary and that leadership programs were no substitute for attention to underlying structures. He called for interventionist policies, but he seems a relatively lonely voice (Stilwell, 2000). Louder is the chorus singing for a 'levelling' of the 'playing field', not with the aim of supporting the regions, but rather by way of removing the benefit obtained, particularly by farmers, from taxation concessions (see, for example, Davenport et al., 1991).

Conclusion

Like our agricultural industries, our country towns are polarising. The smaller, more remote, inland communities are in rapid decline. While the converse is largely true – the larger towns and cities which are better connected to metropolitan Australia and have more diversified economies are prospering – this is by no means the full picture. Some of the most rapidly developing places suffer substantial social problems. Those areas and communities which are declining demographically and socially are also those for which any advantage that might accrue from postmodernisation is likely to be the most elusive.

Here, we see the contradictions of globalisation brought into focus. Alongside a promise of the generation of wealth comes a certainty that deprivation and poverty will accompany it. Along with the opportunities for global marketing comes vulnerability to forces of global investment. And to take those opportunities and potentially escape vulnerability, regional communities need new infrastructural expenditures. These expenditures do not come from governments which are unwilling to plan for the future. But planning for the future means having a vision. When the only vision is the market, planning takes a back seat. Indeed, no planning is the recipe for the continuation of the current social and demographic downward spiral.

Globalisation is pushing much of regional Australia away from what it knows it does best into an economic system in which it has inherent structural and cultural disadvantages. Neoliberal policies are only worsening those disadvantages, as they place an ever-increasing burden of development on to the shoulders of individuals and communities. The inevitable result is a deepening of the chasms between those people and communities which have inherent advantages and those which do not. Disparities in terms of advantage do not necessarily produce disparities in outcomes, however. It is quite feasible that some communities will extract themselves from the spiral of decline, whether it be by retaining their traditional links with agriculture or by venturing into postmodernity. This is the scenario written for them by neoliberal thinking. It is one which places responsibility for the future of regional Australia on the shoulders of regional people. To help foresee the outcome of this approach, it is important to understand how regional people experience their lives and communities in the context of change in their relationships with metropolitan and global actors. Their reflexivity becomes very important.

Further Reading

Newton, P. W. and Bell, M. (eds) (1996) *Population Shift: Mobility and Change in Australia*, Canberra: Australian Government Publishing Service.
 – presents analyses of population changes as they affect regional Australia
Beer, A., Bolam, A. and Maude, A. (1994) *Beyond the Capitals: Urban Growth in Regional Australia*, Canberra: Australian Government Publishing Service.
 – covers population and associated change in the larger regional towns and cities
Sidoti, C. (1999) *Bush Talks*, Sydney: Human Rights and Equal Opportunity Commission.
 – a report on consultations with regional people highlighting social injustices
Stilwell, F. (2000) *Changing Track: A New Political Economic Direction for Australia*, Sydney: Pluto Press.
 – looks at regional decline in the context of globalisation and neoliberalism

Our analysis of reflexivity is developed now by moving to an examination of regional communities. In doing so we lose the industry focus on agriculture and farming. For the purposes of the analysis we set aside the concept of liminality, but retain our focus on social relations and power nevertheless. We continue to look for the impacts of 'global misfortune' on the prospects for people to obtain secure prosperity in an equitable society. Once again our sights are set on vulnerability to neoliberalism and globalisation, but this time in combination with aspects of another element of misfortune: the legacy of colonialism. This draws our attention to the relationship between regional Australia and metropolitan Australia, the latter consisting of the capital cities as centres of economic activity and dominance.

Again we consider the economic theory which supports neoliberalism. It is ironic that neoliberal policies, which place the burden of social and economic development on the shoulders of people and communities, are founded on an economic perspective which offers a very limited understanding of how people and communities act. At best, neoliberalism appears ignorant of the experiences and reactions of people. At worst, it leads to blaming regional dwellers for their economic and social misfortune. This is a product of inherent individualism with an implicit denial of social structure.

To the extent that it is based on rational action theory, the economics of regional development assumes that one or more calculating individuals can be responsible for the poverty or prosperity of towns. This interpretation has not been so easy to accept historically because so much of regional Australia is a product of government intervention, but in a neoliberal climate, with the arms of government being dismantled, it becomes increasingly attractive. But is it reasonable? Does the system within which regional dwellers pursue their economic and social interests permit such a degree of individual influence? This chapter examines the individualism of neoliberal thinking and the economic theory which supports it before discussing the current and historical experience of regional dwellers through restructuring, and offering some conceptual tools for analysis of their reflexivity and capacity to act. It concludes with some brief analysis of that reflexivity and voice.

Economic Individualism

There is a view of regional development which claims that its successes can always be traced back to the skills and efforts of one person. Sometimes this view is stated directly. Robson (1992: 21) states, after some analysis of regional development, that 'it is clear from these experiences that things happen in a community because someone is passionate about making them happen'. It is self-evident that development must be carried out by people. It is a necessary condition, but it is not necessarily sufficient to regard it in isolation from the circumstances in which people carry on development.

Others state the individualistic view less directly in terms of what is needed to stimulate development. For example, Stoeckel (1992) concludes that rural communities presently lack, and therefore need, the characteristics of people who are deemed necessary for progress. These characteristics include vision, leadership and motivation. Curiously, such writers also advocate a bottom-up approach to development, seeking to entrust local development to local people, those same local people who apparently lack vision, leadership and motivation. The bottom-up approach is also appealing because it removes much of the task of government, but it sees the top–bottom relationship only in terms of government (top) and people (bottom). A bottom-up approach is seen as an alternative to government support with the individual actor being paramount (Gough, 1996).

There was hardly a word written about regional development in the late 1990s Australia which did not exhort people to take their futures in hand, because nobody else will (see, for examples, Bureau of Industry Economics, 1994; Industry Commission, 1994; Martin, 1996; R. Powell, 1996, 1997). This aim is not unreasonable in itself, but when it fails to consider the prospects and possibilities facing regional people, it is lacking in reason. The call is often for Local Enterprise Initiatives (LEIs). This approach has been found to have a strong utopian element contained in the assumptions of its proponents (Syrett, 1993: 528). It sometimes comes with caveats. After a discussion about the 'tyranny of the macro', Sorensen (1993b: 236) argues that self-help 'has a lot going for it'. He goes on, however, to point out that LEIs are unlikely to work everywhere due to an uneven distribution of resources. Shaffer (1995) adds an element of social structure and organisation to those resources. The regional development literature has not resolved these contradictions. Regarded overall, it still appears to say to country people that they are on their own but are subservient to forces which they cannot control.

Fischer (1998) takes a complementary position when he claims that the government has tamed the macro forces so that rural communities can get on with their own development. Here we encounter the contradiction implicit in the claim that global forces are controlled by a government whose policy is to minimise intervention. This observation is made all the more difficult for country people when the person making the claim is expected to represent their interests. It is not consistent with the evidence presented in the previous chapter on restructuring. Moreover, it is not consistent with regional people's experience of restructuring.

Their experience is rather one of unconstrained international forces which governments cannot, or are unwilling to, do anything to direct. Not even this rhetoric attempts to claim that country people have any power other than that which they can exercise in a market where there are obviously more powerful actors present. This can only lead to the conclusion that the political party which was supposedly established to represent regional people – the National Party – is likely to encounter such profound contradictions that it would find it difficult to claim representation of regional interests without attracting controversy, if not opposition, in the regions. This point is supported by political events, such as voter defection to the One Nation Party, hostility shown by some people to National Party leadership during the 1998 Federal election campaign and the results of the 1999 Victorian election.

What can regional dwellers do to alter the trajectory of regional restructuring amid globalisation? The first step towards answering this question lies in considering what they have been doing, in many situations, for 150 years. While this will show the strategies which people have adopted to cope with adversity and change, it will also enable us to develop an understanding of the cultural tradition which has grown with this struggle.

Some Regional Histories

Among the countless historical writings about regional Australia, very few have attempted to see regional history from the perspectives of regional dwellers and the relationships in which their society is embedded. This leaves a large void for those attempting a reflexive analysis of current issues. While there is value in a detached view, histories which do not accommodate the regional dwellers' perspectives and admit the reflexivity of regional people effectively leave them out altogether. By not allowing for their reflexivity, or moreover by not considering their interests, the possibility of understanding their situation and the action which can be seen to ensue from it is denied.

There have been exceptions. Gammage (1986) and Gray (1991) present historical analyses which portray change in rural economy and society from local perspectives in inland agriculture-based towns, while Kennedy (1981) and Metcalfe (1988) offer the local perspective in mining towns. Such local analyses offer opportunities to capture the events of history as they directly affect people and so aid understanding of how people saw those events and responded to them. This is impossible when history is addressed at a national scale. It is constrained at the scale of individual biography by the necessity to explicate the situations of individuals, leaving it necessary to examine people in the contexts of their communities. We will therefore focus particularly on the work of Gray (on Cowra, New South Wales) and Gammage (on Narrandera, New South Wales).

Cowra and Narrandera

The Shire of Cowra had a population of about 12 000 in the mid-1980s, with about two-thirds being resident in the town and the remainder in villages and on farms. Cowra has not been seriously threatened by decline. Having a reliable water supply for irrigation and being only 300 kilometres from Sydney and an hour's drive from each of the cities of Orange and Bathurst, it benefits from a secure, mixed economy and proximity to larger centres. But its economy has been based on agricultural production, as has that of Narrandera Shire. Narrandera is smaller, more distant from Sydney and is perhaps less diversified despite proximity to the Murrumbidgee Irrigation Area. It may appear more likely to suffer decline. Nevertheless, both shires display the reflexivity and resistance of local people when their histories are analysed with regard for the local perspective.

Gray (1991) sees the post-European settlement history of Cowra in terms of four stages: European settlement, development and dispersal, the rise of commerce and services, and centralisation and resistance. These stages culminate in the period when fundamental restructuring was signalled in the mid-1980s, although it is instructive to see the extent of changes experienced much earlier. These periods of time are referred to as phases, rather than stages or periods, because they overlap. Instead of thinking of them as periods of time, it is better to consider them as processes through which Cowra has passed.

The early European settlement of the Cowra district is characterised by the accumulation of vast resources in the hands of a small number of people: the 'squatters', so-called because they were able to occupy large areas of unfenced land without necessarily having legal title. Land was, however, officially granted in the late 1820s, and from the 1830s the number of squatters and their holdings grew. Each property developed around a small settlement with its own flour mill. In the 1840s a township started to grow at a crossing of the Lachlan River. In 1847 a group of landholders proposed the establishment of a township and sale of allotments. The town received a boost from traffic to the Lambing Flat goldfield, but by 1871 it could still only claim a population of 265. Cowra was still dominated by large landholders.

The second phase began after the New South Wales (Colonial) Government resolved to permit intensive settlement by way of 'free selection' on land which was held by the squatters. Although first enacted in 1861, the new laws had little effect until the mid-1870s. Nevertheless, the new settlers set about developing most of the Cowra district into intensive farming land, replacing much of the extensive grazing carried on by the squatters. From the early 1880s, substantially as a result of government action and with an enthusiastic response from settlers, the population of Cowra and its district grew by a factor of seven in thirty years. The town's economy expanded with the population as banks, stores, hotels and other businesses proliferated. The squatters lost their ascendancy in the community through this period. Many organisations were established under the leadership of townspeople, but the older landholding families remained prominent. Their presence created an undercurrent of conflict, as they were said to be reluctant to support developments such as the extension of the railway to Cowra. But as Gammage (1986: 217) points out, rural railways 'were built to serve men in Sydney who equated progress with the economic advancement of the metropolis'. He also argues that local people misunderstood this process, thinking that the railways were being built for them.

Just who benefited most from 'free selection' and the development it precipitated is a matter for conjecture. While the legislators' intentions may well have been honourable, there is no doubt that the nature of rural progress was defined more by urban-based institutions which profited from the growth of commerce (see Gray, 1991: 30). A drive for expansion of family farming and rural populations along with it was to last for a hundred years through closer settlement schemes, particularly those aimed at resettling war veterans in the early 1920s and late 1940s. Governments had become quite aggressive by the 1950s, resuming land from remaining large properties. By the 1960s closer settlement was winding down but had not been forgotten. Gray (1991) notes Cowra's local newspaper reporting in 1968 that the leader of the New South Wales opposition Labor Party complained about the cessation of closer settlement. Some large properties had survived as such in relative terms and the owners of others had taken opportunities to expand, so large properties remained. But their existence was barely an issue. Gray (1991) identifies the key feature of the process of dispersal as the creation of a new class of small employers with their employees forming a working class. The Labor Party became active, but so did farmer organisations.

The third phase, the rise of commerce and services, saw the development of locally-owned manufacturing industry, the further expansion of local businesses and the establishment of local government. Employment in agriculture continued to dominate the labour market, but census statistics in the 1920s and 1930s showed large proportions of the workforce as employers or self-employed, suggesting substantial local autonomy (Gray, 1991: 33). Gray warns, however, that while many business and industrial enterprises had been established by local people, others were branches of firms based elsewhere. Moreover, Cowra was still financially reliant on Sydney and depended on government for vital services, notably rail trans-portation. It is also notable that a shire council was established to provide services in the town's rural hinterland, but unlike the Cowra Municipality which was established on local ini-tiative, the Shire was created by the State government to achieve its own objectives.

Gammage offers examples of constraint on local decision-making and action from the earliest times into the 1980s. Both townspeople and farmers have become used to having their life-chances determined by decisions made in metropolitan centres, as Stayner (1990a: 36) argues with respect to 'railway town'. However, government decisions also brought Cowra a large dam across the Lachlan River, manufacturing industry during World War II and a migrant camp after the war. City-based financial institutions facilitated other development. Neverthe-less, the investment of the Cowra people's savings has always been controlled from the city.

A question-mark loomed over the district's continued growth soon after World War II. The 1947 Census revealed that the population of Cowra's rural hinterland, including its vil-lages, had declined by almost 2000 people. Closer settlement was again advocated and adopted, but by the 1960s it had lost all momentum. Decentralisation, or redistribution of population against the trend of metropolitan-focused urbanisation, was offered by the State government. However, it came with a publicised reminder that it was intended to solve Sydney's problems, not Cowra's. (It has been affirmed as ineffective from either perspective – Stilwell, 1993; 1994.) Cowra people would then be less likely to repeat the mistake made by those whom Gammage (1986) identified as deceived about the purpose of the development of railways in the Riverina.

The process of centralisation could be seen as long ago as the free selection period when local businesses were occasionally bought by non-local investors. It became most apparent, along with resistance to it, in the post-World War II period. The first indicator came with the announcement that a large department store, which had been continuously owned and oper-ated by local people in Cowra's main street, had been sold to a city company. A little later Cowra's only remaining flour mill was similarly sold and was then closed. Local utilities came under the control of outside organisations, or the threat of it. The 1950s saw many such occur-rences. The 1960s appear to have offered some respite but by the mid-1970s sales and closures were occurring again and continued, in threat or actuality, into the 1980s and 1990s. Gam-mage (1986: 219) recounts instances of big business closing operations in Narrandera with 'devastating' consequences. (Bolam (1994) reports a strong shift from local towards national and international ownership of manufacturing industry in the New South Wales central west between 1920 and 1990.)

Both Cowra and Narrandera resisted. Cowra's local newspaper called upon district people to support local businesses. As early as 1928 discussion took place about establishing a locally-owned and operated abattoir. It opened, with 50 per cent local ownership, in 1970. Community opposition almost succeeded in preventing the sale of the newspaper to a chain. Such initiative secured assistance to establish the Japanese Garden for which Cowra is known nationally and overseas. Cowra also obtained a large foreign-owned wool scouring factory. Per-haps its most notable effort came in the 1990s after the closure of its largest industrial employer, a vegetable cannery, by its new transnational owner. A group of local investors suc-ceeded in re-establishing the plant as a local business, albeit on a smaller scale. Gammage reports the spawning of various progress and promotion associations around Narrandera Shire. Unlike Cowra, they included a 'new state movement' and efforts to obtain greater power for local government in order to combat centralisation. The weakness of local government was also observed in Cowra.

Meanwhile, the relationship between town and country in the Cowra district had been reversed. Off-farm employment combined with the loss of farm employment meant a decreasing proportion of the workforce was in farming. While the town workforce was growing by 65 per cent between 1947 and 1986, that of the rural hinterland grew by 6 per cent. Employment and self-employment have remained a strong feature of the local economy despite centralisation and substantial reliance on large industry. The various arms of government, when combined with large industry, employed one-third of Cowra's workforce in 1986, when government alone employed more people than there were farmers in the Shire.

The most foreboding turnaround, however, was that by the State government. In 1983 it moved towards limiting the growth of small farms and encouraging the growth of large ones. This indirectly precipitated public uproar in Cowra. When local businesses with interests in land sales heard of the proposed clause that was to go into the Shire's planning document, which intended to require consent from the Council for hobby farm development, they touched off what is still referred to as Cowra's biggest local political controversy. People took very little prompting to protest against what they saw as a potential threat to theirs and/or their children's ability to acquire a farm. They turned against their own local council for apparently supporting the State government and succeeded in having the provision diluted, but not changed in substance. This was another illustration of the weakness of local government in its relations with State government departments, somewhat ironically in this case because the plan was put forward by the State claiming it to be a means of devolving power to local communities. There was no prospect of a return to closer settlement which by then was long-forgotten as an issue. Gray (1991: 41) concludes that 'the most powerful feature of the history of Cowra Shire is the importance of political decisions made in Sydney in the middle of last century, which, more than any other factor, sent Cowra on a course toward growth and prosperity'. The thrust of those decisions was maintained for one hundred years until reversed in the early 1980s. There was no sign of supportive legislation in any way resembling the closer settlement Acts. At the beginning of the rise of Australian neoliberalism, Cowra found itself alone.

Cowra people felt their isolation, and they identified apparent enemies within and without. Such issues as the planning matter discussed above are shown by Gray to distract attention from real social inequities, but not necessarily glaring inequalities, arising from the local social structure. These included lesser provision of services to working-class parts of town, women and Indigenous people. Some local people, notably those with business and farming interests who are also more likely to have extra local connections and access to capital, were relatively advantaged. It was their interpretation of Cowra's situation and their interests which were more readily respected and widely shared. Cowra people attached great significance to their local community. Business and farming people formed a kind of elite, and were better able than others to use this localism, either intentionally or unintentionally, for their own purposes in debate over local issues.

While Cowra and Narrandera people were well aware of their reliance on and subservience to metropolitan Australia, they went about resisting urban interests quite vigorously, but they did so in terms created and maintained by urban interests led by local elites. Gammage (1986: 221) concluded:

> The bush never got the population to hold political supremacy in Australia. It was settled when the industrial revolution was centralizing economic power, and when colonial governments were exercising unprecedented economic and political control. As well country people tied themselves willingly to an export economy, welcomed urban notions of civilization, and accepted material and cultural dependence as the price of progress. They let the tendrils of urban attachment thicken largely unresisted, devoting themselves instead to the task progress assigned to them – the conquest of the bush.

Gammage also describes a history of agricultural productivism and its impact on the Riverina landscape. The energy put into resisting centralisation appears insignificant alongside that put into the production treadmill. It is notable that Gammage could reach these conclusions despite the existence, and at times, significant influence in State and federal politics, of a political party formed from the anger of rural dwellers towards metropolitan dominance consistently avowing the purpose of representing regional interests.

Broken Hill and Kurri Kurri

Regional mining communities suffer centralisation most directly. In the historical examples offered by Kennedy (1981) and Metcalfe (1988), the communities are basically constituted of the working class, as senior mining company managers and owners choose to live elsewhere. Kennedy saw the foundations of the very strong tradition of unionism in Broken Hill embedded in its relationship with the city as it is affected by remoteness. The town's main employer, the Broken Hill Proprietary Company, in its early years had little involvement in community matters amid a climate described by Kennedy as alienation. He attributed this to the mines being controlled by absentee directors who knew nothing about the town's problems (1981: 119).

Despite being much closer to Sydney and more particularly Newcastle, the Hunter Valley mining community described by Metcalfe (1988) shared Broken Hill's social distance from company management and developed a strong class consciousness. The community's resistance was also industrial, facilitated by unions and on occasion being marred by violence often becoming what Metcalfe likens to larrikinism. Community life was profoundly affected by the industrial situation of a large proportion of local people, upon whose wages the institutions of community and the township depended. Similar depictions have been offered by Kriegler (1980) and Williams (1981). The dependency of mining communities and the relative powerlessness of their local authorities amid mine closure is illustrated, with Australian examples, by Neil et al. (1992).

Indigenous Communities

Claims have been made about high levels of autonomy obtained by Indigenous communities in northern Australia through deliberate attempts by government since the 1960s to provide devolution of responsibility to Indigenous people for Indigenous people. There is no doubt that changes have been made to the governance of these communities. Wolfe (1989) reported that some local decision-making had occurred amid development of a degree of local self-reliance. However, Mowbray (n.d.) sees the establishment of Aboriginal councils as tokenistic. All power to make significant change still resides ultimately with government departments in Darwin.

Leaders and Interests

Individuals are important throughout this analysis. Local entrepreneurs and political leaders appear frequently and their influence is recorded. This influence can be found readily in terms of local affairs and events, but not so easily in terms of affecting the relationships in which local development is embedded. What has mattered in all cases is the relationship between communities and outside institutions. This offers no comfort to those who seek to interpret the futures of regional communities as resting in the hands of visionary, entrepreneurial leaders. It also offers little to rural people who have placed their faith in local leaders to manage their dealings with the public and private institutions of metropolitan Australia in ways which would further regional interests. When it is seen how popular local definition of those dealings can relatively advantage some community members (who might be described as local elites), the reflexivity of regional community members becomes highly problematic.

The Relationship between Metropolitan and Regional Australia

Rural people have an image of their relationship with metropolitan Australia which is reflected in their ideological countrymindedness. The image is optimistic only at its most benign and possibly ill-founded. They have 'got on with the job' which metropolitan Australia has defined for them. The city has offered support for what it wants them to do, and while occasionally able to dress that support in ways which made it resemble a gift, has not been able to eliminate the concern among rural people that government and management from the city were working against them, even though they could firmly believe that they were doing the right thing by themselves and their nation. Now that support has been withdrawn under neoliberal thinking. As Economou (1997: 9) put it: 'for so much of what had comprised the regional economy reflected the ascendancy of state interventionism in Australian policy-making from as far back as colonial times'. Dollery and Soul (2000: 161) see the domination of cities over regional states and organisations as a prominent feature of modern industrial societies.

Nobody should be surprised that regional people would seek radical change when confronted by governments which appear no longer to support the principles behind their regional presence, not only because neoliberalism poses a new threat, but also because they have been struggling with the inconsistencies of dependency and countrymindedness for generations. Whichever large private and public investment or legislative undertaking in regional Australia one cares to choose, it is easy to question who ultimately benefits from it. The free selection and closer settlement Acts allowed people to develop farming, but they were moved to do so in ways which locked them into recurring and, for many, inevitably devastating economic and environmental crises while metropolitan commerce prospered. The railways facilitated this process, focusing on the metropolitan centres and making it possible for government and business control to come from them. Small-town industries and businesses were established with hopes for continued expansion, but since they remained small they were easy pickings for larger statewide and national firms, ultimately offering the latter easy means of expansion. Local government was given so few powers and such meagre capacity for revenue-raising that it has never been able to assert local interests in much more than token measures.

Certainly metropolitan Australia has made substantial regional investments, but for whom? Even the Snowy Mountains Scheme and the other great river damming projects, with their consequent irrigation-based industries, are now being questioned in terms of their capacity to support a regional population in the long term. There is evidence from New Zealand that sites of booming development in rural tourism suffer from loss of local control of commerce and the relative disadvantage for local people in the labour market (Phillips and Campbell, 1993). O'Connor and Stimson (1996) use the work of Parsons (1995) to show how the supply of food to the metropolitan population via supermarkets, while obviously based on rural production, is increasingly controlled from Sydney and Melbourne throughout its entire process. The pre-eminence of metropolitan Australia seems impossible to challenge. And when one considers how advantage might accrue to some local people who are able to access external capital or otherwise gain advantage from the development of hotel and supermarket chains, the likelihood of social bifurcation among attenuating local class structures emerges more clearly.

What of political forces, particularly the National Party but also the occasionally-elected representatives of minor parties (notably One Nation) and independents (notably, at the time of writing, the particularly successful Tony Windsor from Tamworth, New South Wales)? They may at times have either direct or indirect influence on political agendas. But they operate in a political arena where, without a substantial gerrymander, regional representatives will remain a diminishing minority. Moreover, they must negotiate the contradictions resulting from liminality and affecting farmer organisations, as discussed in chapter 5. But perhaps most importantly, they work under an ideological climate in which neoliberalism has been allowed virtually to eliminate all other perspectives. The neoliberal juggernaut continues by providing easy interpretation of local issues acceptable across the local social spectrum, cementing regional–metropolitan relations rather than changing them.

Dependency

The concept of dependency is frequently mentioned in writing about metropolitan–regional relations. The demographic processes discussed above have been viewed in the light of a 'core–periphery' or 'centre–periphery' model (see Stilwell, 1974: chapter 4) highlighting the contingency of regional development in a capitalist system which concentrates investment and resources in the largest cities. Australia had urbanised before extensive rural development occurred, and the consequent centralisation prevented the development of inland settlements which were economically and politically strong enough to become independent, even during the gold-rush period and among mining towns like Broken Hill. Consequently, inland regional communities have been able to do little to arrest the demographic trends discussed above, as they remained dependent on the metropolitan centres.

The relationship between metropolitan and regional Australia lends itself to analysis in terms of dependency theory, with the latter being seen as a 'periphery' dependent on the former, which becomes a 'core'. Dependency theory stems from the work of A. G. Frank on international development and has been used to explain the lagging economies of Third World nations. It has been criticised, however, for being overly structuralist and reductionist: not accommodating variation in relationships among countries as it sees systemic dependency as the totality of rich country – poor country relations and concealing resistance to the dominance of the industrialised 'north'. Despite these criticisms, some writers still see value in its application to metropolitan–regional relations. Does the core–periphery conceptualisation retain validity in the era of globalisation?

Dependency was identified as the basis of the relationship between metropolitan United States and a small American town by Vidich and Bensman (1960) in work seen as a precursor to international dependency theory (Young, 1996). Vidich and Bensman claim to expose the dependency and subjugation of local bureaucrats in their lack of control over local decision-making, determined as it is by the statewide and national policies of their organisations. This is a central feature of the revelation that small-town life in the United States is not like that of the democratic, autonomous community which Americans have idolised. One might wonder how Americans could retain such a view of small-town life when one considers what Australians know of the history of decline and resistance among their towns, but the United States does not share Australia's history of centralised industrial development and of centralised administration. American local government has enjoyed far wider powers than its Australian counterpart. While Gramling and Freudenberg (1990) could reasonably discuss the extent to which local resource-dependent communities were reliant on their externally-owned and managed resource extraction industries, it would seem pointless to conduct such research on, for example, the mining communities of the Pilbara in the north-west of Western Australia.

The concept of dependency has been applied more recently to relationships between resource-based communities and 'urban cores'. Smith and Steel (1995) attempt to show a dependency relationship between local economies based on agriculture, forestry and tourism in rural Oregon and the city of Portland. They describe 'controls' which the urban core has over the rural periphery, including those over information and the rules of development, in a way which is reminiscent of Narrandera and Cowra. Knapp (1995) saw these advantages as enabling what could appear as a conspiracy against regional interests. Profits are returned from regional industries to urban owners but corporations seldom transfer their most advanced technologies to regional operations. He concluded that regional communities lack both economic and political power.

This conceptualisation is incomplete, despite the apparent dependency illustrated by the histories of both Cowra and Narrandera and any number of small mining settlements as well as the overseas evidence. The problem is that regional communities have exerted some influence from time to time and benefited from it, even if much of that benefit has not been equitably distributed, has now been largely exhausted and what remains may not be sustainable in the long term. We need to look behind dependency. An approach which permits analysis of the processes and exchanges involved in the metropolitan–regional relationship is required.

Power and Interests

The relationship between metropolitan and regional Australia entails an element of power. One approach to power involves looking for people who are able to make others do something which they would not otherwise do. Gammage's (1986) historical example of Narrandera awaiting State action before sand could be cleared from the main street, and Gray's (1991) more contemporary instances, offer cases of local people beholden to central (State) authority. But our interest in the metropolitan–regional relationship was initially fired by the observation that regional areas are lagging in growth and development, are economically disadvantaged and some small settlements are disappearing altogether. The core has a capacity to attract the development which the periphery lacks. Regional discontent is certainly not just a matter of people resenting being told what to do.

Interests
It is hypothetically possible that regional communities could be entirely dependent, be told what to do with regard to just about everything and prosper at the same time. Many regional people have enjoyed prosperity. However, Australia's regional demographic and economic history indicates that prosperity has not necessarily followed from dependency. The point that it can suggests that we should consider another view of power. An alternative was suggested by Lukes (1974: 34) when he wrote: 'I have defined the concept of power by saying that A exercises power over B when A affects B in a manner contrary to B's interests'. Power is exerted in ways which are much more subtle than telling others what to do and seeing them obey, or determining the conditions in which they may act. While this approach has more direct application to individuals or organisations, it can cast light on the complexity of metropolitan–regional power relations, particularly by raising the problem of specifying interests. It becomes essential to specify what people's interests are and how they do or do not come to be appreciated and fulfilled.

Determining the nature of anybody's interests, including one's own, is an uncertain and hazardous reflexive endeavour. Who is to say that growth and economic development really do serve the interests of regional dwellers who might attach value to an unaffected lifestyle? Here we confront the relativism problem raised in chapter 3. Perceptions of interests are cultural products. Specifications or imputations of the interests of regional dwellers made by metropolitan dwellers are no more than that, as indeed are the definitions of interests adopted by the regional dwellers themselves.

We must ascertain the extent to which regional interests have been served by the metropolitan–regional relationship in order to understand it, but we have no singular means of defining what those interests might be. Moreover, we must admit the possibility that the metropolitan–regional relationship itself has been influential in determining the cultural construction of interests. Gammage (1986) hinted at such effects in his comment that Narrandera people accepted an urban image of progress. Gray (1991) argued that localism defined a common interest for Cowra people across the social spectrum. This resonates with Lawrence's (1987) view of farmers as struggling to define their own ambiguous class position and the point made in chapter 5 about the liminality of farming.

Sociological research has related interests to social class location (see, for example, Barnes, 1977). The class position of regional people has multiple dimensions. It has an over-arching spatial element which can, as in the case of isolated mining communities, intensify perceptions of class, or among agriculture-based towns, smother perceptions of local class under a cushion of localistic egalitarianism (see Dempsey, 1990 as well as Gray, 1991). This appears especially hazardous with regard to rural people.

Gray et al. (1997) considered this problem and opted for a pragmatic solution based on the work of Nielsen (1977), Saunders (1983) and Wiggins (1987). This drew attention to basic need. Wiggins (1987) offered the example of the motorists who could be seen to have an interest in the extension of urban freeways, but their basic interest lay in access to urban facil-ities and services. Gray et al. (1997) offered the example of the farmer who could be seen to need to increase production, but could also be seen to have a 'vital interest' in maintaining a long-term source of family income. This is a development of Saunders' (1983) advocacy of looking for situations which were obvious threats to well-being in order to determine when somebody's interests were threatened. But the above examples illustrate how cultural con-struction renders the process of interest perception questionable and raises the possibility that some may be advantaged by the ways in which others perceive their interests, as apparently enjoyed by Cowra's elites (Gray, 1991). This is what Share (1995) alluded to when he dis-cussed the work of those writers who saw countrymindedness, like agrarianism, as a weapon for those who subjugated rural people to urban organisations and institutions. The metropoli-tan–regional relationship as discussed above and in the previous chapter appears to be one in which metropolitan interests are served at least rather more consistently than those of the regions, and the efforts of regional dwellers to assert their interests have had little effect. It is reasonable, however, to expect that those whose class position gives them greater access to both local and extra-local capital will retain a degree of privilege in an increasingly bifurcated local society.

Community Resistance

The concept of resistance focuses attention on power relations in which equalisation or rever-sal of those relationships is not occurring despite the activity of those whose interests are suf-fering. It refers to action which alters the quality of power relations but not the direction of dominance. The historical analyses of four regional communities discussed above confirmed a long tradition of resistance. Some of the more optimistic analyses of regional development also confirm that resistance is an appropriate concept. Hudson (1989) related a process of 'adaptation' to changing circumstances, not one of forcing change to those circumstances. Kerby and Gorman (1994) set out some analysis of the social conditions necessary for commu-nity economic development. They titled their publication *Changing by Choice*. Kerby and Parish (1997) analysed the process of change, as described above, which the same area had experienced. One might reasonably ask if the changes made were by the choice of local people. One could answer 'yes', but the circumstances in which people made their choices were not of their making. This experience resonates with that of the people of Cowra and Narrandera. People have made a lot of choices, but the power relationship has strengthened with no sign of reversal.

The tenor of resistance may have changed since the late 1980s. While we have not carried out an exhaustive analysis, it seems reasonable to propose that reports of resistance referring to attempts to deflect the diminution of government employment and services (such as Jones, 1987) are becoming less frequent and those extolling local business-based recovery (like Hodge, 1999) are appearing more often. This could be because many places have lost their government employment and services altogether. Or it may be that local entrepreneurship is beginning to flourish, whether stimulated by neoliberal rhetoric or do-or-die economic necessity. Again this should not be taken as a reversal of the metropolitan–regional relationship, even for those places which are seeing some employment growth. There are many which are not.

Resistance in the form of economic action has taken four paths. These could be described as addressing government, corporate business (exogenous), local business (endogenous) and community action. They are not mutually exclusive: resistance can be directed towards more than one at a time. Cowra and Narrandera both illustrate resistance to government downsizing decisions. Pawson and Scott (1992a; 1992b) analysed similar actions during rural restructuring in New Zealand. Cowra also demonstrates resistance to corporate decisions and attempts to steer them, including the attraction of the wool scour and the action of local business in the resurrection of its biggest industry (see also Cahill (1995) and Powell (1996) for analysis of Cowra's experience). The latter example also illustrates an aspect of community action, because local government was closely involved. Lake (1996) described a successful local business established by women. Wildman et al. (1990) reported an encouraging attempt to revitalise a small Queensland town and concluded that both attracting government investment and fostering local initiatives are important.

Resistance which is purely community-based includes the many Local Enterprise Trading Systems (LETS) which have been established in rural communities in Australia and elsewhere to facilitate local trade, provide support for local initiatives (Croft, 1994; Pacione, 1997) and prevent financial leakage from the community. They are said to be quite effective (Williams, 1996) and are perhaps the purest form of community-based resistance. In contrast to many business initiatives, including many of those described by Cahill (1995) and to a minor degree that described by Lake (1996) which received external support, LETS are relatively independent. They are more independent than the Canadian community bond scheme which was established by a provincial government initiative but is community-led (see Parsons, 1993) and the United States' *Community Reinvestment Act* which requires financial institutions to take account of local financial needs (see Green and Cowell, 1994). Their independence can potentially be circumscribed by the state, a point illustrated by the decision of the Commonwealth Government to exempt LETS from social security means-testing (Williams, 1996).

Rural co-operatives are not new, particularly those which market agricultural products, sell equipment and supplies to farmers and process farmers' product, but they are appearing in new circumstances. The community of Yeoval, NSW, formed a co-operative to resurrect their local hospital (Sidoti, 1999). The restoration of banking services through community organisation is another example of community-based resistance through co-operation, although often in the form of a joint project with external partners and therefore substantially exogenous (see

Sexton, 1999). On 6 March 1999 the Wagga Wagga *Daily Advertiser* carried a large page 1 head-line: 'Grand Day: Coleambally Celebrates Opening Of Its Own Bank'. It reported a crowd of 300 'locals', of a stated town population of 600, at the opening ceremony. A community group had succeeded in raising $350 000 to establish the bank, but it could only do so with the support of the Bendigo Bank, an interstate institution, but one with regional origins. The report mentioned that 50 per cent of net profits were to be returned to the local community. This offers a powerful contrast to the previous service provided by a large banking corporation even if it is not by any means entirely endogenous and hence independent. It is also better based in the local community than are the credit unions, based in the larger centres, which are taking over banking abandoned by the national banks in the smaller towns (see Dick, 1998). Bendigo itself has re-established its own stock exchange, first launched during the 1850s gold rushes, with support from the Bendigo Bank. The local development trusts being established following the 1999 Regional Summit are basically local initiatives which aim to keep local resources local with some government support.

However, the question of interests remains. This is most apparent with regard to development with an exogenous element. Barrow and Hall (1995) studied the impact of an office of the American Express company in Brighton, England. They noted that while their findings did not concur with other studies of manufacturing plants, they were able to conclude that the effects of American Express were generally beneficial to the local economy. The implied uncertainty was heightened when the sponsorship of the research by American Express was acknowledged, but that aside, the point is that exogenous economic development is always under a cloud from a local perspective. Gringeri (1993) reported from the United States that local employment was boosted by local efforts to develop 'industrial homeworking', or using the Australian term, 'outwork'. While it created employment for women, their work amounted to cheap labour for the non-local employer who did not have to offer normal industrial protection under the women's terms of employment. Further, their work reinforced gender socialisation which placed women's work in the home. More importantly for the present argument, the locality acted 'essentially as a conduit for capital to enter the community on its own terms' (Gringeri, 1993: 50). This point was made in principle by Ife (1995) when he wrote that relying on attracting industry involved reliance on the same system which was at the root of the local community's disadvantage. Riedel (1999) sounded a (probably unintended) warning by pointing to the attractiveness of low workforce costs for businesses who might establish call centres in regional situations. One might be tempted to envisage the creation of industries which in class and local-external relationship terms are comparable with those described by Kennedy (1981) and Metcalfe (1988).

There is no case analysis of a situation exactly parallel to that indicated by Gringeri in Australia, but there are some which raise the same issue: the extent to which action to attract exogenous development ultimately serves local interests. The issue is also raised by the observations of Gammage and Gray with regard to the ways in which urban organisations have steered rural development to serve their own interests while apparently working for the bush. There are notable instances of conflict within communities over less subtle intrusions of urban interests. Wild (1983) documented a local community rising against its local government when the latter agreed to a Victorian government proposal to establish a waste dump in their locality. The council was forced to back down. A similar scenario was enacted in the southern

New South Wales town of Corowa in the early 1990s and another took place in the late 1990s around the town of Ardlethan in the northern Riverina. Similar conflicts have arisen in the United States (Spies et al., 1998). Gray (1991) records a different situation: one in which some community members, who could reasonably be described as lower middle and working class, were disadvantaged by a development (a wool scour) but could not make their concerns sufficiently heard to halt or change it. These problems can be traced to institutional features of local government. Wild (1983) highlighted elitism of membership and Gray (1991) pointed to the ways in which issues are, or are not, raised and acted upon. This is not to say that local government fails to participate in regional resistance. It was intimately involved in the renaissance of Cowra's largest industry. Cahill (1995) argued that involvement of, but not necessarily leadership or control by, local government is one of ten key components of successful endogenous development. Local government has lobbied for compulsory social impact assessments of all State and federal government policies (Baum, 1996; Wearne, 1996).

While it is not difficult to imagine circumstances in which exogenous development is detrimental to local interests, especially when there is competition among communities to attract it, the Cowra case suggests that similar caution should be applied to endogenous development. We cannot be certain that local democracy will take all interests into account in development issues. This should not place all resistance under suspicion, however. Chisholm (1994; 1995) took an optimistic view after initially reporting the demise of a vital local industry based on a co-operative. He attributed the rescue of Leeton to a coalition of local government, a regional development board and community groups that apparently found solutions which served the community well. Tonts (1996) indicated similar outcomes for some Western Australian towns, but not for others. Not all towns will be equally capable of forming coalitions like that described by Chisholm. As Wallner et al. (1996) pointed out, capacities to organise undertakings like LETS are not evenly distributed across space. It should not be assumed that any or all local interests will necessarily be served by either exogenous or endogenous development, nor should it be assumed that all communities are equally capable of resistance. The result of resistance is likely to be uneven among communities, and possibly uneven within community populations, because of their variable capacities to act, but also because even small communities can be culturally and structurally pluralistic. It is often very difficult for communities to determine collectively where the best interests of their members lie with respect to the whole community and each of its members.

Nevertheless, it is instructive to note that the resistance identified and discussed above has been that of collectivities, not individuals. This is something to which individualistic economic analysis would be quite blind. It leaves us with the possible conclusion that the effort to change the course of rural restructuring under neoliberalism is not necessarily coming so much from the efforts of individual entrepreneurs as the economics of neoliberalism would advocate, but rather from groups of people reflecting on their structural circumstances.

The Presentation and Interpretation of Development Issues

Resistance is itself highly problematic, not just because it does not change power relations. That it may or may not happen in any given situation is problematic enough; more so is the point that if it does happen, it may or may not serve those who carry it out. This makes perception of power relations and the ways in which community members' interests might or might not be served crucial to regional reflexivity. Ideally we would begin to explain these dilemmas by means of ethnographic analysis of communities and their responses to dependency and uneven development. Research has been carried out for community studies such as that by Wild (1978, 1983) and Gray (1991). While indicators of reflexivity are only narrow by-products of these studies, they remain important because they demonstrate the significance of institutions as well as social structure and ideology. They are also able to track the processes through which interests are perceived and acted upon or ignored.

Another aspect of regional reflexivity can be examined by means of content analysis of newspapers. This shows how the relationship between regional and metropolitan Australia is presented for interpretation by regional people. It indicates the range of issues being placed before regional people and can also illustrate the meanings which they attach to those issues. It starts to help us answer the crucial questions of whether or not people do perceive their structural dilemmas and if they do, how they might attempt to extricate themselves from them. It is not possible by this means to explore in detail the processes of reflection and resistance in social interaction and the ways this may be related to class or other structural position, but it is feasible to consider interpretations of events and ideologies related to collective action and individualism as we see how dependency and power are presented by local media.

We have carried out some such analysis by first reading *The Land* from January 1997 to July 1998 and the Wagga Wagga *Daily Advertiser* from June to July 1998. Items which raised regional development issues or pertained in some way to the metropolitan–regional power relationship were noted and subsequently coded in terms of the issue or dimension of the metropolitan–regional relationship. The following presentation of analysis commences with a view of the range of issues presented in articles and an editorial examining explanations and interpretations of regional issues. It goes on to look at material indicating resistance and how it is viewed.

Articles recount the regional experience of restructuring and neoliberalism and make associations with 'economic rationalism', both public and private. They cover:

- crowded meetings about the future of health services (*The Land*, Country Life Supplement, 9 January 1997: 5)
- a 'special report' on health issues covering 'the doctor shortage', the 'hospitals crisis' and aged care, spanning three issues of *The Land* in June 1997
- implications of health service cuts for health and town viability (Wagga Wagga *Daily Advertiser*, Monday, 8 June 1998: 5)
- fears of bank closures (such as 'Hillston Fears Its Last Bank Branch Will Fall' in *The Land*, Country Life Supplement, 24 July 1997: 3)
- the isolation of children refused a government transport subsidy (*The Land*, 14 May 1998: 24)
- the inadequacy of telecommunications (*The Land*, 14 May 1998: 25; 28 May 1998: 25; 4 June 1998: 12
- the difficulties encountered by rural private schools (*The Land*, Education Guide, 24 June 1998: 5)

- loss of railway employment (Wagga Wagga *Daily Advertiser*, 4 June 1998: 3)
- fear of the impact of milk market deregulation (Wagga Wagga *Daily Advertiser*, 25 June 1998: 1)
- closure of a Civil Aviation Safety Authority office (Wagga Wagga *Daily Advertiser*, 26 June 1998: 3)
- closure of factory by transnational corporation (Wagga Wagga *Daily Advertiser*, 2 July 1998: 3).

In each case, it was made clear that these events were caused by external forces over which the local community had no control. This was made explicit in the last-mentioned article, where a local councillor was quoted as showing a clear indication of a feeling of powerlessness: 'just another example of economic rationalism: private enterprise can do what it likes and there's not a lot the community can do about it. It's another example of foreign investors looking after their shareholders while the local community doesn't get much of a look in'.

The structural relationship, in terms akin to dependency, was frequently presented in analysis of news. The editorial of *The Land* (29 May 1997: 14) argued that attracting large-scale exogenous development was the only saviour for rural communities:

> Much as some of us might like to preserve the essentially agricultural flavour and culture of country towns, the figures tell us starkly that any town dependent on dryland agricultural service industry for its prosperity is doomed to suffer an inexorable decline ... Without the circuit-breaking effect created by a new industry, people will continue to drift to larger regional centres and to the capital cities ...

It also cautioned against allowing environmental considerations to prevent establishment of a gold mine. The same editorial also cautioned against privatisation of New South Wales' electricity supply. A later editorial in *The Land* (24 July 1997: 18) confronted an issue which reflects the history of inland development. Local government in western New South Wales wants to establish an international freight airport to bypass Sydney, but 'vested interests in Sydney will oppose the Parkes plan [which] will also give the bush freedom from Sydney's costly airport infrastructure and muddled signals from overseas consumers to local farmers'. Here we see countrymindedness with its potential to ignore and possibly exclude a class dimension from view. The interests implicitly acknowledged extended only to those of agricultural and industrial capital, both local and extra-local. There was also implicit suggestion of common interest between the local community and extra-local industry, indicating a tension within countryminded ideology.

The 'countryminded' quest for rural independence remains apparent as it was through the histories of Cowra and Narrandera. It remains fiercely sought but seen as unattainable, or at best very difficult to attain due to structural impediments. There are, however, numerous reports of resistance in the newspapers studied. Some of these are highly individualistic. A report in the Wagga Wagga *Daily Advertiser* of Friday, 26 June 1998 mentioned two people establishing businesses in a small Riverina town. 'How Betty Inspired A Town' is the headline of an article about a successful business person who had struggled against great adversity to restore a family business after personal tragedy (*The Land*, Country Life, 17 July 1997: 8). An article on the same page was about another successful small business, but attributed success in part to the support of the town. The next page attributed a resurgence, including the return of young people, in another town to 'small town pride'. It contained eight photographs of local people in their businesses. A kind of communal individualism was apparent in an article which attributed attempts to rejuvenate a town to collective self-help (*The Land*, Country Life, 11 September 1997: 3). There are many articles which make one of these interpretations, including: 'Local Community Rallies To Keep Matong On The Map' (*The Land*, Country Life, 25 December 1997: 51); 'How Mudgee Gave Itself' (*The Land*, 1 January 1998: 6); 'Hyden: Wheatbelt Whistlestop No More' (*The Land*, 26 February 1998: 5).

All of these reports presented a positive view of resistance, in apparent tension with the view of dependence on exogenous investment. One letter to the editor of *The Land* (21 August 1997: 15) blamed town decline on the unwillingness of people to support their community by shopping locally. Two weeks later another letter claimed that the author of the first one lacked any understanding: that the failure of towns was not their own fault but rather that of government which had failed to deliver a 'level playing field'. Structural interpretations, of whatever kind, are ever-present, but they do not delve into local social structures.

Of a different kind are those articles that more readily acknowledge the power relationship which encompasses them. Rather than presenting success as dependent on the strength of individual and/or collective will, 'Jerilderie Fights To Keep Hospital' (*The Land*, 16 April 1998: 16) set out a confrontation between health service management and the town's residents in which the latter were plainly disadvantaged. They are also different from articles which indicate that a town's revival has been brought about by settlement of people from the city who have money to invest (such as 'City Folk Revitalise Bush Town', *The Land*, 28 May 1998: 51), and those which attribute revitalisation to investment by a large corporation from out of town (such as 'Coolah's Comeback', *The Land Magazine*, 4 June 1998: 4), or both of these factors ('Why Corowa's Growing In Leaps And Bounds', *The Land Magazine*, 2 July 1998: 4). In these cases the agendas remain beyond the grasp of local people. But not necessarily in all cases. 'Health Campaigner Has Beaten The Odds' (Wagga Wagga *Daily Advertiser*, Monday, 8 June 1998: 6) tells of the success of a woman who campaigned for a mobile mammography service. She was the wife of a State member of parliament. All of these articles, except for the last-mentioned, indicate a situation in which either local people are at a continuing disadvantage or the extent to which their interests will ultimately be served is open to question.

The tensions between idealistic faith in self-help and the realities of the agendas of development and the potential for real development to serve rural local interests are as apparent here as their counterparts were in chapter 5's analysis of the liminality of farming. The problem for farmers and townspeople, posed by neoliberalism regardless of class position, is that it prescribes change in ways which accord with their ideals yet obscure and potentially threaten their interests. This was set out by a resident of a small, relatively remote, New South Wales town in a letter to the editor of *The Land* (16 January 1997: 15) which pointed out that country people, among others, have enthusiastically supported neoliberalism:

For years Australians have bucketed public-provided services and argued that they should become more efficient and business-like ... The banks are being very businesslike – look how well their shareholders are doing. The manager of Australia Post or any other government agency is under similar instructions to close branches that do not 'pay' and we, via our elected representatives, have been responsible for the cutbacks.

To rural people who see the economic activity around them, in town and country, very predominantly in the hands of small business people, being efficient and businesslike makes sense at the same time as it obscures local social structures and thereby fosters the localism which can underpin resistance. But the rhetoric has had the unintended consequence of supporting an ideology which has removed the economic and demographic bases for many of their businesses upon which all community members have been dependent.

Conclusion

Regional people are made aware that their interests are not being served by their relationship with metropolitan Australia at the same time as they are reminded of development possibilities which only metropolitan organisations can offer. Sometimes these are presented as the only possibilities for survival – unless, that is, communities can find the means to achieve successful endogenous development. The only place to look is, according to both neoliberal rhetoric and rural belief in self-reliance, the individual. The same rhetoric supports faith in the competitive individual entrepreneur as the saviour of rural communities. But alongside it comes praise for the collective. At the same time, the interests of individuals are readily obscured in a climate of localistic countrymindedness. These tensions make it very difficult for regional reflexivity to determine where the interests of regional people lie in terms of their relationships within and among their communities and between metropolitan and regional organisations and institutions.

Regional reflexivity continually turns attention to metropolitan arenas. In those arenas, regional interests do not determine agendas. Even in what might appear to be the local arena offered by local government, the agenda of development is seldom determined by local interests. The urban image of progress is still imposed and sometimes accepted, indicating an hegemonic power relationship with regional Australia, despite the existence of nominal political representation. That they are confronted by an urban image might be apparent to rural people when they see metropolitan organisations advocating regional development aimed at increased production which will feed metropolitan industry and commerce, but increasingly rural people are expected to live without the same level of services, indeed without the attributes of full citizenship, which metropolitan people expect. This, in the ideological climate provided by the traditional belief in the individual which is continually recalled in neoliberal rhetoric and policy formulation, risks a degree of self-exploitation among all regional dwellers, as was noted to be commonplace among farm families amid the liminality of farming. When those arenas are either exclusive in membership and participation, or narrow in the range of issues they confront, they cannot be expected to foster the strength of community which neoliberal community rhetoric prescribes.

We are arguing that regional reflexivity has been constrained by the ideological and institutional hegemony of its relationship with metropolitan Australia. But might we be failing our own demand for our own reflexivity? Might rural individualism be so important to regional people that their opportunities for individual advancement, such as they exist, are more important than respect for their well-being, their rights and citizenship? It does not take much pragmatism to accept that the contradictions in such an argument are obvious. Taking opportunities is dependent on capacities like health and education. In a rural society which has often made the interests of the collective quite apparent and organised its members voluntarily to serve each other, a tension between the individual and the collective has always been present. The individual has always depended on the community, and vice versa. Moreover, productive community action can be of an economically irrational kind, such as when people voluntarily contribute more than they can expect to gain from involvement. Rural individualism has its limits in social practice and in ideology, something which the ever-present images of community action alongside personal achievement help to confirm. These tensions are further explored in chapter 9.

What might change resistance into an equalisation or reversal of the metropolitan–regional power relationship? The answer to this question lies in resolution of the tensions between individualism and collectivism amid local and extra-local structural relations, but it also requires a clear perception of the political arenas into which resistance is channelled and the ways in which issues are addressed and agendas are constructed. Thinking along these lines leads to confrontation with the nature of our institutions of government and politics.

Further Reading

Dempsey, K. (1990) Smalltown: A Study of Social Inequality, Cohesion and Belonging, Melbourne: Oxford University Press.
  – a comprehensive social analysis of a rural town covering elements of social division and cohesion in the context of beliefs about community life and relations
Gammage, B. (1986) Narrandera Shire, Narrandera: Narrandera Shire Council.
  – an award-winning history which portrays a rural community in its environmental and political contexts
Stilwell, F. (2000) Changing Track: A New Political Economic Direction for Australia, Sydney: Pluto Press.
  – discusses individualism in a context of neoliberal economic policy
Wild, R. (1983) Heathcote, Sydney: Allen & Unwin.
  – describes and analyses the processes through which a community opposed its own leaders, in the form of a local government council, when they appeared to favour metropolitan interests

The challenges facing rural and regional Australia include finding a pathway to the transformation of rural production into a form which is ecologically sustainable. It would seem imperative that Australians extricate themselves from the legacy of European farming practices. In a globalising world economy, pressures are being exerted on nations like Australia which 'force' regions to exploit their people and natural resources in ways which will perpetuate that legacy. It is necessary, however, to consider this problem globally, in the sense that what have been seen as productivity and efficiency gains must be considered alongside societal benefits and environmental security. In this chapter we introduce the third element of misfortune: that which threatens the bio-physical foundations of rural economy and society.

Once again we see neoliberalism and reflexivity emerging as important themes. Under neoliberalism, Australian governments have been unable or unwilling to intervene to challenge forces associated with globalisation. Australia's future is viewed by our governments as being intimately tied to the global economy and its corporate players. Governments find it difficult to challenge such authority through increased interventions – although many appear quite prepared to provide funding for community-based activities to address environmental concerns. Will these initiatives be the solution Australia is seeking to these very real and growing problems? In this chapter we consider the damage caused by past and current agricultural practices, before evaluating alternative options.

Colonial Agriculture: Compromising the Australian Landscape

Following European colonisation of Australia attempts were made to ensure the fledgling convict outpost would be self-sufficient in food and would therefore not be a drain on the British government; and then – at a time when the Blue Mountains were crossed and the inland pastures were secured by 'squatters' and later purchased by both squatters and ex-miners – to assist in the provision of Britain's food and fibre needs. There was also an overwhelming desire by the colonists for British animals, plants and, moreover, for a British-style landscape. The more the Australian landscape was tamed and fashioned to look like the green and rolling hills of Britain, the more 'progress' was deemed to have been made (see Dovers, 1992; Dryzek, 1997). As the sheep empires developed during the first fifty years of white settlement, it was clear that Australia had the 'right' combination of factors for success in pastoralism: open country that could be grazed with relatively little clearing; relatively mild winters which reduced the need for shelter; minimal need for stock management; and a high value commodity (wool) which, apart from the shearing of sheep, could be produced with relatively little labour (Dovers, 1992). Despite its effect on the environment, and its destruction of entire Indigenous modes of production and consumption (Wickham, 1998), pastoral expansion was heralded as the key to continued prosperity as a 'colonial complementarity' developed between Britain and the former settlements of Australia (McMichael, 1997).

'Free selection' – a form of land reform which sought both to reduce the power of the 'squattocracy' as well as to provide a basis for 'family farm' agriculture – was attempted from the 1860s with mixed success (see Davidson, 1981). Those settling the lands once used for open grazing were now – with limited skill in agriculture, limited capital, and the need to farm intensively to make a living – 'forced' by circumstances to clear the land and to engage in agricultural practices which were unsuited to the climate, soil types and vegetation. Reeve (1988: 10) has reported that the exhaustion of soils through overcropping was reported as early as 1820. Floods, droughts and fires were only some of the misfortunes of this and later periods of farming and grazing. The others were the unstable market for which products were destined, and the limited knowledge of the landscape and its biophysical potential (Dovers, 1992). Severe soil erosion, 'scalded' plains and the replacement of suitable pasture species with woody weeds and less palatable grasses were the immediate consequences of the settlement of semi-arid lands to take advantage of what proved to be a series of short-lived increases in wool prices from the 1880s to the 1930s (Dovers, 1992; Wickham, 1998).

Despite the booms and busts in pastoralism and agriculture, Australia continued from the mid-nineteenth century to the mid-twentieth century to rely upon its coastal and inland farming regions for export income. This necessitated the continued destruction of native vegetation. Ringbarking was the favoured means of tree removal during the 1800s. While those on the land saw positive benefits of new streams and creeks developing as a consequence of tree clearing (Reeve, 1988) we recognise today that this 'extra' water had its downside in severe gully erosion and salinisation.

By the early twentieth century it was recognised that the impacts of tree clearing, overstocking, overgrazing, the bare fallowing of soil, together with the introduction of rabbits and exotic vegetation such as the prickly pear had caused enormous environmental damage. Yet, rising prices for wool and wheat ensured that the pursuit of 'family farming' would continue unabated. According to Dovers (1992) the establishment of the Commonwealth Wheat Board, Soldier Settlement Schemes, and the general state support for farming provided a strong basis for continued agricultural and pastoral activity, with farming moving further into the arid parts of the nation. The 'problems' of agriculture were not to be solved by abandoning certain practices, but by intensifying them or introducing new ones which carried the authority of 'modern science'.

It has been argued by Raby (1996) that adaptability and innovation – both 'driven' by the market imperative of profitability – were the keys to Australia's success as an agricultural exporting nation, and that 'such creativity was essential for the profitable exploitation of the land's riches'. 'Profitable exploitation' is an apt phrase here. For while Raby refers to the combination of technical and institutional creativity as the main features of the 'making' of rural Australia, what has subsequently been shown is that it has also been its unmaking. Under Federation the Australian States retained responsibility for primary production. Each recognised not only that the further expansion of agriculture would require scientific research, but that if they were to remain internationally competitive they would need to develop an elaborate system of farm extension.

During the 1930s – and with graphic recognition of the dustbowl conditions caused, in part, by the farmers' responses to falling prices in the Depression – government action was taken to seek solutions to Australia's natural resource problems. Why? The problem had become highly visible in the misery of family farming in the Depression years, and was shared by the urban population who saw the visible signs of an unsustainable agriculture in the dust-storm clouds that passed through the capital cities of the nation. It was this concern about a national problem – the generalised nature of environmental 'risk' – that was the basis for popular action. While State governments continued to pursue research and extension, the Federal government went one step further by ensuring its Council for Scientific and Industrial Research (CSIR, later to become the CSIRO) studied the problems of land management (see Reeve, 1988: 45). Unfortunately, this did little to address the underlying causes of unsustainable agricultural practices. For example, in South Australia in the late 1930s a committee recommended that clearing of land be suspended, that revegetation be encouraged and that contour banks be employed on ploughed slopes. What it did not comment upon was the widespread use of bare fallowing for wheat production – the cause of much of the soil loss and more general gully and other erosion (see Reeve, 1988: 50). The basic problem of the conflict between private need (increased output from privately-held property) versus public benefit (the conservation of natural resources on those properties and the more general preservation of the environment) was at the heart of the dilemma then, as it is now.

After World War II the pronounced and accumulated problems of environmental degradation were viewed as a national concern. Legislation at the State level sought to enforce rehabilitation of damaged areas via soil conservation measures. But the markets again had their way with policy. From 1950 to the mid-1970s agriculture prospered. It was a period of economic expansion and the creation of considerable wealth, albeit under the mantle of state protection and subsidisation. Britain demanded Australia's food and fibre as it tried to build its postwar economy. Australia's domestic market burgeoned via migration and the baby boom. The rise of Japan as a major importer of Australian agricultural production buoyed the farm economy. Finally, the government's belief that decentralisation of population would be healthy both for regional development and for defence ensured that rural and regional Australia shared in the benefits which were part of postwar prosperity (see Lawrence, 1987).

In most States the areas sown to cropping grew. Sheep and beef numbers increased dramatically and new lands – often in the more marginal climatic areas – were brought into production. The requirement was to supply the marketplace and to ensure economic growth through agricultural (and later, mining) exports. To allow this to occur the contradictory legislative demands to conserve the soil, yet to intensify farming (and to clear new lands, yet to preserve biodiversity), served largely to foster among primary producers an attitude that they could do what they wished with their land. The subsidies and concessions which farmers 'won' from the urban taxpayers were used to provide new chemical inputs, and new machinery, to further 'exploit' the nation's resources.

What Australia currently boasts is a farming and grazing industry of some 115 000 commercial enterprises occupying about 60 per cent of the country's landmass and consuming 72 per cent of the nation's water. Its gross farm gate value in 1998–99 was $28 billion, but when input costs of $24.1 billion are taken out, the net value of agriculture to the nation stands at $3.9 billion (National Farmers' Federation and Australian Conservation Foundation, 2000; Price, 2000). Land degradation is estimated to cost the nation some $3.5 billion annually, and according to the NFF and the Australian Conservation Foundation, over $6 billion will be needed each year for at least ten years to combat environmental degradation (*Australian*, 19 August 2000: 23; AIFF/ACF, 2000; Standing Committee on Environment, Recreation and

Arts, 2001: 11). This system of production would not only seem financially suspect, but also environmentally unsustainable. What has underpinned this system? Why has Australia persisted with it? Are there alternatives?

The Entrenchment of Productivist Agriculture

Australian agriculture was in the past, as it is now, driven by the forces of capital accumulation. Capitalism ensures that, while regulation might be necessary to smooth the contours of capitalist development, owners of the means of production are more or less free to use combinations of capital and labour in ways which will ensure profit. Profit is essential to continued 'reproduction' of the enterprise. Growth in technology is viewed as the key to increased profit. Fundamental to technological development has been the application of science – something which, up until recent decades, has been largely underwritten by the state. Yet, a great many of the environmental problems faced by regional Australia are a direct outcome of the application of science within the framework of capitalism (see Lawrence, 1987). Basically, the application of science has placed farmers on a technological treadmill, one which requires the use of ever-increasing and potent chemicals and artificial fertilisers to ensure continuity of production (Lawrence, 1987; Hindmarsh, 1994; Gray and Phillips, 1996; Black et al., 1999; Drummond and Marsden, 1999; but for criticism see Buttel, 1998). It has also contributed to increased specialisation, and scale, in agriculture (Foster and Magdoff, 1998).

'Reductionism' has become a pejorative term used to describe scientific approaches which seek to obtain 'true' knowledge by breaking entities into their component parts and explaining behaviour as a result of the structure and actions of those components. In biology, for example, reductionism occurs when scientists attempt to explain the actions of organisms by studying the 'elementary physio-chemical processes occurring at the level of atoms and molecules' (see Wills, 1998: 66). Once components are identified, larger-scale processes can be controlled via manipulation of those components (Crook, 1998). Importantly, this approach has been seductive: modern science has progressed up to this point by applying such techniques. The problem here is that a more holistic understanding of the entire organism is usually forsaken, and the details of the micro-level processes are viewed as the best means science has for explaining biological behaviour (Ho, 1998).

The twisted thinking which ignores the integrity of biological systems and the complexities of human/natural resource relations remains a solid part of modern agriculture. In seeking to overcome falling profits (usually resulting from world oversupply, itself a product of a largely anarchic system which fails to meet widespread human need) scientists look at the individual 'components' of the system of agriculture. Crops are sprayed with chemicals to prevent insects from devouring the plants; artificial fertilisers are spread on fields to maximise plant growth; animals are placed in feedlots to maximise the food-to-meat conversion ratio; and so on. By looking at the discrete elements of production rather than the entire system, the outcomes are more virulent pests, fertiliser/chemical pollution of the environment, and animal waste in vast quantities – all contributing to the continuation of an unsustainable agriculture. The 'experts'

– those at least partly responsible for the current trends – implicitly treat the non-expert world as 'epistemically vacuous' (see Wynne, 1996; and see also Grove-White, 1996). It appears local knowledges have little place in science.

It is sobering to remember that the 'environment' was not part of political discourse in Australia until the 1960s (Dryzek, 1997). Since then the environmental consequences of pro-ductivist agriculture have been shown to be quite profound and there has been an effort by the state to embrace environmental issues. Ecology was similarly not viewed as an accepted disci-pline until relatively recently. What ecologists have been able to show is that environmental degradation is not an accident. Rather, it is seen to follow logically from the structure of pro-duction and the application of reductionist science and its agricultural corollary – the intensi-fication/industrialisation of modern farming (Drummond and Marsden, 1999). Here are some of the main features:

- The separation of people from the land, as well as animals from pastures, creates the require-ment for the application of nutrients. In the absence of the recycling of human waste (which is accumulated in, and disposed of from, the cities), the farms must depend upon synthetic nutrients
- Monocultures are a consequence of the economic desirability for specialisation in crop production (there are equivalents with animal specialisation in feedlot beef and inten-sive pig and poultry production). Because they are simplified agronomic systems mono-cultures encourage pests in vast proportions. This, in turn, requires widespread chemical applications
- The development of agrichemicals including their shipping and application is highly energy-intensive. Furthermore, synthetic fertilisers, such as nitrogen, are derived from non-renewable resources, the production of which contributes to global warming
- When applied to farmlands, the soluble fertilisers, herbicides and pesticides usually produce the desired effect of increased output, but they do little to ensure that soil structure is enhanced. In fact, since there is no longer any need to gain nutrients from rotation of crops, soil quality deteriorates. These chemical applications also have the unintended conse-quences of stream contamination and the destruction of natural habitats
- Pesticides can also produce resistance in insects and other pests. The farmer is then left with little choice but to apply ever-more-toxic chemicals in subsequent seasons thereby exacer-bating downstream effects, placing both the farmer and farmworker at a significant health risk, and contaminating foodstuffs destined for the marketplace. In the United States between 50 and 70 per cent of nutrients that reach surface waters have been derived from fertilisers. The high nitrate levels in some waterways and drinking wells have been associ-ated with stomach, bladder and oesophageal cancers in adults. They also cause algal blooms which are themselves poisonous to wildlife, stock and to humans (Altieri, 1998)
- Where animals are separated from the land and produced under large-scale 'factory farm' conditions there is the need to supplement their diets with a variety of antibiotics. These sometimes find their way into the food cycle. And, in some more dramatic cases the feeding of animal dung or offal to other species, within systems of intensive production, leads to quite serious problems for both animals and humans (as with spongiform encephalopathy – the so-called 'mad cow' disease)

- Despite the previous productivity benefits associated with a monocultural system of production, the efficiency of applied agrichemical inputs is decreasing and the yields in most crops have reached a plateau (see Altieri, 1998). While this might mean the questioning of the entire system of production based on scientific, but faulty, logic, the challenge for science is interpreted as one of finding novel ways to make plants respond better. The harnessing of molecular biology is seen as the next logical step, but the environmental consequences of widespread application of genetically-modified organisms is seen by many as an environmental threat (see Ho, 1998; Altieri, 2000; Hindmarsh and Lawrence, 2001)
- The 'generalisation' of competition as a result of globalisation has tended to increase specialisation along with the environmentally-damaging 'externalities' as agrifood networks seek to escape state-based regulation which might limit their profit-making opportunities (Buttel, 1998; Burch, forthcoming).

When expert knowledge is wedded to a reductionist paradigm, funded by private capital, endorsed by the state, and generalised through processes of globalisation, the scientific discoveries which follow will be biased toward the perpetuation of a system which strengthens global agribusiness while marginalising and eliminating alternative approaches (Grove-White, 1996; Drummond and Marsden, 1999; Held et al., 1999). It would appear unlikely that the emerging global order has the capacity to produce sustainable outcomes on a world scale (see Buttel, 1998).

Environmental Degradation in Australia

The current practices of Australia's farmers and graziers have been shown to be unsustainable in the longer term (Conacher and Conacher, 1995; Vanclay and Lawrence, 1995; Price, 1998; AFFA, 1999). Australia is the world's driest continent with seven-tenths of its landmass classified as arid or semi-arid. Although only 10 per cent is classed as arable, some 60 per cent is used for agriculture or grazing. The soils are old and weathered. They are of low fertility and highly susceptible to erosion. This might not, in conditions where soil formation rates are high, present a problem. The reality is that for most of the continent, soil formation is virtually non-existent (Price, 1998). On present estimates Australia accounts for about 20 per cent of soil loss worldwide, and from an area only 5 per cent of the world's total (Lowe, 1998: 73).

Since European settlement some 70 per cent of Australia's native vegetation has been cleared or thinned, much of this – with the aid of modern technology – in the past fifty years. Clearing is occurring three times faster than planting (Stone, 1999). It is estimated that the 2.5 million hectares of Australian land affected by salinity will grow to more than 15.5 million hectares if current farming and land clearing practices are not halted. It is believed to be only a matter of decades until more than 50 per cent of native woodland bird populations will have become extinct (National Farmers' Federation and Australian Conservation Foundation, 2000).

The Murray–Darling Basin (MDB) is of particular concern. Stretching from Charleville to Adelaide it is widely regarded as the nation's most productive agricultural region. It has also been described as Australia's largest 'sewer', containing the nation's most degraded lands and waterways (see Lawrence and Vanclay, 1992). The safety of domestic as well as stock water is under constant threat from algal blooms (there were some fifty outbreaks in 1997 (see Bowmer, 1998)). Tree clearing, together with 'high tech', productivist, agricultural practices have resulted in extensive salinity and soil degradation. Declining yields, fewer crop varieties and the death of vital micro-organisms in the soil are but some of the consequences. Reduction in biodiversity, and species decline have been others. Within the MDB some thirty-seven plant species and twenty-two species of birds and reptiles are presently on the endangered list. Half of the native vegetation in the MDB has disappeared while less than a tenth survives in the sheep-wheat region (MDB Ministerial Council, 1990; Vanclay and Lawrence, 1995).

The loss of natural vegetation and wildlife and of biodiversity is very difficult to 'cost' in monetary terms, but once a particular species is removed the ecosystem is altered in fundamental ways. As Friedmann (2000) has suggested, the protection of polycultural ecosystems is essential to environmental integrity and human progress. Lest we think this is a major problem for Australia alone, McMurtry (1998: 152) has reminded us:

> The world's system of food supply is dominated by a few corporately owned product-lines in a narrow range of artificially cultivated environmental conditions. Of seventy-five types of vegetables available at the beginning of the twentieth century, about 97 per cent of the varieties of each type are now extinct. At the same time thousands of local varieties of rice, wheat, and maize (and potato) ... have been eliminated. In India, for example, thirty thousand different varieties of rice have been replaced by ten varieties across three-quarters of this diverse country.

It is not only biodiversity that is of concern as productivist agriculture takes hold. Waterways are polluted, salinisation increases as trees are felled, and pesticide applications increase. To return to the MDB, there are severe problems with its water due, largely, to intensive irrigation and poor farming practices. In dry seasons, the salinity levels in bores have been found to exceed those recommended by the World Health Organization (Beale and Fray, 1990). It is estimated that the Murray River carries over 1.3 million tonnes of salt each year and there has been concern about the safety and quality of Adelaide's water supply (*Australian*, 12 April 2000: 7). Turbidity, industrial waste and sewage, agrichemicals and weeds and toxic blue-green algae affect the MDB's rivers and creeks.

An inescapable outcome of the processes of soil and water degradation has been a reduction in farm income of millions of dollars per annum. Landscape amenity is also lost (AFFA, 1999). On top of this millions of dollars are spent attempting to overcome or ameliorate environmental degradation. The Federal government's most recent $1.5 billion plan to address dryland salinity and to improve water quality has been criticised by the CSIRO for failing to tackle the main concern: continued unsustainable use of natural resources. Growing more trees to arrest salinity should not occur independently of the introduction of new cropping systems (for example, use of deep rooting crops which capture water) and the supplementation of farm incomes with monies earned from the adoption of more ecologically-sound practices (*Australian*, 12 October 2000: 2).

Part of the problem relates to difficulties in perception by those using resources (Barr and Cary, 2000). In the case of water-use by individual farmers, incremental pollution or land abuse may seem minor – only to prove disastrous when they impact downstream. Rural producers may not be able to 'see' the problem because it is cumulative and its effects are felt well beyond the farm paddock. The annual cost of unsustainable farming (*Australian*, 19 August 2000: 23) includes: waterlogging and salinity ($380m); soil erosion, compaction and structural decline ($280m); acidification ($300m); loss of applied fertilisers ($250m); and the treatment of deteriorating water supplies ($450m) (Price, 1998; *Australian*, 19 August 2000: 23). Over 60 per cent of broadacre and dairy farmers have reported 'significant' land degradation on their properties (Gleeson and Topp, 1997). In addition to this, Robertson (1997) reported that approximately 80 per cent of broadacre agriculture was unprofitable during the 1990s suggesting the futility of continuing with a system of production which both degrades the natural resource base, and fails to provide a decent income to producers.

It is true that these problems are being addressed both on and off the farm. Doubts have been raised as to whether the current support by government via Landcare, Bushcare, other Natural Heritage Trust funded projects and other schemes will be sufficient to overcome the complexity of problems which have developed over generations of farming with the Federal government looking for innovative and alternative ways of managing the nation's natural resources (AFFA, 1999; 2000; Standing Committee on Environment, Recreation and the Arts, 2001). Some of the suggestions for better resource management include:

- Placing taxes on foods so that consumers pay the 'real cost' of food production, and those taxes are paid directly back to regional groups to initiate sustainable development
- Banning the clearing of all native vegetation for a ten-year period
- Requiring all landholders to develop integrated farm plans within a specified period
- Allowing only those landholders with integrated farm plans to access government agency – and other – support
- Providing incentives to landholders via stewardship payments
- Developing, through action learning groups involved in systems-based approaches to problem solving, an understanding of regional problems and issues and initiating plans to address them
- Incorporating Indigenous ideas and practices into landscape management
- Moving from 'farm management' to 'ecosystem management' – removing current farming and grazing activities from the landscape, and growing trees (for salinity control and as part of carbon trading). Carbon trading is expected to be a $100 billion a year industry worldwide within the next decade
- Making funding available to regional catchment groups to develop and implement community-owned strategies for sustainability (see *Courier Mail*, 25 March 1998: 4; Goldney and Bauer, 1998; Ison, 1998; Midmore, 1998; Robertson and Pratley, 1998; Sachs et al., 1998; AFFA, 1999, 2000; *Australian*, 20 November 1999: 23; Langton, 2000; NFF/ACF, 2000; Standing Committee on Environment, Recreation and the Arts, 2001).

Since the 1990s Australian governments have begun to recognise the increasing severity of environmental degradation (AFFA, 2000). They have expressed support for the principles of ecologically sustainable development (see Diesendorf and Hamilton, 1997) and have encouraged rural producers to adopt better management practices. One national farm survey (see Reeve and Black, 1993) has shown that some 90 per cent of Australian producers acknowledge that agricultural land is degraded, 83 per cent believe they have an obligation to the wider community to manage land wisely, and 77 per cent indicate they are prepared to reduce their income slightly to improve environmental outcomes. The attitudes might be the right ones, but they come up against another – that of maximising profit which is the over-riding goal of some 60 per cent of Australian producers (see Reeve and Black, 1993). The latter subsumes the former, with resources continuing to be (mis)managed by producers who are either unable or unwilling to alter the current trajectory of productivist agriculture.

Farmers face pressures that flow from changes in the global agrifood system and from the subsequent responses of Federal and State governments (Burch et al., 1996; 1998; 1999). Transnational capital is ensuring that Australian agriculture is 'market responsive'. By the early 1990s sophisticated management regimes and the application of inputs from industrial agribusiness already allowed just one-fifth of farmers to produce about four-fifths of Australian agricultural output (*Australian Farm Journal*, February 1992).

The 'struggling' farmers are often aware of how they can alter production to reduce environmental degradation, but sometimes this requires substantial investment which may not be possible. Instead, producers place the short-term objective of staying in farming ahead of wider considerations of long-term sustainability (Cameron and Elix, 1991; Vanclay and Lawrence, 1995), with some knowingly 'exploiting' resources as a means of fulfilling their main aim of continuing in farming. As Drummond and Marsden (1999: 214–15) have sug-gested of the Australian sugar industry:

> The outcome of (modernisation) has been a range of increasingly profound environmental impacts and the progressively severe exploitation and eventual disenfranchisement of a large number of farmers ... It is easy enough to under-stand why individual farmers faced with unserviceable levels of debt tend to resort to pragmatic measures with scant regard for their long term in often desperate attempts to meet their immediate commitments ... The dynamic and transforma-tional nature of the global sugar economy has been a significant causal factor underpinning unsustainable events in Queensland.

This statement is as true of most agricultural industries as it is of sugar. The point is, continued exploitation of natural resources can be 'rational' in terms of the producer's immediate goal to stay in agriculture, even though it might be completely irrational from a broader perspective (see Vanclay and Lawrence, 1994).

Genetic Engineering: The Latest in Productivist Agriculture?

One of the key questions of the new millennium is whether or not biotechnologies can pro-vide the key to sustainable agriculture. Another is: can organic agriculture be part of any realistic 'future' for farming? If the answer to the first is 'yes', and to the second 'yes', then a third is: can there be an environmentally-friendly biotechnology which can aid organics to produce a genuinely sustainable agriculture? It appears that governments are endorsing a 'biotech future' without giving consideration to the latter two questions.

While conventional breeding programs have enabled scientists to make incremental improvements to crops, pastures and animals, biotechnology – and specifically genetic engineering as the most potent new tool in the biotechnologist's laboratory – promises quite spectacular gains in output and efficiency for farmers facing the pressures of international competition. Australia might be 'left behind as a competitor and exporter' if it fails to embrace genetic engineering (*Australian Farm Journal*, December 1998: 32). The food industry – responsible for converting, storing, packing and selling the products of agriculture – faces many of the same pressures as the farmers. It has to compete with overseas products often 'dumped' on international markets, and must find means of ensuring that exported foods remain appealing to consumers in distant locations. This means preventing spoilage, increasing shelf life, and enhancing flavour – all within a competitive pricing regime. Here, genetic engineering is being heralded as a revolutionary new way to attain efficiency gains in farming and food processing along with environmental improvements.

The promises of the application of modern biotechnologies in the agricultural and food industries include: improved plant and animal health (including resistance of plants and animals to diseases, pests and environmental extremes); the production efficiency of crops, pastures and animals; production efficiencies in food processing; improvement to the quality of food and agricultural products; development of new products and processes (such as novel foods and biological pesticides); enhanced animal welfare; and benefits to the environment through the reduction in the use of pesticides and fertilisers (Krimsky and Wrubel, 1996; Lee, 1992; Biotechnology Australia, 1999; Lyons and Lawrence, 1999).

The promises are spectacular, with many people standing in awe of the productive power of bio-science. The genetic engineers have been busy in their laboratories inventing new and unusual transgenic combinations: inserting pea genes into rice (to add new protein), trout genes into catfish (to increase the growth of the latter), flounder genes into a tomato (to increase shelf life and improve flavour), and chicken genes into a potato (to increase disease resistance) (see Norton et al., 1998). They have bred a 'headless frog', whose organs will grow as long as the body is fed intravenously (Hindmarsh et al., 1998: 5). What should be remembered is that increases in output together with increases in production efficiency not only allow for, but actively enhance, the current trajectory of productivist agriculture. While some of the experiments appear to be capable of moving producers away from chemical dependency, and of improving the environment, others appear to reinforce broader tendencies towards specialisation, intensification and increasing agricultural surpluses (see Lyons and Lawrence, 1999; Hindmarsh and Lawrence, 2001).

There is a particular concern that genetically-engineered products will become part of the seed/chemical packages of large transnational corporations and that genetic engineering will conform to, rather than challenge and overcome, agriculture's present chemical reliance (Hindmarsh et al., 1998; Australian Conservation Foundation, 1999). There is also the concern that through recent World Trade Organization agreements (such as the Sanitary and

Phytosanitary Standards and the Agreement on Trade Related Intellectual Property (TRIPS)) the stage is being set for a corporate-driven 'second green revolution' which will spread biotechnology, and genetically-modified foods, globally (Shrybman, 1999).

Many biotechnologists believe their experiments are destined to be the saviour of humankind as world population burgeons, demand for food increases, and greater pressure is placed on the environment, while ecologists argue that agrosystem health will be further compromised as transgenic crops lead to insect resistance, to the reduction of biodiversity and ecosystem complexity, threaten soil biota and create so-called 'superweeds' (see Altieri, 2000). Yet, many biotechnologists consider that the people opposing genetic engineering are simply ignorant of the technology, that information campaigns are necessary to 'educate' the public, or that 'lead in' time is needed for countries such as Japan and those of Europe to accept the genetically modified products (see for example, Peacock, 1994; 1998). What does the public think of such work?

From work undertaken in Australia (see Norton, 1998) and from overseas (INRA, 1991; Nottingham, 1998) it would appear that while people approve of certain scientific activities (bacterial and plant biotechnologies, and genetic engineering for human and animal health, for example), they are very much less supportive of the genetic manipulation of foods. Findings from an A. C. Nielsen poll in Australia revealed that only 27 per cent of Australians surveyed indicated that they would buy genetically modified foods (*Sydney Morning Herald*, 24 July 2000: 1). If European and North American results can be taken as a guide, the more that people are informed of the genetic engineering of food, the less they are prepared to support it – the opposite, in other words, of what has been predicted by the bio-scientists. Consumers are demanding 'natural' products. They appear to be increasingly concerned about both the moral acceptability, and potential risks, of some new products and processes (Decima Research, 1993; Wagner et al., 1997) and seem to be highly sceptical of the supposed benefits of genetically engineered foods (Norton, 1998). Importantly, there is evidence that the public in Australia and overseas want all biotechnologically-derived foods labelled (Norton, 1998; Australian Conservation Foundation, 1999) so that they can make informed choices in the supermarket aisles.

What the scientists generally fail to appreciate is that we now live in what has been termed a 'risk society' (Beck, 1992; 2000). In the previous 'industrial' society concerns were for a fair distribution of wealth, but in a risk society the so-called externalities of technological development affect entire regions of the world, and people cannot escape from potential harm because of their wealth, class or political connections. Risk society is confronted by the consequences of the products of its own making. When a cloud from a nuclear meltdown spreads across the countryside it has the potential to damage everything in its way (spatially) and for many years (temporally). All citizens are subject to risk, whether it be from pollutants in drinking water and in streams, from chemical residues on foods, or from toxins in the air (Beck, 1992; Crook, 1998). That these may not be readily perceived, that they are 'hidden' from view, makes them even more invidious. People become anxious about their health and that of their children, and there is a particular concern about the growth of agro-industrialism and its ecological impacts (McMichael, 1997). They become suspicious of a science that promises much, but produces side-effects which may act to destroy life itself.

Greening and the Organic Option

What has been confirmed by sociologists and which (some would suggest) is a direct response to risk, is the progressive 'greening' of western society (Harper, 1993; Brand, 1997). In seeking to minimise risk, voters are demanding that governments embark on pro-environmental programs which not only address previous environmental destruction but will also prevent further damage from occurring. 'Greening' is employed to describe the process of change in the guiding ideologies and socio-economic practices of people and communities as they incorporate concerns about environmental health (see Burch et al., 1999). It is not to be confused with the 'simple' lifestyle so much desired by libertarian 'back to nature' movements, but has at its centre a technical and aesthetically sophisticated appreciation of the need for alternative energy sources, reduction in pollution, and improvement of human health and life-chances (see Brand, 1997).

A growing environmental consciousness is linked directly to the evolution of the 'ecological citizen', someone who:

> takes responsibility for the place where he or she lives, understands the importance of making collective decisions regarding the commons, seeks to contribute to the common good, identifies with bioregions and ecosystems rather than obsolete nation-states or transnational corporations, considers the wider impact of his or her actions, is committed to mutual and collaborative community building ... and acts according to his or her convictions (Thomashow, 1995: 139).

The consumption of organic products has been connected with these changes. Yet, organic producers face the wrath of those who want to ensure organics retains its marginalised position, so that there is no doubt in the minds of governments or consumers about the need for continuation with high-production chemical farming. In his provocatively titled *Saving the Planet with Pesticides and Plastic*, Avery (1995) argued that organic farming produces lower and erratic yields, is incapable of sustaining soil fertility, increases soil erosion, cannot result in any 'natural' balance between production and pests, and has no ability whatsoever of providing a foundation for feeding the world's burgeoning population. These assumptions would appear to be shared by a large number of scientists who tend to believe that organic production is a quaint, self-sufficient option for 'greenies', and that export-producing nations could never base their export income upon organics. Indeed, Youngberg et al. (1993: 298) have suggested that organic agriculture is a 'primitive, backward, nonproductive, unscientific technology suitable only for the nostalgic and disaffected back-to-the-landers of the 1970s'.

The organic movement can be viewed as a good example of the transition from modernity to reflexive modernity, characterised by the politicisation of consumption and of science, and 'doing one's own thing' as part of individualisation (see Beck, 1992; but see, for a different interpretation, Kaltoft, 1999). A 'green' environmental consciousness – present in Australia as much as anywhere else in the world – has encouraged the development of what are perceived to be less-polluting forms of farming (Thomashow 1995; Eder, 1996). In this sense, western 'greening' has allowed organics to emerge as a realistic alternative to conventional agriculture.

The world market for organic foods is estimated to be some $15 billion but this is expected to grow to $100 billion toward the end of the first decade of this century (see Segger, 1997). Demand for organic foods has been increasing at an annual rate of between 20 and 30 per cent in Australia (*Acres Australia*, July 2000: 1). Currently there are only about 2000 registered organic producers/retailers/wholesalers/exporters handling some $200–250 million in produce per year (Kinnear, 1999). Approximately $30–40 million is currently exported. Yet, consumers who purchase organics will pay up to 35 per cent more for those foods over conventionally produced foods for reasons of perceived personal health, to avoid the supposed risks of eating 'factory' foods, and for a more sustainable environment. If organic foods were the same price as conventionally-produced foods, some 6 in 10 consumers would purchase organic products instead of those produced by conventional agriculture (see Kinnear, 1999).

Two related factors – health/food security issues and the rise of 'green protectionism' (see Campbell and Coombes, 1999; Lakin and Shannon, 1999) – are viewed as important elements in the move to organics. Premium prices for organic foods in countries like Japan (where the market is estimated to be some A$40 billion) has demonstrated to Australian and New Zealand producers, and particularly New Zealand transnationals, that the export of organics is an important 'keyhole' market channel (see Monk, 1999; Penfold and Miyan, 1998). Despite this, growth has been limited in Australia. A prediction at the beginning of the 1990s that some 2.5 per cent of Australia's broadacre farm land would be turned over to organic production (Hassal and Associates, 1990) appears to have fallen well short of the mark (see Lyons and Lawrence, 1999). In contrast, in New Zealand, transnational companies are imploring rural producers to convert to the new corporate-linked form of organic production.

Is Australia failing to see the future? It appears that the processing and retailing sectors of corporate agribusiness are beginning to lose interest in genetically modified foods and appear to believe the marketing of 'clean and green' foods will provide the best basis for long-term profit-making. This so-called 'corporate greening' is not happening by accident, but rather, in accordance with the explicit demands of consumers. With their strict production guidelines and chemical-free status, organic products are viewed by the supermarket chains as one of the best means of obtaining premiums on foods sold in their stores (see Burch et al., 1998). Companies, such as the United Kingdom's Sainsbury, have accepted that they must move back into the chain of production and distribution to ensure that the products on their shelves are grown in ways that prevent soil loss, reduce chemical use, and are transported in ways which limit the use of fossil fuels (see Burch et al., 1999). While it is probably best to be largely cynical about the 'real' meaning of such corporate greening (see Beder, 1997) it does appear, *prima facie*, to represent a positive outcome for producers, consumers and the environment.

There is another element in the move toward organics – that of 'green protectionism'. According to New Zealand social scientists Hugh Campbell and Brad Coombes (1999) (but also see also Price, 1998; *Background Briefing*, 1999), there is evidence that as a global free(er) trade regime emerges, some nations wanting to protect their producers will resort to non-tariff trade barriers. Green protectionism includes reducing so-called maximum residue levels for chemicals in imported products and claiming that imported products are produced in environmentally suspect ways (Campbell and Liepins, 1999). One of these might be whether food imports are 'non-polluted', where pollution might be extended to include the presence of genetically-modified materials. A nation such as New Zealand would be well placed to declare itself 'GMO Free' (free of genetically modified organisms) to take greater advantage of its already well-defined clean and green image. Like New Zealand, Australia's products are destined for increasingly demanding, yet fickle, markets. New Zealand appears to have chosen an 'organic' course and Australia a 'biotechnological' course. It is too early to tell which might prove the more strategically viable for Australia's farmers and regional communities.

A final point relates to the policies of the World Trade Organization (WTO) – the body which replaced the General Agreement on Tariffs and Trade (GATT) in 1995 as the global entity responsible for developing and enforcing trade rules. The new Millennium Round (the so-called Seattle Round, or 'Green' Round) will commit its 137 members to certain actions. Australia argues, as it has in the past, that trade barriers should be reduced (it is estimated that if all trade barriers were removed Australia would receive an extra $7.5 billion in benefits, and the world some $1 trillion (*Australian*, 27 November 1999: 1)) The Europeans, in particular, argue that they are not protecting farmers through subsidisation, but rather protecting rural village life and the environment. The Europeans have advanced the argument that Australia is 'subsidising' agricultural production by allowing producers to exploit the environment (*Background Briefing*, 27 June 1999). The phrase used for imposing costs on the environment by farming unsustainably and, in so doing, subsidising exports is termed 'ecological dumping' (Hamilton, 1996a). If, as appears to be the case, the WTO has the power to ban food exports from nations which are deemed to be involved in 'ecological dumping', or are viewed as farming in an unsustainable manner, what might this mean for Australian exports? One might then expect organic production to have a major competitive advantage over productivist agriculture.

The challenge for Australia will be to identify those elements of biotechnology which are unambiguously acceptable to consumers, farmers, and other stakeholders, and to find ways to harness those new technologies in aiding the organics industry to become more financially viable, and for farming to become more sustainable. Indeed, without this (some would say 'unholy') alliance there is little prospect that consumers will obtain the foods they want, or that agriculture will address the environmental and other problems it currently faces. There would be no greater irony for Australia's agricultural and food industries than that of the achievement of spectacular productivity and efficiency gains obtained from genetic engineering – in the context of widespread and deep-seated consumer rejection of those products.

The Prospects for Sustainable Agriculture in Australia

At present sustainability is an ill-defined concept. What, precisely, needs to be sustained? And at what level? These are questions which beg answers (Eder, 1996; Price, 1998; Dale and Bellamy, 1998; Pepperdine and Ewing, forthcoming). Are we talking of a 'self-sustained economy' – one which would reject *any* form of resource depletion? Given that products such as oil, coal and gas are non-renewable resources we would need to develop alternative sources of energy, or abandon existing economic and social arrangements which require the continued supply of these resources. There is no question that such alternative energy sources are necessary. Yet, most people who mention 'sustainability' really refer to a situation which would sustain their own living standards while improving, or at least not harming, the existing natural environment. So sustainability is already a normative concept. We like what we have now (our living standards and our forests and lakes and waterways) and we want to retain it all (see Dryzek, 1997: 132; Sachs et al., 1998). For those who recognise the rapacious nature of economic systems based on ideologies of growth, this situation is untenable. One theory, then, suggests that since growth is an essential part of capitalism, and capitalism requires ever greater use of resources to counter falling rates of profit and ensure competitive advantage, it will be impossible to talk of 'sustainability' in a growth economy (O'Connor, 1994). Yet, any movement back to peasant-like self-sufficiency has virtually no appeal to people who appreciate the benefits of modern living and who gauge individual success by accumulation of the commodities of industrialisation.

An alternative, powerful, suggestion has been made by Friedmann (2000: 1): grow what is good for the earth; eat what is good to grow; and live in relationships which make the first two possible. Friedmann observes that while these are reasonably simple ideas, they seem to be difficult to achieve in a world where industrial monocultures stifle people's ability to imagine (and embrace) polycultural communities. In somewhat more utilitarian terms, Yearley (1996: 130–1) has defined a social arrangement which is now arguably the future basis for economic production. 'Sustainable development' will be:

> a form of socioeconomic advancement which can continue indefinitely without exhausting the world's resources or overburdening the ability of natural systems to cope with pollution. The key point is often expressed through analogy, by saying that sustainable development means living off the interest of the Earth's natural productivity, without gnawing away at the capital.

This is a laudable sentiment, but it needs refinement. Without falling into the trap of creating 'dualisms' (Goodman, 1997) there is some benefit in considering at least two differing approaches to sustainability (see table 8.1). We could equally call these positions 'reformist' (see McManus, 1999) and 'radical'.

Leaving aside the unsubtle way in which positions are 'typecast' in such a typology, together with the particularly difficult problems of operationalising notions of intergenerational distribution and risk aversion (see Drummond and Marsden, 1999), what is captured in table 8.1 is the very different discourses which are emerging about agriculture (see Palmer and Quinn, 1997) and sustainability (see Dryzek, 1997), as well as the possible agendas which might need to be put in place to ensure sustainable outcomes. Australian governments have embraced and legitimised many elements of 'reformist' sustainability (see left-hand column of table 8.1). Here, discourses contain reference to population pressures, to 'spaceship earth', to the need for 'expert advice' and 'impact assessment'. In a policy sense these ideas find their way into approaches such as 'environmental managerialism' (Redclift, 1987) or what is currently emerging in Europe – 'ecological modernisation' (Dryzek, 1997). These approaches tend to overlook the multidimensional nature of sustainable development (Drummond and

Table 8.1 Different approaches to sustainability

Reformist Sustainability	Radical Sustainability
Anthropocentric – aim is to prevent human society suffering the consequences of environmental degradation	Environment-focused – promotion of an economy and society in harmony with the environment
Acceptance of reductionist science and modern technology	Questioning of reductionist science: desire for 'green' technologies
Intergenerational distribution treated separately	Intergenerational distribution integral to sustainability
Low environmental risk aversion	High environmental risk aversion
Marginal changes to existing systems and institutions required	Shift to new systems and institutions, including new ways of thinking
Sustainability achieved alongside current processes of globalisation	Bioregionalism/localism as the first step in sustainable development: globalisation to be held in check

Sources: Adapted from Hodge and Dunn (1992) reported in Drummond and Marsden, 1999; Dryzek, 1997; Sachs et al. 1998; McManus, 1999.

Marsden, 1999: 206). They tend to trust and involve the experts rather than to seek community involvement, and they form part of a retreat from strong policy initiatives (see Diesendorf and Hamilton, 1997). Moreover, the delivery of policy suffers from the conundrum of administrative rationalism: the more disciplined and focused the organisation or agency, the less likely it is to be able to respond in innovative and clever ways to the complex problems with which it must deal (see Dryzek, 1997: 82, after Torgerson and Paehlke, 1990: 9–10).

A move away from this reformist approach was heralded by the 1999 discussion paper *Managing Natural Resources in Rural Australia for a Sustainable Future* produced by the Federal government's Department of Agriculture, Fisheries and Forestry – Australia (AFFA). It sought to provide a new framework for resource management – one based upon community, business and government partnerships; establishment of appropriate institutional arrangements to devolve authority and power to regional organisations; the empowering of communities to act to bring about sustainable development; to build upon the ethos of Landcare; and to provide incentives and market-based instruments to improve the condition of the nation's resource base (AFFA, 1999). These and other suggestions were subsequently endorsed by the Australian public (see AFFA, 2000) and in the Federal government's National Action Plan for Salinity and Water Quality in Australia (see report in *Australian*, 12 October 2000).

While the community partnership focus is an important new development and represents a serious attempt to engage regional stakeholders with the 'realities' of environmental degradation, it fails to acknowledge the root cause of the problems the nation faces. It fails to understand the trajectory of productivist agriculture and provides few clues as to how regions might abandon unsustainable trajectories. So, while its 'solutions' – about community self-help, empowering the regions, providing regional structures for decision-making, and so forth – are clearly of a more 'radical' type, they do nothing to address the many contradictions of current practices. The whole thrust is one based on the slow reform of a system in desperate need of immediate and profound change. And it is one which the government would like to base on voluntary organisations.

Furthermore, as Barr and Cary (2000: 34) argue persuasively, it is unlikely that 'community action' by itself will generate the needed changes in rural areas. First, given the complex nature of decision-making in farming, there is only a certain extent to which the 'stewardship ethic' can be harnessed to drive the profound changes necessary in thinking and behaviour. Second, many producers, often in the face of evidence to the contrary, perceive environmental problems to be greater on neighbouring properties than on their own. They fail to act. Third, Landcare cannot be expected to be any more widely accepted and effective than it is at present. It is a voluntary scheme which does not accord with the value sets of all rural producers. Only one-third of the nation's producers have been motivated to join Landcare groups and moreover, there is nothing in the Landcare 'movement' to alter the trajectory of productivism. With resource depletion resulting from the nature of property ownership – one in which producers believe they have rights to do as they wish with their own resources in order to maintain an income – no amount of 'moral suasion' or voluntary compliance is likely to alter the present system of production, and therefore to achieve sustainability (Reeve, 1997). Beilin (1997) has suggested that while Landcare increases women's visibility, it acts to limit their role as change agents by prescribing certain activities, while avoiding others. Bailey (1997) and Morrissey and Lawrence (1997) have identified the fissures within Landcare groups, and the way power is exercised at the local level to ensure that groups are either free from, or marginalise, any 'green' agenda which might challenge agricultural practices. In this sense, Landcare is a conservative approach to resource management which denies that local elites can capture the agenda (Gray, 1992) and neglects the pressing need for strong state involvement in the regulation of resources (Buttel, 1998). Fourth, the 'vast majority of broadacre farm businesses do not produce sufficient surpluses to allow for reasonable living standards' (Barr and Cary, 2000: 34), let alone for new investment in resource protection. It is for these reasons that the structural conditions contributing to environmental degradation must be addressed if progress is to be made.

While the approach presented in this book has features of both columns of table 8.1, it certainly favours that of radical sustainability. We have argued that the present directions and structure of science and technology must be questioned; that it is no longer possible to consider the economy and society separately from the environment; and that regional Australia's problems of environmental degradation and rural community decline relate directly to the institutional arrangements currently in place (see Mobbs and Dovers, 1999). A move to new institutional structures and processes would appear to be essential to bring about positive change (see chapter 10). There is a sense of urgency associated with those adhering to the ideas associated with radical sustainability. It would be argued – in contradistinction to AFFA – that 'fundamental' alteration to natural resource management may mean abandoning some institutional structures, not working with them in the hope of 'improving' them.

If sustainability can be considered as a process rather than some fixed 'end point' (see Williams, 1993; Buttel, 1998) then it makes sense to focus, as Drummond and Marsden (1999) have done, upon sustainability trajectories. They criticise the current preoccupation with seeking definitional certitude for a concept as slippery as sustainability as being largely unproductive. Time is spent on securing the best definitions, when what is required is an understanding of development trajectories which produce particular (that is more sustainable, or less sustainable) outcomes. Thus, unsustainable practices are those which are unambiguously more exploitative than those that preceded them. Practices and processes which reduce biodiversity, increase soil erosion, place more chemicals in the environment and increase water turbidity or soil salinity are clearly part of a move to a less sustainable environment. In contrast, the growth of trees, the increase in soil organic matter, retention of remnant vegetation, and increasing levels of micro- and macrobiotic life in soils and waterways would be considered to be features of a more sustainable trajectory (see Grimes et al., 1998; Pratley and Robertson, 1998). The simple principle is that there should be no threat to the integrity of eco-systems (Lowe, 1998: 71). Many rural and regional stakeholders are coming to understand this. It is not difficult, in fact, to produce indicators which are agreed upon by regional stakeholders as those showing the growth or otherwise in sustainable practices (see Taylor et al., 1999; Pepperdine, 2000; Lockie et al., forthcoming). Why, then might unsustainable practices continue?

It has been argued that while there may be a growing awareness of environmental issues and a growing desire to address the actual impacts of environmental degradation, there has been a failure to understand the causes of the problem in Australia (Lawrence et al., 1992; Drummond and Marsden, 1999; Barr and Cary, 2000). It is one thing to clean up a creek or plant more trees, quite another to identify the factors responsible for the widespread and cumulative degradation which are *not* being addressed by local efforts. If the present policies deal with symptoms rather than with causes and if, through deregulation in the context of globalisation, they act to devalue family farm-based agriculture and 'force' producers to act in individually rational ways which are socially irrational, it is unlikely that we will ever move from the current unsustainable trajectories.

It is worth considering Buttel's (1998: 281) point in relation to needed actions from the state:

> Sustainability is in large part a public good ... Similar to other public goods, sustainability must be achieved largely through state action. A cornerstone in the shift toward more sustainable societies will almost invariably be the establishment of incentives (particularly through carbon and other green taxes, polluter-pays principles, and various externality-internalization market mechanisms) and regulations that make unsustainable behaviours costly and that encourage the development of appropriate technologies.

One of the reasons policy has failed to deliver in terms of sustainability is that it tends to compartmentalise 'economy', 'environment' and 'society', rather than understanding the complex linkages between all three. Giving priority to the 'environment' still falls into the same trap. For a number of years we have sought to use the terms 'sustainable rural community' and 'sustainable community development' (see, for example Lawrence, 1990; 1995) as a reminder to those who see sustainability only in environmental or economic terms, as a reminder that there is a social dimension to the debate about future options. Quite simply, natural resource problems have been caused by the actions of people, and it is through an understanding of people's attitudes, values, individual and group behaviour, and the responses made under particular circumstances (that is, within institutional structures and signals) that the keys to solving the problem of environmental degradation will be found.

What is generally recognised is that an integrated approach to regional development will greatly benefit the people of rural Australia and particularly farmers (Lawrence, 1998; Dore and Woodhill, 1999; Woodhill, 1999; AFFA, 1999; 2000). Sustainability of the natural resource base, and of communities, must be the goal. The advantages will be felt Australia-wide, but particularly in the regions. First and most obviously the resource base will remain intact and so provide a stable basis for continued production. Second, the abandoning of environmentally harmful practices will ultimately mean the removal of chemicals from the system. Farmers should save on inputs, thus lowering costs of production and increasing international competitiveness. Third, with 'cleaner' food as one outcome new markets may open up both domestically and abroad. Fourth, some of the new sustainable practices are likely to be labour intensive (and knowledge intensive) which may actually swell numbers involved in agriculture and new service industries, providing new vitality to regional communities. Fifth, some areas will be deemed unsuitable for existing forms of agriculture. Farmers may be retrained by a government which identifies the importance of land and water management as a means of returning degraded environments to their former state. Just as in Europe (see Commins, 1990) farmers may come to see themselves, and be seen by the state, as caretakers of wilderness areas, guides for visitors to the outback or as park rangers (see Lawrence, 1987). Again, this represents new work options in rural areas – part of the so-called 'green' jobs which might arise from altered forms of agricultural production. Sixth, instead of structural adjustment monies being employed in an effort to reduce farm numbers, they might be diverted into schemes which assist producers to engage in cooperative schemes such as syndication or in organic production. A tax rebate might be provided to those whose farming practices are deemed sustainable. AFFA has even suggested the creation of a Land-bank, bringing to the discussion table a 'radical' suggestion made at least a decade earlier (Lawrence, 1987).

Such actions would not only show that the state is behind the move to a more sustainable agriculture but would also show that the state is actually promoting and legitimising certain sustainable options. (It would also be mirroring what is happening in Europe.) This will not simply be about 'picking winners' – something governments are reluctant to do (see Anderson, 1999) – but the state would be intervening to encourage practices which are objectively more sustainable than current ones.

The difficulty with the above suggestions is that they contradict current moves toward a more deregulated system of production and that of endorsing high tech agribusiness-driven solutions to economic problems in farming (Lawrence, 1987; Drummond and Marsden, 1999). Government policy will, in other words, be required to alter significantly to accommodate sustainability. If the sale of much of Telstra and the subsequent creation of the Natural Heritage Trust is to be remembered in a positive way, it might be for the strong refocusing of attention on regional sustainability. That this is not yet perceived to be an outcome represents a failure of government to connect the elements of sustainability and to empower people at the local level to look for local and novel solutions to the problems of catchments.

As we will argue in chapter 10, it is at the regional level of problem identification and decision-making that much of the future 'promise' lies. This realisation has come late in the day for Australia (see AFFA, 1999) but at least it *has* come! Australia must decide how best to assist these regional bodies to function.

Conclusion

This chapter has provided an overview of the environmental dilemma faced by Australia: to continue with an environmentally-unsound productivist agriculture which is consistent with our predetermined 'colonial' role of providing bulk commodities to an unknown global market, or to alter, in a fundamental way, that trajectory. The two choices which are currently presented to Australians are those of moving to a genetically-engineered future for Australian agriculture, or to build a foundation on organic production. A more ambitious 'third' option is to combine the best of biotechnology to assist the development of the organics industry. This is not fanciful. There are techniques within biotechnology which, from the consumers' point of view, are not controversial. Importantly, they do not necessitate creating transgenic plants and animals.

The question raised by those who believe that any 'biotechnology' compromises the integrity of organics is: can organic production in its existing form provide a sound basis for a future agriculture in Australia? The answer which we have at present is 'no'. Some compromise must be reached between the organic purists and the biotechnological elite. This is not the place to outline the contours of engagement, but it is the place to suggest that biotechnology will not go away, that consumers do not want to eat genetically modified foods, and that organic production will struggle unless it can both increase its penetration of consumer markets, and can claim to be the basis for sustainable agriculture.

Past rounds of environmental degradation have not necessarily been caused by neoliberalism. Rather, neoliberalism can be viewed as acting to perpetuate tendencies within capitalism toward environmental destruction. Environmental degradation is serious and widespread. It will not be overcome until there is a move toward the delegitimisation and replacement of current agricultural practices. This might, to the surprise of some, not come from local recognition that land and water management has had some 'negative' outcomes, nor of national recognition that production is occurring in an unsustainable manner, but from the decisions of global regulatory bodies which prevent Australian farm output from entering the world market because it is produced in an unsustainable manner.

We have raised the spectre of green protectionism as a legitimate, worldwide, consumer response to the manipulation of foods by science and industry – both bent on increasing profits in the production and processing sides of agriculture. 'Greening' is viewed as a widespread suspicion of chemical agriculture, and the products that result therefrom. It is seen to be a part of the emerging risk society, where consumers, in their reflexivity, reject the view that more science will provide for increased food security, and where there is a search for alternatives to what is viewed as factory farming and its 'artificial' foods. That Australian governments have been extremely slow to appreciate this is just one more aspect of the nation's global misfortune.

Further Reading

Beder, S. (1996) *The Nature of Sustainable Development*, Second Edition, Melbourne: Scribe.
  – proposes a model for environmental sustainability
Hindmarsh, R., and Lawrence, G. (eds) (2001) *Altered Genes II: The Future*, Melbourne: Scribe.
  – a critical approach to biotechnology
Lawrence, G., Higgins, V. and Lockie, S. (eds) (2001) *Environment, Society and Natural Resource Management: Theoretical Perspectives from Australasia and the Americas*, Cheltenham: Edward Elgar.
  – a collection of papers discussing a range of perspectives on the relationships between society and the natural environment, and the ways those relationships might be managed
White, M. (1997) *Listen ... Our Land is Crying*, Sydney: Kangaroo Press.
  – depicts Australia's rural environmental problems with a plea for change in practices
Yearley, S. (1996) *Sociology, Environmentalism, Globalization: Reinventing the Globe*, London: Sage.
  – discusses perspectives on the relationship between globalisation and the bio-physical environment

We have seen the ways in which regional Australia is bifurcating into two kinds of society. One is globally connected and prosperous while the other is languishing under globalisation and its political concomitant: neoliberalism. We have also seen that regional people are resisting the effects of their dependency and the impacts of uneven development. They appear fixed on a trajectory which maintains an unsustainable productivism. Despite continued resistance they remain constrained by liminality and difficulty in obtaining a reflexivity which will provide a course towards fundamental change to the extent demanded by sustainability. What we are yet to consider is the process of cultural change through which that reflexivity may or may not grow and find direction. It is also worth considering cultural change for its own sake; in order to answer very reasonable questions about the survival of the reality in which Australia's rural cultural tradition has developed.

This chapter examines cultural change, drawing on the term 'detraditionalisation' to delineate possible interpretations and ramifications of cultural change rather than necessarily confirm that any particular path is being followed. In using the concept of 'detraditionalisation', we again encounter the issues of relativism and reflexivity, including that raised by the 'Russian doll' analogy mentioned in chapter 3. Rapid change is occurring in Australian rural culture. More complex questions surround the problem of reflexivity. One question is whether or not regional dwellers are changing their culture and being changed by it in ways that will enable them to break free from metropolitan hegemony and productivism. The concept of detraditionalisation helps us to consider that possibility. Further complexity arises with consideration of the possibility that cultural change is breaking down the institutions and practices which have sustained rural culture. Still more difficulty is encountered when one considers the problem of relativism in the light of the possibility that detraditionalisation is breaking down both the cultural underpinnings which have made rural society distinguishably rural, alongside economic and social processes of restructuring, and the urban–rural differentiation which enables us to confirm reflectively that rural society actually exists as a lived experience. In some ways, we may be seeing the end of rural Australia as we have known it.

We raise three questions:
- are rural people obtaining the reflexivity which is said to come with detraditionalisation and moving to a post-traditional or postmodern society?
- is detraditionalisation destroying rurality's cultural and social distinctiveness, including its social bonding systems, and thereby creating a kind of anomie or normlessness?
- is detraditionalisation also destroying rurality and/or creating a new rurality which is detached from that faced by rural people?

Rural Tradition in the Context of Globalisation

The concept of tradition has from time to time been applied by rural sociologists, but not perhaps as extensively as one might expect, given that agriculture has been seen as an indicative component of 'traditional' societies. Rural societies are often thought to retain features of premodern cultures which are significant to their reflexivity. While industrial societies can be seen as having developed from premodernity (or tradition) through modernisation and now to be entering postmodernity, rural societies have remained in a partly, but not completely, premodern or traditional state associated with their marginal class position, or liminality. The concept of detraditionalisation prompts exploration of any such change in its widest ramifications, drawing attention to the possibility that it could be affecting the underpinnings of rural society in the same way in which changes from premodernity to modernity, or modernity to postmodernity, have affected capitalism and capitalist society.

Early sociological investigations discovered what were thought to be some of the essential characteristics of rural life which were associated with, but not confined to, agriculture. The concept of tradition has been closely and erroneously tied to the concept of the 'rural' by interpreters of early sociologists – notably Ferdinand Toennies. In seeking to understand the vast processes of industrialisation and urbanisation of the eighteenth and nineteenth centuries and with concern for the type of society which was developing, Toennies contrasted traditional and emerging social relations, finding that strong social bonds had been displaced by an impersonal and contractual form of association. This idea was developed into one of the notoriously misleading 'dualisms' of sociology by implying that rural life has retained tradition which would otherwise have been eliminated by urbanisation (see Bell and Newby, 1971). While it is wrong to draw such a simple historical contrast, it is reasonable to propose that people do struggle to retain features of their culture during urbanisation and industrialisation.

In 1994 Buttel contrasted two currently prominent perspectives in the sociology of agriculture: the 'globalisation' and 'local diversity' approaches which bring this struggle into view. The globalisation approach illuminates the structural forces of change, emanating from the interests of transnational capital, while the local diversity view sees the responses which people make to those forces. The globalisation approach focuses on markets and institutions, while the local diversity view sees ideas and culture, including the interactions between cultural change and restructuring.

While confirmation or refutation that farms are being subsumed by capital, either national or transnational, has been difficult to achieve, there is evidence of a process of struggle at the levels of community, family and individual which may have some significance in the broader process of change. The 'coping strategies' literature attributes significance to the people involved in farming (see, for example, Gray et al., 1993). Applications of regulation theory and the concept of a 'contested terrain' have cast light on local farm and community level resistance to global forces acting through capital and the state (Campbell, 1994), providing a global–local dimension to the kinds of reflection and resistance discussed in chapter 7. Global forces may appear to be homogenising, but people's experiences of them may differ.

While global structures can be identified now, global cultures may be only emerging and doing so differently among local communities. Giddens (1994: 101) argues, consistently with Pahl (1998), that under modernisation and consequent ultimate loss of community attachment, local social practices change, becoming 'relics or habits', but remain significant. Featherstone (1993) argues that even amid the forces of transnational media and cultures of consumption, local cultures will remain strong as they provide avenues for the retention and development of personal identities. Kennedy (1997), for example, sees regional communities asserting their tradition in the wake of economic devastation after the moratorium on cod fishing which destroyed the economic basis enjoyed by many Newfoundland communities for centuries. The ways in which tradition is asserted may be very significant to the course of globalisation and its effect on regional society.

The Nature of Tradition

Tradition can be viewed as an historical object or practice, a set of beliefs about the past or an invention of the present claiming to represent the past. The notion of an historical process involving a handing down of culture through the generations is the only essential element. It can encompass 'all accomplished patterns of the human mind, all patterns of belief or modes of thinking, all achieved patterns of social relationships, all technical practices, and all physical artifacts or natural objects' (Shils, 1981: 16). It is also important to note that beliefs about objects and practices as well as the objects and practices themselves can be seen as traditions.

Much of the debate about tradition has centred on the nature of 'traditional' societies. Sometimes tradition is seen as a virtue or even as essential to what gives meaning to life, and at other times it is seen as a hindrance to desired change. Giddens sees tradition as having 'guardians' and a binding force which contains moral and emotional prescriptions connected with a taken-for-granted truth. Tradition in this view is an organising medium for collective memory. This implies that any agent, in a process of social reconstruction of the past, who is able to conduct the organisation of collective memory is placed in a position of power. The guardians are agents of the power of unquestionable truth. In this formulation, the nature of the society is not of such direct concern as the power apparatuses within which tradition is moulded. Tradition, however, remains contestable. MacIntyre (1984: 144) sees conflict as essential, claiming that 'a living tradition then is an historically extended, socially embodied argument, and an argument precisely in part about the goods which constitute that tradition'. Reflexivity arises in the contexts of such argument.

Tradition can be intentionally constructed, or invented (Hobsbawm, 1984), by those powerful enough to win the argument or set an agenda which constricts it. Shils' approach to tradition could not accommodate traditions like the notorious examples of Scottish regalia and the 'ploughman's lunch', which reputedly lack the long historical roots that his definition requires. Giddens, however, takes a different view, believing that what is seen to be authentic is more important than what is authentic. Giddens sees tradition as a medium of identity, fulfilling a personal need for assurance that the world is as it is and remains predictable, or 'ontological security'. The possibility that tradition can become, or be constructed as, a significant resource in power relationships emerges further. Tradition is an important attribute of the relationship between individual people and their society.

Tradition is of interest to analysts of change in farming for three reasons, not including the point that traditional societies have often been seen as consisting predominantly of farmers. As a medium of identity, tradition enables people to act as social beings. When tradition clashes with structure, adverse effects are felt. 'Social dissatisfaction, agrarian political protest, stress symptoms and mental illness in the farming community can be interpreted as expression of their inclusion in alien and in part contradictory social structures' (Pongratz, 1990: 10). Contrarily, tradition also legitimates power structures. When examined together, these attributes of tradition constitute a third reason: it offers a window on reflexivity and the agency which is missing from the globalisation perspective at the same time as it is independent of issues relating to spatial variation.

Theories of Detraditionalisation

In the late 1990s much attention was given to detraditionalisation, of which reflexivity is said to be a central feature. It frees people from social structures and makes them monitor themselves in a process which, on the surface, would appear to give power to individuals (Lash and Urry, 1994: 4). This idea leaves little room for determinant globalisation. Rather, it trains attention on the ways in which people reflect on structures, and act on the basis of such reflection, suggesting an hypothesis to the effect that rural people are achieving a reflexivity which could lead to ideological and social change. This might offer a straightforward way ahead, were it not also for the ambiguity of the structural position of farmers and the dependency of regional communities. The questions still hanging over subsumption theory highlight the persistence of this problem at the same time as they highlight its significance. Subsumption could be seen to hang on reflexivity, each denying the other. If there is no process towards subsumption, there is little to be reflexive about.

While Lash and Urry (1994) see detraditionalisation as individualisation, Shils (1981) sees it as rationalisation fuelled by an ideology of individualism. Either way, its outcome is the replacement of one tradition with another, rather than replacement of tradition with another basis for social organisation. Giddens (1994) sees modernisation as a process of retraditionalisation – not detraditionalisation with rationalisation as Shils suggests – because tradition has been essential to the legitimation of state power. In Giddens' view traditions can even flourish under modernisation because they succeed in defending taken-for-granted truth while avoiding threats amid political competition. Modernity makes adherents justify traditions.

Will emerging traditions become available to everybody? Will all those people who are trying to find an identity in a retraditionalising society necessarily succeed in doing so and be able to participate fully in it? Not necessarily – as some theoreticians and empirical researchers have alerted us. Do individuals escape the authority of tradition altogether? Can new traditions coexist with old, and if so, are they equally strongly adhered to? Heelas (1996) holds that detraditionalisation entails the decline of the belief in the pre-given or natural orders of things. Individual people are themselves called upon to exercise authority in the face of the disorder and contingency which is thereby generated. '"Voice" is displaced from established sources, coming to rest with the self' (Heelas, 1996: 2). If this is so, contrary to Giddens' view, individuals may lose all opportunity to be 'informed by all those sustained voices of external authority which – alone – can give enough "shape" to our lives to enable us to act as identifiable subjects' (Heelas, 119: 9). The questions above boil down to one of determining whether or not there are accepted modes of belief and behaviour which individuals can call upon to shape their own lives.

Farming Tradition

Research focuses on three features of farming tradition: agrarian identity and ideology; social relationships dependent on farming; and farm practices including succession, inheritance and farm knowledge. Farm inheritance is perhaps central to these elements of tradition. The passing of farms, or at least the farming vocation, from generation to generation has sustained the farming tradition alongside an idealised view of agriculture. Agrarian ideology, as discussed in chapter 6, takes an idyllic view of farming life, placing value on self-reliance, frugality, community participation, hard work and stewardship, and avowing a fundamental economic and social role for agriculture. The practice of inheritance along with isolation, differentiation and mutual interdependence has sustained particular forms of social relationships. Knowledge of farming, sometimes known as 'indigenous technical knowledge' (Kloppenburg, 1992) or 'local knowledge' is also transmitted across generations.

Each of these characteristics gives meaning to the practice of farming. Moreover, they create expectations which people can have of themselves and others. The practice of farming has its guardians. Within local communities and across rural Australia it has its iconic individuals, some of whom, like Sir Sidney Kidman and, in a related field, R. M. Williams, have become Giddens' 'guardians'. But when those icons no longer appear to offer a clear relationship with the lived experience of rural people, when the truth of their image of rurality becomes questionable, the reflexivity of detraditionalisation also becomes part of the practice of rural living.

The Detraditionalisation of Farming

Given the importance of tradition to social organisation and the interest which rural sociology has shown in the changing social organisation of agriculture, it is perhaps surprising that farming tradition has not been prominent in the analysis of rural change. This inattention can be explained by the structuralism of the political economy models which gained favour in the 1970s and 1980s. During the twenty-first century in Australia the effects of the degradation of farm land, along with other ecological processes, will depend at least in part on reflexivity associated with detraditionalisation. If enough farmers reflect on their traditional practices associated with productivism as well as the social structural conditions which marginalise them, and change in those structural conditions ensues, there may be prospects for some trend reversals.

Farmers have found their own way through processes of detraditionalisation. The Giddens model would propose that they have defended elements of tradition, redefining them as necessary. They have pursued productivism and persevered on a high-input treadmill, but have retained the family basis of farm operation. Through a rising individualism which has seen state support wither, they have retained their family and community ideology. There is little indication that farming tradition is disappearing. But it is certainly under pressure to change.

Pressure to change, following Shils, can be endogenous or exogenous. That is, it can come either from inside or outside the tradition. In the case of farming as it undergoes rapid change, however, it may be difficult to distinguish between the two. What appears to be exogenous might soon, after negotiation and adaptation, become endogenous. It is necessary to be alert to evidence of the intensification of expressions of cultures, remembering that expressions and affirmations of culture, and culture as the traditional lived experience associated with a particular social structural condition, are different things. Sidney Kidman as the image of the heroic battler who made good through seemingly intolerable conditions and

R. M. Williams as the supplier of the quality equipment needed to achieve such feats, are not the stuff of survival through the globalisation of Australian agriculture in the twenty-first century. Although the entrepreneurship implicit in these two 'legends' is still called for, different qualities and skills are also said to be required. 'Battling' and risk-taking are no longer enough.

Adapting Share et al. (1991), it may be fruitful to consider detraditionalisation in terms of vertical and horizontal orientations. Vertical forces are those of subsumption which push farming into agricultural commodity chains; those which precipitate questioning of traditional practices, ideologies and knowledge. Horizontal forces act spatially, commonly arising from population migration, and change community relations. Ward and Lowe (1994) saw forces of change in both dimensions under globalisation and broader economic restructuring which is placing pressure on intergenerational farm transfer and the migration of environmentally-conscious people concerned about farm practices into farming areas. Yruela (1995) concluded that Spain had lost its traditional rural culture completely through change in both dimensions.

Newcomers

Australian research has shown that community interaction suffers as newcomers from the city, seeking a 'rural lifestyle', do not participate in traditional institutions and are thought, at least by 'locals', not to possess environmental values consistent with farming (Kelly, 1994; Passfield et al., 1996). For Kelly (1994) those same locals, in a peri-urban area, would seek to retain the option of selling land to newcomers at the prices they are apparently willing to pay, thereby confronting themselves with a challenge to their own culture and further rendering their community liable to depiction as 'postagricultural'. Marginalisation of traditional culture as a lived experience appears to be inevitable, yet all parties retain an interest in expression and affirmation of that culture. But one must question its durability in such circumstances. Watkins and Champion (1991) were concerned with change arising from the movement of former urban dwellers into rural areas in Britain. In some of these circumstances, developing social relations can depend on competing identities and processes of identity formation at different geographical levels, such as when urban emigrants bring a national identity, as English people have done in rural Wales, but local identity constructs are also significant (Cloke et al., 1998). Rogers (1991) found that the practice of traditional extended family farming strengthened during the immigration of urban dwellers. The newcomers had challenged old elites, but they used and thereby reinforced traditional claims to status. Such competition can be said to give meaning to community identities and relationships (Marsden et al., 1993).

It can also lead to conflict. In the United States, Salamon and Tornatore (1994) gave the postagricultural community they studied the pseudonym of 'Splitville', such is the extent of social division following an influx of urban poor. The newcomers felt that their property should be granted respect regardless of its use and appearance, contradicting a traditional system of social standing which holds a tidy home to be an indicator of good citizenship. The 'old-timers' found the newcomers to lack a spirit of community. The two groups do not interact, leaving a locality profoundly divided socially. The assertion of tradition which developed during earlier periods of successful farming and associated activity may be stronger than ever among its adherents, but social division is the inevitable result. Again, the durability of the traditional culture is under question, but this is not always necessarily so. Fisher (1997) showed that people moving into a rural area and establishing a new business or even an industry (in this case, craft production) can be marginalised. All that can be said is that tradition comes under question and a power struggle ensues.

Power struggles could also develop over guardianship, rather than the attributes of tradition. This seems eminently possible when tourism is a force for asserting tradition; when the traditions of rural production are turned into resources for the promotion of rural consumption. It was pointed out in chapter 6 that while tourism industries can promote local growth, the benefits do not necessarily flow to the local population. It is also acknowledged that immigrant managers and workers in a tourism industry can bring challenges to local tradition in much the same way as other urban emigrants (Derrett, 1997), some forms of tourism can appropriate tradition constructed over generations of production into commodities for consumption. Control over such appropriations has obvious potential to generate friction, especially if guardianship is claimed by immigrants. Diversification of a local economy can sometimes involve a loss of local control in more direct ways, as tourism was found to imply in a New Zealand community when urban-based firms came to dominate the local economy (Phillips and Campbell, 1993) and alternative industries similarly brought loss of control to local economies traditionally dominated by sugar production in Central Queensland, thereby removing influence over the local community from the cane growers.

If the guardians of tradition and the ideals and images they purvey can retain an uncontradicted counterpart in reality, adherents of tradition would seem more likely to assert their culture, be able to define the local culture and exclude those defined as not adhering to it. They may be able to do so despite contradictions amid the assertions, as Gray (1991) found when many members of a rural community could proclaim family farming ideals and have their protests heard while others with greater problems were ignored. Such situations strengthen tradition, at least temporarily. As apparently occurred in 'Splitville', a stalemate is also possible. Detraditionalisation is a process consisting of power struggles which will not necessarily be resolved in any particular direction, but the process of restructuring, and the real counterparts to tradition, will eventually prevail. The result may be reconstruction of tradition into a form which will survive, and possibly strengthen. But the descendants of those who constructed the traditions of production will lose their capacity when tradition becomes a commodity for consumption.

Australian farmers are facing forces of detraditionalisation which are mostly vertical. The movement of urban dwellers into rural areas is occurring, but not on a large scale overall (see chapter 6). What is making the traditions of production more tenuous, or liable to reconstruction, is the inability of producers to perpetuate them under the rigours of restructuring. The vertical processes are combining with the horizontal.

Farm Succession and Inheritance

Studies of vertical detraditionalisation among farmers make impacts on the specific dimensions of rural tradition more apparent. Intergenerational transfer is the basis of farming practice, including gender relations in the farm family. Stayner (1997b) finds from a large (1250)

Australian sample survey of farms that although 72 per cent of male farmers and 42 per cent of female farmers have grown up on farms, only 41 per cent of parents are encouraging their children to continue in farming. The fact that 29 per cent of Stayner's respondents have had their farms in their families for at least three generations indicates that farm inheritance has remained a common practice for a long period, without being universal. It would appear, however, likely to decline. This could have substantial implications – both cultural and immediately practical. It is often thought that, despite the supposed plundering associated with productivism, there is an image of the family farming system as one which promotes sustainability through values, specifically those associated with the stewardship of land.

Succession maintains tradition by providing an instrument to transmit beliefs, values and practices as well as ensuring a continued supply of labour to the farm. Voyce (1997) claims that the desire for intergenerational transfer is what keeps the family farming system going. With family and community relations, it also provides a conduit for knowledge which may be significant to farm practices: the ways in which farms are operated either through processes of decision and consequent action or merely by habit. While Australian farming tradition has been drawn from Europe, it has never contained the strong 'peasant mentality' identified by Bohler and Hildenbrand (1990), but the importance of the farm and the commitment of family members to it have been features of Australian rural culture. The value placed on succession can remain strong even when, as Gamble et al. (1995) report, families do little to arrange it formally, leaving it as an assumed, unspoken and inevitable practice. It would seem likely that Australian farm communities lack the 'common purpose' (Symes and Appleton, 1986: 359) which had been a feature of English farm communities, associated with strong local networks and family continuity. As in Europe (Symes and Appleton, 1986) there is evidence of less value being placed by 'modern' families on continuity of the farm in the family as they place greater value on farming as a business (Hannibal et al., 1991). As succession declines as a practice, so will the community ties on which the value placed on succession is partly founded. The significant change occurring in Australia may be one of reality rather than values, but it can have effects in either form.

In terms of direct effects from intergenerational transfer, one might expect that farmers who anticipate that at least one of their offspring will continue operation of their farm would be more interested in its long-term viability. Moreover, those farms which have been taken on as a career by a younger family member may receive the benefit of new ideas, possibly drawn from educational opportunities not available to the older generation. The presence of a successor on a farm also simply provides more labour, thereby reducing the costs of effecting change in a farm's operation. European research has found that older farmers who have successors are more likely to seek to ensure that their farm is well-developed, so that their heirs will take over a productive operation (Potter and Lobley, 1992a; 1992b). Providing a productive farm for an heir means bequeathing one that does not have degraded land. Somewhat ironically when applied to Australia, this implies that those farmers with successors may be just as likely to conserve their land, the opposite of Potter and Lobley's (1992a; 1992b) finding that those with successors are more likely to exploit it for higher production. Such is the dilemma for Australian farmers who might seek a more profitable operation for their heirs but may be just as concerned about ensuring that land degradation does not render their asset unproductive.

There is evidence to suggest that the condition of land will deteriorate, and land degradation correspondingly accelerate, with the decline in farm succession and inheritance tradition. Gray and Crockett (1998) and Gray et al. (2000) use different data sets from mixed farming areas to show how farms with a successor present are likely to display greater use of conservation techniques. They also find tradition to be more important than economic factors. Gray and Crockett (1998) conclude that the more important characteristics of farms which would appear more likely than others to take action to deal with catchment management problems are large farm size and family operation with an expectation of succession, underpinned by value placed on the farm and its development. The less important characteristics are: large value of production, high farm income (some farmers with high incomes scored very low in terms of carrying out catchment management work), high levels of education and youthfulness of operators.

They conclude that increasing farm size could have potentially beneficial effects on farm environments. But if it occurs at the expense of those factors which help farmers to retain their long-term perspective, underpinned by traditional farming values associated with succession, it could be counter-productive. Similarly, a youthful and educated farm workforce could be an increasing resource enabling catchment management initiatives. But if this threatens the long-term perspective taken by farmers it could also be counter-productive. When tradition is taken into account it is perhaps not surprising that it is the long-term considerations which are important, much more important than short-term factors like annual income. This field of research has received little attention, but the point being made here does receive some backwards support from Powell (1997) who sees no reason why non-family farms would be any better for the environment. It appears that as detraditionalisation reaches the principal cultural underpinning of the family farm system, environmental effects could be substantial.

Pluriactivity

Chapter 4 pointed to the growth of off-farm work, as an aspect of farm pluriactivity, as directly affecting the culture of farming, notably including the social relationships implicit in family farming. Off-farm work coupled with declining farm incomes could, however, remove some faith in family farming as the family farm is no longer seen to provide the potential for a satisfactory family income. Although some of the farmers interviewed by Gray et al. (1993) for the 1992 study described in chapter 5 would have liked to stay on their farms for longer than they planned to, about one quarter did not plan to retain their farms until retirement. Farming may also be seen, when coupled to off-farm work, to be a source of stress and an unstable family environment. It is ironic that many farmers take off-farm work in order to support the farm for their family, but in doing so threaten the stability of family relationships (Gray et al. 1993, Gray and Lawrence, 1996).

Pile (1990) found that farmers did not want to return to old practices but they wanted a redefined tradition to survive, taking them off production treadmills. This is hardly surprising given the discussion in chapter 5. It is broadly supported by Shucksmith (1993) who found Scottish farmers to be reluctant to move toward the postproductivist era proposed by European policies. Farmers are finding, however, that the meaning of farming is changing. A tension becomes apparent as restructuring separates the ideal of farming from that of family life and intergenerational transfer is questioned. Change in meanings, upon reflection of structural conditions, avoids a 'motivation crisis' (see Pile, 1990: 177) as farmers adopt patterns of meaning common in other parts of society.

Alternative farm enterprises can also fuel such personal crises. Pile (1990) found tension between traditional and modern values as farmers were pressured to allow non-agricultural uses of their land. Hinrichs (1995) points to the tensions which arise when farmers are confronted with a decision to retain old technology and maintain their farms for consumption rather than production. The emergence of postproductivist agriculture in Europe and North America has extended the influence of metropolitan centres through the demand of their populations for sites of consumption rather than of production. The new form of control is much more personally direct than that of production systems which are mediated by markets, even under processes of subsumption, as the consumers of tourism bring their needs right to the farm, converting it, or part of it, from private into public space.

In this way, escape from the productivist treadmill may not bring an end to subservience. As Hinrichs points out, consumption of what remains a finite resource can create a new treadmill. This time the treadmill would be cultural, as well as economic or technical, in the attempts to sustain the experiences desired by tourists. Most important of all, however, it means that, just as the productivist system of agriculture was built on an urban image of progress, so the postproductivist system will be built on an urban image of rural tradition. This would do nothing to avoid the contradictions in rural tradition to which Pongratz (1990) attributes many of the stresses inherent in rural liminality.

While chapter 4 made the point that alternative farm enterprises are often controlled by women, the patriarchal nature of farm family relationships appears to be persisting. However, when one considers patriarchy from its cultural concomitant, masculinity, one can see possible ground for change. Younger women and those who work off-farm tend to resist the roles prescribed under patriarchy despite strong conservative community values (Alston, 1995). These values are maintained by a hegemonic masculinity which defines good farm practice as the domain of men. Masculine ideology defines men as farmers and women as adjuncts, holding that only men have the necessary qualities to be good farmers. Moreover, men who are seen to rely on women for contributions outside the home and garden are defined as inadequate, even though women have made extensive contributions to farm work (Phillips, 1998).

Masculinity confronts greater contradictions still, under the postproduction model of agriculture. The operation of businesses by women 'on the side' is not new. As the financial condition of farms has deteriorated it has remained possible for men to treat the fact that the family became dependent on the 'side' business as a kind of joke. But when farming itself comes to be defined as the maintenance of a tradition so obviously constructed by and for urban consumers, and managed by women, the threat to masculine identity becomes more profound. As Francis (1994) would argue, such contradictions become seeds of change.

This is a clear case of retraditionalisation based on individualisation. In such a process change must be led, at least symbolically, in order to remain a viable tradition, one which sustains a viable society. The additional question for rural people is whether or not they can provide that leadership, and hence become the guardians of their own culture. To do so requires reflexivity in order to identify their culture and the sources of it. With the possibility that women may find ways of negotiating the dilemma identified by Kubik and Sterling (1998) (see Chapter 5) and challenge the hegemony of productivism in its relationship with the hegemony of masculinity, this most profound rural cultural change may direct reflexivity towards a new and more sustainable practice of farming.

Farmer Knowledge

The knowledge dimension of detraditionalisation provides an approach to the question of reflexivity. Reflective pressure to abandon Fordist productivism, along the environmentalist lines suggested by Giddens, has also been revealed by Ward (1993). The technological tread-mill requires farmers to add technical knowledge to their own stock, without, however, necessarily questioning it. The continuing value of local knowledge has been extensively debated (see Kloppenburg, 1992). It would be naive to say that replacement of knowledge which has been transmitted through the generations with 'scientific' knowledge is part of detraditional-isation. This is due to an inherent capacity for farmers to think reflectively. This capacity is provided by their own transmitted knowledge and their relationships with the agents of 'scientific' knowledge. Resistance to the knowledge propagated by the state can be seen as a feature of resistance to the colonisation of knowledge by agribusiness 'science' under capitalist productivism (Kubik and Stirling, 1998).

    This is a power relationship which can also be explored at the level of social interaction in everyday life by applying the concept of the 'deferential dialectic'. Newby (1975) saw deference as a form of social interaction, potentially identifiable among individual people, in the context of a power relationship. The relationship between farmers and the agents of the agricultural sciences (what we will call the 'techno-elite') is one of dependence. Farmers depend on technology and knowledge of how to use it. They are also, however, independent property owners who can, in theory at least and as far as government regulation allows, ignore the prescriptions of science. They are sometimes aware, quite reasonably, that it might be in their interests to do so. This creates a dialectical relationship – one in which opposing forces meet and produce a synthesis.

    The relationship depends on the opposition of the processes of differentiation and identification. Powerful actors must maintain the perception among subordinates that there are important differences between them. The techno-elite must offer constant reminders that they have a knowledge which farmers lack, and that their knowledge is of a different kind. These reminders need not deny that farmers have knowledge of their own. That would be unacceptable to farmers. The techno-elite must, however, continually remind farmers that there is a knowledge other than their own on which they depend. This occurs at a cultural level through advertising. Chemical products are presented in an almost mystical form, with information about how to use them but very little explanation of how they work. At the level of social interaction, the techno-elite maintain their demeanour by claiming total knowledge. This becomes apparent when threatened. There is a story, possibly apocryphal but neverthe-less meaningful, of an agronomist who made mistakes during a field day presentation. Another agronomist present corrected the errors before the assembled farmers, to be told later by the presenter with some force that the work of an agronomist should never be publicly questioned. The presenter had feared destruction of the deferential relationship.

The techno-elite must also maintain belief in an identification of interests. If interests were perceived to conflict, an atmosphere of distrust could develop and the team-like image of the farmer–techno-elite relationship fail. At the cultural level, advertising again offers reminders that, for example, the 'local bloke' is there to help all local farmers pull through hard times. At a more intimate level, farmers compete for the attention of agronomists, especially as services are declining with the withdrawal of state support. Having an attentive agronomist is a sign that a farmer has attained some status among other farmers. There might also be an element of unintended and unconscious coercion. Farmers who are able to obtain the highly valued attention of an agronomist would not want to lose that attention by not being seen to follow the advice offered. There is a tension inherent in the dialectical deferential relationship, but it does provide a built-in reflexive component in farming tradition.

Postproductivism could resolve that tension in favour of the farmer in some cases where the traditional knowledge becomes the basis of farm operation. Among the data collected during the interviews described in chapter 5 there arise instances of reflection on fundamental change; conceptual thinking about farming which would challenge productivism:

> Change is the hardest thing to accept and understand. In fact at one of the meetings I went to in town you could see that we were victims of our own perspective, and this is true. The way that we see things is an old way, things are changing.
> *(Male farmer aged 55 with secondary education)*

> It has made me sort of less dependent on agriculture. And it has made me look elsewhere … And one of the things – the very interesting things that we on the land are discussing these sort of issues – is that I now see the farm as something that has value as a space … it's very strategically located between Melbourne and Sydney, and it's very easy to get to either of those places. I think (you know) in generations to come it will have considerable value for future generations as a very pleasant space.
> *(Male aged 51 with non-agricultural tertiary education)*

However, as argued above, stepping into 'postmodern' options like tourism will not necessarily place control of practice in the hands of the farmer. It will, rather, create a new relationship: that between farmer and tourist consumer. And if that relationship calls upon new means of expressing a reconstructed tradition beyond the knowledge of farmers, appropriators of 'scientific' knowledge may again enter the relationship.

Values

There is some evidence that a more entrepreneurial ethic is developing. This suggests that a discourse has emerged through which the meaning of farming may be reconstructed. Production treadmills are being questioned alongside the validity of non-local knowledge (Gray et al., 1995). These processes suggest a degree of reflexivity, as tradition is being questioned. But calls for farmers to act, in one way or another, in a more businesslike manner (see, for example, Stoeckel, 1998) are very common. As discussed in chapter 5, these are often based on an assumption that farming tradition is about retaining 'lifestyle' values in contrast to 'modern' farming which is moved by business values. It might be argued, however, as Lasley et al. (1992) does with respect to the United States, that the values base for the construction of large-scale agriculture was created in 'business' terms by nineteenth century Land Acts. The image of farming which has dominated agriculture has been one in which farmers operate businesses in order to provide urban industry with the raw materials it needs as efficiently as possible. It is hard to conceive that their success in doing so could be motivated only by the desire to experience a particular lifestyle. As chapter 5 argues, this idea is based on simplistic, supposedly dichotomous, analysis of the values of farming people without regard to the macro- and micro-social relationships involved. In productivist terms, the reflexivity which farmers demonstrate in questioning the treadmill could be seen as a rejection of 'business' values. This presents another instance of the tensions of liminality creating a built-in reflexivity and a struggle to assert an autonomous tradition.

The Trajectory of Change

The detraditionalisation of farming presents indications of postmodern reflexivity. Some authors believe 'reflexive modernity' is occurring – in terms of the breakdown of oppressive social structures. But it also points to evidence of loss of tradition bringing heightened environmental problems and the replacement of one process of urban domination with another, as the image of rurality becomes that determined by the consumption habits of urban dwellers rather than the production demands of urban interests. Along with all of these come tensions which will have impacts among farm families and communities.

Farming people are continuing their traditional assertions of knowledge as they struggle to maintain the basis of transmission, by intergenerational succession, of that knowledge and its associated values. The replacement being proposed, in terms of a rationalised farm 'business', run on corporate principles if not actually a joint-stock company, is problematic for many of them. It is not a model which comes from their experience, or which their tradition would enable them to control. In their liminality, farm families have always dealt with such tensions. With the rise of pluriactivity, those tensions become more profound.

Rather than destroying all of farming's cultural distinctiveness, the process of detraditionalisation is apparently reasserting it, but not in a way which would offer greater rural autonomy. Rural culture is being reconstructed in the same dependent relationship which regional Australia has suffered and it promises to perpetuate that relationship. Moreover, it is doing so in a way which cedes control of the process very directly to urban interests – so directly that it poses a threat to the identity of farming people. While this may also threaten the oppressive gender relations and the lack of acknowledgement of the contribution of rural women, it will also bring uncertainty of identity for both men and women. The image of rurality which farm tourism is creating is one far removed from the experience of very many farming people, especially those unable to profit from it. Even further removed is the 'rural' environment created by urban interests to suit the tastes of urban dwellers seeking rurality as they 'imagine' it to be (see Till, 1993).

Such radical change reminds us of Giddens' warning about fundamentalism. Farming tradition involves a strong element of reflection. The contradictions of liminality make that inevitable but also problematic as individuals are cast loose from the structures which provided some security amid marginality. While there is an argument in favour of reflexivity, it must be accompanied by a warning that as a reaction to powerlessness it can prompt hostility and even violence. American rural vigilantism has been attributed to such conditions (Stock, 1996), and while Australia does not have such a strong tradition of anti-government sentiment, the grounds for fundamentalism are certainly fertile.

The Detraditionalisation of Rural Community

Alongside the values and practices of farming lie the necessary social relationships within which culture is sustained and reconstructed. The discussion above touched on social relationships, but it remains now to focus on community, or the context in which those relationships are enacted through the habits of everyday life among farm families and in towns. The rural idyll, a foundation for rural values and ideology, describes a social climate where relationships in town and country are close, positive and mutually supportive. Australian rural communities have revealed a strong ideology of localism, or belief among people that their own locality is significant to them (Gray, 1991), a sense of attachment to their local community (Dempsey, 1990) and a capacity for united action (Wild, 1983; Poiner, 1990). Bonds based on sentiment, or communion, have also been apparent. Behind the perseverance of such tradition can lie kinship relations, propinquity facilitating interaction and the sharing of symbols (Hall et al., 1984; Cohen, 1985; Gray, 1991). To put the point more fashionably, it might be expected that Australian rural communities, and possibly also smaller regional centres, would possess significant social capital. But is this so?

Social capital is often usefully defined as the 'glue' which binds people into community and societal relations, enabling them to act together spontaneously and voluntarily for collective benefit (see definitions by Cox (1995) and Gain (1996), the latter focusing specifically on rural issues). Falk and Harrison (1998) and Cavaye (2000) include networks, norms and trust relations in their definition. All of the above quote the work of Putnam (1993) in which he found positive association between social capital and the strength of regional development. Social capital is seen to consist of reciprocities based on egalitarian social interaction and the trust which develops with it.

Given the pervasiveness of rural ideology, it would not be surprising to find suggestions that detraditionalisation involves the loss of social capital rather than its construction. In this regard, detraditionalisation is made complex with the observation that rural tradition is a source of personal social capital in the form of belief in self-reliance which logically contradicts any need for collective social capital. Moreover, collective social capital is tempered by rules of association which distinguish public from private. It is built on social interaction which is constrained by traditional rules pertaining to many aspects of rural life, but perhaps most notably to gender relations, leadership and private property.

Social capital can be seen to accrue to both communities and individuals: communities as they display collective solidarity based on mutual goals, egalitarianism and trust (collective social capital), and individuals as they display a capacity for interaction while retaining autonomy and social standing (personal social capital). Collective social capital is essential to the maintenance of a democratic community in the same way that it is to democratic society (Cox, 1995). Gain (1996) applied this point to rural development. But neither of these writers distinguishes personal from collective social capital which may themselves be mutually contradictory. Autonomy and social standing, which are associated by rural tradition with self-reliance, are not always consistent with mutual goals, egalitarianism and trust. This creates an obvious tension between policies and programs which espouse individualism, self-reliance, market solutions and competition and those which rely on collective action and co-operation. This tension is fuelled by elements of rural tradition (Stone, 1994). There is also an inherent tension for analysts of social capital. Social networks, bonding and trust can be resources for communities, but they can also be appropriated by powerful members of those communities.

Personal Social Capital

Rural culture is drawn upon by both individual and community. Individuals call upon it to define their personal self-worth, as was indicated by the concept of the 'good farmer'. Rural people have often been thought of, and have collectively thought of themselves as, individualistically self-reliant while being responsible community members. Gray and Phillips (1996) argue that pressure on traditions of farm succession and inheritance and belief in self-reliance amid rising economic and environmental pressure will change rural tradition, but those traditions continue to provide individuals with the moral strength and motivation for the continuation of family-based farming. This is so because they provide farmers with means of attaining social standing (Phillips and Gray, 1995).

The future of personal social capital takes on special importance, given the nexus identified by Stone (1994) and Gray and Phillips (1996) between community, agrarianism and land degradation. The individualism of the 'farmers' creed' can militate against the co-operative action necessary to address environmental problems, like water quality deterioration and soil salination, which cross farm boundaries. Agrarian culture contains this contradiction: farm people expect themselves to be independent and self-reliant and their property to be private at the same time as they place great importance on their community and its organisations. But the necessity to confront financial and environmental problems has led to pressure on traditional gender relations (as families become more dependent on off-farm income generated by women), leadership (as diversification of farm operations and local self-reliance have increased) and the institution of private property (as collective environmental problems have emerged). At the same time, the deterioration of social capital affects the social relations in which the value of intergenerational succession is confirmed.

Collective Social Capital

Collective social capital is said to be destroyed by restructuring as population decline and work demands make local organisations, in which social relations are enacted and trust relations enabled, unviable. Although Gray et al. (1993) did not find leaving organisations to be common among coping strategies, Stone (1994) argues that it is a serious problem associated with restructuring. Rationalisation associated with neoliberalism can change the basis of relationships by destroying 'weak ties' (being other than kin and similar 'strong ties' in which mutuality might be strong but feelings and actions not necessarily positive) (Granovetter, 1972) which sustain community (Gray et al., 1998). Community studies, such as Wild (1983) and Poiner (1990) have, in the past, shown how communities can band together to fight an external threat despite the individualism implicit in agrarian faith in self-reliance. Nevertheless, there is uncertainty in the literature about the effects of restructuring on community activity and hence on community responses to it.

Social capital depends on the maintenance and the use of communication networks. It is perhaps ironic that technological developments which are often said to facilitate communication have been found to threaten social capital. In a remote area of New South Wales, Epps (1996) found that the elimination of the manual telephone exchange and the associated termination of routine radio calls had reduced contact among community members. The old party line, in particular, provided a local information exchange. Allen and Dillman (1994) found the same. This is, however, a rather more subtle problem than that of communities like 'Splitville' which are suffering social division. In principle, however, it could have more serious implications. Gray and Phillips (1996) and Gray et al. (2000) discuss a relationship between social interaction and intergenerational transfer, with ultimate implications for sustainable farming practices (as mentioned earlier in this chapter). A broad association of this kind is supported by American evidence in Lyson and Barham (1998).

There is evidence of a growing lack of trust in rural institutions. Wild (1983) found a lack of trust in the local government, as did Gray (1991). Indications of further loss of trust through restructuring have also appeared. Evidence was collected during the interviews conducted for the 1992 and 1996 studies described in chapter 5.

> I could name some of the old fellows at the [agribusiness] that we would just go and ask things and they would tell us – and we would trust them – and every word they said we would trust. And these days, you don't.
> *(Male farmer aged 55 with secondary education)*

This was echoed by a 55-year-old woman with primary education:

> it leaves a bad taste in my mouth – it leaves me with much to be desired from accountants – mistrust of bank managers – and advice from banks. I just hate banks.

According to a 59-year-old male farmer with tertiary agricultural education:

> [The effect of the crisis has been that it] made me bitter.
>   *Interviewer:* Want to say why ?
>   Well, it started … I used to take a lot of notice from the government and the agriculture department and I tried to switch from dairying to beef and I used to go to

the seminars. Last October was the last time I went, they said there, that in twenty years, beef was going to be good, but it hasn't been so good. From then on I never trusted anyone.

The 1996 (drought) study found that community life was, by necessity, being neglected as people had to work longer hours; but also threatening is the social division which was found to arise from the bureaucratisation (rationalisation) of drought relief payments (Gray et al., 1998). Local people were becoming instruments of state administration as they were asked to participate in nominating farm families for assistance. Application of criteria were problematic because of geographic variability in rainfall and variation in the availability of records. This led to conflict, especially if less-deserving people were seen to be nominated while those with more serious problems were neglected. People found both situations distressing. This added a local dimension to a rising level of distrust among farm people, which had traditionally been focused on metropolitan-based government.

There has also been, in contrast, an indication of renewed collective social capital in the form of some resurgence of co-operative selling organisations for the domestic market since the Australian Wheat Board's domestic marketing monopoly was eliminated. The dramatic and apparently spontaneous rise of Landcare groups also suggests that collective social capital is strong. One might also make that claim on the basis of the rapid rise of the One Nation Party, despite that organisation's passion for raising divisions and its internal problems (see Lawrence et al., 1999).

The strength of local rural social capital has, however, always been questionable due to the presence of social divisions in rural communities. There are social factors inherent in rural communities in addition to the agrarian faith in individual self-reliance and commodification of time which make for division and hence limit the capacity of communities to take lasting collective action. The collective social capital of communities has always been contingent on the maintenance of collective identity and egalitarianism – if not social equality. Despite popular images of rural communities as sites of social interaction, trust and mutual support, there has long been extensive evidence of social division, both cultural and structural. These problems can only worsen as restructuring bifurcates rural society.

Structural Differentiation

The most obvious structural cleavage is that between town and country. Dempsey (1990) found a latent antagonism between town business people and farmers which could be traced back to 1930s Victorian government legislation which abolished farmers' debts. Confrontation is avoided, Dempsey argued, because the town business people do need farmers economically and socially. Gray (1991: 141) depicted the relationship between town and farm people as a 'deferential dialectic', in which the tension inherent in the contradiction between identification and differentiation of interests and cultural attributes is managed with claims about dependency by farmers and deference by townspeople.

This dimension can be represented within the towns, particularly where farm family members take up town employment due to the financial incapacity of their farm. This applies particularly to men, who have been found to retain their agrarian values in the quite different social milieux of factories (Kidman, 1991). Industrial relations in rural communities have always been difficult for employees as unions have suffered distrust in an ideological climate more favourable to agrarian ideals of self-reliance. Winson (1997) found that even older workers, who had been abused by employers and acknowledged the help of unions, tended to attribute the issues to the laziness of workers and found ways to blame the unions. In Australia this tension has been managed by generalising antagonism to that between country and city (Francis, 1993). It is nevertheless inherently more difficult for a working class to draw on the social capital of a community under these conditions.

While the town and country division is the most obvious dimension of structural differentiation, there can be substantial and increasing differences in property and wealth among farm families. Structural differentiation among farm families does not have the cultural consequences of the town–country division. This is partly due to denial of difference, with people relating an egalitarian belief, acknowledging only rural–metropolitan differences as having significance. But it is also due to possession of land: the symbol of status accepted by both town and country dwellers. Both structural divisions among farmers and between farm and town people can be profound, but the differences between town and country are those which have the most significant cultural consequences in terms of social division.

Nevertheless, there is vast evidence of controversy, conflict and distrust over economic development in country towns, as in communities in general (Donovan, 1993; Cox and Wood, 1994; Ramsay, 1996) which can affect country as well as town (see Cocklin and Wall, 1997 and, in Australia, Gravell, 1993). Town populations can also be highly stratified in terms of gender, class, race and ethnicity. This has been amply demonstrated in Australian community studies. Gray (1991) saw structural differentiation in terms of power. In particular, business and farm people were more able than others to make local politics work in their interests, by raising issues and having them acted upon. Those issues related to the more traditional functions of local government and, as narrowly defined by farm and business interests, local economic development. Women, Indigenous people and working-class people had particular difficulties. This was explained partly in terms of community social structures and cultural tradition, but the institution of local government and the culture surrounding it also contributed. Many Australian rural community studies have revealed political elitism. Higgins (1998) considered the possibility that restructuring may have weakened the power base of farm interests, but like Gray (1991), he found the ideological hegemony enjoyed by farm interests to be resilient, and likely to be sustained.

Cultural Differentiation

Town–country cultural differentiation is illustrated culturally in terms of the status system. Dempsey (1990), Gray (1991), Oxley (1978) and Poiner (1990) analysed the status ladders of rural communities which encompass both town and country. All three studies found farmers at the top of a status ladder as identified by local people, while town-dwelling workers were at the bottom. Gray (1991) found some town dwellers who felt that farmers could be aloof, snobbish and arrogant in their belief that the town depended on them, while a farmer said that town business people treated farmers with contempt, believing them to be slow-witted.

The idea of rural communities lacking collective social capital runs counter to the popular image of them as friendly and co-operative. The latter image has been severely damaged by community studies like those of Dempsey (1990) and Gray (1991). But the work of Metcalfe (1988) offers a contrast with a local society which was in itself egalitarian, co-operative and capable of strong collective action, based as it was on the class homogeneity of mine workers. There is no doubt that collective social capital has the potential to be very strong in rural/regional communities, but its strength should not be assumed. And as Oxley (1978) has shown, that strength can be a product of negotiating the meanings of difference: community members may display a strong egalitarianism but its exhibition is subject to delicate rules of behaviour which acknowledge inequality at the same time. Egalitarianism is not always strong enough to deny inequality, especially where inequitable power relations become apparent to community members and trust breaks down. Without the capacity of egalitarianism, or the belief in fundamental equality of individuals despite their social attributes, to enable interaction across social boundaries, collective social capital could not accrue to any community. This needs only slight qualification in the light of argument that perception of a common threat can lead to an implicit denial of difference and even a reversal of behaviour (Cohen, 1982). Threats are usually temporary and are therefore unlikely, unless cumulative, to contribute to detraditionalisation. This view is supported by evidence from Wild (1983) who found that previous social relationships were restored after a community achieved its victory over State government.

To the extent that Australia's rural communities have possessed collective social capital, it is impossible to judge it either as a positive or a negative feature of rural tradition. Certainly, local social interaction has maintained the culture in which intergenerational succession and land stewardship have been valued (Gray and Phillips, 1996; Gray et al., 2000). Social capital has been drawn upon in times of personal difficulty and common threat (Oxley, 1978; Poiner, 1990). But it has also been drawn upon to maintain the dominance of elites and effectively devalue the interests of others. This comments not just on rural tradition, but also on the institutions in which interests are expressed, or not expressed.

With the social capital of rural communities appearing to have been traditionally so dubious and tenuous, it would be unwise to claim that, in net terms, restructuring is having a detrimental effect on it. But detraditionalisation itself may be having a detrimental effect on both personal and collective social capital. Just as it appears to pose a threat to the cultural underpinnings of the stewardship of land, so it could, by raising the prominence of fundamentalism, be threatening the egalitarianism upon which collective social capital has depended. In that way, rurality itself is being fundamentally redefined. Yet again there is another side. Those strong community bonds which keep class conflict suppressed and denied could be applied to achieve the opposite. And traditional reflexivity could question productivism. The rise of rural feminism adds hope for radical change. But, in this instance, change can bring threats to personal social capital and the maintenance of identity.

The End of Rural Australia?

Farming tradition is not dying. Any contrast between a disappearing traditional farm-based society and a rationalised or subsumed modernity or a postmodern utopia offers just another unnecessary dualism. Tradition is more fruitfully seen as a medium through which the demands of globalisation are interpreted and responded to. Tradition is itself reconstructed through that interpretation and response. The problem lies in the nature of that interpretation and the direction of response.

The rural Australia of the agrarian ideal, to the extent that it ever existed, is coming to an end. The notion of large numbers of families contenting themselves indefinitely by working their own land in a European manner for themselves and their subsequent generations was rendered impossible at the outset by productivism in combination with the natural environment. Nevertheless, that notion has been proclaimed as the reality of Australian rurality. And the loudest and proudest voices have been those of rural people in their attempts to contradict the very contradictions of their own liminality. Detraditionalisation is opening a way to reflect on that predicament. But at the moment the indications are that, apart from the glimmer from rural feminism and the persistence of a reflexive tradition in farm management, there is little questioning of those aspects of tradition which sustain productivism and structural differentiation. Retraditionalisation seems to be reconstructing agrarian images in alliance with metropolitan interests and the forces of globalisation. At the same time, collective social capital is being eroded and continues to be misdirected.

It seems that, rather than obtaining a new reflexivity which will help farmers to come to terms with their structural position, some are being directed inwards. They are seeing economic and social bifurcation further threaten their capacity to reflect upon and respond to globalisation. In seeking to renew their identity, some are narrowing their social relations as they resort to fundamentalism, throwing away what collective social capital they possess and diving into normlessness with all the accompanying stress of coping with loss of identity. As they reach towards agrarianism they cannot deny that the possibility of attaining agrarian ideals is becoming more remote. At the same time, the postmodern economy is creating expressions of the idyll upon which agrarianism relies in forms over which they have little control. Their rurality, always founded on an urban ideal, is being taken from them. The rurality of the twenty-first century will not be that created following the urban-inspired land legislation of the nineteenth. The 'real' rural may be that which is served directly to the urban customer. In that sense it will cease to be rural in the form which rural people have come to regard as their own culture.

While this proclaims an end to the Australia of rural people's culture, it need not be judged to be harmful. Removal of such features as masculine hegemony, agricultural productivism and social differentiation may not be lamented. They do not constitute necessary attributes of any culture. The challenge for rural people now is to find ways of preserving those aspects of their culture which will sustain it at the same time as they reconstruct it in ways which will turn globalisation in their favour. The challenge is to create their own institutions in which they can modify the negative and retain the positive aspects of their tradition.

Further Reading

Heelas, P., Lash, S. and Morris, P. (eds) (1996) *Detradiionalization: Critical Reflections on Authority and Identity*, Oxford: Blackwell.
  – a collection of papers discussing the theory of detraditionalisation and its implications
Lees, J. (ed.) (1997) *A Legacy Under Threat? Family Farming in Australia*, Armidale: University of New England Press.
  – accounts of cultural as well as structural change in farming
Marsden, T., Murdoch, J., Lowe, P., Munton, R. and Flynn, A. (1993) *Constructing the Country-side*, London: UCL Press.
  – depicts rurality as a cultural construction
Pile, S. (1990) *The Private Farmer: Transformation and Legitimation in Advanced Capitalist Agriculture*, Aldershot: Dartmouth Press.
  – examines the process of change in the meaning of farming associated with restructuring

Australia's regional society is saddled with limited reflective capacity and an interminable powerlessness in its relationship with metropolitan Australia. The contrast with a global city, like Sydney and Australia's other major, globalising, urban places, is pronounced. The agendas of regional Australia are being written for it by people who are part of a globalising system to which regional dwellers have very limited access. Yet they are hearing that it is up to them: they can choose to restructure their economy, their community and their lives or they can effectively lose access to Australia's economy and society with all its rights and benefits of citizenship – which is happening to many of them anyway. They are in a sense being told that they must postmodernise before they have access to modernity, before they acquire the resources to progress beyond their liminality. Certainly, there are some who have sufficient personal and economic capital to enable them to make that advance. But this does not seem to be helping the majority. We are seeing, instead, the creation of an economically bifurcated and socially divided regional society.

Two factors make the escape from global misfortune especially problematic. The first is the ideological climate in which neoliberalism is promulgated. It makes reflexivity difficult. However, neoliberalism is internally unstable. The second consists of the biophysical and political/economic environments in which regional people must operate. But there are alternatives. This chapter returns to another element of global misfortune: the legacy of colonial development and administration. It focuses on inconsistencies and contradictions in neoliberalism before discussing changes which can foster reflexivity and provide resources needed to escape global misfortune.

Neoliberal Hegemony

Neoliberalism appears as a juggernaut with hegemonic power. Its accompanying political rhetoric seems to make it irresistible. It can turn regional people against the institutions which have traditionally supported them, but which are currently labelled as bureaucratic and inefficient. This is nowhere clearer than among the government railway systems and to a lesser degree among the deregulated, privatised or simply abolished agricultural marketing support organisations. The kinds of policies which were praised as promoting individual liberty by fostering a small farming system for 100 years from the 1860s have been repudiated since the 1980s as a threat to individual liberty. But neoliberalism weakens the social fabric upon which its own policies rely. Its hegemony must be examined before considering its capacity for self-destruction.

The Attractiveness of Individualism
Identification of inadequate human resources as the source of regional problems is compatible with a view expressed by regional people and agencies. Issues like lack of adaptability, motivation and leadership were raised during consultations conducted by the Rural Industries Research and Development Corporation (Martin, 1996). This view is quite compatible with rural people's view of themselves as self-reliant: if we had the right people amongst us, we could do it. Russell (1999) focuses on leadership as the solution to regional development proclaiming,

in a way which would appeal to adherents of rural ideology (the self-reliance aspect of which the same paper decries) that people, particularly leaders, are what will make the difference.

It might be quite correct to point to the volatility of seats in the House of Representatives since 1987 (Economou, 1997). But if regional people and agencies are happy implicitly to deny their structural relationship with metropolitan Australia and their dependency amid globalisation, a claim that it is necessarily a good thing for regional people cannot be justified. Their liminality, once again, can be seen to constrain them, despite their countrymindedness and the capacity of National Party leaders to remind them of it while espousing neoliberalism. Under these conditions, plus the howls of critics who point to failed regional growth-centre policies, a move back towards interventionist, structural solutions would seem very unlikely. The grasp which regional people have on their relationship with metropolitan Australia can be released by neoliberal rhetoric whenever neoliberal leadership desires. This ideology stokes the fires of countrymindedness and in so doing ignites the fierce independence which underpins and justifies neoliberal economics, but fails comprehensively to deliver a satisfactory future for regional dwellers.

Devolution or Subservience?

The prospects for regional people influencing policy may paradoxically be reduced while they appear to increase, although people are not necessarily totally powerless as individuals. Local and other voluntary organisations have become facilitators of many government services. In the regional context, the accompanying acceptance of individualism and self-reliance in welfare deinstitutionalisation and 'partnership' development are obvious potential instances of rural ideology legitimating self-exploitation among farmers and farm families as well as other sections of regional Australia. But are there real counterparts to the rhetoric of devolution?

Since the late 1970s Australian governments have sought to divest themselves of much responsibility for the provision of social services, preferring to use what they see as a reserve pool of labour and expertise, mostly that of women, which is available in 'the community' (Meekosha and Mowbray, 1995). In this way, people come to participate in the exercise of state power (see Kelsey, 1995 and Murdoch and Abram, 1998 for New Zealand and British illustrations). They are 'enabled' – by obtaining skills and other attributes from which they can benefit – at the same time as they are subjected more firmly to a relationship of power (Burchell, 1996; Rose, 1996). From this perspective, government can become rather sinister at the same time as it appears to promote individual liberty (Rose and Miller, 1992). The acceptance of 'partnerships' between local and regional voluntary organisations and central (in Australia both State and Federal) governments also offers potential examples. The most prominent of these is called the Federal 'Rural Partnership Program'. It sets out principles which provide that all rural programs will be administered in partnership arrangements with local or regional organisations.

A master–servant relationship between local and central agency has always prevailed in Australia. The ways in which local government is subordinate to, and is indeed a product of, the States is sufficient evidence, but it is also reasonable to add the many types of voluntary organisations which have been established to accept responsibilities which the States would prefer to be without. Australian local government was created to be subservient (see Chapman and Wood, 1984). In 1993 there was some relaxation of the New South Wales legislation which exhaustively prescribed the powers of local government, such that councils could decide what activities they might undertake. Nevertheless, they remain seriously constrained by the State government's power to limit their revenue-raising. Only in Victoria has a State government passed responsibility for regional development to local government and even then the former retains control over policy development (Senate Employment, Workplace Relations, Small Business and Education References Committee, 1999). These changes might be better described as decentralisation, which maintains subservience while taking on some appearance of devolution.

Neoliberal Inconsistencies

The juggernaut is vulnerable. Emy (1998) points to a possibility that neoliberalism, with its promotion of materialist values, if not greed, alongside the fragmentation of institutions and rising inequality, can bring about the return of what it despises most, regulation under a state apparatus. This may seem difficult to imagine in a rural ideological climate, but the affinity between rural ideology and neoliberalism contains many uncertainties.

The Instability of Decentralisation

It remains reasonable to ask if there is anything in the process of decentralisation which regional communities can grasp in order to work toward autonomous development. Decentralisation is very convenient for government: it legitimates withdrawal of funding while pointing to community incapacity in the event of adverse results. However, might the prospects for reflection on metropolitan–regional relationships be increasing as people are brought closer to the ways in which central power is exerted?

Community 'capacity-building' strategies may become significant in ways not intended by the state. Where government experts are charged with the role of defining the contours of community engagement, the result can be co-optation amid decentralisation (Cavaye, 2000). However, 'capacity building' is facilitated by enhancing social capital and providing the community with the necessary technical skills, resources and knowledge required to support their actions. This is frequently seen as 'empowerment' and must bear some potential to promote reflection on structural relationships. It could also be proposed that while decentralisation might appear to offer local autonomy and hence destroy the basis for countrymindedness, reflective popular perception that decentralisation is just a smokescreen for state dominance could have the opposite, rather destabilising effect on the neoliberal agenda. All of this, for example, could be said of Landcare.

However, this process of empowerment is potentially disintegrating, depleting rather than expanding social capital to the extent to which it ignores community social structures. Social exclusion can ensue for those who do not embrace the approach of, or decisions resulting from, local community action. Existing power relations in the community may be reinforced rather than challenged in such circumstances. The community which has been 'empowered' may be a conservative sub-group which already has local dominance. The regions are in a condition of social fragmentation yet the state places its faith in those increasingly fragmented communities literally to change their worlds. This would seem to be a recipe for instability rather than secure development.

The Creation and Destruction of Social Capacity

While neoliberalism promotes individualism, it relies on social organisation. There is a large quantity of research which has argued that a strong civil society, or social capital, is an essential ingredient in development (see Kilpatrick and Bell, 1998 as an Australian example). This argument is made on the grounds that co-operation and collective action, based on active networks and relationships of trust, are very important to economic development and environmental sustainability.

A look at Australian rural policies suggests that while some communities may develop social capital, others destroy it, despite retaining the rhetoric of partnership and participation. For example, the old Rural Adjustment Scheme and its successor 'Agriculture – Advancing Australia' contain elements which may activate an exclusion mechanism: they deny assistance to families whose farm is deemed not to be viable (itself a potential blow to personal social capital), but provide support to other families seeking to buy their property. While Landcare has been found to promote the social capital upon which it depends (Lockie, 1995), other programs, notably those aimed at entrepreneurial economic development, remain highly individualistic. Applications of National Competition Policy, occurring when local organisations are dispensed with under 'compulsory competitive tendering' by local government, are having the same effect (see discussion in Gray and Lawrence, 2000b). As Fitzgerald (1996) saw it, restructuring combined with the imposition of user-pays principles in government programs is devaluing citizenship and destroying social capital as only those who can participate in the market are able to participate in their community.

Reflexivity and Social Change

Neoliberalism may seem to be a coherent philosophy, but it contains contradictions. It depends on its capacity to interpret people's interests for them and to create a smokescreen of liberty to cover its enlistment of volunteers to organise in its cause. However, the community basis of local authority contains the seeds of its own destruction when market-satisfied individuality is placed above collective, community interests. In addition, while globalisation appears unstoppable, the interaction of global and local forces may promote local or regional cultures at the expense of the national, hence precipitating the destruction of the cultural basis of the nation state upon which the regions have depended. This point requires confirmation, but uncertainty remains the only certainty (see Marris, 1996 for an extensive discussion). Giddens (1996: 226) made the point with respect to the institution of the family: 'The wholesale expansion of a market society, however, is a prime force promoting those very disintegrative forces affecting family life which neoliberalism, wearing its fundamentalist hat, diagnoses and so vigorously opposes'.

The only directions for regional reflexivity being offered by political movements at the end of the twentieth century were neoliberalism and fundamentalism. Globalisation is imposing the inconsistencies of neoliberalism on regional people, leaving many of them grasping at fundamentalism in an attempt to unite a society by dividing it. Anxieties amid detraditionalisation can create a new fundamentalism. It arises when people react radically to the expansion of modernity and attempt to defend tradition as possessing the only authentic claims to truth. Neoliberalism offers a formula, through individualism, suppposedly to find truth. But fundamentalism brings more than a refusal to change as its adherents deny all reason to engage in dialogue and hence threaten an important quality of democracy: its capacity for resolving issues (Giddens, 1996). The contradiction in fundamentalist reflexivity becomes apparent. Claims to truth based on tradition are contested in a reflexive environment, and the authenticity of tradition is lost once it can be seen to be contestable.

But reflexivity is unlikely to emerge without risk and anxiety. To obtain autonomy from relative powerlessness, regional people must, by definition, change their relationship with metropolitan Australia. In its precariousness the reconstitution and redefinition of the activities of the nation state might offer them an opportunity to do so. But first they must see their situation in terms of that relationship – viewing themselves as subject to formal political institutions rather than just participants in them. To the extent that decentralisation fosters social capital, it may create conditions in which reflection on the structural relationship between the region and the metropole will occur.

What of countrymindedness? Does it not represent a tradition of reflexivity which could create a stable pathway to change? It may, to the extent that it indicates appreciation of the metropolitan-regional relationship. But countrymindedness has served to direct energy into the formal institutions, most obviously the National Party which has itself become an instrument of the neoliberal view. The significance of the National Party seems likely to diminish as it is propelled toward destruction by its own reliance on the rural communitarian traditions which its neoliberal policies are threatening, much in the way that the British Thatcher government created the conditions of its own demise by bemoaning social disintegration at the same time as it promoted individualism (see Giddens, 1996). The election of independents, including local mayors, and strong support for the One Nation Party at the expense of the National Party in the 1999 New South Wales election offered evidence of debilitation in the National Party. The rise of neoliberalism has deepened the contradictions faced by the National Party since the early 1980s when Costar and Woodward (1985) concluded that it had a secure future. Even those successful expressions and eventually political actions, such as adjustments to economic and social policies made at the behest of rural organisations, have also served to reconstruct the same arenas in which their subjugation is maintained. Such has been the direction of countrymindedness as the fuel for political representation.

However, countrymindedness and the existing political organisations may be capable of change. Or more promisingly, new, non-fundamentalist movements may arise in order to make change. Pixley (1998) reminds us that although neoliberalism works by co-opting social movements into the service of capital, some, like feminism and labour (although doubt may be cast on Landcare – see Martin and Halpin, 1998) have made important, progressive, contributions throughout Australian history. Stilwell (2000) sees such movements as foci for development of alternatives to the neoliberal globalisation path, especially if they can achieve enhanced coordination.

Regional Australia has participated in many social movements. Regional communities are vulnerable now because, in their liminality and reflective failures including lurches into fundamentalism, their social movements are very easily co-opted by neoliberalism. They are functioning very well, though not always perfectly, for global capital. Government has largely succeeded in applying its arts to this end. In these circumstances there appears to be no accessible place for a reflective regional people to participate in steering government towards policies which work for them. The regional revolution has to find new ways of using the apparatus of democracy, ways which are not inspired by interpretations made under metropolitan hegemony. Under the latter they fail to reflect adequately on the conditions of power. How can regional people develop a true reflexivity and bring what we might term a 'revolutionary change' to the current circumstances of marginalisation?

The task is to formulate an agenda which will facilitate the pursuit of radical change toward sustainability in all its dimensions. This involves a search for a pathway towards the conditions in which reflexivity can become unconstrained and the dependency relationship modified as productivism is rejected in favour of sustainability. This will obviously require change, using 'new thinking'. This new way of thinking (sociologically, with an eye to globalisation, postmodernisation and reflexivity amid power relations) focuses on the potential which people have and seek as social, rather than individual, actors needing equity, or a 'fair go' for their own and subsequent generations.

Developing Alternatives to Productivism and Neoliberal Countrymindedness

Regional people need avenues to promote and influence planning. Planning implies rejection of neoliberal market worship. Under neoliberalism, there is no overall plan for socio-economic development in regional Australia, and certainly no effective form of, or avenue for, planning by the regions themselves. Governments continue to witness city-based and coastal development without knowing what to do to assist those communities apparently being left behind. This centralising force appears to run counter to the principle that economic opportunity should be spread evenly. People who have been isolated, disempowered and suspicious of distant governments will need sufficient resources to prepare local plans, to develop local options, and to engage in a host of otherwise unfamiliar economic and social activities. Many will simply have to think differently and take on greater responsibility for themselves and their communities, aware that they cannot expect central governments to assist them.

In terms of service delivery, it must be recognised that, in the absence of a broad commitment to development policy which aims to provide resources to regional areas, there will continue to be uneven development, unmet needs, inappropriate servicing and the continuation of the social disadvantage which is a consequence of spatial polarisation (Rolley and Humphreys, 1993; Cheers, 1998; Stehlik and Lawrence, 1999). Without a fundamental commitment to the health and welfare of regional Australians, 'efficiencies' may be achieved via small modifications to service delivery, but nothing at all will be done to meet the needs of these citizens, or to reverse social bifurcation.

At State and federal levels there remain some remnants of an egalitarian ethos in policymaking. Policies based upon principles of social justice seek to ensure that Australians have equality of access no matter what State they reside in, and no matter what their background.

Thus, for example, social security is available to all those deemed to be in need: geographical location is considered to be irrelevant. Similarly, university education is – in theory at least – available to all who are qualified to enrol and can afford to pay any required fees. The tax system applies throughout the nation, as do those laws protecting the rights of citizens. Telecommunications is another area where the parameters have been established nationally and there are means for 'fiscal equalisation', or spatially distributing taxation revenue among governments according, at least partly, to need. While fundamental and important, these policy principles do not alone create conditions conducive to social justice.

How to confront the wider processes which create and reproduce social inequalities (both across Australia and between urban and regional sectors within Australia) remains a policy issue. Specifically how, in the face of tendencies toward the concentration and central-isation of capital in mining and agriculture, toward rationalisation in business and in govern-ment service provision and toward further environmental degradation, can regional development policies – those aimed at reversing these tendencies – be rethought in a way which affords them priority?

Sustainable Regional Development

The challenge for regional Australia at the beginning of the twenty-first century is not just to fix its social and economic policies, but rather to build socially, economically and environ-mentally strong communities which have the necessary linkages with global capital, but which have a prospect beyond this season's price for traditional products like coal, beef or wheat. Such communities need to be aware of the impacts of development not only in relation to job creation and welfare, but also upon the fragile ecosystems of the continent. The concept of 'sustainable regional development' (SRD), encompassing all the interests of regional dwellers, is being advanced to address the full breadth of issues and the relations among them (Lowe and Murdoch, 1993; Lawrence, 1998; Dore and Woodhill, 1999; Dovers and Mobbs, 1999; Mobbs and Dovers, 1999). Like those voices seeking greater infrastructure and business support for regional Australia, there are advocates for SRD. But unlike those advocating more interventionist regional policies, SRD supporters are gaining prominence.

There has been much discussion about 'sustainable' development in Australia. This has been consistent with an environmental imperative both to ensure that natural resource devel-opment occurs within ecological limits, and to address the undesirable 'downstream' effects (such as environmental pollution) caused through previous rounds of resource (mis)use (see AFFA, 1999; Dovers and Mobbs, 1999; Mobbs and Dovers, 1999). Sustainable resource-use options have become central to the study and practice of land and water management within Australia. Current models for natural resources management and community activity have been found wanting.

What has been missing is an appreciation of the interconnections between biophysical and social phenomena at the catchment or regional level – connections which act either to facilitate, or to hinder, sustainable development. Conceptual developments in relation to globalisation and the environment will best emerge from research at a spatial level where interactions among environmental, social and economic factors can be examined. Some studies, such as those of Barr (1999) and Barr et al. (1999), have indicated that farm structural adjustment and land degradation are interrelated and can be made visible by research which focuses on local and regional (catchment) levels. However, this only establishes the importance of an integrated approach to sustainability and suggests a research basis for it. The means by which regional interests can be pursued sustainably amid globalisation remain obscure.

Dore and Woodhill (1999) sought better ways to integrate economic development and management of natural resources in the pursuit of SRD. They also sought to examine the current and potential roles and capacities of various regional organisations in relation to SRD, and to assess and contribute to the improvement of communication networks of regional organisations – both within, and between, regions. They concluded that the best way to bring about desirable development in the regions (including rural and remote areas) will be through joint State/Federal regional initiatives which target regional 'self-help' options – the familiar neoliberal ethos.

However, they acknowledge that specific programs should allow regional initiatives to be at the forefront of economic and social development, to overcome the otherwise apparent tensions which arise from attempts by three existing levels of government to support change at the local level. It is at the regional level that the connections between community viability, economic development, and environmental integrity are best understood, and planning decisions made. At the start of the twenty-first century what are missing are regional decision-making and management structures which require that power be devolved to the regions allowing them to have either meaning or effect, and people's organisational 'capacity' be raised so that they can be given effect. This view has at least been implicitly acknowledged in the important discussion paper produced by the National Natural Resource Management Task Force (AFFA, 1999).

In their overview of regional development initiatives throughout Australia, Dore and Woodhill (1999) noted that global trends including the rise of neoliberalism, the declining relevance of 'old' political ideologies and structures, the emergence of new forms of governance based upon democratic participation, together with the imperative of sustainable development were altering, fundamentally, the ways that nation states conduct their business. Perhaps optimistically, these global trends were viewed as providing a new logic for the proliferation of regional planning initiatives. Recent directions in public policy in Australia – toward user-pays, local and State government reform, creation of regional bodies, the 'community participation' thrust – are all said to reinforce the growth of regionally-based initiatives aimed at solving the problems of social decline and environmental degradation. Although the Dore and Woodhill report was largely silent about the current problems faced by, and new mechanisms (such as those mentioned earlier) to assist, regional communities, it nevertheless argued – and justified the case for – regional initiatives as a catalyst for development of rural and remote Australia. Again, this theme was a strong feature of the Federal government's discussion paper on natural resource management, one which is now part of policy (see AFFA, 2000).

Dore and Woodhill (1999) found rural and regional people not to have well-developed skills in conceptualising the future, utilising new communication technologies, managing productive links with corporate bodies, or designing new strategies for community growth. This is what so-called 'community capacity building' activities seek to redress, but they risk the short-sightedness of neoliberal individualism while retaining the practical attractiveness of people-based rather than collective community strategies. While such an argument might be used further to justify the retreat by the state, it might also be seen as a call for government to be strategic in its investment in communities so that local or regional autonomy might develop. One way to begin to ensure that dependency is not recreated is to build equitable partnerships between communities and agencies, with the community determining its priorities, and the state providing the technical support that the community requires. This implies a change in governance towards regional/local autonomy. Dore and Woodhill acknowledge the governance issues, but there is a danger that they will be ignored, in practice if not in rhetoric, in a neoliberal ideological climate.

Full understanding of 'local' or regional human and environmental systems in the context of the 'global' at a practical level has become a major theoretical challenge, as it offers a first step toward integrated policy development. Research and community activities such as that conducted at the Institute for Sustainable Regional Development at Central Queensland University (under joint funding provided by the Queensland State Government, and by the University) and the Centre for Rural Social Research at Charles Sturt University, are starting points. Indeed, if the Kemp *White Paper on Higher Education* is anything to go by, many such organisations might spontaneously arise in regional Australia (see Kemp, 1999) to help refocus the research of the non-metropolitan universities on the problems of the regions. But the main issue for all should be to discover the 'ingredients' for sustainable regional development – that is, to identify the most sustainable production options as well as the causes of regional economic and social growth and decline. For while we have seen some benefits, overseas, of many models for local action based on community development principles, and while Australia has now embraced this approach, it still remains tied to the ideological foundations of neoliberalism at a policy level.

Overseas research suggests that sustainable regional development has the following preconditions. It will:

- require an integrated, holistic approach to policy which recognises interconnections between the environment, society and the economy and which seeks to break down artificial and constraining structures which impede regional decision-making;
- satisfy present and future needs for material well-being for people, while addressing ecological issues and the emerging cultures;
- not be based upon a nationally-determined 'blueprint'. It will vary from place to place according to demands of people, the environment and the economy – and have an ability to be responsive, flexible and resilient;
- not be driven by a set of technical or economic goals which exist independently of local people. Participation is crucial in ensuring ownership of outcomes;
- ·fail – if left to centralised planners and other 'experts'. It must engage everyday experience and respect the genuine needs and priorities of local citizens (Brawley, 1994; Dore and Woodhill, 1999).

This is consistent with the move to bottom-up rather than top-down planning, but power relations remain a concern. Dale and Bellamy (1998) and Dore and Woodhill (1999) discuss the issue of power. While 'consultation' is the word normally used when governments act (through agencies) at the regional level, this does not even represent decentralisation. Stakeholder groups are often brought together within regions, and asked their views, and then, following this 'consultation period', action is taken by agencies with little consideration of the local groups. This is, in effect, top-down planning using 'consultation' as a convenient device to give a community face to government decision-making. The reason this occurs at present is that there is no agreed planning framework for regional Australia. This is hardly surprising given that neoliberalism has attacked regionalism at the same time as it denies the need for planning.

Frameworks for negotiation among development interests and a capacity for government to serve the interests of the regions appear to be sadly lacking in Australia. A first step would be for natural resource and primary industry agencies of the States, along with regional universities, to actively (re)focus their activities at the regional level. Yet, at a time of increasingly scarce resources in both sectors, there is little will, or capacity, to act to support the regional groups. This is a form of institutional failure (see Price, 1998). Research indicates that regional organisations often lack the social capital to enable them to interact in purposeful ways (Cavaye, 1999b). Again, when people are expected to undertake a complex activity like regional planning but are not provided with the intellectual tools or support mechanisms to help them in the task, the result is often confusion, despair and hostility. There is also the issue of the global and the local. If regions are managed as economic resources, there is the danger that global capital will take advantage of regions competing with each other, and lowering environmental standards, to obtain much needed investment (see Lawrence, 1978; Lawrence, 1987; 1999a; 1999b; Beilin, forthcoming).

If, in contrast, the regions are capable of articulating with local, national and global capital in a manner which brings in investment dollars while achieving social and environmental sustainability, then their future is likely to be much more secure. While some of the above analysis might be interpreted as positioning regional citizens as victims of large-scale movements of capital, this does not have to be so in reality. Indeed, we must recognise that regional citizens are active players whose efforts can affect local conditions and circumstances in ways which can enhance development. They remain vulnerable because of the narrow economic base of production, ongoing environmental degradation, the continued threat of service rationalisation, the emigration (and non-replacement) of young and/or talented leaders and others, declining social capital, the absence of institutions in which they can define and pursue their interests, and the lack of an integrated rural development policy at the State or federal level.

National Economics (2000) provided some very useful suggestions for those governments desiring (daring?) to reverse regional polarisation. Governments should plan nationally so that no region is left behind. Repopulation of the regions was also viewed as essential. Strategic economic investments need to be made in partnership with business. An example provided was the decision by the New South Wales government that 4 per cent of the portfolio of the State superannuation board should go into regional development. Regional economic development agencies need to be strengthened and their future placed on a more secure footing. It is at the regional level, we argue, that industry network clusters will form and bring long-term benefits to citizens. Information technologies must become more widespread. Regional business and communities must develop digital skills. Governments must assist communities to harness new planning tools, and to strengthen the social capital of citizens through regional information systems, and through the revitalisation of libraries and community centres. Finally, governments at all levels must better co-ordinate their services. They must also foster a strong 'vision' for the future of non-metropolitan Australia (see National Economics, 2000: vi–vii). The future is seen as a *regional* future. It is about regions being supported on an equitable basis by government at the national level. Beer (2000) argued that there were still avenues for government to promote regional development through existing institutions.

There are now numerous lists of the characteristics of successful communities derived from experiences in the United States, United Kingdom, New Zealand and Australia. Unfortunately many of these characteristics are either difficult or impossible to measure – something demanding more research in the Australian context. More importantly, many are highly problematic in that they may appear to indicate the presence of social capital, but that social capital can be weakened by division and be appropriated by some people to serve exclusive interests. They do, however, give an approach to what is needed for rural and remote communities to develop themselves. According to research (Kelty, 1993; Shaffer, 1994; Larcombe, 1998; Cavaye, 1999a; 1999b; Dore and Woodhill, 1999) the characteristics of successful communities include those of:

Social Capital
- the ability of people to assess the positive and negative qualities of community life;
- widespread participation in community decision-making;
- a co-operative, inclusive, community spirit formed of trusting social relationships;
- acceptance of women and minority groups as participants and leaders;
- a strong presence of traditional institutions that are integral to community life but adaptable to a reflexive role amid changing local and external relationships;
- a conviction that, ultimately, the local or regional community must be substantially responsible for its own destiny.

Human Capital
- knowledge, skill and ability to assess the community's best options;
- strong support for, and belief in the creative role of, education;
- knowledge and appreciation of the region's biophysical limits;
- planning for power to be transferred, over time, to a younger generation of participants and leaders;
- experimentation with local approaches to community service delivery;
- a widespread and sophisticated use of information resources;
- acceptance of outside financial and other assistance to support local initiatives.

Economic Capital
- investment in the region by local businesses and institutions;
- a co-ordinated, meaningful and focused economic development program;
- a realistic appraisal of future economic opportunities.

While Australia's urban communities might succeed without many of these features – driven as they are by the momentum of population growth, private economic activity and government infrastructural investment – growth of the regions is likely to occur only when most of these key features are present. And, as suggested above, much of the future investment by the state must be in people and communities, with the purpose of enhancing human and social capital. Local and regional communities do not have the resources to acquire the elements essential to their futures without support from central government. Some of the external mechanisms, those which central governments can assist in delivering, are:

- the provision of support for social learning and reflection on local–global relationships which can lead to effective reflexivity, including formulation of an implementation plan;
- acceptance by government that specific infrastructure will need to be provided regionally for national benefit, such as communication services and high-speed railway services, in line with the plan generated regionally;
- greater articulation between government, industry and environmental organisations in the co-ordination of investment activities;
- progressive 'empowerment' via community involvement in planning, and enhanced local (political) activity aimed at securing the most assistance from government and private investment;
- new skill development and learning options, including enhanced reflective capacity via educational institutions and more informal training activities;
- the strengthening of social capital through encouragement of local people to improve their community interaction and by the fostering of local institutions through which genuinely inclusive and trusting social relationships can emerge (see discussions in Dore and Wood-hill, 1999; Mobbs and Dovers, 1999; Stehlik and Lawrence, 1999).

This implies a greater degree of government intervention and a capacity among regional communities to direct that intervention. Although questionable with regard to the extent of local autonomy they bestow, models like that of the European 'Leader' program are worth considering (see Westholme et al., 1999; Ray, 2000).

Some Limitations of Sustainable Regional Development

None of these proposals involves the certain creation of a setting in which rural and regional people can be empowered by developing their own reflexivity and challenging their dependency. Most offer only limited hope for significant reversal of the depletion of social capital. It is instructive to consider different historical circumstances.

There is a great contrast between the reflective social and cultural condition of regional Australia at the beginning of the twenty-first century and what it was half a century previously. Coombs (1981) described the approach taken to post-World War II development. It was a time of optimism stimulated, obviously, by the end of the war. It was a time of 'catchment management' in places like the Tennessee Valley in the United States. It was a time of resources shortage amid a rapid increase in the rate of family formation bringing demand for housing and household goods. It was also a time of optimism for rural industries. Coombs' (1981: 59–61) words are worthy of extensive quotation. He refers to a plurality of ideas from planning, architecture and the arts among others:

> These intellectual and emotional influences were at work in the community gener-ally. In various parts of Australia, voluntary groups were being formed to discuss their relevance to the local scene and urge upon governments the need to plan for the effective development of the country's resources and to involve those locally concerned in that process.

He mentions the Murray Valley specifically:

> The Murray was one of the few Australian rivers with great irrigation potential, some of which had been already realised. However, with that irrigation, residents saw increasing salinity, soil erosion, forest destruction, silting of water storages, and similar problems. They believed that only co-ordinated planning, in which the residents themselves were involved, backed by adequate and comprehensive research could break through the State jealousies and bureaucratic barriers to realise the full potential of the valley as a context for human settlement.

Local planning and development organisations appeared and grew spontaneously. It was these groups which initiated contact with governments, rather than being prompted into exis-tence by governments:

> The larger of these organisations tended to be interested primarily in the potential for integrated development offered by planning on a regional basis, and in the desire to emphasise the distinctive character and autonomy of their particular region. The potential of community planning did not stop at the planning stage. Other community groups saw themselves as taking part, together with govern-ment at the various levels, in the physical process of creating the facilities needed by their communities.

Remember, Coombs is talking here of an initiative instituted some forty or so years ago. Integrated planning for sustainability and community–government partnerships in develop-ment are not new ideas and as ideas they are not products of government alone.

This sprouting of community solidarity and initiative was also revealed by Gray (1991) in the context of the development of a country town during the same period. It was a time which neoliberal ideologues might wish to be repeated, except that the community energy came from collective ideals, not individualism. Those ideals were products of pluralistic debate, not imposition of and resignation to such a narrow set of principles and beliefs as that represented by neoliberalism and propelled by globalisation. It is particularly noteworthy that, contrary to what one might expect given the environmental degradation of the last fifty years, it appears that local people were aware of the dangers of unsustainable development. Why they did not pursue a more sustainable development path is open to interpretation.

A broader approach to sustainable regional development than that generally advocated is required. We must add substantial change in, if not reversal of, those policies which destroy social, human and economic capital and the environment they all depend on. The impacts of neoliberalism on regional economies and population through the withdrawal of support and services and the neglect of infrastructure have been raised in earlier chapters. The absence of identification of regional structural problems and the deleterious effect of agency fragmentation, competition policy and bureaucratisation continue to prohibit endogenous reflection and action despite the stated intentions of various governments to develop the kinds of mechanisms described above. Policy must seek to restore the conditions for endogenous collective action.

Some Principles for the Direction of People-Oriented Policy

People-focused policy retains potential to create conditions in which regional people can move their society towards greater equality and sustainability, in line with the characteristics of successful communities listed above, just as the rhetoric of neoliberalism would claim but cannot deliver. The basic principles of such policy are that it provides regional people with the resources necessary to:
- build their social, economic and human capital;
- develop their reflexivity, so that they can make cultural as well as structural adjustments into postproductivism;
- take advantage of globalisation in ways which address their own interests; and that it provides regional people with the institutions in which:
  - their reflexivity can develop;
  - their regional social capital can grow;
  - their cultural distinctiveness can be expressed and developed;
  - resources to cope with and challenge globalisation can be autonomously developed;
  - their interests are raised autonomously as agendas for deliberation in national arenas.

Autonomy, social capital, reflexivity and education are all central to this scheme. To establish these principles we must provide an institutional framework supported by a culture which builds and maintains genuine social capital in ways which enable autonomous development and reflexivity within the constraints of globalisation.

The Weakness of a Communitarian Solution

The models presented earlier set out a solution with many characteristics of communitarianism: a means of implementing SRD by looking to 'community' to give teeth to the rhetoric of local self-help. This has much appeal, both for those who seek regional autonomy and those who seek to avoid central government commitment to funding support. It moves a step beyond the notion of partnership, while most policy prescriptions offered so far do not go beyond decentralisation into devolution. It has problems, however.

Communitarianism is attractive in that it tries to offer an antidote to individualism. But as a political movement it struggles with serious problems which can be brought to our attention by rural detraditionalisation – its reliance on tradition to restore the primacy of the collective. As Gutman (1992) among others explains, structuralist critics of liberalism point to social inequality but communitarian critics tend to focus on lack of tradition and sources of identity as underpinning societal and moral decay. In doing so they risk advocating the recreation of the oppressive structures which both socially-conscious communitarians and liberals would all decry. Communitarianism reaches for sources of collectivity, and in doing so risks attaching itself to those which would threaten the social capital it depends on.

A communitarian solution to regional inequality and social bifurcation would propose endogenous collective action. Social capital may be important to collective action, but as we have seen, it has traditionally been fractured by local social inequalities and is being further eroded by neoliberal policies. Loss of social capital may prohibit a communitarian solution. However, as argued in chapter 9, care must be taken when lamenting the decline of social capital, for it is a dangerous commodity. Might trust cease to be social capital if it forms the basis of a political growth (or grant) machine (Molotch, 1976; Molotch and Logan, 1988; Low, 1994) which makes local politics work for capital but ignores other interests? When does 'embedded corporatism' (Perucci, 1994) or business-community symbiosis (Tosterud, 1998) become exclusion and elitism? Local government in its present form is not conducive to the development of genuine collective social capital. The same might be so of local and regional organisations like Integrated Catchment Management Committees and even Landcare.

A communitarian approach, based on existing institutions and organisations, would have grossly uncertain outcomes, except for an apparently high probability of uneven development. Dependence on social capital adds to uncertainty because there is no reason to expect it to be evenly distributed in regional Australia. As argued in chapter 9, it can be found to be very strong in some circumstances, dependent on localised social and economic histories, but weak in others. Where autonomy and tradition accompany each other, genuine autonomous development is conceivable (see Musyck, 1995), but there are few such instances in Australia. (The often-mentioned example of Broome in remote Western Australia comes to mind: a community with sufficient economic and political power to have itself exempted from the White Australia Policy.) Other situations, such as those described in chapter 7, are very different.

Institutional Incapacity

Australian communitarianism does not provide a design for an institutional framework. The only text approaching the issue (Latham, 1998) fails to deal with it and leans back on local government. There are no viable existing alternatives. Regional local government is fragmented and disparate. There are many councils, especially in those States which, unlike Victoria, have not been aggressively amalgamating councils. While some cover large regional cities and are relatively economically strong, others are small, in terms of the size of their operation rather than the area covered, and economically weak.

Nevertheless, on the face of it, local government appears to be the institution offering the best arena in which to develop such a framework, despite its contradictory relationships with collective social capital as implied by its local leadership being concomitant with elitism based on rural conservatism. If they were aware of the elitism of local government as revealed in Australian community studies, critics of communitarianism may be horrified by such a suggestion. Communitarianism could well lead to very undemocratic outcomes under existing institutions, in much the way that a return to what are seen as traditional family values, as implied by those advocating a strengthening of the institution of the family, would entrench patriarchy. Hence it will be necessary, as advocated by Gutman (1992), to think in terms of creating entirely new institutions, rather than returning to or adjusting old ones.

Up to this time, local government has applied itself to provision of, at best, a narrow range of social services and it has undertaken little activity in either economic or environmental development (though rather more in the former than the latter) – despite having planning and various regulatory powers, such as weed control. There are well-known contradictory examples, such as the activity of Orange City Council in human services and the generally greater involvement of Victorian councils in human services. Local government has failed because State governments have not allocated responsibilities and powers to local government in these fields and have enforced restraint on local revenue-raising and hence capacities to take initiatives, despite widening potential powers. Steps have been taken to broaden the planning perspectives of rural councils, such as the requirement of the New South Wales government that all councils prepare social plans. But local government has been severely constrained financially and produced disappointing outcomes. Furthermore, local government's vision, constrained by conservatism and in some situations what are effectively local dynasties, has continued to be limited, and it has remained highly sceptical about embracing activities which it views as belonging to other levels of government and which risk imposing new commitments on ratepayers (Garlick, 1997; Self, 1997).

Much has been written about the value of co-operation among councils. This includes the way in which regional organisations of councils have managed to sustain an element of regionalism along with the advantages of sharing resources and co-ordination of activities. This is an important but difficult issue, due to the tendency of local authorities to compete with each other (European Association of Development Agencies, 1995), a tendency which is promoted by central government programs which offer support on a competitive basis (and direct policy intervention, such as competition policy in Australia).

The fragmentation of local government is cross-cut by the fragmentation of the agencies of governance. If one could conceive that central governments had at any time been fearful of regional institutions, one might be tempted to describe the tradition of regional governance in Australia as having been built on divide-and-conquer principles. As discussed above, governance has been implemented in regional Australia by co-opting local energies, but rather than create singular local institutions, the different agencies of central government have each created separate local organisations to administer their policies and programs. This results in a plethora of local organisations in regional communities (recognised as a hindrance to the development of sustainable agriculture by Williams and Walcott (1998)), which are constituted by, and sometimes whose members are appointed by, central government. Examples include Hospital Boards, Rural Lands Protection Boards and Catchment Management Committees and, in some States, Regional Development Boards. There are those like Landcare groups and Rural Counselling Committees that are more spontaneous, but they are all accountable to central government. These locally-based organisations lie alongside industry-based groups, such that farmers and others can become involved in extraordinary numbers of them and, as a consequence, suffer 'burnout'. Reale (1998) counted thirteen organisations involved with one industry in one locality. Each of these operates independently of the others, although there might be overlapping memberships.

The possibilities for duplication of functions, or at least claims by opponents of duplication, are high in these circumstances, a factor to which Martin (1998) attributes the demise of the Keating government's Regional Development Organisations. Among local organisations, local government is usually seen to be paramount. It is also seen as the (albeit sometimes unreliable) advocate for the local community (Gray, 1991). The principles of place management, as advocated by Latham (1998) are worth considering as an antidote to fragmentation, but would not necessarily foster autonomy. They might, however, offer stepping stones to creation of genuine regional institutions.

Fragmentation, combined with the subservience of local government to central government, leaves no opportunity for even the largest communities to obtain some co-ordinated control of local affairs. And there seems little prospect for change unless radical policies like place management are seriously considered as a starting point. This remains so despite the implicit identification of the problems of fragmentation by advocates of co-ordination, applying the 'whole-of-government' approach, like Laurance (1999), Senate Employment, Workplace Relations, Small Business and Education References Committee (1999), Anderson and MacDonald (1999) and Northern Summit participants (at Katherine in 2000).

From time to time one or other of the State governments proposes amalgamation of local government councils on the grounds of obtaining economies of scale. These almost always encounter strong local resistance, despite the lack of local resources and existing interdependence (as noted by Searston and Searston (1998) and Sorensen and Epps (1995)). (For an illustration of the issues, see James (1996).) This has also occurred with other organisations, including New South Wales' Rural Lands Protection Boards. Resistance need not be surprising when one considers the tradition of competition between rural communities, nurtured on sports fields and confirmed in the scramble for development. It is also an affirmation of collective social capital. New South Wales required some councils to amalgamate in 1980 and in the late 1990s called for volunteers to amalgate, but obtained little interest. South Australia has amalgamated councils, but Victoria chose to do so by force. At the same time it replaced elected councillors with appointed administrators. The administrators have since been replaced by elected councillors in all but one case, where a majority of voters in a referendum sought to keep the administrators. Such is the regard in which local government is held, and consequently such is its weakness. There is evidence that the larger the rural/remote shire, the more likely that human service delivery will be compromised (Stehlik and Lawrence, 1999).

Spatial enlargement will have no effect on functional fragmentation and will not necessarily impact on relative autonomy.

Prospects for Regional Autonomy

When one compares the historical and social regionality of Europe with that of Australia the prospects for any degree of regional autonomy in the latter appear non-existent. It is difficult to compare regions which, having long histories, were drawn together relatively recently to form nation states. Other such places have long traditions of cultural and economic autonomy which can result in an independent and prosperous region (see, for example, Musyck, 1995). Australian non-metropolitan regions are creations of nation states and urban capital. Their tradition, as argued throughout this book, borders on that of total subservience.

Regionalism will have to obtain, at very least, drastic modification of regional governance to provide an institution capable of reflecting on and pursuing regional interests: a drastic restructuring of Australia's system of governance. Dore and Woodhill (1999) acknowledge that radical institutional change may be necessary for long-term sustainability. Curiously, they stop short of advocating it in the short term. Senate Employment, Workplace Relations, Small Business and Education References Committee (1999, chapter 6: 15) hints at the issue but then sidesteps it with the sentence: 'The Committee sees no public gain from a wrangle about powers based on constitutional considerations'. This may be a recollection of the problems encountered by the Whitlam model of regionalism, but other approaches might not be ruled out in this way. The Australian Constitution explicitly permits what might be the most drastic form of regionalism, the formation of new States.

A reflective communitarianism may hold some prospect for autonomous regional development amid globalisation, but development must be placed in a system which does not sustain the traditional power element in the metropolitan–regional relationship. 'Going global' will not reduce uncertainty and unevenness of development. But as Australia presently has a very high degree of centralisation by reasonable international comparison (Jones, 1993) – something which increased in the 1990s (Mathews and Grewal, 1997) – there may be some room for optimism. For example, O'Toole (1998) advocated perceiving regions as cities, but did not set out a clear program either to establish these 'cities' or to take advantage of them.

A Regional Solution

Communitarian approaches suffer a two-dimensional problem. The only institutions available to create an arena in which the interests of regional dwellers can be debated, defined and expressed are not capable of such activity due to their fragmentation and subservience to central authority. Moreover, attempts to create stronger local institutions are either opposed locally or are prescribed centrally in ways which risk the elimination of what exists of local democracy. Imposition of place management may help to defeat fragmentation but will not do much for autonomy. This first dimension appears almost insuperable.

The second dimension of this problem might, however, lead us eventually toward a solution. We cannot look to existing local institutions. Even if they were strong enough, under their present structures, cultures and systems they would remain a threat to local collective social capital rather than either a builder or an equitable appropriator of it. The construction of collective social capital is unlikely to occur within an institution resembling existing local government, as it promotes distrust rather than trust. But a move towards a pluralistic and participatory form of regional organisation, with a high degree of autonomy, would foster social capital and strengthen the reflexivity which would consequently strengthen challenges to central authority.

How can we expect such collectivism to spring from vulnerability and resignation to neoliberalism? We are confronted with a chicken and egg problem. Should attention be focused on building collective social capital in order to enable regional institutions to fight for autonomy just as they struggle to find a place in the global economy, or should central governments, State and Federal, work together to create new institutions in which collective social capital can grow, thereby creating conditions for regional organisations to seek autonomy? The latter offers a more stable solution.

The feasibility of institutional change stems from the emergence of regional conglomerates (see Dale and Bellamy, 1998; Mobbs and Dovers, 1999) which have been formed precisely because of the failure of local government to see beyond the immediate town or shire and address the problems of sustainability. These institutions are currently, but perhaps unwittingly, challenging the future role of local government in developing a truly sustainable regional community. This is not to say that these organisations are necessarily autonomous. Even the comprehensive catchment management organisations, such as those of Victoria and New South Wales, remain answerable to State government. Nevertheless, there is an apparent tension here for State governments which would like to preserve their divide-and-conquer strategy. Do they look for ways of providing new forms of support to local government to help it to carry out – in a centrally-determined and long-term fashion – the social service activities and 'capacity building' demanded at the local level, or do they look toward stronger regional bodies to bring about co-ordinated and sustainable development, involving improved decision-making about a variety of issues, including some particularly difficult ones which central government might prefer to devolve? Planning at the catchment level (or at a regional level representing the amalgamations of shires and city councils) is viewed or at least mooted by both State and Federal governments as crucial to the future well-being of both non-metropolitan Australians and of the environment. We argue that there is now a spatially-based choice for supporting all service delivery: that between aiding local government and harnessing the energy of emerging regional bodies while progressively strengthening them. This, of necessity, will be a political decision. In our view, it is at the regional level that real 'empowerment' can occur: local government is not equipped, in an age of reflexive modernisation and globalisation, to be the catalyst for change at the regional level.

Centrally-directed change from local to regional government is essential. Despite the currently fashionable discourse about social capital, Australia cannot count on being able to build it to the extent that it will provide the necessary catalyst. It remains a spontaneous construction through informal and habitual processes of social interaction. It may seem ironic, but following the analysis of Filion (1998), it is reasonable to suppose that the most significant contribution of community economic development, under neoliberal resource starvation, may ultimately arise in terms of collective social capital born of necessity despite individualism, something without which they are less likely to succeed (McQuaid, 1997). Nevertheless, it is essential to the sustainability of regional action and autonomy. The process of social capital creation is also potentially far more complex.

Regional Social Capital

Approaches to social capital must acknowledge both its relationship to social structure and its cultural construction. Temptation to see it in individualistic terms, which are more amenable to policy intervention, should be avoided. The current fashion for 'capacity-building' (Murray and Dunn, 1995) risks individualism if it is allowed to focus on leadership and learning, both of which are receiving research attention and are obviously more amenable to policy intervention than the spontaneity of collective social capital. Leadership has been identified as a problem for Australian rural communities by Epps and Sorensen (1996) and Sorensen and Epps (1996), as have the policy-oriented pronouncements discussed above. However, it may often be difficult to differentiate leadership from elitism, and as Gemmill and Oakley (1997) claimed, it is reasonable to question the need for leadership. Might it be a myth which serves only to allow people to avoid taking responsibility for themselves at the same time as it enables others to dominate them?

Alongside the concept of leadership we sometimes read of the need for 'visioning', a procedure in which a selection of enlightened individuals define a development trajectory for communities. While promoted as collaborative, 'visioning' requires leaders. 'Innovative, creative solutions that meet the changing times are developed through the interaction of leaders and citizens working toward common goals' (Ayres, 1996: 21). When combined with leadership, the possibility for elite control of the agenda of local development, with consequent erosion of social capital, becomes clear. The possibilities for regionalism to serve only the interests of regional elites, as identified by Lovering (1999) under British 'new regionalism' policy, should be avoided. Reflexivity may be applied to the rhetoric of development, just as it has traditionally been applied to the rhetoric of agricultural technology, to effect critique of leadership and visioning as solutions.

Association of the concepts of learning and social capital is implicit in the group learning techniques of agricultural extension. When viewed as extension, it is also implicit in Landcare, Coast Care and Bush Care. It is also implicit in much community development activity, although when notions of education and 'best practice' are replaced with those of awareness of and sensitivity to culture and its diversity, the character of the association changes (the approach of Mobbs (1998) is one such). Even the most 'bottom-up' extension models can still be bound by the culture of productivism and its relationship to agribusiness. Ironically, however, it is top-down extension, that which engages the 'deferential dialectic' discussed in chapter 9, which is most likely to promote both personal and social capital. It does so by creating an 'other', an entity to which collective identity can be contrasted. The 'bottom-up' approaches, while using collective social capital, risk depleting it if, as local government is apt to do, they create a local organisation but lose relations of trust by failing to identify firmly with local interests.

Learning as an approach to social capital is rather less insidious, but it still presents issues related to individualism and elitism. Bawden (1998) saw learning as the currency of social capital. But learning from what, or more importantly, from whom? Who sets the learning agenda? Is it permitting reflection on interests? If learning is seen as an individualistic process of exchange, as is the case in the classroom, it can do nothing for collective social capital as, in fact, it cannot whenever power relationships are involved (the exception being resistance to power). Where learning is carried out in group contexts there is danger that the group will form an elite in a community. This possibility is not accounted for by advocates like Kilpatrick et al. (1998), as indeed it would be difficult to account for outside a substantial community study. The approach of Falk and Harrison (1998) in which they acknowledged assumptions about the relationship between learning and collective social capital, is more encouraging. Ultimately, the basic problem is how to give regions the autonomy to build their own social capital.

There is an extensive literature on the building of collective social capital, or 'community-building' rather than capacity-building. All, to varying degrees, recognise that collective social capital is indeed collective rather than individual (see Carroll, 1996). Some seek a non-materialist approach based on rich cultural tradition (see examples in Rajan, 1993). Some focus on institutional arrangements (Ostrom, 1994). Others, like Allen and Dillman (1994) recognise the spontaneity of social capital but also see possibilities for its intentional construction. Events believed to raise social capital are recounted (as by Radford, 1996).

All this literature should be questioned in terms of its confirmation that social capital was in fact built rather than merely used, depleted or appropriated. It is sometimes claimed that one outcome of Landcare, perhaps its most significant outcome, has been the construction of social capital, but it is impossible to know, in the absence of a comprehensive longitudinal study, if it really has grown. It may have actually reduced collective social capital by creating division between Landcare members and non-members, those who adopt its prescriptions versus those who do not. As Myers and Macnaghten (1998) revealed, crisis rhetoric, with which Landcare tends to be surrounded, does not foster collective social capital. It is also wise to ask to what purposes appropriated social capital might be put to serve whose interests. All attempts to build social capital should proceed with caution.

Regional Government

Intervention in the construction of social capital should be aimed at removing the threats to it from social inequality and division. One step towards removing these threats is taken with the establishment of genuinely pluralistic, participatory regional government. Such government will also have the capacity for social analysis and policy development, presently lacking in local government. It might follow the example of integrated local area planning and social planning as required of local councils by the government of New South Wales. These are, however, legislative prescriptions aimed at existing local government. Regional government (or if Australia went in a parallel direction, new States) must be based on social capital which is not necessarily based on social equality, but rather on equity and definitely not elitism. In this way, reflexivity will not be blocked in its response to the structures of gender, class and race/ethnicity. This will open a conservative rural culture, steeped in an agrarianism and filled with contradictions by liminality, to a questioning of productivism, masculinity and exclusion.

There is also a spatial dimension to social capital within regions. Regional, rather than local community cultures will also flourish with an institutional base which retains focus on the 'otherness' of metropolitan and global entities. Interdependence within regions can focus attention on regional spatial inequalities. Reflexivity should be allowed to retain its 'countryminded' focus, but in a way which does not maintain existing power relations within or among regions or between regional and metropolitan Australia. Regional institutions and organisations must defragment and obtain sufficient resources. This is predicated on a reflexivity which focuses on the forces which seek to 'divide and conquer' and obscure the benefits of co-operation and collaboration. It is feasible that communities which have a long tradition of competition will reflect on their relationship to urban capital. Fitzgerald (1991) asked if it were possible that working-class members of a community would see themselves as sharing an interest with those of another community even though the communities were competing to retain industry. In principle, local consciousness and action in individual communities in regional Australia could, as Fitzgerald found, foster action at the wider level, but only when reflexivity dispenses with current versions of countrymindedness and aims its arrows directly at the source of dependency – regional dependency on national and global capital, rather than the governments which serve capital. Here lies the potential seed for reflexivity amid globalisation.

Institutional Change

It will, however, all require institutional change. Regional dwellers, even those in the larger towns and cities, are caught in a double-bind. Their high level of ownership of property gives them a stake in their locality. Furthermore, the belief in the institution of private property heightens their sensitivity to property issues (see the discussion about the effects of planning in Gray (1991)). They dare not, or do not wish to, do anything to threaten property values (Gray, 1993). Hence, they are very vulnerable to the 'growth machine' politics of local elites (Molotch, 1976) and find it particularly difficult to resist the offerings of agribusiness and other forms of capital including perpetuated productivism. In so doing they enter relationships which ultimately perpetuate their dependency and environmental degradation.

As Varnam et al. (1990) showed, it is most unlikely that the frequent appeals by rural people to the city for assistance on the basis of agrarian arguments will ever be heard. City people may take an interest when they see farmers suffering during flood or drought, but their voluntary acceptance of a necessity for higher food prices in order to support farmers is most unlikely. It is not surprising that deregulation and associated promises of lower food prices have not been questioned by city people. Appeals to city voters, within existing political institutions are fruitless. Appeals to rural voters within the same institutions are equally fruitless, as

illustrated by the failure of the Country Summit Alliance at the 1999 New South Wales election. But appeals on the basis of local and regional representation are not, as illustrated by the
strong performances of some independents at that election.

For this reason it is essential that institutions of regional government be equipped to
take responsibility for well-being in all the communities in their spheres of influence. Orfield
(1997) presents a model developed in United States cities through which central and outer
city authorities recognised and acted to ameliorate the social disasters which followed deindustrialisation in the inner suburbs (see Wacquant, 1995 for a particularly horrifying account
of these situations). They did so because they recognised a mutual interest in the well-being of
the entire city. There is no reason why a similar logic could not be accepted by regional government and applied in all its socio-spatial dimensions, provided that genuinely pluralistic
regional institutions and organisations are established. This realisation of common interests
across regions is essential to the implementation of regional, autonomous institutions of government, lest it be opposed by those from smaller settlements who would fear a new, intra-
regional dimension to dependency under the power of larger towns and cities.

With regard to fundamental institutional change, Australia faces two choices. The first
is to create regional entities with no legal status, but which articulate with the three levels of
government. A second is to create permanent structures that have the power to make decisions and enact rules – ensuring that when the regional community makes decisions, those
decisions lead to on-ground actions. The latter, we believe, represents real empowerment and
is the only viable way to counteract the urbocentric nature of policy making, and the current
failures of government to deal with regional social, economic and environmental degradation.

Governments at the local, State and Federal levels now accept the view of ecologists
that the 'bio-region' should be the logical base for decision-making about natural resource and
socio-political issues (Kim and Weaver, 1994; Forman, 1995; Dore and Woodhill, 1999;
Dovers and Mobbs, 1999; Mobbs and Dovers, 1999; Brunckhorst and Coop, forthcoming).
The region is viewed as the 'natural' spatial entity for resource management largely because
people can view themselves as members of a bio-physical catchment or subcatchment and can
therefore understand how the use of natural resources in one area affects another (AFFA,
1999). However, 'bio-regionalism' has suffered criticism (Jennings and Moore, 1999) and the
division of Australia into regions for development purposes has always been problematic.

Regionalism, of course, presupposes drastic change to Australian federalism. But the
establishment of regions, or even new States, has often been discussed. The Whitlam government's regionalisation failed after fervent opposition from the States. There have been
attempts by regional people to create new States which have also failed. What is mooted in
this book is fundamentally different. It has been developed from a regional perspective on
regional problems, in a context of globalisation with its impact on national sovereignty and an
imperative for sustainability. It is also based on the proposed growth of regional institutions
driven in part by popular reflexivity.

Despite historical failures, regionalism has never been off the public agenda entirely.
Optimistic advocates of radical change (such as Tanner (1999) and Dennis Altman (quoted
by Byrski, 1998)) are accompanied by pessimistic advocates (like John Button with regard to
the short term at least (also quoted by Byrski, 1998)). But there is a strongly held and reason-

able view that Australia's present three-tier system of government is inappropriate to a global-ised world. It is also inappropriate to the interests of regional Australians. And might State governments be more likely to recognise it as such at a time when the regions are declining as a source of wealth and growing as a source of inequality and uncertainty? The new state move-ments of the 1920s and 1930s and into the 1960s (see Crowley, 1985) arose during times of long-term optimism for rural industries, pre-dating current concerns about sustainability. Now our regional areas are depicted as long-term liabilities rather than long-term assets.

A more recent advocate (Stilwell, 2000) sees regional government as essential to addressing regional inequities and, while not claiming it to be likely to occur in the first decade of the twenty-first century, does see it as viable in the longer term. He describes two proposed geographical models, one of which was offered by the Kelty Taskforce on Regional Development (1993). Stilwell argues that land taxation could be used by a regional system to steer development away from the cities. Moreover, he says it would provide the only economic means of addressing uneven development. He acknowledges that effects on sustainability would have to be considered and that strong central authority over international trade policies would be needed to prevent destructive competition among regions for investment, as decried by Amin (1999). Regionalism is presented as a radical but straightforward solution to the problems of sustainable development.

Equity and Sustainability

The institutions of government are not the only significant resources needed. We argued earlier that central government must continue to support the development of regional infra-structure. This extends to the provision of facilities in which reflexivity can develop, specifically in educational institutions, alongside social capital. The inequalities and ideologies of rural and regional Australians have been discussed extensively in earlier chapters. Their entrench-ment in cultures will make them difficult for rural and regional people to reflect upon. While asserting the need for autonomous reflexivity, we acknowledge that exogenously introduced educational practices are as necessary to the development of autonomous reflexivity as they are to the development of their economic and environmental resources.

It is important that we recognise that rural Australia has a distinctive culture, but one which is not of its own making and which is being appropriated by the dominant urban culture anyway. The forces for cultural change are present, particularly in feminism. While it is hard to predict that rural feminism will move towards a wholesale rejection of productivism, at least it has the capacity to question the dominant masculinist paradigm and to create collective social capital. The current fashion for seeking cultural change is misguided to the extent that cultural change is already happening. Is it not reasonable to expect questioning of the agrarian values of independence and self-reliance when co-operation and collective class action start to appear essential for the survival of families on their farms? To a large extent reflexivity only requires the maintenance of the rural social fabric in order to survive. This should not, how-ever, be seen as a purely endogenous activity. As this book has shown, outsiders' views can be illuminating as they reinterpret cultures for their adherents, and in so doing, help those people to judge the good and the bad in their cultures for themselves; in other words, so that they accept the challenge of postmodern reflexivity.

Reflexivity and the growth of social capital are essential, but under a regional model of government the notion of social equity is predicated upon maintenance of fiscal equalisation. Fiscal equalisation has been shown to prevent a drift toward centralisation and federal disintegration in Canada when compared to the United States (Theret, 1999). Regionalisation for sustainability must be built on models and practices of fiscal equalisation which are based on sustainability criteria, not just crude population statistics. Current models of fiscal equalisation for distribution of Commonwealth funds to the States and local government are a little more sophisticated than this, but much needs to be done to place the distribution of funds on a sustainability basis among regions. The creation of 'enterprise zones', based upon a US model, is heralded as a possible solution to Australia's regional problems (NIEIR, 2001). It certainly represents one means by which fiscal equalisation can be attempted. But enterprise zones are almost exclusively focused on economic growth, not sustainable regional development. It is as if social benefits and environmental security will flow automatically from a host of taxation breaks and investment incentives – both linked to enhanced forms of local government cooperation (see NIEIR, 2001). We believe such an approach (a legacy of the 'old thinking') is naive and would provide a partial solution, at best. Moreover, unless taxation law is attuned to the objectives of regional fiscal equalisation very little positive change will occur in regional Australia.

Might some change be achievable in the short term? Australia can move forward by applying the principles set out above and adopting the recommendations from Dore and Woodhill aimed at sustainable regional development. One step towards doing so is to recognise that rural Australia remains an asset though dependent, that central support for it is essential and that fragmentation is helping to maintain helplessness through dependency. The establishment of 'partnerships' will not change that relationship. A parallel step involves recognising that neoliberalism is destroying rural society, or creating the conditions for its disintegration as inevitably as productivism is destroying its natural environment.

Australia's regions are those of the nation, not the States. Hence regionalism must be accepted by the States as primarily a national issue to be worked on jointly. We would accept that it is most unlikely to proceed as radical change. Rather, we advocate a process involving initial modification of existing institutions, despite their shortcomings. Neither regionalism nor reflexivity is likely to develop quickly. Nevertheless, governments should undertake, in the short term, to work towards the following longer-term actions. They should:

- provide substantial incentives for local government reconstruction/transformation, applying the Orfield (1997) principles to promote consideration of local as well as regional interests, so that viable regional entities can be created, from the initiative of regional people, with cultures fostering pluralistic democracy and social equity;
- once formed, give substantial power to these organisations to allow planning for population growth, economic development, and environmental management on a regional basis;
- facilitate co-ordination throughout each region with new initiatives in telecommunications, transport, health, education, culture and the environment alongside elimination of the forces depleting social capital as they bolster inequality;

- identify those regions experiencing major social disadvantage, economic inequality or environmental deterioration and close the gaps through fiscal equalisation. This will also be achieved by identifying mechanisms which aid and reward regions in their quest for sustainability;
- set up a national network of co-ordination between the regions to allow for new ideas and approaches to be readily generalised when they prove worthwhile and foster a national regional consciousness from which regional interests are powerfully expressed and conflicts negotiated;
- ensure each region has adequate tertiary education and research facilities and establish within regional higher educational institutions (including TAFE) United States-style 'land grant' responsibilities to foster local development through reflective 'people-focused' training, accreditation and interaction. While the granting of land would not be the purpose here, funding to facilitate and co-ordinate local socio-economic development would be. Their mission would be to stimulate and underpin sustainable regional development at the same time as they generate social capital;
- put in place mechanisms that will prevent the state 'decommissioning' the regions if there is any change in government at the State or Federal level.

We stress that, other than by way of the long-held principle of fiscal equalisation and the imperative for sustainability, we are not advocating special treatment of rural and regional dwellers in the long term. We adhere to the principle that like each of the States, the regions of Australia should work with each other, valuing each other's contribution to their own self-sustainability. We also stress our view that, despite all the threats to social capital discussed above, we see rural communities at local and regional level as capable of fostering social equity and inclusion among all people and localities. As Wahlquist (1999) points out, citing the success of New South Wales member of parliament Tony Windsor who rejected One Nation Party racism, rural people appreciate that the strength of their communities lies in their inclusivity. As discussed earlier, egalitarianism amid social inequality, which has impacts on everyday life of a kind not experienced in the larger cities, sustains a delicate and fallible, but persistent, inclusivity. It is social bifurcation amid the changes of restructuring imposed by globalisation along the neoliberal path which poses the greatest threat to such inclusivity.

And a role for the communities, other than subscribing to the above? Exhortations to develop themselves, have 'visions' or find leaders may provide minimal excitement and opportunity, but – without the devolution of decision-making power and provision of the resources necessary to give effect to that power – they border on the futile. Rather, we advocate reflection on global structures and globalising cultures. As globalisation diminishes the autonomy of nations, so might it be seen as appropriate for regions or localities to form their own networks for global action. Rural Australians are by no means the only people who depend on unsustainable agricultural systems resulting from productivism. Nor are they the only people with an interest in 'clean and green' agriculture. Community organisation can extend beyond national boundaries and market role, as evidenced by the achievements of organisations like Greenpeace and Amnesty International and the current and historical struggles of the trade union movement. Wiseman (1998: 145) saw some potential in such movements as an anti-dote to the 'beggar-thy-neighbour' or 'race to the bottom' process among local communities amid globalisation. It is conceivable that transnational capital might occasionally see a mutual interest in such activities, based on the example of the actions of Sainsbury's (UK) super-market chain against genetically modified foods. National governments are no longer the only potential source of support for rural interests.

Our exhortations to regional people to take opportunities offered by globalisation might resemble neoliberal rhetoric. But we see social and political opportunities, not just chances for businesses to make profits. We see opportunities, in part, coming from developing a reflexivity which will illuminate the contradictions of neoliberalism and the social disasters to come from ignoring social inequity and injustice. We see opportunities from global connectedness and reflection on social and environmental conditions on a global scale. We also see opportunities emanating from the rush by governments to destroy their capacity to govern while attempting to maintain that capacity with institutions based on rhetoric, the inconsistencies and contra-dictions of which will inevitably become apparent to a reflexive population. The opportunity for creating the institutions necessary to SRD can only arise through that reflexivity. Recent political instability is only the first hint that governments cannot ignore these processes.

What of our own reflexivity? We are sure readers will recognise that, as regional dwellers, we are caught in the same double-bind as our neighbours.

Further Reading

Agriculture, Forestry and Fisheries – Australia (AFFA) (2000) Steering Committee Report to Australian Governments on the Public Response to Managing Natural Resources in Rural Australia for a Sustainable Future: a Discussion Paper for Developing National Policy, Canberra: AFFA.
– government thinking on pathways toward sustainable regional development
Cavaye, J. (2000) Our Community, Our Future: a Guide to Rural Community Development, Brisbane: Department of Primary Industries.
– an overview of community development models, including new approaches
Dore, J. and Woodhill, J. (1999) Sustainable Regional Development: Final Report, Canberra: Greening Australia.
– defines and proposes means of achieving sustainable regional development
Stilwell, F. (2000) Changing Track: A New Political Economic Direction for Australia, Sydney: Pluto Press.
– discusses models for regional government and issues surrounding them
Winter, I. (ed.) (2000) Social Capital and Public Policy in Australia, Melbourne: Australian Institute of Family Studies.
– a collection of papers discussing the problems and prospects for the development of social capital as a means of addressing social problems
Wiseman, J. (1998) Global Nation? Australia and the Politics of Globalisation, Cambridge: Cambridge University Press.
– suggests local and regional potential for addressing globalisation

Bibliography

Acres Australia, 6, 8 July 2000; 5 August 1991: 14.

Agriculture, Forestry and Fisheries, Australia (AFFA) (2000) *Steering Committee Report to Australian Governments on the Public Response to Managing Natural Resources in Rural Australia for a Sustainable Future: A Discussion Paper for Developing National Policy*, AFFA, Canberra, July.

—— (1999) *Managing Natural Resources in Rural Australia for a Sustainable Future: A Discussion Paper for Developing a National Policy*, Canberra: AFFA.

Albrecht, D. (1998) 'The Industrial Transformation of Farm Communities: Implications for Family Structure and Socioeconomic Conditions', *Rural Sociology*, 63, 1: 51–64.

—— (1997) 'The Changing Structure of US Agriculture: Dualism Out, Industrialism In', *Rural Sociology*, 62, 4: 474–90.

Albrow, M. (1990) 'Introduction', in Albrow, M. and King, E. (eds) *Globalisation, Knowledge and Society*, London: Sage.

Alexander, I. and Jones, R. (1997) 'Some Days Too Far Away: Service Provision in Rural Esperance, W.A.', in Bliss, E. (ed.) *Proceedings of the Second Joint Conference of the Institute of Australian Geographers and the New Zealand Geographical Society*, Hobart: January: 119–21.

Alexander, M. (1998) 'The Rise of Globalism in the International World Economy: Bringing Sociological Analysis Back In', in Alexander, M., Harding, S., Harrison, P., Kendall, G., Skrbis, Z. and Western, J. (eds) *Refashioning Sociology: Responses to a New World Order*, Proceedings of the Annual Conference of the Australian Sociological Association, Brisbane: 232–7.

Alexandra, J. and Eyre, D. (1993) 'Water and Environment', in Johnson, M. and Rix, S. *Water in Australia: Managing Economic, Environmental and Community Reform*, Sydney: Pluto Press: 85–120.

Allen, J. and Dillman, D. (1994) *Against All Odds: Rural Community in the Information Age*, Boulder: Westview Press.

Alston, M. (1999) 'Surviving in Rural Communities: a Blueprint for the New Millennium', *Proceedings of the Country Matters Conference*, Canberra: Bureau of Rural Sciences, W2 (1).

—— (1998) 'Farm Women and Their Work: Why is it Not Recognised?' *Journal of Sociology*, 34, 1: 23–34.

—— (1997) 'Socio-cultural Factors and Family Farming', in Lees, J. (ed.) *A Legacy Under Threat? Family Farming in Australia*, Armidale: University of New England Press: 99–119.

—— (1996) 'Backs to the Wall: Rural Women Make Formidable Activists', in Lawrence, G., Lyons, K. and Momtaz, S. (eds) *Social Change in Rural Australia: Perspectives from the Social Sciences*, Rural Social and Economic Research Centre, Rockhampton, Queensland: Central Queensland University: 77–84.

—— (1995) *Women on the Land: The Hidden Heart of Rural Australia*, Sydney: University of New South Wales Press.

Altieri, M. (2000) 'The Ecological Impacts of Transgenic Crops on Agroecosystem Health', *Ecosystem Health* 6, 1: 13–23.

—— (1998) 'Ecological Impacts of Industrial Agriculture and the Possibility for Truly Sustainable Farming', in Magdoff, F., Buttel, F. and Foster, J. (eds) *Hungry for Profit: Agriculture, Food and Ecology*, New York: Monthly Review Press: 60–71.

—— (1998) 'Ecological Impacts of Industrial Agriculture and the Possibilities for Truly Sustainable Farming', *Monthly Review*, 50, 3, July–August: 60–71.

Amin, A. (1999) 'An Institutionalist Perspective on Regional Economic Development', *International Journal of Urban and Regional Research*, 23, 2: 365–78.

Anderson, J. (1999) 'Foundation for the Future of Regional Australia', Media Release from the Deputy Prime Minister and Minister for Transport and Regional Services, 28 October, www.nolg.gov.au/regional/summit/media/anderson/a160_99.htm

—— (1998) 'Start Talkin': Anderson's Vision for the Bush', *The Land*, 29 October: 17.

Anderson, J. and MacDonald, I. (1999) 'Regional Australia: Meeting the Challenges', *Ministerial Statements*, Canberra: Parliament of Australia.

Anosike, N. and Coughenour, C. M. (1990) 'The Socioeconomic Basis of Farm Enterprise Diversification Decisions', *Rural Sociology*, 55, 1: 1–24.

Appadurai, A. (1990) 'Disjuncture and Difference in the Global Cultural Economy', in Featherstone, M. (ed.) *Global Culture*, London: Sage: 295–310.

Argent, N. M. and Rolley, F. (2000) 'Financial Exclusion in Rural and Remote New South Wales, Australia; a Geography of Bank Branch Rationalisation, 1981–98', *Australian Geographical Studies*, 38, 2: 182–203.

Australasian Biotechnology, 8, 2: 81–3.

Australian, 12 October 2000; 12 September 2000; 19 August 2000: 23; 12 April 2000; 27 November 1999; 20 November 1999; 2 October 1996.

Australian Broadcasting Corporation (1999) 'Report on Dairy Farmer Organization's Stated Attitude to Industry Deregulation', *The Country Hour*, 10 December 1999.

Australian Bureau of Statistics (1998) *Household Use of Information Technology, Australia*, Cat. No. 8146.0, Canberra: ABS.

Australian Conservation Foundation (1999) 'Say "No!" to Gene Tech's Bitter Harvest', Supplement to *Habitat*, June.

Australian Farm Journal, 8, 10, December 1998; February 1992.

Australian Institute of Health and Welfare (1998) *Health in Rural and Remote Australia*, Canberra: Australian Institute for Health and Welfare.

Australian Magazine, 9 September 2000.

Australian Rural Adjustment Unit (1981) *Submission from the Australian Rural Adjustment Unit to the Working Group preparing a Policy Discussion Paper on Agriculture*, Armidale: University of New England.

Avery, D. (1995) *Saving the Planet with Pesticides and Plastic: The Environmental Triumph of High-Yield Farming*, Indianapolis: Hudson Institute.

Ayres, J. (1996) 'Essential Elements of Strategic Visioning', in Norman, W. (ed.) *Community Strategic Visioning Programs*, Westport, CT: Praeger: 21–36.

Bachrach, P. and Baratz, M. S. (1970) *Power and Poverty*, New York: Oxford University Press.

Background Briefing, 'The Starvation of Sustenance', ABC Radio, 27 June 1999.

Badcock, B. (1997) 'Recently Observed Polarising Tendencies and Australian Cities', *Australian Geographical Studies*, 35, 3: 243–59.

Bailey, M. (1997) 'Landcare: Myth or Reality?', in Lockie, S. and Vanclay, F. (eds) *Critical Landcare*, Wagga Wagga, NSW: Centre for Rural Social Research: 129–42.

Banks, J. and Marsden, T. (1997) 'Reregulating the UK Dairy Industry: The Changing Nature of Competitive Space', *Sociologia Ruralis*, 37, 3: 382–404.

Barber, J. (1998) 'Rural Disadvantage in the Distribution of South Australian Home and Community Care Funding', *Australian Journal of Social Issues*, 33, 3: 231–9.

Barlett, P. (1993) *American Dreams, Rural Realities: Family Farms in Crisis*, Chapel Hill, NC: University of North Carolina Press.

Barnes, B. (1977) *Interests and the Growth of Knowledge*, London: Routledge and Kegan Paul.

Barr, N. (1999) 'Structural Adjustment to Facilitate Implementation of Integrated Catchment Management Plans in Mixed Farming Areas', in Jones, P. (ed.) *1998 Dryland Forum, Toowoomba: Proceedings of the Dryland Forum of MDBC Natural Resources Management Strategy Funded Projects, Toowoomba, November, 1998*, Canberra: Murray–Darling Basin Commission: 69–75.

Barr, N. and Cary, J. (2000) *Influencing Improved Natural Resource Management on Farms: a Guide to Understanding Factors Influencing the Adoption of Sustainable Resource Practices*, Canberra: Bureau of Rural Sciences.

Barr, N., Gray, I. and Anderson, N. (1999) 'Structural Adjustment and the Implementation of Catchment Management Plans', *Report Prepared for the Murray–Darling Basin Commission Project D7028: Structural Adjustment to Facilitate Implementation of Integrated Catchment Management Plans in Mixed Farming Areas*, Canberra: Murray–Darling Basin Commission.

Barrow, M. and Hall, M. (1995) 'The Impact of a Large Multinational Organization on a Small Local Economy', *Regional Studies*, 29, 7: 635–53.

Baum, N. (1996) 'The Local Government Perspective', in *Rural Communities Looking Ahead, Proceedings of a Rural Social Policy Conference*, Sydney: New South Wales Council of Social Service: 88–9.

Baumgardt, B. and Martin, M. (eds) (1991) *Agricultural Biotechnology: Issues and Choices*, Indiana: Purdue University Agricultural Experiment Station.

Bawden, R. (1998) 'Life Beyond Economics: Learning Systems and Social Capital', in Falk, I. (ed.) *Learning Communities, Regional Sustainability and the Learning Society*, Conference Proceedings, Volume 1, 13–20 June, 1998, Launceston: Centre for Research and Learning in Regional Australia: 13–18.

Beal, D. and Ralston, D. (1998) 'Economic and Social Impacts of the Closure of the Only Bank in Australian Rural Communities', in Staples, M. and Millmow, A. (eds) *Studies in Australian Rural Economic Development*, Wagga Wagga, NSW: Centre for Rural Social Research, Charles Sturt University: 51–61.

Beale, B. and Fray, P. (1990) *The Vanishing Continent*, Sydney: Hodder & Stoughton.

Beck, U. (2000) *What is Globalization?* Cambridge: Polity.

—— (1996) 'Risk Society and the Provident State', in Lash, S., Szerszynski, B. and Wynne, B. (eds) *Risk, Environment and Modernity: Towards a New Ecology*, London: Sage: 27–43.

——(1992) *Risk Society*, London: Sage.

Beck, U., Giddens, A. and Lash, S. (1994) *Reflexive Modernization: Politics, Tradition and Aesthetics in the Modern Social Order*, Cambridge: Polity Press.

Beder, S. (1997) *Global Spin: The Corporate Assault on Environmentalism*, Melbourne: Scribe Publications.

—— (1996) *The Nature of Sustainable Development*, 2nd edn, Melbourne: Scribe.

Beer, A. (2000) 'Regional Policy and Development in Australia: Running Out of Solutions?' in Pritchard, B. and McManus, P. (eds) *Land of Discontent: the Dynamics of Change in Rural and Regional Australia*, Sydney: University of New South Wales Press: 169–94.

—— (1998) 'Economic Rationalism and the Decline of Local Economic Development in Australia', *Local Economy*, May: 51–63.

Beer, A., Bolam, A. and Maude, A. (1994) *Beyond the Capitals: Urban Growth in Regional Australia*, Canberra: Australian Government Publishing Service.

Beeson, M. and Firth, A. (1998) 'Neoliberalism as a Political Rationality: Australian Public Policy Since the 1980s', *Journal of Sociology*, 34, 3: 215–31.

Beggs, J., Haines, V. and Hurlbert, J. (1996) 'Revisiting the Rural–Urban Contrast: Personal Networks in Nonmetropolitan and Metropolitan Settings', *Rural Sociology*, 61, 2: 306–25.

Beilin, R. (forthcoming) 'The Brave New Order: Power, Visibility and the Everyday Landscapes of Australian Farmers', in Lawrence, G., Higgins, V., and Lockie, S. (eds) *Environment, Society and Natural Resource Management: Theoretical Perspectives from Australasia and the Americas*, Cheltenham, UK: Edward Elgar.

Beilin, R. (1997) 'The Construction of Women in Landcare: Does it Make a Difference?', in Lockie, S. and Vanclay, F. (eds) *Critical Landcare*, Wagga Wagga, NSW: Centre for Rural Social Research, Charles Sturt University: 57–70.

Bell, C. and Newby, H. (1971) *Community Studies*, London: Allen & Unwin.

Bell, D. (1993) *Communitarianism and its Critics*, Oxford: Clarendon Press.

Bell, J., Pandey, U. and Brooks, M. (1992) *A Conceptual Framework for the Sociological Study of Stress in Farming*, Armidale: Department of Sociology, University of New England.

Bell, M. (1995) *Internal Migration in Australia 1986–1991: Overview Report*, Canberra: Bureau of Immigration, Multicultural and Population Research, Australian Government Publishing Service.

—— (1992) 'The Fruit of Difference: The Rural–Urban Continuum as a System of Identity', *Rural Sociology*, 57, 1: 65–82.

Belyea, M. and Lobao, L. (1990) 'Psychosocial Consequences of Agricultural Transformation: The Farm Crisis and Depression', *Rural Sociology*, 55, 1: 58–75.

Bendix, R. (1966) *From Max Weber: An Intellectual Portrait*, London: Methuen.

Benedyka, S. (1998) 'Working Experience: Factors Affecting Employment Change in Dubbo', in *Proceedings of the National Agricultural and Resource Outlook Conference*, Canberra: Australian Bureau of Agricultural and Resource Economics: 71–4.

Beus, C. and Dunlap, R. (1994) 'Endorsement of Agrarian Ideology and Adherence to Agricultural Paradigms', *Rural Sociology*, 59, 3: 462–84.

Bevin, S. (1994) 'The Role of Local Government in Economic Development – The New Zealand Experience', *Regional Policy and Practice*, 3, 1: 35–9.

Biotechnology Australia (1999) *Developing Australia's Biotechnology Future*, Canberra: Commonwealth of Australia.

Bishop, T. (1997) 'Financial Reforms', in Dollery, B. and Marshall, N. (eds) *Australian Local Government: Reform and Renewal*, Melbourne: Macmillan: 172–88.

Bjornlund, H. and McKay, J. (1999) 'Do Permanent Water Markets Facilitate Farm Adjustment and Structural Change Within Irrigation Communities?', *Rural Society*, 9, 3: 555–71.

Black, A., Duff, J., Saggers, S. and Baines, P. (1999) *Rural Communities and Rural Social Research Issues: Priorities for Research: Draft Discussion Paper,* Perth: Centre for Social Research, Edith Cowan University.

Blanc, M. and Mackinnon, N. (1990) 'Gender Relations and the Family Farm in Western Europe', *Journal of Rural Studies*, 6, 4: 401–5.

Blekesaune, A. (1991) 'Changes in Ways of Making a Living Among Norwegian Farmers 1975–1990', *Sociologia Ruralis*, 31, 1: 48–57.

Bohler, K. and Hildenbrand, B. (1990) 'Farm Families Between Tradition and Modernity', *Sociologia Ruralis*, 30, 1: 18–33.

Bolam, A. (1994) 'Small Urban Australia: Central in the National Economy But Still Peripheral in Policy', *Australian Geographer*, 25, 2: 125–32.

Bonanno, A., Busch, L., Friedland, W., Gouveia, L. and Mingione, E. (eds) (1994) *From Columbus to ConAgra: the Globalisation of Agriculture and Food*, Kansas: University Press of Kansas.

Bonner, K. (1998) 'Reflexivity, Sociology and the Rural–Urban Distinction', *Canadian Review of Sociology and Anthropology*, 35, 2: 165–89.

Botterill, L. (2000) 'Government Responses to Farm Poverty: The Policy Development Process', *Rural Society*, 10, 1: 15–27.

—— (1999) 'Farm Welfare: The Policy Development Process', paper prepared for the Bureau of Rural Sciences 'Country Matters' Conference, Canberra, 20–21 May.

Boucher, S., Flynn, A. and Lowe, P. (1991) 'The Politics of Rural Enterprise: A British Case Study', in Whatmore, S., Lowe, P. and Marsden, T. (eds) *Rural Enterprise: Shifting Perspectives on Small-Scale Production*, London: David Fulton: 120–40.

Bourke, L. (1997) 'Preserving Agricultural Land in Times of Urbanisation: Impacts on a Regional Culture in Pennsylvania', in Mules, W. and Miller, H. (eds) *Mapping Regional Cultures*, Rockhampton, Queensland: Rural Social and Economic Research Centre, Central Queensland University: 84–96.

Bowler, I., Clark, G., Crockett, A., Ilbery, B. and Shaw, A. (1996) 'The Development of Alternative Farm Enterprises: A Study of Family Labour Farms in the Northern Pennines of England', *Journal of Rural Studies*, 12, 3: 285–95.

Bowmer, K. (1998) 'Water: Quality and Quantity', in Pratley, J. and Robertson, A. (eds) *Agriculture and the Environmental Imperative*, Melbourne: CSIRO: 35–69.

Brand, K. (1997) 'Environmental Consciousness and Behaviour: the Greening of Lifestyles', in Redclift, M. and Woodgate, G. (eds) *The International Handbook of Environmental Sociology*, United Kingdom: Edward Elgar: 204–17.

Brawley, E. (1994) 'Social and Community Development: Basic Principles and Current Trends', paper delivered at the International Conference on Issues Affecting Rural Communities, Townsville: James Cook University.

Brecher, J. and Costello, T. (1994) *Global Village or Global Pillage: Economic Reconstruction from the Bottom Up*, Boston: South End Press.

Brownhill, D. (1997) Speech to the National Agricultural Outlook Conference, Canberra: ABARE.

Brunckhorst, D. and Coop, P. (forthcoming) 'The Influence of Social Eco-logics in Shaping Novel Resource Governance Frameworks', in Lawrence, G., Higgins, V. and Lockie, S. (eds) *Environment, Society and Natural Resource Management: Theoretical Perspectives from Australasia and the Americas*, Cheltenham, UK: Edward Elgar.

Bryant, L. (1997) Understanding Pluriactivity: Pluriactive Patterns and Subjective Constructions of Pluriactivity in South Australia, unpublished doctoral thesis, Flinders University of South Australia.

Bryson, L. and Mowbray, M. (1981) 'Community: The Spray-On Solution', *Australian Journal of Social Issues*, 16, 4: 255–67.

Budge, T. (1996) 'Population Decline in Victoria and Tasmania', in Newton, P. and Bell, M. (eds) *Population Shift: Mobility and Change in Australia*, Canberra: Australian Government Publishing Service: 192–204.

Burch, D. (forthcoming) *The Political Economy of Agri-food Restructuring*, Report to the Government of Thailand, Nathan: Griffith University.

Burch, D., Goss, J. and Lawrence, G. (eds)(1999) *Restructuring Global and Regional Agricultures: Transformations in Australasian Economies and Spaces*, Aldershot: Ashgate.

Burch, D., Lawrence, G., Rickson, R. and Goss, J. (eds) (1998) *Australasian Food and Farming in a Globalised Economy: Recent Developments and Future Prospects*, Melbourne: Department of Geography and Environmental Science, Monash University.

Burch, D., Rickson, R. and Annels, R. (1992) 'The Growth of Agribusiness: Environmental and Social Implications of Contract Farming', in Lawrence, G., Vanclay, F. and Furze, B. (eds) *Agriculture, Environment and Society*, Melbourne: Macmillan: 259–79.

Burch, D., Rickson, R. and Lawrence, G. (eds) (1996) *Globalization and Agri-food Restructuring: Perspectives from the Australasia Region*, Aldershot: Avebury.

Burchell, G. (1996) 'Liberal Government and Techniques of the Self', in Barry, A., Osborne, T. and Rose, N. (eds) *Foucault and Political Reason: Liberalism, Neo-Liberalism and Rationalities of Government*, Chicago: University of Chicago Press: 19–36.

Burdon, Alan (1996) 'Commonwealth Government Assistance for Adjustment in Agriculture', in *Australian Rural Policy Papers 1990–95*, Canberra: Australian Government Publishing Service: 1–48.

Bureau of Industry Economics (1994) *Regional Development: Patterns and Policy Implications*, Canberra: Australian Government Publishing Service.

Burnley, I., Murphy, P. and Fagan, R. (1997) *Immigration and Australian Cities*, Sydney: Federation Press.

Buttel, F. (2000) 'Some Reflections on Late Twentieth Century Agrarian Political Economy', paper presented to the 10th World Congress of Rural Sociology, Rio de Janeiro, 30 July–5 August.

—— (1998) 'Some Observations on States, World Orders, and the Politics of Sustainability', *Organisation and Environment*, 11, 3, September: 261–86.

—— (1994) 'Agricultural Change, Rural Society and the State in the Late Twentieth Century', in Symes, D. and Jansen, A. (eds) *Agricultural Restructuring and Rural Change in Europe*, Wageningen Studies in Sociology, 37, Wageningen: Agricultural University: 13–31.

Buxton, G. (1985) '1870–1890', in Crowley, F. (ed.) *A New History of Australia*, Melbourne: Heinemann: 165–215.

Byrski, L. (1998) *The Way Ahead: Prominent Australians Talk about the Future of Our Nation*, Sydney: New Holland.

Cahill, G. (1995) *Growing Your Own Community: Successful Adjustment Strategies for Rural Communities*, Bendigo: Agriculture Victoria.

Cameron, J. and Elix, J. (1991) *Recovering Ground*, Melbourne: Australian Conservation Foundation.

Campagne, P., Carrere, G. and Valceschini, E. (1990) 'Three Agricultural Regions of France: Three Types of Pluriactivity', *Journal of Rural Studies*, 6, 4: 415–22.

Campbell, H. (1994) Regulation and Crisis in New Zealand Agriculture: The Case of Ashburton County, 1984–1992, unpublished PhD thesis, Wagga Wagga, NSW: Charles Sturt University.

Campbell, H. and Coombes, B. (1999) 'Green Protectionism and Organic Food Exporting from New Zealand: Crisis Experiments in the Breakdown of Fordist Trade and Agricultural Policies', *Rural Sociology*, 64, 2, June: 302–19.

Campbell, H. and Liepins, R. (1999) 'The Development of Organic Standards in New Zealand: Evaluating the Evolution of Organic Certification During Export-Led Development', paper presented at the XVIII Congress of the European Society for Rural Sociology, Lund, Sweden, 24–28 August.

Campbell, H. and Phillips, E. (1993) 'The Uncoupling Thesis: A Critical Appraisal', *Regional Journal of Social Issues*, 27: 47–9.

Campbell, K. (1985) 'Changing Institutions, Processes and Issues in the Formation of Australian Agricultural Policy', *Australian Journal of Agricultural Economics*, 29, 3: 210–29.

Carroll, J. and Manne, R. (eds) (1992) *Shutdown: the Failure of Economic Rationalism*, Melbourne: Text.

Carroll, M. (1996) 'Building Community', in *Rural Communities Looking Ahead, Proceedings of a Rural Social Policy Conference*, Sydney: New South Wales Council of Social Service: 78–81.

Cavaye, J. (2000) *Our Community, Our Future: A Guide to Rural Community Development*, Brisbane: Department of Primary Industries, Queensland.

—— (1999a) The Role of Government in Community Capacity Building, unpublished manuscript, Department of Primary Industries, Rockhampton, Queensland.

—— (1999b) 'The Role of Public Agencies in Helping Rural Communities Build Social Capital', paper presented at the International Symposium on Society and Resource Management, Brisbane: University of Queensland, July.

Chapman, R. and Wood, M. (1984) *Australian Local Government: The Federal Dimension*, Sydney: George Allen & Unwin.

Cheers, B. (1998) *Welfare Bushed: Social Care in Rural Australia*, Aldershot: Ashgate.

Cheru, F. (1996) 'New Social Movements: Democratic Struggles and Human Rights in Africa', in Mittelman, J. (ed.) *Globalisation: Critical Reflections*, Boulder: Lynne Rienner: 145–64.

Chew, S. (1995) 'Environmental Transformations: Accumulation, Ecological Crisis, and Social Movements', in Smith, D. and Borocz, J. (eds) *A New World Order? Global Transformations in the Late Twentieth Century*, Connecticut: Praeger: 201–15.

Chiappe, M. B. and Flora, C. B. (1998) 'Gendered Elements of the Alternative Agriculture Paradigm', *Rural Society*, 63, 3: 372–93.

Chisholm, D. (1995) 'Maintaining a Sustainable Economic Base in Rural Towns: A Case Study of Leeton', *Australian Geographer*, 26, 2: 156–63.

—— (1994) 'The Letona Crisis', *Rural Society*, 4, 1: 2–5.

Claridge, C. (1999) 'Rural Women, Decision Making and Leadership Within Environmental and Landcare Groups', *Rural Society*, 8, 3: 183–95.

Clark, D., Ilbery, B. and Berkeley, N. (1995) 'Telematics and Rural Businesses: An Evaluation of Uses, Potentials and Policy Implications', *Regional Studies*, 29, 2: 171–80.

Clarke, P. and Little, J. (1997) *Contested Countryside Cultures*, London: Routledge.

Cloke, P. (1997) 'Editorial: Country Backwater to Virtual Village? Rural Studies and the "Cultural Turn"', *Journal of Rural Studies*, 13, 4: 367–75.

Cloke, P. and Thrift, N. (1994) 'Refiguring the Rural', in Cloke, P., Doel, M., Matless, D., Phillips, M. and Thrift, N., *Writing the Rural: Five Cultural Geographies*, London: Paul Chapman Publishing: 1–5.

Cloke, P., Doel, M., Matless, D., Phillips, M. and Thrift, N. (1994) *Writing the Rural: Five Cultural Geographies*, London: Paul Chapman Publishing.

Cloke, P., Goodwin, M. and Milbourne, P. (1998) 'Cultural Change and Conflict in Rural Wales: Competing Constructs of Identity', *Environment and Planning A*, 30, 3: 463–80.

Cocklin, C. and Wall, M. (1997) 'Contested Rural Futures: New Zealand's East Coast Forestry Project', *Journal of Rural Studies*, 13, 2: 149–62.

Cohen, A. (1985) *The Symbolic Construction of Community*, London: Ellis Horwood/Tavistock.

Cohen, A. (1982) 'Blockade: A Case Study of Local Consciousness in an Extra Local Event', in Cohen, A.
     (ed.) *Belonging: Identity and Social Organisation in British Rural Cultures*, Manchester: Manchester Uni-
     versity Press: 292–321.
Coleman, W. and Skogstad, G. (1995) 'Neo-Liberalism, Policy Networks and Policy Change: Agricultural
     Policy Reform in Australia and Canada', *Australian Journal of Political Science*, 30: 242–63.
Collingridge, M. (1991) 'What is Wrong with Rural Social and Community Services?', *Rural Society* 1, 2: 2–6.
—— (1989) 'Editorial', *Rural Welfare Research Bulletin*, 1.
Colliver, R. (1998) *Better Planning for Rural Development*, Canberra: Rural Industries Research and Develop-
     ment Corporation.
Commins, P. (1990) 'Restructuring Agriculture in Advanced Societies: Transformation, Crisis and
     Responses', in Marsden, T., Lowe, P. and Whatmore, S. (eds) *Rural Restructuring: Global Processes and
     their Responses*, London: David Fulton: 45–76.
Commonwealth Department of Housing and Regional Development (1994) *Working Nation: Policies and Pro-
     grams*, Canberra: Australian Government Publishing Service.
Commonwealth Scientific and Industrial Research Organisation (CSIRO) (1991) *Australia's Environment and
     Its Natural Resources*, Canberra: CSIRO.
Conacher, A. and Conacher, J. (1995) *Rural Land Degradation in Australia*, Melbourne: Oxford University Press.
Connors, T. (1996) *To Speak with One Voice: The Quest by Australian Farmers for Federal Unity*, National Farm-
     ers' Federation, Canberra.
Connors, T. (1998) 'Farmers Can Solve their Problems by Themselves', *Australian Farm Journal*, 8, 9: 16–17.
Coombs, H. C. (1981) *Trial Balance*, Melbourne: Macmillan.
Corby, D., Walker, G. and Murphy, T. (1998) 'Investment Returns in the Central West', in Staples, M. and
     Millmow, A. (eds) *Studies in Australian Rural Economic Development*, Centre for Rural Social Research,
     Wagga Wagga, NSW: Charles Sturt University: 81–8.
Costar, B. and Woodward, D. (1985) 'Conclusion', in Costar, B. and Woodward, D. *Country to National: Aus-
     tralian Rural Politics and Beyond*, Sydney: George Allen & Unwin: 135–8.
Courier Mail, 14 December 1999: 4; 25 March 1998: 4; 18 March 1999.
Cowell, D. and Green, G. (1994) 'Community Attachment and Spending Location: The Importance of Place
     in Household Consumption', *Social Science Quarterly*, 75, 3: 637–55.
Cox, E. (1995) *A Truly Civil Society: the 1995 Boyer Lectures*, Sydney: ABC Books.
Cox, K. and Wood, A. (1994) 'Local Government and Local Economic Development in the United States',
     Regional Studies, 28, 6: 640–5.
Cox, R. (1996) 'A Perspective of Globalisation', in Mittelman, J. (ed.) *Globalisation: Critical Reflections*, Boul-
     der: Lynne Rienner: 21–32.
—— (1991) 'The Global Political Economy and Social Choice', in Drache, D. and Gertler, M. (eds) *The New
     Era of Global Competition: State Policy and Market Power*, Montreal: McGill-Queen's University Press:
     335–49.
Craig, R. and Phillips, K. (1983) 'Agrarian Ideology in Australia and the United States', *Rural Sociology*, 48, 3:
     409–20.
Cribb, J. (1994) 'The Unsettling of Australia: Disturbing Trends on the Way to 2001', *Australian Magazine*,
     12–13 February: 10–16.
Croft, J. (1994) 'Community Bond Issue – a Capital LETSystem', *Rural Society*, 3, 4: 13–15.
Crook, S. (1998) 'Biotechnology, Risk and Sociocultural (Dis)order', in Hindmarsh, R., Lawrence, G. and
     Norton, J. (eds) *Altered Genes – Reconstructing Nature: The Debate*, Sydney: Allen & Unwin: 132–44.
Crook, S., Pakulski, J. and Waters, M. (1992) *Postmodernization: Change in Advanced Society*, London: Sage.
Crowley, F. (ed.) (1985) *A New History of Australia*, Melbourne: Heinemann.
Dale, A. (1998) 'Essential Elements of a Successful Regional Plan', in Grimes, J., Lawrence, G. and Stehlik, D.
     (eds) *Sustainable Futures: Towards a Catchment Management Strategy for the Central Queensland Region*,
     Rockhampton, Queensland: Institute for Sustainable Regional Development: 15–27.
Dale, A. and Bellamy, J. (1998) *Regional Resource Use Planning in Rangelands: An Australian Review*, Canberra:
     Land and Water Resources Research and Development Corporation.

Dale, A., Bellamy, J., MacLeod, N., Lowes, D., Bischof, R., Cowell, S., Howlett, C. and Said, A. (1998) *Regional Resource Use Planning in Rangelands: An Australian Review*, Canberra: Land and Water Resources Research and Development Corporation.

Davenport, S., Lynch, J. and Douglas, R. (1991) 'Country Towns and Fluctuating Rural Fortunes – Is There a Case for Assistance?', *Review of Marketing and Agricultural Economics*, 59, 3: 255–70.

Davidson, A. (1997) 'The Dilemma of the Middle: Restructuring of the Dairy Industry in New South Wales', *Rural Society*, 7, 2: 17–27.

Davidson, A. and Schwarzweller, H. (1995) 'Marginality and Uneven Development: The Decline of Dairying in Michigan's North Country', *Sociologia Ruralis*, 35, 1: 40–66.

Davidson, B. (1981) *European Farming in Australia*, Amsterdam: Elsevier.

Davidson, B. and Lees, J. (1993) *An Investigation of Poverty in Rural and Remote Regions of Australia*, Armidale: The Rural Development Centre, University of New England.

Dawson, B. (1994) 'Rural Employment in Australia', *Rural Society*, 4, 2: 14–21.

Dean, M. (1999) *Governmentality: Foucault, Power and Social Structure*, Sage: London.

de Haan, L. (2000) 'Globalization, Localization and Sustainable Livelihood', *Sociologia Ruralis*, 40, 3: 339–65.

De Vries, W. (1990) 'Pluriactivity and Changing Household Relations in the Land van Maas en Waal, The Netherlands', *Journal of Rural Studies*, 6, 4: 423–8.

Decima Research (1993) *Final Report to the Canadian Institute of Biotechnology on Public Attitudes towards Biotechnology*, Ottawa: Canadian Institution of Biotechnology.

Dempsey, K. (1992) *A Man's Town: Inequality Between Men and Women in Rural Australia*, Melbourne: Oxford University Press.

—— (1990) *Smalltown: A Study of Social Inequality, Cohesion and Belonging*, Melbourne: Oxford University Press.

Department of Foreign Affairs and Trade (1998) *Submission to the Productivity Commission Inquiry into the Impact of Competition Policy Reforms on Rural and Regional Australia*, Canberra.

Department of Industry, Technology and Regional Development (1992) *Human and Community Resources for Regional Economic Development*, Canberra: Australian Government Publishing Service.

Department of Land and Water Conservation (NSW) (1995) *WEST 2000 Where is it up to? The Strategies in Summary*, Dubbo: Department of Land and Water Conservation.

Derrett, R. (1997) 'Socio-Cultural Considerations for Regional Tourism Policy and Planning', *Regional and Enterprise Development Network Newsletter*, 2, 3: 1–2.

Devonport City Council (1998) *Impact of Competition Policy Reforms on Rural and Regional Australia, Submission to Productivity Commission Inquiry*, Devonport: Devonport City Council.

Dick, A. (1998) 'Towns Reap the Benefits from Bush Push', *The Land*, 14 May: 27.

Diesendorf, M. and Hamilton, C. (eds) (1997) *Human Ecology, Human Economy: Ideas for an Ecologically Sustainable Future*, Sydney: Allen & Unwin.

Disney, J. (1990) 'Roles for Government in Urban and Regional Development', in *Economic Planning and Advisory Council, Regional Policies: Future Directions*, Canberra: Australian Government Publishing Service.

Dollery, B. and Marshall, N. (eds) (1997) *Australian Local Government: Reform and Renewal*, Melbourne: Macmillan.

Dollery, B. and Soul, S. (2000) 'A Note on Australian Local Government and Regional Economic and Social Inequalities', *Australian Journal of Social Issues*, 35, 2: 159–68.

Donovan, T. (1993) 'Community Controversy and the Adoption of Economic Development Policies', *Social Science Quarterly*, 74, 2: 386–402.

Dore, J. and Woodhill, J. (1999) *Sustainable Regional Development: Executive Summary of the Final Report*, Canberra: Greening Australia.

—— (1999) *Sustainable Regional Development: Final Report*, Canberra: Greening Australia.

Dovers, S. (1992) 'The History of Natural Resource Use in Rural Australia: Practicalities and Ideologies', in Lawrence, G., Vanclay, F. and Furze, B. (eds) *Agriculture, Environment and Society: Contemporary Issues for Australia*, Melbourne: Macmillan: 1–18.

Dovers, S. and Mobbs, C. (1999) 'Towards the Development of Principles for Adaptive Regional Natural Resource Management', paper presented at the International Symposium on Society and Resource Management, Brisbane: University of Queensland, 8 July.

Dow, G. (2000) 'Economic Rationalism Versus the Community: Reflections on Social Democracy', *Australian Journal of Social Issues*, 34, 3: 209–29.

Drache, D. and Gertler, M. (1991) 'The World Economy and the Nation-State: The New International Order', in Drache, D. and Gertler, M. (eds) *The New Era of Global Competition: State Policy and Market Power*, Montreal: McGill-Queen's University Press: 3–25.

Drought Policy Review Task Force (1990) *Managing for Drought, Final Report*, Canberra: Australian Government Publishing Service.

Drummond, I. (1996) 'Conditions of Unsustainability in the Australian Sugar Industry', *Geoforum*, 27, 3: 345–54.

Drummond, I. and Marsden, T. (1999) *The Condition of Sustainability*, London: Routledge.

Drysdale, R. (1991) 'Aged Migration to Coastal and Inland Centres in NSW', *Australian Geographical Studies*, 29, 2: 268–84.

Dryzek, J. (1997) *The Politics of the Earth: Environmental Discourses*, New York: Oxford University Press.

Duncan, S., Volk, R. and Lewis, R. (1988) 'The Influence of Financial Stressors upon Farm Husbands' and Wives' Well-Being and Family Life Satisfaction', in Marotz-Baden, R., Hennon, C. and Brubaker, R. (eds) *Families in Rural America: Stress, Adaptation and Revitalization*, St Paul: National Council on Family Relations: 32–9.

Easdown, W. (1999) 'The Social Infrastructure Needed to Develop Rural Internet Use in Southern Queensland', *Rural Society*, 9, 3: 585–99.

Economou, N. (1997) 'Is the Tide Turning? The Politics of Sustainable Growth in Regional Australia', paper presented to the Sustainable Economic Growth in Regional Australia Conference, Geelong: September.

Eder, K. (1996) *The Social Construction of Nature: A Sociology of Ecological Enlightenment*, London: Sage.

Efstratoglou-Todoulou, S. (1990) 'Pluriactivity in Different Socio-Economic Contexts: a Test of the Push–Pull Hypothesis in Greek Farming', *Journal of Rural Studies*, 6, 4: 407–13.

Elix, J. and Lambert, J. (1998) *Missed Opportunities: Harnessing the Potential of Women in Australian Agriculture*, Canberra: Rural Industries Research and Development Corporation.

Ellison, N. (1997) 'Towards a New Social Politics: Citizenship and Reflexivity in Late Modernity', *Sociology*, 31, 4: 697–717.

Emy, H. (1998) 'States, Markets and the Global Dimension: An Overview of Certain Issues in Political Economy', in Smyth, P. and Cass, B. (eds) *Contesting the Australian Way*, Cambridge: Cambridge University Press: 17–37.

Epps, R. (1996) 'Technological Change and Communications in a Sparsely Settled Community: A Case Study in Remote Rural Australia', in Lawrence, G., Lyons, K. and Momtaz, S. (eds) *Social Change in Rural Australia: Perspectives from the Social Sciences*, Rockhampton, Queensland: Rural Social and Economic Research Centre, Central Queensland University: 106–18.

Epps, R. and Sorensen, A. (1996) 'The Nature of Leadership in Rural Australia: A Case Study of Four Central Western Queensland Towns', in Lawrence, G., Lyons, K. and Momtaz, S. (eds) *Social Change in Rural Australia: Perspectives from the Social Sciences*, Rockhampton, Queensland: Rural Social and Economic Research Centre, Central Queensland University: 154–66.

Essex, S. and Brown, G. (1997) 'The Emergence of Post-Suburban Landscapes on the North Coast of New South Wales', *International Journal of Urban and Regional Research*, 21, 2: 259–85.

European Association of Development Agencies (1995) *Creation, Development and Management of RDAs: Does it Have to be so Difficult?* Lismore: Centre for Australian Regional Enterprise and Development.

Evans, J. and Ilbery, B. (1993) 'The Pluriactivity, Part-Time Farming, and Farm Diversification Debate', *Environment and Planning A*, 25, 7: 945–59.

Evans, N. and Ilbery, B. (1996) 'Exploring the Influence of Farm-Based Pluriactivity on Gender Relations in Capitalist Agriculture', *Sociologia Ruralis*, 36, 1: 74–92.

—— (1992) 'Farm-based Accommodation and the Restructuring of Agriculture: Evidence from Three English Counties', *Journal of Rural Studies*, 8, 1: 85–96.

Everitt, J. and Annis, R. (1992) 'The Sustainability of Prairie Rural Communities', in Bowler, I., Bryant, C. and Nellis, M. (eds), *Contemporary Rural Systems in Transition*, vol. 2, Wallingford, Oxford: CAB International.

Fairweather, J. (1995) 'Dilemmas and Decisions Over On- or Off-farm Work', *Rural Society*, 5, 1: 6–19.

Falk, I. and Harrison, L. (1998) *Indicators of Social Capital: Social Capital as the Product of Local Interactive Learning Processes*, Discussion Paper D4/1998, Launceston: Centre for Research and Learning in Regional Australia.

Featherstone, M. (1993) 'Global and Local Cultures', in Bird, J., Curtis, B., Putnam, T., Robertson, G. and Tickner, L. (eds) *Mapping the Futures: Local Cultures, Global Change*, London: Routledge: 169–87.

Featherstone, M., Lash, S. and Roberston, R. (eds) (1995) *Global Modernities*, London: Sage.

Filion, P. (1998) 'Potential and Limitations of Community Economic Development: Individual Initiative and Collective Action in a Post-Fordist Context', *Environment and Planning A*, 30, 6: 1101–23.

Fischer, T. (1998) 'Australia's Rural Prospects for 2000 and Beyond', in Staples, M. and Millmow, A. (eds) *Studies in Australian Rural Economic Development*, Wagga Wagga, NSW: Centre for Rural Social Research, Charles Sturt University: 5–8.

Fisher, B. (1999) 'Outlook 99 – Commodity Overview', paper presented to the 1999 Agriculture and Resources Outlook Conference, Canberra.

Fisher, C. (1997) '"I Bought My First Saw with My Maternity Benefit": Craft Production in West Wales and the Home as the Space of (Re)production', in Clarke, P. and Little, J. (eds) *Contested Countryside Cultures*, London: Routledge: 232–51.

Fitchen, J. (1995) 'Spatial Redistribution of Poverty Through Migration of Poor People to Depressed Rural Communities', *Rural Sociology*, 60, 2: 181–201.

—— (1991) *Endangered Spaces, Enduring Places: Change, Identity, and Survival in Rural America*, Westview, Boulder.

Fitzgerald, J. (1991) 'Class As Community: the New Dynamics of Social Change', *Environment and Planning D: Society and Space*, 9, 1: 117–28.

Fitzgerald, R. (1996) 'Sustainable Development and Rural Structural Adjustment', in *Rural Communities Looking Ahead, Proceedings of a Rural Social Policy Conference*, Sydney: New South Wales Council of Social Service: 42–8.

Forman, R. (1995) *Land Mosaics: The Ecology of Landscapes and Regions*, Cambridge: Cambridge University Press.

Foster, J. and Magdoff, F. (1998) 'Liebig, Marx, and the Depletion of Soil Fertility: Relevance for Today's Agriculture', *Monthly Review*, 50, 3, July–August: 32–45.

Francis, D. (1994) *Family Agriculture: Tradition and Transformation*, London: Earthscan Publications.

Francis, R. (1993) 'Representations of Restructuring in the Meat-Packing Industry of Victoria', *Environment and Planning A*, 25, 12: 1725–42.

Freudenberg, W. (1991) 'Rural–Urban Differences in Environmental Concern: A Closer Look', *Sociological Inquiry*, 61, 2: 167–98.

Friedmann, H. (2000) 'Eating in the Gardens of Gaia: Envisioning Polycultural Communities', paper presented to the 10th World Congress of Rural Sociology, Rio de Janeiro, 30 July–5 August.

—— (1993) 'The Political Economy of Food: A Global Crisis', *New Left Review*, 197, January–February: 29–57.

—— (1991) 'Changes in the International Division of Labor: Agri-food Complexes and Export Agriculture', in Friedland, W., Busch, L., Buttel, F. and Rudy, A. (eds) *Toward a New Political Economy of Agriculture*, Boulder: Westview: 65–93.

Friedmann, H. and McMichael, P. (1989) 'Agriculture and the State System: the Rise and Decline of National Agricultures, 1870 to the Present', *Sociologia Ruralis* 29: 93–117.

Fuller, A. (1990) 'From Part-Time Farming to Pluriactivity: A Decade of Change in Rural Europe', *Journal of Rural Studies*, 6, 4: 361–73.

Gain, L. (1996) 'Equity in Social Policy', in *Rural Communities Looking Ahead, Proceedings of a Rural Social Policy Conference*, Sydney: New South Wales Council of Social Service: 19–23.

Gallent, N., Jones, R. and Allen, C. (1998) 'Local Concerns and Regional Devolution: Observations from Wales', *Regional Studies*, 32, 2: 181–6.

Gamble, D., Blunden, S., Kuhn-White, L., Voyce, M. and Loftus, J. (1995) 'Transfer of the Family Farm Business in a Changing Rural Society', Canberra: Rural Industries Research and Development Corporation.

Gammage, B. (1986) *Narrandera Shire*, Narrandera: Narrandera Shire Council.

Garcia, L. (1998) 'Home Violence Orders Soar', *Sydney Morning Herald*, 20 October: 1.

Garlick, S. (1997) 'Regional Economic Development: New Partnership Challenges for Local Government', in Dollery, B. and Marshall, N. (eds) *Australian Local Government: Reform and Renewal*, Melbourne: Macmillan, 276–93.

Garnaut, J. (1998) 'Earning Money Off the Farm', *ABARE Update*, 13 (April): 3.

—— (1997) *Issues in the Delivery of Commonwealth Social Support Programs for Farm Families*, ABARE Research Report 97.7, Canberra: Australian Bureau of Agricultural and Resource Economics.

Garnaut, J. and Lim-Applegate, H. (1998) 'People in Farming', *ABARE Research Report*, 98.6, Canberra: Australian Bureau of Agricultural and Resource Economics.

—— (1997) 'Farmers: The New Generation', in *Farm Surveys Report, 1997*, Australian Bureau of Agricultural and Resrouce Economics, Canberra: 22–25.

Garnaut, J., Rasheed, C. and Rodriguez, G. (1999) *Farmers at Work: The Gender Division*, Canberra: Australian Bureau of Agricultural and Resource Economics.

Gasson, R., Crow, G., Errington, A., Hutson, J., Marsden, T. and Winter, D. (1988) 'The Farm as a Family Business: A Review', *Journal of Agricultural Economics*, 39, 1: 1–41.

Gemmill, G. and Oakley, J. (1997) 'Leadership: An Alienating Social Myth', in Grint, K. (ed.) *Leadership: Comtemporary and Critical Approaches*, Oxford: Oxford University Press: 272–88.

Geno, B. (1998) 'Gender Based Differences in Approaches to Managing Farms Sustainably', paper presented to the Sixth Conference of the Agri-Food Research Network, Rockhampton, Queensland, August.

—— (1997) *Literature Review of Small Towns in Australia*, Lismore: Centre for Australian Regional and Enterprise Development.

Gibson-Graham, J. (1994) 'Reflections on Regions, the White Paper and a New Class Politics of Distribution', *Australian Geographer*, 25, 2: 148–53.

Giddens, A. (1996) *In Defence of Sociology: Essays, Interpretations and Rejoinders*, Cambridge: Polity Press.

—— (1994) 'Living in a Post-Traditional Society', in Beck, U., Giddens, A. and Lash, S. *Reflexive Modernization: Politics, Tradition and Aesthetics in the Modern Social Order*, Oxford: Blackwell: 56–109.

Gill, S. (1996) 'Globalisation, Democratisation, and the Politics of Indifference', in Mittelman, J. (ed.) *Globalisation: Critical Reflections*, Boulder: Lynne Rienner: 205–28.

Gleeson, T. and Topp, V. (1997) 'Broadacre Farming Today – Forces for Change', in Australian Bureau of Agricultural and Resource Economics, *Outlook 97, Volume 2, Agriculture, Proceedings of the National Agricultural and Resources Outlook Conference*, Canberra: Australian Bureau of Agricultural and Resource Economics: 53–66.

Godden, D. (1997) *Agricultural and Resource Policy: Principles and Practice*, Melbourne: Oxford University Press.

Goetz, S. and Debertin, D. (1996) 'Rural Population Decline in the 1980s: Impacts of Farm Structure and Federal Farm Programs', *American Journal of Agricultural Economics*, 78, 3: 517–29.

Goldney, D. and Bauer, J. (1998) 'Integrating Conservation and Agricultural Production: Fantasy or Imperative?', in Pratley, J. and Robertson, A. (eds) *Agriculture and the Environmental Imperative*, Melbourne: CSIRO: 15–34.

Goodman, D. (1997) 'World-scale Processes and Agro-food Systems: Critique and Research Needs', *Review of International Political Economy*, 4, 4: 663–87.

Goodman, D. and Watts, M. (1994) 'Reconfiguring the Rural or Fording the Divide?: Capitalist Restructuring and the Global Agro-Food System', *Journal of Peasant Studies*, 22, 1, October: 1–49.

Goodman, D., Sorj, B. and Wilkinson, J. (1987) *From Farming to Biotechnology: a Theory of Agro-Industrial Development*, Oxford: Basil Blackwell.

Goody, J. (1997) 'Industrial Food: Towards the Development of a World Cuisine', in Counihan, C. and van Esterik, P. (eds) *Food and Culture*, London: Routledge: 338–56.

Gough, A. (1996) 'Self Employment Development Through Local Enterprise', in *Rural Communities Looking Ahead, Proceedings of a Rural Social Policy Conference*, Sydney: New South Wales Council of Social Service: 84.

Gow, J. (1997) 'Commonwealth Drought Policy: 1989–1995. A Case Study of Economic Rationalism', *Australian Journal of Social Issues*, 32, 3: 273–82.

—— (1994) 'Farm Structural Adjustment – An Everyday Imperative, Incorporating Comments On Lawrence', *Rural Society* , 4, 2: 9–13.

Gramling, R. and Freudenberg, W. (1990) 'A Closer Look at "Local Control": Communities, Commodities and the Collapse of the Coast', *Rural Sociology*, 55, 4: 541–58.

Granovetter, M. (1972) 'The Strength of Weak Ties', *American Journal of Sociology*, 78, 6: 1360–80.

Gravell, K. (1993) 'A Bridge Too Far?: Community Power Structures on Victoria's Raymond Island', *Rural Society*, 4, 2: 2–8.

Gray, I. (1994) 'The Changing Structure of Rural Communities', *Rural Society*, 4, 3: 17–21.

—— (1993) 'Power, Community and Locality: An Empirical Researcher's Perspective on a Theoretical Debate', *Annual Conference of the British Sociological Association*, Colchester, England: University of Essex.

—— (1992) 'Power Relations in Rural Communities: Implications for Environmental Management', in Lawrence, G., Vanclay, F. and Furze, B. (eds) *Agriculture, Environment and Society: Contemporary Issues for Australia*, Melbourne: Macmillan: 141–56.

—— (1991) *Politics in Place: Social Power Relations in an Australian Country Town*, Cambridge: Cambridge University Press.

Gray, I. and Crockett, J. (1998) 'Producer Profiles Based on Survey Data from the Middle Murrumbidgee Catchment', *Report to the Murray–Darling Basin Commission*, Wagga Wagga, NSW: Centre for Rural Social Research, Charles Sturt University.

Gray, I. and Lawrence, G. (1996) 'Predictors of Stress Among Australian Farmers', *Australian Journal of Social Issues*, 31, 2: 173–89.

—— (2000) 'Capacity Building, Governance and Uncertainty for Australian Rural Communities', paper presented to the Conference on Community Capacity Building for Development, Ho Chi Minh City, December.

Gray, I. and Phillips, E. (1996) 'Sustainability and the Restructuring of Tradition: A Comparative Analysis of Three Rural Localities', in Lawrence, G., Lyons, K. and Momtaz, S. (eds) *Social Change in Rural Australia: Perspectives from the Social Sciences*, Rockhampton, Queensland: Rural Social and Economic Research Centre, Central Queensland University: 276–89.

Gray, I., Dunn, A. and Phillips, E. (1997) 'Power, Interests and the Extension of Sustainable Agriculture', *Sociologia Ruralis*, 37, 1: 97–113.

Gray, I., Dunn, P., Kelly, B. and Williams, C. (1991) *Immigrant Settlement in Country Areas*, Canberra: Australian Government Publishing Service.

Gray, I., Lawrence, G. and Dunn, A. (1993) *Coping with Change: Australian Farmers in the 1990s*, Wagga Wagga, NSW: Centre for Rural Social Research, Charles Sturt University.

Gray, I., Phillips, E., Ampt, P. and Dunn, A. (1995) 'Awareness or Beguilement: Farmers' Perceptions of Change', in Share, P. (ed.) *Beyond Countrymindedness: Communications, Culture and Ideology in Rural Areas*, Key Papers 4, Wagga Wagga, NSW: Centre for Rural Social Research, Charles Sturt University: 53–69.

Gray, I., Phillips, E. and Dunn, A. (forthcoming) 'Aspects of Rural Culture and the Use of Conservation Farming', in Shulman, A. and Price, R. (eds) *Adoption of Sustainable Resource Management Practices*, vol. 2, Canberra: Land and Water Resources Research and Development Corporation.

Gray, I., Stehlik, D., Lawrence, G. and Bulis, H. (1998) 'Community, Communion and Drought in Rural Australia', *Journal of the Community Development Society*, 29, 1: 23–37.

Green, G. P. and Cowell, D. K. (1994) 'Community Reinvestment and Local Economic Development in Rural Areas', *Journal of the Community Development Society*, 25, 2: 229–45.

Grimes, J., Lawrence, G. and Stehlik, D. (eds) (1998) *Sustainable Futures: Towards a Catchment Management Strategy for the Central Queensland Region*, Rockhampton, Queensland: Institute for Sustainable Regional Development.

Grimson, M. (1998) *Rural Health Policy*, Barton: National Farmers' Federation.

Gringeri, C. (1993) 'Inscribing Gender in Rural Development: Industrial Homework in Two Midwestern Communities', *Rural Sociology*, 58, 1: 30–52.

Grove-White, R. (1996) 'Environmental Knowledge and Public Policy Needs: On Humanising the Research Agenda', in Lash, S., Szerszynski, B. and Wynne, B. (eds) *Risk, Environment and Modernity: Towards a New Ecology*, London: Sage: 267–86.

Gruidl, J. and Walzer, N. (1995) 'Does Local Economic Development Policy Affect Community Employment Growth?' *Journal of the Community Development Society*, 23, 2: 53–65.

Grunseit, A., Lupton, D., Crawford, J., Kippax, S. and Noble, J. (1995) 'The Country Versus the City: Differences Between Rural and Urban Tertiary Students on HIV/AIDS Knowledge, Belief and Attitudes', *Australian Journal of Social Issues*, 30, 4: 389–404.

Gutman, A. (1992) 'Communitarian Critics of Liberalism', in Avineri, S. and de Shalit, A. (eds) *Communitarianism and Individualism*, New York: Oxford University Press: 120–36.

Hall, R., Thorns, D. and Willmott, W. (1984) 'Community, Class and Kinship: Bases for Collective Action Within Localities', *Environment and Planning D: Society and Space*, 2, 2: 201–15.

Halpin, D. and Martin, P. (1999) 'Representing and Managing Farmers' Interests in Australia', *Sociologia Ruralis*, 39, 1: 78–99.

—— (1996) 'Agrarianism and Farmer Representation: Ideology in Australian Agriculture', in Lawrence, G., Lyons, K. and Momtaz, S. (eds) *Social Change in Rural Australia: Perspectives from the Social Sciences*, Rockhampton, Queensland: Rural Social and Economic Research Centre, Central Queensland University: 9–24.

Hamilton, C. (1996a) 'Globalisation and the Working People: the End of Post-War Consensus', paper delivered at the ANZAAS Conference, Canberra, 3 October.

—— (1996b) 'Economic Rationalism in the Bush', paper presented to the Department of Primary Industries and Energy, Canberra, 19 November.

Hampel, B., Holdsworth, R. and Boldero, J. (1995) 'Urban/Rural Differences in Environmental Consciousness', *Rural Society*, 5, 4: 13–20.

Hannibal, M., Gamble, D. and Murray, A. (1991) *West Moreton Dairy Insight: A Collaborative Inquiry*, Melbourne: University of Western Sydney and the Australian Dairy Research and Development Corporation.

Harper, S. (ed.) (1993) *The Greening of Rural Policy: International Perspectives*, London: Belhaven Press.

Harrison, L. (1993) 'The Impact of the Agricultural Industry on the Rural Economy – Tracking the Spatial Distribution of the Farm Inputs and Outputs', *Journal of Rural Studies*, 9, 1: 81–8.

Haslam-McKenzie, F. (1998) 'Statistical Boundaries: A Means by which the Realities of Rural Decline in the Western Australian Wheatbelt have been Hidden', in Staples, M. and Millmow, A. (eds) *Studies in Australian Rural Economic Development*, Wagga Wagga, NSW: Centre for Rural Social Research, Charles Sturt University: 41–50.

Hassall and Associates (1990) *The Market for Australian Produced Organic Food*, Canberra: Rural Industries Research and Development Corporation.

Heelas, P. (1996) 'Detraditionalization and its Rivals', in Heelas, P., Lash, S. and Morris, P. (eds) *Detraditionalization: Critical Reflections on Authority and Identity*, Oxford: Blackwell: 1–20.

Heelas, P., Lash, S. and Morris, P. (1996) *Detraditionalization: Critical Reflections on Authority and Identity*, Oxford: Blackwell.

Held, D., McGrew, A., Goldblatt, D. and Perraton, J. (1999) *Global Transformations: Politics, Economics and Culture*, Cambridge: Polity.

Henshall Hansen Associates (1988) *Small Towns in Victoria*, Melbourne: Victorian Department of Agriculture and Rural Affairs.

Herbert-Cheshire, L. (2001) 'Governance, "Local" Knowledge, and the Adoption of Sustainable Farming Practices', in Lawrence, G., Higgins, V. and Lockie, S. (eds) *Environment, Society and Natural Resource Management: Theoretical Perspectives from Australasia and the Americas*, Edward Elgar, Cheltenham, UK.

—— (2000) 'Contemporary Strategies for Rural Community Development in Australia: a Governmentality Perspective', *Journal of Rural Studies*, 16, 2: 203–15.

Hermann, V. and Uttitz, P. (1990) '"If Only I Didn't Enjoy Being a Farmer!" Attitudes and Opinions of Monoactive and Pluriactive Farmers', *Sociologia Ruralis*, 30, 1: 62–75.

Higgins, V. (1998) '"Self-Reliance", Governance and Environmental "Management": A Case Study of the Rural Adjustment Scheme', paper presented to the Sixth Conference of the Agri-Food Research Network, Rockhampton, Queensland, August.

—— (1998) 'Breaking Down the Divisions? A Case Study of Political Power and Changing Rural Local Government Representation', *Rural Society*, 7, 3/4: 51–8.

Higgins, V., Lockie, S. and Lawrence, G. (2001) '"Changing People to Change Things"': Building Capacity for Self–help in Natural Resource Management – A Governmentality Perspective', in Lawrence, G., Higgins, V. and Lockie, S. (eds) *Environment, Society and Natural Resource Management: Theoretical Perspectives from Australasia and the Americas*, Edward Elgar, Cheltenham, UK.

Hillier, J. and McManus, P. (1994) 'Pull up the Drawbridge: Fortress Mentality in the Suburbs', in Gibson, K. and Watson, S. (eds) *Metropolis Now*, Sydney: Pluto Press: 91–101.

Hindess, B. (1988) *Choice, Rationality and Social Theory*, London: Unwin Hyman.

—— (1996a) 'Liberalism, Socialism and Democracy: Variations on a Governmental Theme', in Barry, A., Osborne, T. and Rose, N. (eds) *Foucault and Political Reason: Liberalism, Neo-Liberalism and Rationalities of Government*, Chicago: University of Chicago Press: 64–80.

—— (1996b) *Discourses of Power: From Hobbes to Foucault*, Oxford: Blackwell.

Hindmarsh, R. (1994) Power Relations, Social-Ecocentrism, and Genetic Engineering: Agro-biotechnology in the Australian Context, unpublished doctoral thesis, Nathan: Griffith University.

Hindmarsh, R. and Lawrence, G. (eds) (2001) *Altered Genes II: Reconstructing Nature*, Melbourne: Scribe.

Hindmarsh, R., Lawrence, G. and Norton, J. (eds) (1998) *Altered Genes – Reconstructing Nature: The Debate*, Sydney: Allen & Unwin.

Hinrichs, C. (1995) 'Off the Treadmill? Technology and Tourism in the North American Maple Syrup Industry', *Agriculture and Human Values*, Winter: 39–47.

Ho, M. (1998) *Genetic Engineering, Dream or Nightmare? The Brave New World of Bad Science and Big Business*, Bath: Gateway Books.

Hobsbawm, E. (1984) 'Introduction: Inventing Traditions', in Hobsbawm, E. and Ranger, T. (eds) *The Invention of Tradition*, Cambridge: Cambridge University Press: 1–14.

Hodge, A. (1999) 'Bush Town Comes Through on Kalamazoo', *Weekend Australian*, 20–21 February: 10.

Hodge, I. and Dunn, J. (1992) *Rural Change and Sustainability: a Research Review*, London, ESRC.

Holmes, J. and Day, P. (1995) 'Identity, Lifestyle and Survival: Valuations of South Australian Pastoralists', *Rangeland Journal*, 17, 2: 193–212.

Holmwood, J. and Stewart, A. (1991) *Explanation and Social Theory*, London: Macmillan.

Horner, D. and Reeve, I. (1991) *Telecottages: The Potential for Rural Australia*, Canberra: Australian Government Publishing Service.

Hoy, C. (1998) 'Regional Development IT: Creating Global Opportunities', *Regional and Enterprise and Development Network*, 3, 3: 1.

Hudson, H. (1992) 'Telecommunications Policies for Rural Development', *CIRCIT Policy Research Paper 30*, Melbourne: CIRCIT.

Hudson, P. (1989) 'Change and Adaptation in Four Rural Communities in New England, NSW', *Australian Geographer*, 20, 1: 54–64.

Huggonier, B. (1999) 'Regional Development Tendencies in OECD Countries', keynote paper presented at the Regional Australia Summit, Canberra, October.

Hugo, G. (1996) 'Counterurbanisation', in Newton, P. and Bell, M. (eds) *Population Shift: Mobility and Change in Australia*, Canberra: Australian Government Publishing Service: 126–46.

Hugo, G. (1994) 'The Turnaround in Australia: Some First Observations from the 1991 Census', *Australian Geographer*, 25, 1: 1–17.

Hugo, G. and Smailes, P. (1992) 'Population Dynamics in Rural South Australia', *Journal of Rural Studies*, 8, 1: 29–51.

Hundloe, T. (1997) 'The Value of World Heritage Areas in Sustaining Regional Economies', paper presented to the Sustainable Economic Growth in Regional Australia Conference, Lorne, September.

Hungerford, L. (1996) 'Beyond Sugar: Diversification within the Primary Production Sector in the Wide Bay-Burnett Region', in Cryle, D., Griffin, G. and Stehlik, D. (eds) *Futures for Central Queensland*, Rockhampton, Queensland: Rural Social and Economic Research Centre, Central Queensland University: 27–30.

Hurley, F. (1994) 'The Issue-Attention Cycle and Regional Development: Is It Really Back on the Political Agenda?' *Regional Policy and Practice*, 3, 2: 19–28.

Hurst, P. and Thompson, G. (1996) *Globalisation in Question*, London: Polity Press.

Ife, J. (1995) *Community Development: Creating Community Alternatives – Vision, Analysis and Practice*, Melbourne: Longman.

Industry Commission (1994) *Impediments to Regional Industry Adjustment – Volume One: Report*, Canberra: Australian Government Publishing Service.

INRA (1991) *Opinions of Europeans on Biotechnology in 1991*, Brussels: Commission of the European Communities.

Ison, R. (1998) 'The Search for System', in Michalk, D, and Pratley, J. (eds) *Agronomy – Growing a Greener Future*, Proceedings of the Ninth Australian Agronomy Conference, Wagga Wagga, NSW: Australian Society of Agronomy: 149–58.

Jacob, S., Willits, F. and Jensen, L . (1996) 'Residualism and Rural America: A Decade Later', *Journal of Sociology and Social Welfare*, 23, 3: 151–62.

James, V. (1996) 'Local Government Boundary Reform', *Lower Eyre Peninsula Study Team: Household Survey Report*, City of Port Lincoln.

Jennings, S. and Moore, A. (1999) 'The Rhetoric Behind Regionalism in Natural Resource Management: Myth, Reality and Moving Forward', paper presented at the International Symposium on Society and Resource Management, Brisbane: University of Queensland, 8 July.

Jensen, R. (1998) 'Rural Australia: Past, Present and Future', in Staples, M. and Millmow, A. (eds) *Studies in Australian Rural Economic Development*, Wagga Wagga, NSW: Centre for Rural Social Research, Charles Sturt University: 9–20.

Johansen, S., Kann, F., Orderub, G., Hegrenes, A. and Hovland, I. (1999) *Norwegian Agriculture and Multifunctionality: the Peripheral Dimension*, Oslo: Norwegian Institute for Urban and Regional Research.

Jones, B. (1997) 'Commonwealth Industry Policy and Regional Australia', paper presented to the Sustainable Economic Growth in Regional Australia Conference, Lorne, September.

Jones, J. (1999) 'Personality and Marketing Keys to Agri-Tourism Success', *Australian Farm Journal*, 9, 10: 26–9.

—— (1998) 'Barons of the Bush', *Australian Farm Journal*, 8, 9: 20–44.

Jones, M. (1993) *Transforming Australian Local Government: Making it Work*, Sydney: Allen & Unwin.

Jones, O. and Little, J. (2000) 'Rural Challenge(s): Partnership and New Rural Governance', *Journal of Rural Studies*, 16, 2: 171–83.

Jones, T. (1987) 'Towns Fight to Save Public Service Jobs', *The Land*, 13 August: 6.

Kaltoft, P. (1999) 'Organic Farming in Late Modernity: At the Frontier of Modernity or Opposing Modernity', paper presented at the XVIII Congress of the European Society for Rural Sociology, Lund, Sweden, 24–28 August.

Kanter, R. (1995) *World Class: Thriving Locally in the Global Economy*, New York: Simon & Schuster.

Kapferer, J. (1990) 'Rural Myths and Urban Ideologies', *Australian and New Zealand Journal of Sociology*, 26, 1: 87–106.

Keat, R. and Urry, J. (1975) *Social Theory as Science*, London: Routledge.

Kelly, R. (1994) Changing Land Use in Glenquarry: Change and Continuity, unpublished BA (Hons) thesis, Wagga Wagga, NSW: Charles Sturt University.

Kelly, S. (1987) 'City Folk, Country Folk: Demographic and Attitudinal Urban–Rural Differences', *Family Matters*, 24: 43–5.

Kelsey, J. (1995) *Economic Fundamentalism: The New Zealand Experiment – A World Model for Structural Adjustment?*, London: Pluto Press.

Kelty, B. (1993) *Developing Australia: a Regional Perspective*, Canberra: Australian Government Publishing Service.

Kemp, D. (1999) *White Paper on Higher Education*, Canberra: Australian Government Publishing Service.

Kenkel, M. (1986) 'Stress – Coping – Support in Rural Communities: A Model for Primary Prevention', *American Journal of Community Psychology*, 14, 5: 457–78.

Kennedy, B. (1981) 'How Distance Shaped a Community: Broken Hill's First Ten Years', in Bowman, M. (ed.) *Beyond the City: Case Studies in Community Structure and Development*, Melbourne: Longman Cheshire: 114–26.

Kennedy, J. (1997) 'At the Crossroads: Newfoundland and Labrador Communities in a Changing International Context', *Canadian Review of Sociology and Anthropology*, 34, 3: 297–317.

Kenyon, P. (1996) 'What is Community Economic Development?', in *Rural Communities Looking Ahead, Proceedings of a Rural Social Policy Conference*, Sydney: New South Wales Council of Social Service: 73–6.

Kerby, J. (1992) 'How Stressed are Rural People?' *Rural Society*, 2, 3: 15–16.

Kerby, J. and Gorman, K. (1994) *Changing by Choice: Identifying Mechanisms for Social and Economic Change in the Riverland*, South Australia Department of Primary Industries, Technical Report no. 218.

Kerby, J. and Parish, J. (1997) 'Social, Economic and Environmental Challenges in the Riverland', in *Agriculture, Volume 2, Proceedings of the National Agricultural Outlook Conference*, Canberra: ABARE: 125–37.

Kerridge, K. (1978) 'Value Orientations and Farmer Behaviour: An Exploratory Study', *Quarterly Review of Agricultural Economics*, 31, 1: 61–72.

Kidman, M. (1991) 'New Town Belonging, Believing and Bearing Down', in Alston, M. (ed.) *Family Farming: Australia and New Zealand*, Wagga Wagga, NSW: Centre for Rural Social Research, Charles Sturt University: 33–51.

Kiel, R. (1998) 'Globalization Makes States: Perspectives of Local Governance in the Age of the World City', *Review of International Political Economy* 5, 4: 616–46.

Kilpatrick, S. and Bell, R. (1998) *Support Networks and Trust: How Social Capital Facilitates Economic Outcomes for Small Businesses, Discussion Paper D17/1998*, Launceston: Centre for Research and Learning in Regional Australia.

Kilpatrick, S., Bell, R. and Falk, I. (1998) *Groups of Groups: The Role of Group Learning in Building Social Capital, Discussion Paper D3/1998*, Launceston: Centre for Research and Learning in Regional Australia.

Kim, K. and Weaver, R. (eds) (1994) *Biodiversity and Landscapes: a Paradox of Humanity*, Cambridge: Cambridge University Press.

King, A. (1991) *Culture, Globalisation and the World-System: Contemporary Conditions for the Representation of Identity*, London: Macmillan.

Kinnear, S. (1999) 'Overview of the Organic Industry in Australia', paper presented at the Farming for the Future: Organic Produce for the 21st Century Conference, Mackay, Queensland, 22–23 September.

Kloppenburg, J. (1992) 'Science in Agriculture: A Reply to Molnar, Duffy, Cummins and Van Santen and Flora', *Rural Sociology*, 57, 1: 98–107.

—— (1991) 'Social Theory and the De/Reconstruction of Agricultural Science: Local Knowledge for an Alternative Agriculture', *Rural Sociology*, 56, 4: 519–48.

Knapp, T. (1995) 'Rust in the Wheatbelt: The Social Impacts of Decline in a Rural Kansas Community', *Sociological Inquiry*, 65, 1: 47–66.

Kneen, B. (1995) *Invisible Giant: Cargill and its Transnational Strategies*, London: Pluto Press.

Kriegler, R. (1980) *Working for the Company*, Melbourne: Oxford University Press.

Krimsky, S. and Wrubel, R. (1996) *Agricultural Biotechnology and the Environment: Science, Policy and Social Issues*, Urbana: University of Illinois Press.

Kubik, W. and Stirling, B. (1998) 'Go-For Knowledge: Gender and the Reconstruction of Prairie Farm Work', paper presented to the Annual Meetings of the Rural Sociological Society, Portland, Oregon.

Lake, M. (1996) 'The Woolshed: A Case Study in Rural Enterprise', *Rural Society*, 6, 2: 34–40.

Lakin, M. and Shannon, P. (1999) *Export of Frozen Low-Chemical and Organic Vegetables to East Asia and the European Union, Interim Report to the Horticultural Research and Development Corporation*, Brisbane: Department of Primary Industries.

Land, The, 2 April 1998; 12 February 1998; 5 February 1998.

Land Management Task Force (1995) *Managing for the Future*, Report of the Land Management Task Force, Canberra: Commonwealth of Australia.

Langton, M. (2000) *Burning Questions*, Centre for Indigenous Natural and Cultural Resource Management, NTU, Darwin.

Larcombe, G. (1998) 'Innovative Rural Development, in Office of Rural Communities', *Positive Rural Futures 1998*, Brisbane: Office of Rural Communities.

Lash, S. and Urry, J. (1994) *Economies of Signs and Space*, London: Sage.

Lasley, P., Hoiberg, E. and Bultena, G. (1992) 'Is Sustainable Agriculture an Elixir for Rural Communities? The Community Implications of Sustainable Agriculture', paper presented at Rural Sociological Society Meetings, Pennsylvania State University, State College.

Latham, M. (1998) *Civilising Global Capital: New Thinking for Australian Labor*, Sydney: Allen & Unwin.

Laurance, I. (1999) 'Beyond the Backlash: A National Framework for Regional Delivery of Rural Development', paper presented to the Regional Australia Summit, Canberra.

Lawrence, G. (2000) 'Global Perspectives on Rural Communities: Trends and Patterns', paper presented at the International Landcare Conference, Melbourne, 2–5 March.

—— (1999a) 'Australian Rural Communities in a "Greening" World', keynote address, Regional Landcare and Catchment Management Conference, Boyne Island, Queensland, 29–30 October.

—— (1999b) 'Agri-food Restructuring: a Synthesis of Recent Australian Research', *Rural Sociology*, 64, 2, June: 186–202.

—— (1998) 'The Institute for Sustainable Regional Development', in Grimes, J., Lawrence, G. and Stehlik, D. (eds) *Sustainable Futures: Towards a Catchment Management Strategy for the Central Queensland Region*, Rockhampton, Queensland: Institute for Sustainable Regional Development: 6–8.

—— (1996) 'Rural Australia: Insights and Issues from Contemporary Political Economy', in Lawrence, G., Lyons, K. and Momtaz, S. (eds) *Social Change in Rural Australia*, Rockhampton, Queensland: Rural Social and Economic Research Centre: 332–49.

—— (1995) *Futures for Rural Australia: From Agricultural Productivism to Community Sustainability*, Rockhampton, Queensland: Rural Social and Economic Research Centre.

—— (1992) 'Farm Structural Adjustment: the Imperative of the Nineties?' *Rural Society*, 2, 4: 5–7.

—— (1990) 'The Management of Change in Resource Use and Its Consequences in the Murray–Darling Basin', *Conference of the Community Advisory Committee of the Murray–Darling Basin*, Shepparton, 20–21 November.

—— (1987) *Capitalism and the Countryside: The Rural Crisis in Australia*, Sydney: Pluto.

—— (1978) Regionalism as Internal Imperialism, unpublished Master of Sociology thesis, Madison: University of Wisconsin.

Lawrence, G. and Gray, I. (1997) 'Social Factors Shaping the Australian Sugar Industry', in Keating, B. and Wilson, J. (eds) *Intensive Sugar Cane Production: Meeting the Challenges Beyond 2000*, Oxford: CAB International: 71–86.

Lawrence, G. and Vanclay, F. (1998) 'Gene-biotechnology, the State and Australia's Agri-food Industries', in Hindmarsh, R., Lawrence, G. and Norton, J. (eds) *Altered Genes – Reconstructing Nature: The Debate*, Sydney: Allen & Unwin: 147–59.

—— (1992) 'Agricultural Production and Environmental Degradation in the Murray–Darling Basin', in Lawrence, G., Vanclay, F. and Furze, B. (eds) *Agriculture, Environment and Society: Contemporary Issues for Australia*, Melbourne: Macmillan: 33–59.

Lawrence, G. and Williams, C. (1990) 'The Dynamics of Decline' in Lawrence, G., Cullen, T. and Dunn, P. (eds) *Rural Health and Welfare in Australia*, Melbourne: Arena.

Lawrence, G., Gray, I. and Stehlik, D (1999) 'Changing Spaces: the Effects of Macro-social Forces on Regional Australia', in Kasimis, C. and Papadopoulos, A. (eds) *Local Responses to Global Integration: Toward a New Era of Rural Restructuring*, Aldershot: Ashgate: 63–87.

Lawrence, G., Higgins, V. and Lockie, S. (eds) (2001) *Environment, Society and Natural Resource Management: Theoretical Perspectives from Australasia and the Americas*, London: Edward Elgar.

Lawrence, G., Vanclay, F. and Furze, B. (eds) (1992) *Agriculture, Environment and Society: Contemporary Issues for Australia*, Melbourne: Macmillan.

Lawrence, M. (1997) 'Heartlands or Neglected Geographies? Liminality, Power, and the Hyperreal Rural', *Journal of Rural Studies*, 13, 1: 1–17.

Leach, B. and Winson, A. (1995) 'Bringing "Globalization" Down to Earth: Restructuring and Labour in Rural Communities', *Canadian Review of Sociology and Anthropology*, 32, 3: 341–64.

Lee, M. (1992) *Genetic Manipulation: The Threat or the Glory? Report of House of Representatives Standing Committee on Industry, Science and Technology*, Canberra: Australian Government Publishing Service.

Lees, J. (1997) 'The Origins of the Legacy', in Lees, J. (ed.) *A Legacy Under Threat? Family Farming in Australia*, Armidale: University of New England Press: 1–13.

Lefevre, C. (1998) 'Metropolitan Government and Governance in Western Countries: A Critical Review', *International Journal of Urban and Regional Research*, 22, 1: 9–25.

Le Heron, R. (1993) *Globalized Agriculture: Political Choice*, Oxford: Pergamon Press.

Le Heron, R., Britton, S. and Pawson, E. (1992) 'Introduction', in Britton, S., Le Heron, R. and Pawson, E. (eds) *Changing Places in New Zealand*, Christchurch: New Zealand Geographical Society: 1–16.

Le Heron, R., Cooper, I., Perry, M. and Hayward, D. (1997) 'Commodity System Governance: a New Zealand Discourse', in Taylor, M. and Conti, S. (eds) *Uneven Development: Global and Local Processes*, Aldershot: Avebury: 81–100.

Le Heron, R., Roche, M. and Johnston, T. (1994) 'Pluriactivity: An Exploration of Issues with Reference to New Zealand's Livestock and Fruit Agro–Commodity Systems', *Geoforum*, 25, 2: 155–71.

Leipins, R. and Bradshaw, B. (1999) 'Neo-Liberal Agricultural Discourse in New Zealand: Economy, Culture and Politics Linked', *Sociologa Ruralis*, 39, 4: 563–82.

Lichtblau, K. (1995) 'Sociology and the Diagnosis of the Times or: The Reflexivity of Modernity', *Theory, Culture and Society*, 12, 1: 25–52.

Liepins, R. (1998) 'Fields of Action: Australian Women's Agricultural Activism in the 1990s', *Rural Sociology*, 63, 1: 128–56.

Lindsay, R. and Gleeson, T. (1997) 'Changing Structure of Farming in Australia', *ABARE Current Issues*, 4.

Lippert, N. (1993) *The Spiral Down to Poverty: Rural Communities in Crisis*, ACSJC Occasional Paper No. 15.

Little, J. and Austin, P. (1996) 'Women and the Rural Idyll', *Journal of Rural Studies*, 12, 2: 101–11.

Lloyd, A. and Malcolm, B. (1997) 'Agriculture and the Family Farm in the Economy' in Lees, J. (ed.) *A Legacy Under Threat? Family Farming in Australia*, Armidale: University of New England Press: 59–80.

Lobao, L. and Thomas, P. (1992) 'Political Beliefs in an Era of Economic Decline: Farmers' Attitudes Toward State Economic Intervention, Trade, Food Security', *Rural Sociology*, 57, 4: 453–75.

Lockie, S. (1998) '"Name Your Poison": the Discursive Construction of Chemical Use as Everyday Farming Practice', paper presented to the Sixth Conference of the Agri-Food Research Network, Rockhampton, Queensland, August.

—— (1997) 'Is "Subsumption" Still Relevant? The Question of Control in Australian Broadacre Agriculture', *Rural Society*, 7, 3/4: 27–36.

—— (1997) 'Rural Gender Relations and Landcare', in Vanclay, F. and Lockie, S. (eds) *Critical Landcare*, Key Papers no. 5, Wagga Wagga, NSW: Centre for Rural Social Research, Charles Sturt University: 71–82.

—— (1997) 'Beyond a "Good Thing": Political Interests and the Meaning of Landcare', in Lockie, S. and Vanclay, F. (eds) *Critical Landcare*, Wagga Wagga, NSW: Centre for Rural Social Research: 29–44.

—— (1995) 'Beyond a "Good Thing": Political Interests and the Meaning of Landcare', *Rural Society*, 5, 2/3: 3–12.

Lockie, S. and Burke, L. (eds) (2001) *Rurality Bites: the Social and Environmental Transformation of Rural Australia*, Sydney: Pluto Press.

Lockie, S. and Pritchard, B. (eds) (2001) *Consuming Foods, Sustaining Environments*, Brisbane: Australian Academic Press.

Lockie, S. and Vanclay, F. (eds) (1997) *Critical Landcare*, Wagga Wagga, NSW: Centre for Rural Social Research.

Lockie, S., Dale, A., Taylor, B. and Lawrence, G. (forthcoming) '"Capacity for Change": Testing a Model for the Inclusion of Social Indicators in Australia's National Land and Water Audit', *Society and Natural Resources*.

Loewith, K. (1960) *Gesammelte Abhandlungen. Zur Kritik der Geschichtlichen Existenz*, Stuttgart: Kohlammer.

Lovering, J. (1999) 'Theory Led by Policy: The Inadequacies of the "New Regionalism" (Illustrated from the Case of Wales)', *International Journal of Urban and Regional Research*, 23, 2: 379–95.

Low, N. (1994) 'Growth Machines and Regulation Theory: The Institutional Dimension of the Regulation of Space in Australia', *International Journal of Urban and Regional Research*, 18, 3: 451–69.

Lowe, I. (1998) 'The State of the Australian Environment', in Michalk, D. and Pratley, J. (eds) *Agronomy – Growing a Greener Future, Proceedings of the Ninth Australian Agronomy Conference*, Wagga Wagga, NSW: Australian Society of Agronomy: 69–74.

Lowe, P. and Murdoch, J. (1993) *Rural Sustainable Development: Report for the Rural Development Commission*, London: Rural Development Commission.

Lowe, P., Marsden, T. and Whatmore, S. (1994) 'Changing Regulatory Orders: The Analysis of the Economic Governance of Agriculture', in Lowe, P., Marsden, T. and Whatmore, S. (eds) *Regulating Agriculture*, London: David Fulton Publishers: 1–30.

Lukes, S. (1974) *Power: A Radical View*, London: Macmillan.

Lyle, M. (1998) 'Uniting our Rural Communities: The Millaa Millaa Project', in Falk, I. (ed.) *Learning Communities, Regional Sustainability and the Learning Society*, Conference Proceedings, vol. 2, 13–20 June 1998, Launceston: Centre for Research and Learning in Regional Australia: 232–5.

Lyons, K. and Lawrence, G. (1999) 'Alternative Knowledges, Organic Agriculture and the Biotechnology Debate', *Culture and Agriculture* 21, 2: 1–12.

Lyson, T. (1985) 'Husband and Wife Work Roles and the Organization and Operation of Family Farms', *Journal of Marriage and the Family*, 47, 3: 759–64.

Lyson, T. and Barham, E. (1998) 'Civil Society and Agricultural Sustainability', *Social Science Quarterly*, 79, 3: 554–67.

MacGregor, C. and Fenton, M. (1999) 'Community Values Provide a Mechanism for Measuring Sustainability in Small Rural Communities in Northern Australia', *Proceedings of the Country Matters Conference*, Canberra: Bureau of Rural Sciences, W1 (3).

MacIntyre, A. (1984) 'The Virtues, the Unity of a Human Life and the Concept of a Tradition', in Sandel, M. (ed.) *Liberalism and Its Critics*, Oxford: Basil Blackwell: 125–48.

Mackinnon, N., Bryden, J., Bell, C., Fuller, A. and Spearman, M. (1991) 'Pluriactivity, Structural Change and Farm Household Vulnerability in Western Europe', *Sociologia Ruralis*, 31, 1: 58–71.

Maher, C. and Stimson, R. (1994) *Regional Population Growth in Australia: Nature, Impact and Implications*, Canberra: Bureau of Immigration and Population Research.

Malcolm, B., Sale, P. and Egan, A. (1996) *Agriculture in Australia: an Introduction*, Melbourne: Oxford University Press.

Mansfeld, Y. and Ginosar, O. (1994) 'Determinants of Locals' Perceptions and Attitudes Towards Tourism Development in their Locality', *Geoforum*, 25, 2: 227–48.

Marotz-Baden, R. and Colvin, P. (1986) 'Coping Strategies: Rural Urban Comparison', *Family Relations*, 35, 2: 281–8.

Marris, P. (1996) *The Politics of Uncertainty*, London: Routledge.

Marsden, T., Murdoch, J., Lowe, P., Munton, R. and Flynn, A. (1993) *Constructing the Countryside*, London: University College of London Press.

Marsh, S. and Pannell, D. (1998) 'The Changing Relationship Between Private and Public Sector Agricultural Extension in Australia', *Rural Society*, 8, 2: 133–51.

Marshall, D. (1998) 'Missing the Jackpot? The Proliferation of Gambling in Australia and its Effect on Local Communities', *Australian Geographical Studies*, 36, 3: 237–47.

Marshall, N. (1997) 'Introduction: Themes and Issues in Australian Local Government', in Dollery, B. and Marshall, N. (eds), *Australian Local Government: Reform and Renewal*, Melbourne: Macmillan: 1–14.

Martin, C. (1998) 'Administration: The Missing Element in Regional Development', in Staples, M. and Millmow, A. (eds) *Studies in Australian Rural Economic Development*, Centre for Rural Social Research, Wagga Wagga, NSW: Charles Sturt University: 63–6.

—— (1996) 'The Policy Framework for Change in Regional Areas: A Macro-perspective', *Rural Society*, 6, 2: 41–3.

Martin, H. and Schumann, H. (1997) *The Global Trap: Globalisation and the Assault on Prosperity and Democracy*, London: Zed Books.

Martin, P. (1997) 'The Constitution of Power in Landcare: a Poststructuralist Perspective with Modernist Undertones', in Lockie, S. and Vanclay, F. (eds) *Critical Landcare*, Wagga Wagga, NSW: Centre for Rural Social Research: 45–56.

—— (1996) 'Ownership and Management of Broadacre and Dairy Farms', in *Farm Surveys Report, 1996*, Canberra: Australian Bureau of Agricultural and Resource Economics: 46–7.

Martin, P. and Halpin, D. (1998) 'Landcare as a Politically Relevant New Social Movement?' *Journal of Rural Studies*, 14, 4: 445–57.

Mathews, R. and Grewal, B. (1997) *The Public Sector in Jeopardy: Australian Fiscal Federalism from Whitlam to Keating*, Melbourne: Centre for Strategic Economic Studies, Victoria University.

McGinness, M. (1996) 'Social Issues for Rural and Remote Australia', in *Australian Rural Policy Papers 1990–95*, Canberra: Australian Government Publishing Service: 199–264.

McGrew, A. (1992) 'A Global Society?' in Hall, S., Held, D. and McGrew, A. (eds) *Modernity and Its Futures*, Cambridge: Polity Press.

McKenzie, F. (1999) *Impact of Declining Rural Infrastructure*, Canberra: Rural Industries Research and Development Corporation.

—— (1996) 'Policy Implications of Population Decline', in Newton, P. and Bell, M. (eds) *Population Shift: Mobility and Change in Australia*, Canberra: Australian Government Publishing Service: 205–17.

—— (1994) *Regional Population Decline in Australia: Impact and Policy Implications*, Canberra: Bureau of Immigration and Population Research.

McKinsey and Company (1994) *Lead Local, Compete Global: Unlocking the Growth Potential of Australia's Regions*, Canberra: Australian Government Publishing Service.

McManus, P. (1999) 'Industrial Food Networks and Sustainability', paper presented at the Agri-food VII Conference, Sydney University, 14–16 July.

McMichael, P. (2000) *Development and Social Change: a Global Perspective*, 2nd edn, Thousand Oaks: Pine Forge.

—— (1999) 'Virtual Capitalism and Agri-food Restructuring', in Burch, D., Goss, J. and Lawrence, G. (eds) *Restructuring Global and Regional Agricultures: Transformations in Australasian Agri-food Economies and Spaces*, Aldershot: Ashgate: 3–22.

—— (1997) 'Rethinking Globalisation: The Agrarian Question Revisited', *Review of International Political Economy*, 4, 4: 630–87.

—— (1996) *Development and Social Change: a Global Perspective*, California: Pine Forge.

—— (1995) 'The New Colonialism: Global Regulation and the Restructuring of the Interstate System', in Smith, D. and Borocz, J. (eds) *A New World Order? Global Transformations in the Late Twentieth Century*, Connecticut: Praeger: 37–56.

—— (1984) *Settlers and the Agrarian Question: Foundations of Capitalism in Colonial Australia*, Cambridge: Cambridge University Press.

McMichael, P. and Lawrence, G. (2001) 'Globalising Agriculture: Structures of Constraint for Australian Farming', in Lockie, S. and Bourke, L. (eds) *Rurality Bites: The Social and Environmental Transformation of Rural Australia*, Sydney, Pluto Press.

McMurtry, J. (1998) *Unequal Freedoms: The Global Market as an Ethical System*, Toronto: Garamond Press.

McQuaid, R. (1997) 'Local Enterprise Companies and Rural Development', *Journal of Rural Studies*, 13, 2: 197–212.

Meares, A. (1997) 'Making the Transition from Conventional to Sustainable Agriculture: Gender, Social Movement Participation, and Quality of Life on the Family Farm', *Rural Sociology*, 62, 1: 21–47.

Meekosha, H. and Mowbray, M. (1995) *Community Empowerment: A Reader in Participation and Development*, London: Zed Books.

Metcalfe, A. (1988) *For Freedom and Dignity*, Sydney: Allen & Unwin.

Midmore, D. (1998) 'Agriculture and the Modern Society', *Acres Australia*, 6, 2: April: 33–6.

Miele, M. and Murdoch, J. (2000) 'Fast Food/Slow Food: Standardisation and Differentiation in Culinary Networks', paper presented to the Xth World Congress of Rural Sociology, Rio de Janeiro, 30 July–5 August.

Miller, L. (1996) 'From Contract Farming and Dependency to Control by Transnational Capital: A Case Study in Tasmanian Hops and Agribusiness Power', in Lawrence, G., Lyons, K. and Momtaz, S. (eds) *Social Change in Rural Australia: Perspectives from the Social Sciences*, Rockhampton, Queensland: Rural Social and Economic Research Centre, Central Queensland University: 64–76.

Miller, T. (1993) *The Well-Tempered Self: Citizenship, Culture, and the Postmodern Subject*, Baltimore: Johns Hopkins.

Mittelman, J. (1996a) 'The Dynamics of Globalisation', in Mittelman, J. (ed.) *Globalisation: Critical Reflections*, Boulder: Lynne Rienner: 1–20.

—— (1996b) 'How Does Globalisation Really Work?', in Mittelman, J. (ed.) *Globalisation: Critical Reflections*, Boulder: Lynne Rienner: 229–42.

Mobbs, R. (1998) 'The Self Empowerment of Communities: A Systems Strategy for Rural Community Assessment', in Falk, I. (ed.) *Learning Communities, Regional Sustainability and the Learning Society*, Conference Proceedings, vol. 2, 13–20 June 1998, Launceston: Centre for Research and Learning in Regional Australia: 358–64.

Mobbs, C. and Dovers, S. (1999) *Social, Economic, Legal, Policy and Institutional R&D for Natural Resource Management: Issues and Directions for LWRRDC*, Canberra: Land and Water Resources Research and Development Corporation.

Moffatt, A, (1996) 'Can Regional Australia Benefit from Electronic Information Systems', *Outlook 96*, Canberra: ABARE: 165–74.

Molotch, H. (1976) 'The City as a Growth Machine', *American Journal of Sociology*, 82, 2: 309–30.

Molotch, H. and Logan, J. (1988) 'Tensions in the Growth Machine: Overcoming Resistance to Value-Free Development', in Warren, R. and Lyon, L. (eds) *New Perspectives on the American Community*, Belmont, California: Wadsworth: 274–90.

Monk, A. (1999) 'The Organic Manifesto: Organic Agriculture in the World Food System', in Burch, D., Goss, J. and Lawrence, G. (eds) *Restructuring Global and Regional Agricultures: Transformations in Australasian Agri-food Economies and Spaces*, Aldershot: Ashgate: 75–86.

—— (1998) 'The Australian Organic Basket and the Global Supermarket', in Burch, D., Lawrence, G., Rickson, R. and Goss, J. (eds) *Australasian Food and Farming in Globalised Economy: Recent Developments and Future Prospects*, Melbourne: Monash Publications in Geography Number 50, Monash University: 69–82.

Mooney, P. and Hunt, S. (1996) 'A Repertoire of Interpretations: Master Frames and Ideological Continuity in US Agrarian Reform', *Sociological Quarterly*, 37, 1: 177–97.

Moreira, M. (2000) 'Local Consequences and Responses to Global Integration: the Role of the State and the Less Favoured Zones', paper presented to the Xth World Congress of Rural Sociology, Rio de Janeiro, 30 July–5 August.

Morning Bulletin, 24 March 2001: 9.

Morrisey, P. and Lawrence, G. (1997) 'A Critical Assessment of Landcare in a Region of Central Queensland', in Lockie, S. and Vanclay, F. (eds) *Critical Landcare*, Wagga Wagga, NSW: Centre for Rural Social Research: 217–26.

Mowbray, M. (n.d.) 'State Control or Self-Regulation?: On the Political Economy of Local Government in Remote Aboriginal Townships', in Brealey, T., Neil, C. and Newton, P. (eds) *Resource Communities*, CSIRO: 261–74.

Mules, W. and Miller, H. (eds) (1997) *Mapping Regional Cultures*, Rockhampton: Rural Social and Economic Research Centre, Central Queensland University.

Municipal Association of Victoria (1994) *Cutting the Social Fabric of Rural Communities: A Look at the Impact of Cuts to Government Services on Country Victoria*, Melbourne: Municipal Association of Victoria.

Munton, R. and Marsden, T. (1991) 'Dualism or Diversity in Family Farming? Patterns of Occupancy Change in British Agriculture', *Geoforum*, 22, 1: 105–17.

—— (1990) 'The Rural Restructuring Process: Emerging Divisions of Agricultural Property Rights', *Regional Studies*, 24, 3: 235–45.

Murdoch, J. (1995) 'Governmentality and the Politics of Resistance in U.K. Agriculture: The Case of the Farmers Union of Wales', *Sociologia Ruralis*, 35, 2: 187–205.

Murdoch, J. and Abram, S. (1998) 'Defining the Limits of Community Governance', *Journal of Rural Studies*, 14, 1: 41–50.

Murphy, P. and Watson, S. (1995) 'Winners, Losers and Curate's Eggs: Urban and Regional Outcomes of Australian Economic Restructuring, 1971–1991', *Geoforum*, 26, 4: 337–49.

Murray, M. and Dunn, L. (1995) 'Capacity Building for Rural Development in the United States', *Journal of Rural Studies*, 11, 1: 89–97.

Murray–Darling Basin Ministerial Council (1990) *Natural Resources Management Strategy: Towards a Sustainable Future*, Canberra: Murray–Darling Basin Ministerial Council.

Murrumbidgee River Management Board (1998) *Submission to Productivity Commission Enquiry into the Impact of Competition Policy Reforms on Rural and Regional Australia*, http://.pc.gov.au.

Musgrave, W. (1983) 'Rural Communities: Some Social Issues', *Australian Journal of Agricultural Economics*, 27, 2: 145–51.

Musyck, B. (1995) 'Autonomous Industrialization in South West Flanders (Belgium): Continuity and Transformation', *Regional Studies*, 29, 7: 619–33.

Myers, G. and Macnaghten, P. (1998) 'Rhetorics of Environmental Sustainability: Commonplaces and Places', *Environment and Planning A*, 30, 2: 333–53.

Naisbitt, J. (1994) *Global Paradox: The Bigger the World Economy, the More Powerful the Smaller Players*, Sydney: Allen & Unwin.

Napier, R. (1997) 'Business Structures for the Future', in *Outlook 97, Agriculture, Volume 2, Proceedings of the National Agricultural Outlook Conference*, Canberra: ABARE: 83–92.

Naples, N. (1994) 'Contradictions in Agrarian Ideology: Restructuring Gender, Race-Ethnicity, and Class', *Rural Sociology*, 59, 1: 110–35.

National Economics (2000) *State of the Regions 2000*, Canberra: Australian Local Government Association.

National Farmers' Federation (1998) *Submission to the Productivity Commission Inquiry into the Impact of Competition Policy Reforms on Rural and Regional Australia*, Canberra.

—— (1993) *New Horizons: a Strategy for Australia's Agri-food Industries*, Canberra: National Farmers' Federation.

National Farmers' Federation and Australian Conservation Foundation (NFF/ACF) (2000) *A National Scenario for Strategic Investment*, http://www.nff.org.au/rtc/5point.htm

National Institute of Economic and Industry Research (2001) *Enterprise Zones: Creating Jobs and Prosperity in Regional Australia*, Report to the Institute of Chartered Accountants and the Local Government and Shires Association of NSW, Melbourne: National Institute of Economic and Industry Research.

—— (1998) *State of the Regions: A Report to the Australian Local Government Association 1998 Regional Cooperation and Development Forum*, Melbourne: National Institute of Economic and Industry Research.

National Natural Resource Management Task Force (1999) *Managing Natural Resources in Rural Australia for a Sustainable Future*, Canberra: Agriculture, Forestry and Fisheries – Australia.

National Rural Health Alliance (1997) *Forum Overview, National Rural Health Public Health Forum*, Canberra: National Rural Health Alliance.

Neil, C., Tykklainen, M. and Bradbury, J. (1992) *Coping with Closure: An International Comparison of Mine Town Experiences*, London: Routledge.

Newby, H. (1975) 'The Deferential Dialectic', *Comparative Studies in Society and History*, 17, 2: 139–64.

Newton, P. W. and Bell, M. (eds) (1996) *Population Shift: Mobility and Change in Australia*, Canberra: Australian Government Publishing Service.

Neyland, B. and Kendig, H. (1996) 'Retirement Migration to the Coast', in Newton, P. and Bell, M. (eds) *Population Shift: Mobility and Change in Australia*, Canberra: Australian Government Publishing Service: 364–77.

Nielsen, K. (1977) 'True Needs, Rationality and Emancipation', in R. Fitzgerald (ed.), *Human Needs and Politics*, Sydney: Pergamon: 142–56.

Norton, J. (1998) 'Throwing up Concerns about Novel Foods', in Hindmarsh, R., Lawrence, G., Norton, J. (eds) *Altered Genes – Reconstructing Nature: The Debate*, Sydney: Allen & Unwin: 173–85.

Norton, J., Lawrence, G. and Wood, G. (1998) ' The Australian Public's Perception of Genetically-engineered Foods', *Australasian Biotechnology*, 8, 3, May/June: 172–81.

Nottingham, S. (1998) *Eat Your Genes: How Genetically Modified Food is Entering Our Diet*, Marrickville: Australian Consumers' Association.

NSW Council of Social Service and Office of Social Justice and Youth Policy (1995) *Rural Communities Looking Ahead: An Issues Paper for the New South Wales Rural Social Policy Conference*, Dubbo.

O'Connor, J. (1973) *The Fiscal Crisis of the State*, New York: St Martin's Press.

O'Connor, K. and Stimson, B. (1996) 'Convergence and Divergence of Demographic and Economic Trends', in Newton, P. and Bell, M. (eds) *Population Shift: Mobility and Change in Australia*, Canberra: Australian Government Publishing Service: 108–25.

O'Connor, K., Stimson, R. and Taylor, S. (1998) 'Convergence and Divergence in the Australian Space Economy', *Australian Geographical Studies*, 36, 2: 205–22.

O'Connor, M. (ed.) (1994) *Is Capitalism Sustainable? Political Economy and the Politics of Ecology*, New York: Guilford Press.

O'Hearn, D. (1995) 'Global Restructuring, Transnational Corporations and the "European Periphery": What Has Changed?', in Smith, D. and Borocz, J. (eds) *A New World Order? Global Transformations in the Late Twentieth Century*, Connecticut: Praeger: 71–90.

Olfert, R. (1997) 'Agricultural Structure and Community Viability in Saskatchewan', in *Agriculture, Volume 2, Proceedings of the National Agricultural Outlook Conference*, Canberra: ABARE: 103–10.

Olson, K. and Schellenberg, R. (1986) 'Farm Stressors', *American Journal of Community Psychology*, 14, 5: 555–69.

O'Neill, D. (1999) 'Infrastructure', paper presented to the Regional Australia Summit, Canberra.

Opperman, M. (1994) 'Regional Aspects of Tourism in New Zealand', *Regional Studies*, 28, 2: 155–67.

Orfield, M. (1997) *Metropolitics: A Regional Agenda for Community and Stability*, Washington: Brookings Institution Press.

Ostrom, E. (1994) 'Constituting Social Capital and Collective Action', in Keohane, R. and Ostrom, E. (eds) *Local Commons and Global Interdependence: Heterogeneity and Cooperation in Two Domains*, London: Sage: 1–26.

O'Toole, K. (1999) 'Think Global and Act Local and What Do You Get? The Experience of Small Towns in Victoria', paper presented at Civilising the State: Civil Society, Policy and State Transformation Conference, Deakin University, 6 December.

—— (1998) 'Economic Development in the Green Triangle: A Need for Reassessment in the New International Environment', in Staples, M. and Millmow, A. (eds) *Studies in Australian Rural Economic Development*, Wagga Wagga, NSW: Centre for Rural Social Research, Charles Sturt University: 31–9.

Overbeek, H. (1990) *Global Capitalism and National Decline: the Thatcher Decade in Perspective*, London: Unwin Hyman.

Oxley, H. (1978) *Mateship in Local Organization*, 2nd edn, Brisbane: University of Queensland Press.

Pacione, M. (1997) 'Local Exchange Trading Systems: A Rural Response to the Globalization of Capitalism', *Journal of Rural Studies*, 13, 4: 415–27.

Pahl, R. (1998) 'Friendship: the Social Glue of Contemporary Society?', in Franklin, J. (ed.) *The Politics of Risk Society*, Cambridge: Polity Press: 99–119.

—— (1968) 'The Rural–Urban Continuum', in Pahl, R. (ed.) *Readings in Urban Sociology*, London: Pergamon Press: 263–97.

Palmer, L. and Quinn, H. (1997) 'Farming Discourses: From Baa-lambs to Bar-codes', in Mules, W. and Miller, H. (eds) *Mapping Regional Cultures: Discourses in Social Contexts*, Rockhampton, Queensland: Rural Social and Economic Research Centre: 97–111.

Parham, D., Barnes, P., Roberts, P. and Kennett, S. (2000) *Distribution of the Economic Gains of the 1990s*, Staff Research Paper, Canberra: Productivity Commission.

Paris, C. (1994) 'New Patterns of Urban and Regional Development in Australia: Demographic Restructuring and Economic Change', *International Journal of Urban and Regional Research*, 18, 4: 555–72.

Parsons, G. (1993) 'Community Bonds: A New Approach to Community and Economic Development', *Journal of the Community Development Society*, 24, 2: 196–212.

Parsons, H. (1995) *The Role of the Melbourne Wholesale Fruit and Vegetable Market in Fresh Produce Supply Chains*, Working Paper No. 35, Melbourne: Department of Geography and Environmental Science, Monash University.

Passfield, R., Lawrence, G. and McAllister, J. (1996) 'Not So Sweet: Rural Restructuring and its Community Impact – the Mackay Sugar District, Queensland', in Lawrence, G., Lyons, K. and Momtaz, S. (eds) *Social Change in Rural Australia: Perspectives from the Social Sciences*, Rockhampton, Queensland: Rural Social and Economic Research Centre, Central Queensland University: 188–200.

Paterson, I. (1998) 'Bigger is Better Says Wool Industry Report', *The Land*, no. 3942, 29 October: 8.

Pawson, E. and Scott, G. (1992a) 'Case Study 7.2: Resisting Post Office Closures', in Britton, S., Le Heron, R. and Pawson, E. (eds) *Changing Places in New Zealand*, Christchurch: New Zealand Geographical Society: 170–1.

—— (1992b) 'Community Responses in the West Coast', in Britton, S., Le Heron, R. and Pawson, E. (eds) *Changing Places in New Zealand*, Christchurch: New Zealand Geographical Society: 280–3.

Peacock, J. (1998) 'Implications of Genetic Engineering for Australian Agriculture', in ABARE, *Outlook 98: Additional Papers, Proceedings of the National Agricultural and Resource Outlook Conference*, February, Canberra: ABARE: 67–9.

—— (1994) 'Genetic Engineering of Crop Plants Will Enhance the Quality and Diversity of Foods', *Food Australia*, 46: 379–81.

Penfold, C. and Miyan, M. (1998) 'Organic Agriculture – Now and the Future', in Michalk, D., and Pratley, J. (eds) *Agronomy – Growing a Greener Future, Proceedings of the 9th Australian Agronomy Conference*, Wagga Wagga, NSW: Australian Society of Agronomy: 669–72.

Pepperdine, S. (2000) 'Towards a Framework to Integrate Social Issues in Natural Resource Management', paper presented to the Xth World Congress of Rural Sociology, Rio de Janeiro, 30 July–5 August.

Pepperdine, S. and Ewing, S. (forthcoming) 'Integrating Social Sustainability Considerations in Natural Resource Management', in Higgins, V., Lawrence, G. and Lockie, S. (eds) *Social Sciences in Natural Resource Management: Perspectives from Australasia and the Americas*, Cheltenham, UK: Edward Elgar.

Perkins, H. (1989) 'The Country in the Town: the Role of Real Estate Developers in the Construction of the Meaning of Place', *Journal of Rural Studies*, 5, 1: 61–74.

Perucci, R. (1994) 'Embedded Corporatism: Auto Transplants, the Local State and Community Politics in the Midwest Corridor', *Sociological Quarterly*, 35, 3: 487–505.

Pfeffer, M. and Lapping, M. (1994) 'Farmland Preservation, Development Rights and Theory of the Growth Machine: Views of Planners', *Journal of Rural Studies*, 10: 233–47.

Phelps, B. (1998) 'Genetic Engineering: the Campaign Frontier', in Hindmarsh, R., Lawrence, G. and Norton, J. (eds) *Altered Genes – Reconstructing Nature: The Debate*, Sydney: Allen & Unwin: 186–98.

Phillips, E. (1998) *The Social and Cultural Construction of Farming Practice: 'Good Farming' in Two New South Wales Communities*, unpublished PhD thesis, Wagga Wagga, NSW: Charles Sturt University.

Phillips, E. and Campbell, H. (1993) 'The Contemporary Meaning of Rural Development in New Zealand', *Rural Society*, 3, 2: 9–11.

Phillips, E. and Gray, I. (1995) 'Farming "Practice" as Temporally and Spatially Situated Intersections of Biography, Culture and Social Structure', *Australian Geographer*, 26, 2: 127–32.

Pieterse, J. (1996) 'Globalisation as Hybridization', in Featherstone, M., Lash, S. and Robertson, R. (eds) *Global Modernities*, London: Sage: 45–68.

Pile, S. (1990) *The Private Farmer: Transformation and Legitimation in Advanced Capitalist Agriculture*, Aldershot: Dartmouth Press.

Pinch, S. (1989) 'The Restructuring Thesis and the Study of Public Services', *Environment and Planning A*, 21, 7: 905–26.

Pini, B. (1999) 'The Emerging Economic Rationalist Discourse on Women and Leadership in Australian Agriculture', *Rural Society*, 8, 3: 223–33.

Pinkerton, J., Hassinger, E., and O'Brien, D. (1995) 'Inshopping by Residents of Small Communities', *Rural Sociology*, 60, 3: 467–80.

Pixley, J. (1998) 'Social Movements, Democracy and Conflicts over Institutional Reform', in Smyth, P. and Cass, B. (eds) *Contesting the Australian Way*, Cambridge: Cambridge University Press: 138–53.

Poiner, G. (1990) *The Good Old Rule: Gender and Other Power Relationships in a Rural Community*, Sydney: Sydney University Press.

Pongratz, H. (1990) 'Cultural Tradition and Social Change in Agriculture', *Sociologia Ruralis*, 30, 1: 5–17.

Potter, C. and Lobley, M. (1992a) 'Ageing and Succession on Family Farms: The Impact on Decision-making and Land Use', *Sociologia Ruralis*, 32, 2/3: 317–34.

—— (1992b) 'The Conservation Status and Potential of Elderly Farmers: Results from a Survey in England and Wales', *Journal of Rural Studies*, 8, 2: 133–43.

Powell, J. (1997) 'Resource Development, Environmental Planning and the Family Farm: An Historical Interpretation', in Lees, J. (ed.) *A Legacy Under Threat? Family Farming in Australia*, Armidale: University of New England Press: 147–73.

Powell, R. (1998) 'Agriculture and the Economy', in Michalk, D. and Pratley, J. (eds) *Proceedings of the Ninth Australian Agronomy Conference*, Wagga Wagga, NSW: Australian Society of Agronomy: 13–20.

—— (1997) 'Market Economies and Small Towns', *Regional and Enterprise Development Network*, 2, 1: 1.

—— (1996) 'Succeeding Small Towns in Rural New South Wales', paper presented at the Community Development Society International Conference, Melbourne.

Pratley, J. and Robertson, A. (1998) *Agriculture and the Environmental Imperative*, Melbourne: CSIRO.

Price, P. (1998) 'Sustainability – What Does it Mean, and How Should it be Applied in a Regional Context?', in Grimes, J., Lawrence, G. and Stehlik, D. (eds) *Sustainable Futures: Towards a Catchment Management Strategy for the Central Queensland Region*, Rockhampton, Queensland: Institute for Sustainable Regional Development: 15–27.

Price, R. (2000) 'Redesigning Agricultural Landscapes – Social, Economic and Ecological Imperatives', in Gleeson, T. (ed.) *Participant Essay Series: Draft Proceedings of the Australian Values – Rural Policies Symposium*, Old Parliament House, Canberra, 28–29 August (n.d.)

Pritchard, B. (1999) 'Australia as a Supermarket to Asia? Government, Territory, and Political Economy of the Australian Agri-food System', *Rural Sociology* 64, 2: 284–301.

—— (1998) 'Deregulation and the Growth of Grains Co-operatives', in Burch, D., Lawrence, G., Rickson, R. and Goss, J. (eds) *Australasian Food and Farming in a Globalised Economy: Recent Developments and Future Prospects*, Monash Publications in Geography Number 50, Melbourne: Department of Geography and Environmental Science, Monash University: 43–53.

Pritchard, B. and McManus, P. (eds) (2000) *Land of Discontent: the Dynamics of Change in Rural and Regional Australia*, Sydney: University of New South Wales Press.

Productivity Commission (1999) 'Impact of Competition Policy Reforms on Rural and Regional Australia', *Productivity Commission Inquiry Report No. 8*, Canberra.

Productivity Commission (1998) *Impact of Competition Policy Reforms on Rural and Regional Australia, Inquiry Issues Paper*, Canberra: Productivity Commission.

Pusey, M. (1991) *Economic Rationalism in Australia*, Cambridge: Cambridge University Press.

Putnam, R. (1993) *Making Democracy Work: Civic Traditions in Modern Italy*, Princeton: Princeton University Press.

Raby, G. (1996) *Making Rural Australia: An Economic History of Technical and Institutional Creativity, 1788–1860*, Melbourne: Oxford University Press.

Radford, N. (1996) 'Accepting the Challenge', in *Rural Communities Looking Ahead, Proceedings of a Rural Social Policy Conference*, Sydney: New South Wales Council of Social Service: 85–6.

Rajan, R. (ed.) (1993) *Rebuilding Communities: Experiences and Experiments in Europe*, Dartington: Green Books.

Ramsay, M. (1996) *Community, Culture and Economic Development: The Social Roots of Local Action*, Albany: State University of New York Press.

Ray, C. (2000) 'The EU Leader Programme: Rural Development Laboratory', *Sociologia Ruralis*, 40, 20: 163–71.

—— (1997) 'Towards a Theory of the Dialectic of Local Rural Development within the European Union', *Sociologia Ruralis*, 37, 3: 345–62.

Reale, L. (1998) Rapid Rural Appraisal of the Vegetable Industry in the Murrumbidgee Irrigation Areas, unpublished Master of Applied Science dissertation, Wagga Wagga, NSW: Charles Sturt University.

Redclift, M. (1987) *Sustainable Development: Exploring the Contradictions*, London: Methuen.

Redclift, M. and Woodgate, G. (eds) (1997) *The International Handbook of Environmental Sociology*, Cheltenham: Edward Elgar.

Reed, M. and Gill, A. (1997) 'Tourism, Recreational and Amenity Values in Land Allocation: An Analysis of Institutional Arrangements in the Postproductivist Era', *Environment and Planning A*, 29, 11: 2019–40.

Rees, S., Rodley, G. and Stilwell, F. (eds) (1993) *Beyond the Market: Alternatives to Economic Rationalism*, Sydney: Pluto Press.

Reeve, I. (1997) 'Land Resource Management: Management or Negotiation?', in Lockie, S. and Vanclay, F. (eds) *Critical Landcare*, Wagga Wagga, NSW: Centre for Rural Social Research: 83–96.

—— (1997) 'Property and Participation: An Institutional Analysis of Rural Resource Management and Landcare in Australia', *Rural Society*, 6, 4: 25–35.

—— (1988) *A Squandered Land: 200 Years of Land Degradation in Australia*, Armidale: Rural Development Centre, University of New England.

Reeve, I. and Black, A. (1993) *Australian Farmers' Attitudes to Rural Environmental Issues*, Armidale, NSW: Rural Development Centre, University of New England.

Reis, J., Hespanha, P., Pires, A. and Jacinto, R. (1990) 'How Rural is Agricultural Pluriactivity?', *Journal of Rural Studies*, 6, 4: 395–9.

Retallack, S. (2000) 'After Seattle: Where to Next for the WTO?', *The Ecologist* 30, 2, April: 30–4.

Richardson, R. and Gillespie, A (1996) 'Advanced Communications and Employment Creation in Rural and Peripheral Regions: a Case Study of the Highlands and Islands of Scotland', *Annals of Regional Science*, 30, 1: 91–110.

Riedel, G. (1999) 'Telecom and E-Commerce Opportunities for Regional Australia', keynote paper presented to the Regional Australia Summit, Canberra.

Ritzer, G. (1996) *The McDonaldization of Society*, 2nd edn, California: Pine Forge.

Roberts, I., Doyle, S., Stayner, R., Mues, C. and Gray, A. (1996) 'The Future for Australian Agriculture: Important Issues to 2010', *Outlook 96*, Canberra: ABARE: 55–75.

Robertson, A. and Pratley, J. (1998) 'From Farm Management to Ecosystem Management', in Pratley, J. and Robertson, A. (eds) *Agriculture and the Environmental Imperative*, Melbourne: CSIRO: 243–63.

Robertson, G. (1997) 'Managing the Environment for Profit', in Australian Bureau of Agricultural and Resource Economics, *Outlook 97, Proceedings of the National Agricultural and Resources Outlook Conference*, Canberra: ABARE: 75–9.

Robertson, R. (1996) 'Glocalization: Time–Space and Homogeneity–Heterogeneity', in Featherstone, M., Lash, S. and Robertson, R. (eds) *Global Modernities*, London: Sage: 25–44.

Robson, M. (1992) *Australian Regional Developments: 25. The Hamilton Experience*, Belconnen: Office of Local Government in the Commonwealth Department of Immigration, Local Government and Ethnic Affairs.

Rogers, S. (1991) *Shaping Modern Times in Rural Areas: The Transformation and Reproduction of an Aveyronnais Community*, Princeton: Princeton University Press.

Rolley, F. and Humphreys, J. (1993) 'Rural Welfare – The Human Face of Australia's Countryside', in Sorensen, T. and Epps, R. *Prospects and Policies for Rural Australia*, Melbourne: Longman Cheshire: 241– 57.

Rose, N. (1996) 'Governing "Advanced" Liberal Democracies', in Barry, A., Osborne, T. and Rose, N. (eds) *Foucault and Political Reason: Liberalism, Neo-Liberalism and Rationalities of Government*, Chicago: University of Chicago Press: 37–64

Rose, N. and Miller, P. (1992) 'Political Power Beyond the State: Problematics of Government', *British Journal of Sociology*, 42, 2: 173–205.

Rosenblatt, P. and Keller, L. (1983) 'Economic Vulnerability and Economic Stress in Farm Couples', *Family Relations*, 32, 4: 567–73.

Ross, R. and Trachte, K. (1990) *Global Capitalism: the New Leviathan*, Albany: SUNY Press.

Russell, D. (1999) 'Community and Industry Leadership', paper presented to the Regional Australia Summit, Canberra.

Ruzicka, L. and Choi, C.Y. (1999) 'Youth Suicide in Australia', *Journal of the Australian Population Association*, 16 (1/2): 29–46.

Sachs, W., Loske, R. and Linz, M. (1998) *Greening of the North: a Post-Industrial Blueprint for Ecology and Equity*, London: Zed Books.

Salamon, S. and Tornatore, J. (1994) 'Territory Contested Through Property in a Midwestern Post-Agricultural Community', *Rural Sociology*, 59, 4: 636–54.

Salt, B. (1997) 'Demographic and Cultural Change in the Bush', in *Agriculture, Volume 2, Proceedings of the National Agricultural Outlook Conference*, Canberra: ABARE: 119–24.

—— (1992) *Population Movements in Non-Metropolitan Australia*, Canberra: Australian Government Publishing Service.

Sanderson, S. (1986) 'The Emergence of the "World Steer": Internationalization and Foreign Domination in Latin American Cattle Production', in Tullis, F. and Hollist, W. (eds) *Food, the State and International Political Economy*, Lincoln: University of Nebraska Press.

Sant, M. and Simons, P. (1993) 'Counterurbanization and Coastal Development in New South Wales', *Geoforum*, 24, 3: 291–306.

Santamaria, B. (1997) 'Gambling on a Finance System', *Australian*, 10 May: 25.

Sarantakos, S. (1998) 'Farm Families and City Families', in Sarantakos, S. (ed.) *Quality of Life in Rural Australia*, Wagga Wagga, NSW: Centre for Rural Social Research: 93–103.

Saunders, P. (1983) *Urban Politics: A Sociological Interpretation*, London: Hutchinson.

Scales, B. (1997) 'The Challenge for Regional Australia', paper presented at the Sustainable Economic Growth in Regional Australia Conference, Lorne, September.

Scrase, T. (1995) 'Globalisation, India and the Struggle for Justice', in Smith, D. and Borocz, J. (eds) *A New World Order? Global Transformations in the Late Twentieth Century*, Connecticut: Praeger: 37–56.

Searston, M. and Searston, I. (1998) 'Community Development and Local Government: The Queensland Situation', in Falk, I. (ed.) *Learning Communities, Regional Sustainability and the Learning Society*, Conference Proceedings, vol. 2, 13–20 June 1998, Launceston: Centre for Research and Learning in Regional Australia: 296–302.

Segger, P. (1997) 'World Trade in Organic Foods: A Growing Reality', paper presented at the Future Agenda for Organic Trade, Fifth IFOAM Conference on Trade in Organic Products, Oxford.

Self, P. (1997) 'The Future of Australian Local Government', in Dollery, B. and Marshall, N. (eds) *Australian Local Government: Reform and Renewal*, Melbourne: Macmillan: 297–310.

Senate Employment, Workplace Relations, Small Business and Education References Committee (1999) *Jobs for the Regions: A Report on the Inquiry into Regional Employment and Unemployment*, Canberra: Parliament of Australia.

Sexton, E. (1999) 'Rural Areas Getting Around Bank Closures', *Sydney Morning Herald*, 6 April 1999: 21.

Shaffer, R. (1995) 'Is Sustainable Regional Economic Development Possible?', *Australasian Journal of Regional Studies*, 1, 1: 21–30.

—— (1994) 'Rural Communities and Sustainable Economic Development', in McSwan, D. and McShane, M. (eds) *Issues Affecting Rural Communities, Proceedings of the Conference on Issues Affecting Rural Communities*, Rural Education and Development Centre, James Cook University: 267–71.

Share, P. (1995) 'Beyond Countrymindedness: Representations in the Post-Rural Era', in Share, P. (ed.) *Communications, Culture and Ideology in Rural Areas*, Key Papers 4, Wagga Wagga, NSW: Centre for Rural Social Research, Charles Sturt University: 1–23.

—— (1987) 'The Liminality of Farmers: Class and Gender Relations in Agricultural Populations', *Regional Journal of Social Issues*, 21: 19–40.

Share, P., Campbell, H. and Lawrence, G. (1991) 'The Vertical and Horizontal Restructuring of Rural Regions: Australia and New Zealand', in Alston, M. (ed.) *Family Farming: Australia and New Zealand*, Wagga Wagga, NSW: Centre for Rural Social Research, Charles Sturt University: 1–23.

Shaw, A. (1985) 'History and Development of Australian Agriculture', in Williams, D. (ed.) *Agriculture in the Australian Economy*, Sydney: Sydney University Press: 1–28.

Sheil, H. (1999) 'Transformation: From Despair to Optimism', paper presented to the Regional Australia Summit, Canberra.

Shils, E. (1981) *Tradition*, Chicago: University of Chicago Press.

Shortall, S. (1994) 'Farm Women's Groups: Feminist or Farming or Community Groups, or New Social Movements?', *Sociology*, 28, 1: 279–91.

Shrestha, N. (1997) 'On "What Causes Poverty? A Postmodern View"', *Annals of the Association of American Geographers*, 87, 4: 709–16.

Shrybman, S. (1999) 'The World Trade Organisation: the New World Constitution Laid Bare', *Ecologist*, 29, 4, July: 270–5.

Shucksmith, M. (2000) 'Social Exclusion and Reflexivity: Bounded Choices and Sustainable Livelihoods in Rural Britain', paper presented to the Xth World Congress of Rural Sociology, Rio de Janeiro, 30 July–5 August.

—— (1993) 'Farm Household Behaviour and the Transition to Post-Productivism', *Journal of Agricultural Economics*, 44, 3: 466–78.

Shumpeter, J. (1975) *Capitalism, Socialism and Democracy*, New York: Harper.

Sidoti, C. (1999) *Bush Talks*, Sydney: Human Rights and Equal Opportunity Commission.

Simmons, P. (1993) 'Recent Developments in Commonwealth Drought Policy', *Review of Marketing and Agricultural Economics*, 61, 3: 443–54.

Slee, P. (1988) 'Crisis on the Farm: A Telephone Survey of Rural Stress', *Australian Social Work*, 41, 4: 9–13.

Smailes, P. J. (2000) 'The Diverging Geographies of Social and Business Interaction Patterns: a Case Study of Rural South Australia', *Australian Geographical Studies*, 38, 2: 158–81.

—— (1997) 'Socio-Economic Change and Rural Morale in South Australia, 1982–1993', *Journal of Rural Studies*, 13, 1: 19–42.

—— (1996) 'Accessibility Changes in South Australia and the Country Town Network', in Lawrence, G., Lyons, K. and Momtaz, S. (eds) *Social Change in Rural Australia: Perspectives from the Social Sciences*, Rockhampton, Queensland: Rural Social and Economic Research Centre, Central Queensland University: 119–38.

—— (1991) 'The Impact of the Rural Crisis of 1985–1989 on a Rural Local Government Area', *South Australian Geographical Journal*, 91: 24–45.

Smith, C. and Steel, B. (1995) 'Core-Periphery Relationships of Resource-Based Communities', *Journal of the Community Development Society*, 26, 1: 52–70.

Sorensen, A. (1991) 'Misleading Impressions: The Recession in the Farm Sector and its Impact on Rural Australia', *Policy*, 7, 3: 18–21.

—— (1990) 'Virtuous Cycles of Growth and Vicious Cycles of Decline: Regional Economic Growth in Northern New South Wales', in Walmsley, D. (ed.) *Change and Adjustment in Northern New South Wales*, Armidale: University of New England: 41–59.

Sorensen, A. and Epps, R. (1997) 'The Changing Economic Structure of Four Central Queensland Shires', paper presented at the joint conference of the Institute of Australian Geographers and the New Zealand Geographical Society, Hobart, January.

—— (1996) 'Leadership and Local Development: Dimensions of Leadership in Four Central Queensland Towns', *Journal of Rural Studies*, 12, 2: 113–25.

Sorensen, A. and Weinand, H. (1991) 'Regional Well-Being in Australia Revisited', *Australian Geographical Studies*, 29, 1: 42–70.

Sorensen, T. (1993a) 'Approaches to Policy', in Sorensen, T. and Epps, R (eds) *Prospects and Policies for Rural Australia*, Melbourne: Longman Cheshire: 274–89.

—— (1993b) 'The Future of the Country Town: Strategies for Local Economic Development', in Sorensen, T. and Epps, R. (eds) *Prospects and Policies for Rural Australia*, Melbourne: Longman Cheshire: 201–40.

Sorensen, T. and Epps, R. (1995) 'Local Economic Change in Four Central West Queensland Shires', paper presented to the Annual Conference of the Institute of Australian Geographers, Newcastle, September.

—— (1993) 'An Overview of Economy and Society', in Sorensen, T. and Epps, R. (eds) *Prospects and Policies for Rural Australia*, Melbourne: Longman Cheshire: 7–31.

South Gippsland Shire Council (1998) *Submission to [Productivity Commission] Enquiry into the Impact of Competition Policy Reforms on Rural and Regional Australia*, http://.pc.gov.au.

Spies, S., Murdock, S., White, S., Krannich, R., Wulfhorst, J., Wrigley, K., Leistritz, F., Sell, R. and Thompson, J. (1998) 'Support for Waste Facility Siting: Differences between Community Leaders and Residents', *Rural Sociology*, 63, 1: 65–93.

Squires, V. and Tow, P. (eds) (1991) *Dryland Farming: a Systems Approach*, Sydney: Sydney University Press.

St Clair, J. (1997) 'Going Online in Regional Australia', paper presented to the Sustainable Economic Growth in Regional Australia Conference, Lorne, September.

Stabler, A. and Olfert, J., (1996) *The Changing Role of Rural Communities in an Urbanizing World: Saskatchewan – An Update to 1995*, Canadian Plains Research Centre, University of Regina.

Standing Committee on Environment, Recreation and the Arts (2001) *Coordinating Catchment Management – Inquiry into Catchment Management*, Canberra: House of Representatives.

—— (1990a) *An Economic Development Study of Werris Creek, NSW*, Armidale: Rural Development Centre, University of New England.

—— (1990b) *The Economic Impacts in Wool Prices on a Small Rural Town: Guyra, NSW*, Armidale: Rural Development Centre, University of New England.

Standing Committee on Primary Industries and Regional Services (2000) *Time Running Out: Shaping Regional Australia's Future*, Canberra: House of Representatives.

Stayner, R. (1998) *The Role of the Regional Economy in Farm Adjustment*, Canberra: Rural Industries Research and Development Corporation.

—— (1997a) 'Families and the Farm Adjustment Process', in Lees, J. (ed.) *A Legacy Under Threat? Family Farming in Australia*, Armidale: University of New England Press: 121–45.

—— (1997b) 'Getting into Farming: Family and Financial Factors', in *Agriculture, Volume 2, Proceedings of the National Agricultural Outlook Conference*, Canberra: Australian Bureau of Agricultural and Resource Economics: 111–18.

—— (1994) 'Adjustment on Family Farms', in *Outlook 94: Agriculture*, Canberra: Australian Bureau of Agricultural and Resource Economics: 26–34.

Stayner, R. and Reeve, I. (1990) 'Uncoupling': Relationships Between Agriculture and the Local Economies of Rural Areas in New South Wales*, Armidale: Rural Development Centre, University of New England.

Stehlik, D. and Lawrence, G. (1999) 'Issues Facing Rural and Remote Populations in Queensland', submission to the Queensland Government's Community Services Strategy; Brisbane: Premier's Department, Queensland Government (unpublished paper).

—— (1996) 'A Direction Toward Sustainability? Australian Rural Communities and Care for the Aged', *Journal of the Community Development Society* 27,1: 45–55.

Stehlik, D., Gray, I. and Lawrence, G. (1998) *Australian Farm Families' Experience of Drought in the 1990s: A Sociological Investigation*, Canberra: Rural Industries Research and Development Corporation.

Stewart, J. (1994) *The Lie of the Level Playing Field: Industry Policy and Australia's Future*, Melbourne: Text.

Stilwell, F. (2000) *Changing Track: A New Political Economic Direction for Australia*, Sydney: Pluto Press.

—— (1998) *Going Global? Australian Cities and the Challenge of Globalisation*, Sydney: Department of Geography, University of Sydney.

—— (1994) *Australian Urban and Regional Development: the Policy Challenge*, Research Paper no. 8, 1994, Canberra: Parliamentary Research Service, Parliament of Australia.

—— (1993) *Reshaping Australia: Urban Problems and Policies*, Sydney: Pluto Press.

—— (1992) *Understanding Cities and Regions*, Sydney: Pluto Press.

—— (1974) *Australian Urban and Regional Development*, Sydney: Australia and New Zealand Book Company.

Stimson, R., Baum, S., Mullins, P. and O'Connor, K. (1999) 'Australia's Regional Cities and Towns: Modelling Community Opportunity and Vulnerability', paper presented to the Annual Conference of the Australian and New Zealand Regional Science Association, Newcastle: 19–22 September.

Stock, C. (1996) *Rural Radicals: Righteous Rage in the American Grain*, Ithaca: Cornell University Press.

Stoeckel, A. (1998) 'Farmers Can Solve their Problems by Themselves', *Australian Farm Journal*, 8, 9: 16–17.

—— (1992) *Addressing The Issues of Rural Towns: R&D Opportunities Available for RIRDC to Fund*, Canberra: Rural Industries Research and Development Corporation.

Stokes, H. and Wyn, J. (1998) 'Community Strategies: Addressing the Challenges for Young People Living in Rural Australia', in Falk, I. (ed.) *Learning Communities, Regional Sustainability and the Learning Society*, Conference Proceedings, vol. 2, 13–20 June, 1998, Launceston: Centre for Research and Learning in Regional Australia: 311–21.

Stone, R. (1996) *Sociological Reasoning: Towards a Post-Modern Sociology*, Basingstoke: Macmillan.

Stone, S. (1999) 'Australians Called to Comment on Tree Clearing', Media Release from the Parliamentary Secretary to the Minister for the Environment and Heritage, 2 August.

—— (1994) 'Changing Cultures in the Farming Community', in Cosgrove, L., Evans, D. and Yencken, D. (eds) *Restoring the Land: Environmental Values, Knowledge and Action*, Carlton: Melbourne University Press: 202–19.

Storey, D. (1999) 'Issues of Integration, Participation and Empowerment in Rural Development: The Case of LEADER in the Republic of Ireland', *Journal of Rural Studies*, 15, 3: 307–15.

Strange, M. (1989) *Family Farming: a New Economic Vision*, Lincoln: University of Nebraska Press.

Strange, S. (1998) 'Globaloney?', *Review of International Political Economy* 5, 4, Winter: 704–11.

Stretton, H. and Orchard, L. (1994) *Public Goods, Public Enterprise, Public Choice: Theoretical Foundations of the Contemporary Attack on Government*, London: Macmillan.

Sydney Morning Herald, 24 July 2000.

Symes, D. and Appleton, J. (1986) 'Family Goals and Survival Strategies: The Role of Kinship in an English Upland Farming Community', *Sociologia Ruralis*, 26, 3/4: 345–63.

Syrett, S. (1993) 'Local Economic Initiatives in Portugal: Reality and Rhetoric', *International Journal of Urban and Regional Research*, 17, 4: 527–46.

Tanner, L. (1999) *Open Australia*, Sydney: Pluto Press.

Taskforce on Regional Development (1993) *Developing Australia: A Regional Perspective (Volume One)*, Canberra: Australian Government Publishing Service.

Taylor, B., Lockie, S., Lawrence, G. and Dale, A. (1999) 'Industry Focus Groups – Summary Report', draft submission to the National Land and Water Audit, Rockhampton, Queensland: Centre for Social Science Research.

Taylor, M. (1997) *Bludgers in Grass Castles: Native Title and the Unpaid Debts of the Pastoral Industry*, Resistance Books, Chippendale.

—— (1991) 'Economic Restructuring and Regional Change in Australia', *Australian Geographical Studies*, 29, 2: 255–67.

Teather, E. (1999) 'The Double Bind: Being Female and Being Rural: A Comparative Study of Australia, New Zealand and Canada', *Rural Society*, 8, 3: 209–22.

—— (1992) 'Remote Rural Women's Ideologies, Spaces and Networks: The Example of the Country Women's Association of New South Wales, 1922–1992', *Australian and New Zealand Journal of Sociology*, 28, 3: 369–90.

Teeple, G. (1995) *Globalisation and the Decline of Social Reform*, New Jersey: Humanities Press.

Tewdwr-Jones, M. (1998) 'Rural Government and Community Participation: The Planning Role of Community Councils', *Journal of Rural Studies*, 14, 1: 51–62.

Theret, B. (1999) 'Regionalism and Federalism: A Comparative Analysis of the Regulation of Economic Tensions between Regions by Canadian and American Federal Intergovernmental Transfer Programmes', *International Journal of Urban and Regional Research*, 23, 3: 479–512.

Thomashow, M. (1995) *Ecological Identity: Becoming a Reflective Environmentalist*, Massachusetts: MIT Press.

Thorns, D. (1992) *Fragmenting Societies? A Comparative Analysis of Regional and Urban Development*, London: Routledge.

Tickell, A. and Peck, J. (1995) 'Social Regulation After Fordism: Regulation Theory, Neo-Liberalism and the Global–Local Nexus', *Economy and Society*, 24, 3: 357–86.

Till, K. (1993) 'Neotraditional Towns and Urban Villages: the Cultural Production of a Geography of "Otherness"', *Environment and Planning D: Society and Space*, 11: 709–32.

Timmons, G. (1999) 'Communities Leading Change', paper presented to the Regional Australia Summit, Canberra.

Tomlinson, J. (1999) *Globalization and Culture*, Cambridge: Polity Press.

Tonts, M. (1996) 'Economic Restructuring and Small Town Adjustment: Evidence from the Western Australian Central Wheatbelt', *Rural Society*, 6, 2: 24–33.

Tonts, M. and Jones, R. (1996) 'Rural Restructuring and Uneven Development in the Western Australian Wheatbelt', in Lawrence, G., Lyons, K. and Momtaz, S. (eds) *Social Change in Rural Australia: Perspectives from the Social Sciences*, Rockhampton, Queensland: Rural Social and Economic Research Centre, Central Queensland University: 139–53.

Torgerson, D. and Paehlke, R. (1990) 'Environmental Administration: Revising the Agenda of Inquiry and Practice', in Fischer, F. and Black, M. (eds) *Managing Leviathan: Environmental Politics and the Administrative State*, Ontario: Broadview Press: 7–16.

Tosterud, B. (1998) 'Regional Development Models: Methods of Action', *Regional and Enterprise Development Network*, 3, 2: 1–3.

Townsend, M., Mahoney, M. and Hallebone, E. (2000) 'Countering Rural Policy Impacts: Community Development Initiatives for Local Control', paper presented to the Xth World Congress of Rural Sociology, Sustainable Rural Livelihoods: Building Communities, Protecting Resources, Fostering Human Development, Rio de Janeiro, Brazil, 30 July–5 August.

Van Hook, M. (1987) 'Harvest of Despair: Using the ABCX Model for Farm Families in Crisis', *Social Casework*, 68, 5: 273–8.

Vanclay, F. and Lawrence, G. (1995) *The Environmental Imperative: Eco-social Concerns for Australian Agriculture*, Rockhampton, Queensland: Central Queensland University Press.

—— (1994) 'Farmer Rationality and the Adoption of Environmentally Sound Practices: A Critique of the Assumptions of Traditional Agricultural Extension', *European Journal of Agricultural Education and Extension* 1, 1, April: 59–90.

Varnam, J., Jordan, J. and Epperson, J. (1990) 'Preferences of Citizens for Agricultural Policies: Evidence from a National Survey', *American Journal of Agricultural Economics*, 72, 2: 257–67.

Victorian Catchment and Land Protection Council (1997) *Managing Victoria's Catchments: Partnerships in Action*, Melbourne: Department of Natural Resources and Environment.

Vidich, A. and Bensman, J. (1960) *Small Town in Mass Society*, New York: Doubleday Anchor.

Vinson, A. (1999) *Unequal in Life: The Distribution of Social Disadvantage in Victoria and New South Wales*, Melbourne: Ignatius Centre.

Voyce, M. (1997) 'Inheritance and Family Farm Ownership', in Lees, J. (ed.) *A Legacy Under Threat? Family Farming in Australia*, Armidale: University of New England Press: 199–212.

Wacquant, L. (1995) 'The Ghetto, the State and the New Capitalist Economy', in Kasinitz, P. (ed.) *Metropolis: Centre and Symbol of Our Times*, London: Macmillan: 418–49.

—— (1992) 'Toward a Social Praxeology: The Structure and Logic of Bourdieu's Sociology', in Bourdieu, P. and Wacquant, L. *An Invitation to Reflexive Sociology*, Chicago: University of Chicago Press: 1–59.

Wagner, W., Torgerson, H., Einsiedel, E., Jelsoe, E., Fredickson, H., Lassen, J., Rusanen, T., Boy, D., de Cheveigne, S., Hampel, J., Stathopoulou, A., Allansdottir, A., Midden, C., Nielsen, T., Przestalski, A.,

Twardowski, T., Fjaestad, B., Olsson, S., Olofsson, A., Gaskell, G., Durant, J., Bauer, M. and Liakopoulos, M. (1997) 'Europe Ambivalent on Biotechnology', *Nature*, 387: 845–7.

Wahlquist, A. (1999) 'Demographic and Social Changes in Australia', paper presented to the Regional Australia Summit, Canberra.

Walker, C. and Battye, K. (1996) *Mental Health Effects of the Rural Crisis*, Cowra: Mid Western Mental Health Services and the New South Wales Central West Division of General Practice.

Wallner, H., Narodoslawsky, M. and Moser, F. (1996) 'Islands of Sustainability: A Bottom-Up Approach Towards Sustainable Development', *Environment and Planning A*, 28, 10: 1763–78.

Walmsley, D. and Weinand, H. (1997) 'Fiscal Federalism and Social Well-Being in Australia', *Australian Geographical Studies*, 35, 3: 260–70.

Walmsley, J., Epps, R. and Duncan, C. (1995) *The New South Wales North Coast 1986–1991: Who Moved Where, Why and with What Effect?* Canberra: Bureau of Immigration, Multicultural and Population Research.

Walter, G. (1997) 'Images of Success: How Illinois Farmers Define the Successful Farmer', *Rural Sociology*, 62, 1: 48–68.

Warburton, J., MacDonald, S. and Rosenman, L. (1997) 'Issues of "Retirement" for Rural Men in the Darling Downs Region', *Rural Society*, 7, 2: 29–37.

Ward, N. (1993) 'The Agricultural Treadmill and the Rural Environment in the Post-Productivist Era', *Sociologia Ruralis*, 33, 3/4: 348–64.

Ward, N. and Lowe, P. (1994) 'Shifting Values in Agriculture: The Farm Family and Pollution Regulation', *Journal of Rural Studies*, 10, 2: 173–84.

Waters, M. (1995) *Globalisation*, London: Routledge.

Waterson, D. (1968) *Squatter, Selector and Storekeeper*, Sydney: Sydney University Press.

Watkins, C. and Champion, T. (1991) *People in the Countryside: Studies of Social Change in Rural Britain*, London: Paul Chapman Publishing.

Watson, G. and Johnson, M., (1993) 'Pricing: Cheap Water or an Environmental Perspective', in Johnson, M. and Rix, S. (eds) *Water in Australia: Managing Economic, Environmental and Community Reform*, Sydney: Pluto Press: 212–34.

Watts, R. (1998) 'The Right Thing: Globalisation, the Australian State and the Policy Process', paper presented at the Refashioning Sociology: Responses to a New World Order Conference of the Australian Sociological Association, Brisbane: Queensland University of Technology.

Wearne, J. (1996) 'Local Government in Rural and Remote Communities', in *Rural Communities Looking Ahead, Proceedings of a Rural Social Policy Conference*, Sydney: New South Wales Council of Social Service: 28–31.

Weekend Australian, 28–29 October 2000; 1–2 May 1999; 17–18 December 1994.

Weinand, H. and Lea, D. (1990) 'The Movers and the Stayers: Changes in Population in Northeastern New South Wales', in Walmsley, D. (ed.) *Change and Adjustment in Northern New South Wales*, Armidale: Department of Geography and Planning, University of New England: 61–72.

Welford, R. (1999) 'Environment Report – Blueprint for Queensland', *Media Statement, Queensland Departments of Environment and Heritage, and Natural Resources*, 11 November.

Welsh, R. (1998) 'The Importance of Ownership Arrangements in US Agriculture', *Rural Sociology*, 63, 2: 199–213.

—— (1997) 'Vertical Coordination, Producer Response, and the Locus of Control over Agricultural Production Decisions', *Rural Sociology*, 62, 4: 491–507.

West, B. and Smith, P. (1996) 'Drought, Discourse and Durkheim: a Research Note', *Australian and New Zealand Journal of Sociology*, 32, 1: 93–102.

Westholme, E., Moseley, M. and Stenlas, N. (eds) (1999) *Local Partnerships and Rural Development in Europe*, Cheltenham: Dalarna Research Institute and Cheltenham and Gloucester College of Higher Education.

Weston, R. E. and Cary, J. W. (1979) *A Change for the Better? Stress, Attitudes and Decision-Making of Dairy Farmers, 1976 to 1978*, Melbourne: School of Agriculture and Forestry, University of Melbourne.

Wheatbelt Area Consultative Committee (1998) Submission to Productivity Commission Enquiry into the Impact of Competition Policy Reforms on Rural and Regional Australia, http://.pc.gov.au.

White, M. (1997) *Listen ... Our Land is Crying, Australia's Environment: Problems and Solutions*, Sydney: Kangaroo Press.

Wickham, S. (1998) 'Land Degradation Issues and Management Concerns for Aboriginal Communities of Central Australia', in Michalk, D. and Pratley, J. (eds) *Agronomy – Growing a Greener Future, Proceedings of the Ninth Australian Agronomy Conference*, Wagga Wagga, NSW: Australian Society of Agronomy: 37–44.

Wiggins, D. (1987) *Needs, Values, Truth: Essays in the Philosophy of Value*, Oxford: Basil Blackwell.

Wild, R. (1983) *Heathcote*, Sydney: George Allen & Unwin.

—— (1978) *Bradstow: A Study of Status, Class and Power in a Small Australian Town*, rev. edn, Sydney: Angus & Robertson.

Wildman, P., Moore, R., Baker, G. and Wadley, D. (1990) 'Push from the Bush: Revitalization Strategies for Smaller Rural Towns', *Urban Policy and Research*, 8, 2: 51–9.

Wilkinson, B. (1996) 'Regional Trading Blocs: Fortress Europe versus Fortress North America', in Drache, D. and Gertler, M. (eds) *The New Era of Global Competition: State Policy and Market Power*, Montreal: McGill-Queen's University Press: 51–82.

Williams, C. (1996) 'Local Purchasing Schemes and Rural Development: an Evaluation of Local Exchange and Trading Systems (LETS)', *Journal of Rural Studies*, 12, 3: 231–44.

—— (1981) *Open Cut: The Working Class in an Australian Mining Town*, Sydney: Allen & Unwin.

Williams, M. (1993) 'Sustainability: an Overworked Word?', *Agricultural Science*, 6, 5: 46–8.

Williams, R. (1975) *The Country and the City*, St Albans: Paladin.

Williams, R. and Walcott, J. (1998) 'A Handy Framework for Regional Sustainability – What Can We Learn from People, Models and Aeroplanes?', in Falk, I. (ed.) *Learning Communities, Regional Sustainability and the Learning Society*, Conference Proceedings, vol. 2, 13–20 June, Launceston: Centre for Research and Learning in Regional Australia: 337–43.

Wills, P. (1998) 'Disrupting Evolution: Biotechnology's Real Result', in Hindmarsh, R., Lawrence, G. and Norton, J. (eds) *Altered Genes – Reconstructing Nature: The Debate*, Sydney: Allen & Unwin: 66–80.

Wilson, J., Simpson, I. and Landerman, R. (1994) 'Status Variation on Family Farms: Effects of Crop, Machinery, and Off-Farm Work', *Rural Sociology*, 59, 1: 136–53.

Wilson, P. (1997) 'Building Social Capital: A Learning Agenda for the Twenty-First Century', *Urban Studies*, 34, 5–6: 745–60.

Winson, A. (2000) 'The Sustainability of Manufacturing Dependent Rural Communities: the Impact of Restructuring in Canada During the 1990s', paper presented to the Xth World Congress of Rural Sociology, Rio de Janeiro, 30 July–5 August.

—— (1997) 'Does Class Consciousness Exist in Rural Communities? The Impact of Restructuring and Plant Shutdown in Rural Canada', *Rural Sociology*, 62, 4: 429–53.

Winter, I. (ed.) (2000) *Social Capital and Public Policy in Australia*, Melbourne: Australian Institute of Family Studies.

Wiseman, J. (1998) *Global Nation? Australia and the Politics of Globalisation*, Cambridge: Cambridge University Press.

Wolfe, J. (1989) *That Community Government Mob: Local Government in Small Northern Territory Communities*, Casuarina: North Australia Research Unit.

Woodhill, J. (1999) Sustaining Rural Australia: a Political Economic Critique of Natural Resource Management, unpublished doctoral thesis, Australian National University.

Woodhill, J. and Dore, J. (1997) *Integrated Regional Development: Capitalising on the Learning*, Phase 1 Issues Paper, Canberra: Greening Australia.

Woolhouse, S. (1997) 'Oh, But That's Because We've Only Been Here 10 Years: The Practices of Newly Arrived and Long Established Farm Families in the Great Southern Region, 1970–1995', paper presented at the Joint Conference of the Institute of Australian Geographers and the New Zealand Geographical Society, Hobart, January.

Working Group on Development in Rural Areas (1993) *A Policy Framework for Development in Rural Areas,* Canberra: Department of Primary Industries and Energy.

Wright, V. and Kaine, G. (1997) 'Economic and Market Forces Influencing Land Ownership', in Lees, J. (ed.) *A Legacy Under Threat? Family Farming in Australia,* Armidale: University of New England Press: 81–98.

Wulff, M. and Newton, P. (1996) 'Mobility and Social Justice', in Newton, P. and Bell, M. (eds) *Population Shift: Mobility and Change in Australia,* Canberra: Australian Government Publishing Service: 426–43.

Wynne, B. (1996) 'May the Sheep Safely Graze? A Reflexive View of the Expert–Lay Knowledge Divide', in Lash, S., Szerszynski, B. and Wynne, B. (eds) *Risk, Environment and Modernity: Towards a New Ecology,* London: Sage: 44–83.

Yapa, L. (1997) 'Reply: Why Discourse Matters, Materially', *Annals of the Association of American Geographers,* 87, 4: 717–22.

—— (1996) 'What Causes Poverty?: A Postmodern View', *Annals of the Association of American Geographers,* 86, 4: 707–28.

Yearley, S. (1996) *Sociology, Environmentalism, Globalization: Reinventing the Globe,* London: Sage.

Young, F. (1996) 'Small Town in Mass Society Revisited', *Rural Sociology,* 61, 4: 630–48.

—— (1994) 'The Goldschmidt Hypothesis in Chile', *Rural Sociology,* 59, 1: 154–74.

Youngberg, G., Schaller, N. and Merrigan, K. (1993) 'The Sustainable Agriculture Policy Agenda in the United States: Politics and Prospects', in Allen, P. (ed.) *Food for the Future: Conditions and Contradictions of Sustainability,* New York: John Wiley: 295–318.

Yruela, M. (1995) 'Spanish Rural Society in Transition', *Sociologia Ruralis,* 35, 3/4: 276–96.

Index

agrarianism, 5, 50, 73–4, 77, 163, 173–4, 205
agriculture
    alternative, 75, 151–7, 169
    costs, 145
    extension, 8, 62, 139–40, 201–2
    history, 8–14
    markets, 8, *see also* market forces
    organic, 146, 149–51
    practices, 4, 8, 33, 83, 139, 145, 167–8
    prices, 8, 10
    productivity, 8
    structural change, 8, 11, 53–4,
    sustainable, 83, 140, 145–6, 151–6
    science, 140–1
    technology, 8, 31, 141
    see also policy, productivism, structural adjustment
Agriculture – Advancing Australia, 61, 185
Agriculture, Fisheries and Forestry – Australia (AFFA), 153–7
agrifood sector, 32, 33, 143, 203
Anderson, John *see* Deputy Prime Minister
Australian Bureau of Agricultural and Resource Economics, 39
Australian Country Party *see* National Party

banks, 62–3, 106, 129–30
Bendigo Bank, 130
biodiversity, 144
bioregionalism, 153, 204
biotechnology, 141–3, 146–8
    see also genetic engineering
boards *see* statutory marketing authorities
Bourdieu, Pierre, 47
Britain, *see* United Kingdom
bureaucracy
    Australian, 9
    international, 22
Bureau of Industry Economics, 103, 113

Canada, 39, 108, 129
Canberra, 2
'capacity building' *see* community – development
capitalism, 17, 20–1, 25–7, 30, 34, 37, 192–3
    crises, 26, 29
catchments, 188–9, 202

cities, 2, 6, 44, 97–8, 199, 203, 205
citizen and citizenship, 12, 18, 30, 41, 148, 165
City–Country Alliance, 7
closer settlement, 120–2
Codex Alimentarius, 23
colonialism, 5, 8, 17, 21
commodity chains, 150
communitarianism, 186, 195–6
community, 25, 38, 44, 63, 76, 98, 111, 128–31, 175–7
    change, 156, 173–80
    conflict, 130–1, 165–6, 176
    development, 184, 189–90, 201–2
    division, 176–8
    empowerment, 84, 154, 184, 193
    global, 25
    power relations, 166, 184, 187
    see also social capital
competition policy *see* National Competition Policy
conservation *see* ecological issues
consumerism, 24, 40
contract farming *see* subsumption
cooperatives, 129–30
corporations *see* transnational corporations
'corporate greening', 150
corporatism, 18, 29, 40, 58, 60
Country Party *see* National Party
country towns, 97–9, 108
    histories, 119–23
countrymindedness, 73–4, 124, 133, 186
culture, 18–19, 23–5, 72–4, 160–80
    farm, *see* farm – tradition
    globalised, 24, 25
    regional, 12, 17, 177, 179
    see also detraditionalisation

decentralisation, 110–12, 114, 121, 140, 184–5
    cf devolution 184, 186
deindustrialisation, 39, 40
dependency, 117–36
    on agriculture, 110
    on metropolitan centres, 112–36, 172–3, 186
Deputy Prime Minister, 2
deregulation, 13, 61, 80
    agriculture, 58–60
determinism, 11, 19, 20, 40

detraditionalisation, 160–1, 163, 164–80, 186, 196
devolution, 23, 183, 189, 196
drought, 8, 60, 86, 139, 176
    effects, 66
    policy, 60

ecological issues, 139–57, 164
    tree clearing, 8
    see also sustainability
'ecological modernisation', 152
economic growth, 28, 30
economic rationalism, 42–5, 72
economics and economists 9, 10, 38, 39, 41, 43, 53, 72
education, 9, 40, 62, 105, 168, 193, 205, 207
egalitarianism, 6, 176, 178, 187–8
elites
    global, 19
    local, 122, 124, 202
'empowerment', 188–93, 204
environment, 2, 14, 61–2
environmental degradation, 8, 133, 138–57, 165, 167, 188–9
    see also ecological issues
environmentalism, 29
equity, 205–8
ethnicity, 30
Europe, 9, 10, 40, 56
European Union/Economic Community, 22, 86

family farms, 53–70, 138, 167
farm
    broadacre, 53
    corporate, 8, 53–4
    costs, 66
    diversification, 55
    family, 53, 168–73, 177
    lifestyle, 11
    morale, 69, 169
    numbers, 54
    'problem', 2, 39
    size, 54
    stress, 9, 11, 67–9, 82
    succession, 166–8
    sustainable management, 146, 168
    tradition, 163–4
    treadmill, *see* treadmill
    see also detraditionalisation
farmers
    coping, 54–5, 66, 67–8
    decision-making, 42, 56
    female, 56–7, 67–8, 76, 92, 154
    interests, 31–33, 58, 77–9, 146
    knowledge, 170–1
    male, 67–8, 76
    militancy, 89
    organisations, 7, 42, 76, 77, 78, 89–90, 120
    values, 72–3, 171–2, 178
    voices, 72, 93
    see also National Farmers' Federation, Landcare
federalism, 6, 204
feminisation, 21
feminism, 44, 57
fiscal equalisation, 6, 206–7
Fischer, Tim, 113
food
    and biotechnology, 147–8
    consumption, 32, 33
    organic, 150
    prices, 203
    processed, 32
    'regimes', 31–3
    safety, 150
    see also agrifood sector
Fordism, 33, 110
France, 2, 10
free selection, 74–5, 120, 138–9
fundamentalism, 38, 173, 186

General Agreement on Tariffs and Trade (GATT), 21, 151
    see also World Trade Organization
gender
    identity, 76
    relations, 56–7, 92, 169
    roles, 56, 169
    see also masculinity
genetic engineering, 146–8
    see also biotechnology
Giddens, Anthony, 47, 161–2, 163, 185–7
global cities, 34
globalisation, 12, 13, 17–23, 37, 45, 49, 72, 115, 160–1, 179, 182, 187, 191, 195, 203, 207
Goldschmidt hypothesis, 108
governance, 190
    global, 22
    national, 6, 23
    regional, 191, 197–200
    theory, 44
government
    local, 6, 35, 99, 106, 122, 131, 183–4, 194–200
    regional, 202–3
    state and federal, 182–208
    graziers *see also* pastoral industry
governmentality, 44–5
Great Dividing Range, 8, 65
green movement, *see* environmentalism
'greening', 149–51, 157

Hanson, Pauline, *see* One Nation Party
health, 68–9, 95, 104–5
Hobart, 5
hobby farms, 122

Human Rights and Equal Opportunity Commission, *see* Sidoti, Chris

ideology, 23–5, 37, 72–9, 160–80
    rural, 72–5, 77, 84–5, 91
    see also agrarianism, fundamentalism
Ignatius Centre, 2
Indigenous People, 2, 7, 5, 8, 17, 44, 45, 68, 103, 104–5, 123–4, 177
individualism, 6, 117–18, 131, 133–4, 136, 163, 182–3, 201
industrial conditions, 107, 130
infrastructure, 38, 112, 114, 205
Institute for Health and Welfare, 1
institutions, 41, 154, 188, 196–9, 203–5
    see also governance
interests,
    farmers', 72, 78, 171
    regional, 127, 128, 130, 131–2, 204
    theory, 44, 51, 127–8
international
    debt, 26
    division of labour, 31
    trade *see* trade
internet, 25, 33
    see also telecommunications
irrigation, 61–2, 144
isolation,
    women 82–3

Japan, 17, 22

Labor Party, 6, 7, 120
land
    degradation, 143–6, 167–88
    management, 145, 188–9
    rights, 5
    see also property
Landcare, 145, 154, 185, 196, 198, 201–2
leadership
    community, 2, 124, 201
    farmer organisation, 90
learning, 202
legitimation, 74, 157
    crisis, 29
Liberal Party, 7
liminality, 6, 75, 78, 92, 118, 160–1
Local Enterprise Initiatives (LEIs), 118
Local Enterprise Trading Systems (LETS), 129
local government *see* government – local
localism, 135, 173
Lukes, Steven, 44–5

management, 20,
market forces, 10, 28, 30, 38
Marx, Karl, 48

masculinity, 169
media, 77,
    content analysis of, 132–5
Melbourne, 5
micro-economic reform, 104
migrants, 2, 44, 65
migration
    internal, 95–6, 165
    international, 19, 21, 30
modernity, 19, 161
multifunctionality, 10
Murray–Darling Basin, 143–4

nation state, 18, 19, 21, 22, 24, 30, 32, 35
National Competition Policy, 106–7, 114, 185
National Farmers' Federation, 7, 77–9
National Institute of Economic and Industry Research, 101
National Party, 7, 45, 76–7, 118, 186
National Rural Health Alliance, 68
neoliberalism, 5, 9, 10, 11, 18, 39, 50, 59, 103–4, 129, 138, 182–5
    agricultural policy, 59
    contradictions of, 182, 184–5
    and globalisation, 18, 19, 21, 23
    and individualism, 117, 135
    and natural resource management, 157
    and power, 51, 183
    and reflexivity, 69
    and regions, 103
New South Wales, 5, 191, 197, 198, 202–4
'new right', 9, 40
new states, 6, 122, 203, 205
New Zealand, 86
North American Free Trade Agreement (NAFTA), 22–3
Northern Territory, 5

off-farm income, 66
off-farm work, 2, 55, 56
One Nation Party, 2, 7, 176, 186, 207
organic production, *see* agriculture – organic

pastoralism, 8, 138
    see also squatters
patriarchy, 9, 56, 76, 92, 169
Pauline Hanson's One Nation Party *see* One Nation Party
peri-urban areas, 165
Perth, 97
pluriactivity, 55–6, 168–70
policy
    -making, 9, 37–51, 76
    natural resources, 145, 153
    options, 156, 206
    people-oriented, 38–9, 195

policy (*cont.*)
  regional, 112–14, 189, 193, 200–8
  rural, 10, 27, 58, 185
  see also bureaucracy
political economy, 48
pollution, *see* ecological issues
population
  decline, 96–8
  distribution, 38, 95–8
  growth, 96–7,
  see also migration
post Fordism, 25–38
postmodernism, 37, 46–50, 206
postmodernity
  theory, 27, 37, 50, 109–12
  and towns, 109–12, 115, 160
postproductivism, 160, 168–9, 171, 203
poverty
  global, 21, 28–9
  regional, 38, 99, 102–3
  rural, 65–7, 82
power relations,
  industrial/managerial, 107, 124–5,
  regional–metropolitian, 123, 133, 166, 190–1
  perceptions of, 87–8
  subsumption, 58
  theory, 37, 43, 50, 51, 72–9
  see also dependency
prices *see* agriculture – prices, food – prices
privatisation
  and globalisation, 21
productionist 'treadmill', *see* treadmill
productivism, 8, 141–3
Productivity Commission, 1, 65, 68, 97, 100, 114
property, 5, 18, 203

quality of life, 2
  rural–urban comparison 49
Queensland, 5, 7, 56, 59, 62, 166, 190

rational action theory, 42–3
rationality, 11, 45–50, 69
reflexivity, 12, 41, 160–3, 173, 179–80, 185, 187, 201,
    203, 206
  and collective action, 195
  community, 184
  farmers', 72, 92–3, 169–70
  regional, 136, 185–7, 203, 208
  theory, 37, 45, 47, 48–9, 50, 163
regional
  development, 156, 188–95, 198
  governance, *see* governance
  government, 6
  planning, 9, 187–91
Regional Australia Summit, 1, 113

Regional Development Organisations, 190, 199–201,
    204–7
regions, 22–5, 34, 44
regulation,
  global, 21–2, 31–2
regionalism, 6, 99, 199–201, 204–5
re-regulation, 63
research, 188–9, 190
resistance
  farm, 58, 92
  international, 22
  regional, 41, 121, 128–31
restructuring, 13, 26, 34, 41, 53–70, 75, 80–99, 94
  perspectives, 63–4
  see also agriculture – structural change
'risk society', 140, 148
roads, 9
rural
  ideology *see* ideology – rural, *see also* agrarianism,
      fundamentalism
  idyll, 2, 73
  policy, *see* policy – rural
Rural Adjustment Scheme *see* Agriculture – Advancing
    Australia
rural–urban differentiation, 25, 38, 48–9, 73, 96, 101–2,
    160–1, 176–7
  perceptions of, 85
  'urbocentrism', 66
rurality, 4, 46, 48, 49, 50, 179

salinity *see* soil – salinity
science, legitimacy of , 47
self-help policy, 9, 153, 175, 189
self-reliance, *see* ideology – rural
Sidoti, Chris., 100, 104, 105
social
  bifurcation, 2, 4, 30, 56, 65, 77, 98, 102, 114–15,
      160, 196
  capital, 173–6, 185, 192, 193–6, 200–2, 206
  class, 6, 75, 128
  justice, 105–7
  mobility, 6
  polarisation *see* bifurcation
  policy, 104–8, *see also* policy – rural
  relations, 45, 177
  services, 2, 62–3, 105
  structure, 11, 12
  welfare, 18, 45, 61, 66–7
soil *see* ecological issues
soldier settlement, 74
South Australia, 5
'sponge cities', 97
squatters, 5, 120, 138
states, *see* government – state and federal
statutory marketing authorities, 59–60

stress, *see* farm – stress
structural adjustment, 8, 11, 34, 53, 60–1, 77, *see also*
    agriculture – structural change
subsumption, 57–8
suicide, 68
sustainable development, 31, 141–57, 182–208
Sustainable Regional Development (SRD) *see*
    sustainable development
sustainability, 3, 8, 138–43, 151–7, 159, 187, 188–95,
    205–8
    see also agriculture – sustainable, ecological issues
Sydney, 5

Taskforce on Regional Development, 112–13, 205
Tasmania, 5
technology, 18, 20, 27–8, 30, 40, *see also* agriculture –
    technology, biotechnology
telecommunications, 33, 112, 175, 206
terms of trade, 11
Terra Nullius, 5
Third World, 18
tourism, 4, 10, 56, 111, 166
trade, 21–3
    'green protectionism', 150
trade unions, 6, 17, 18, 27, 35, 78, 207–8
tradition, 162–79
transnational corporations, 18–20, 27, 31–4, 40, 45
transport, 9, 18, 33, 120
treadmill, 4, 53, 58, 164, 169

trees *see* ecological issues

uncoupling, 109–10
unemployment, 21, 29, 100–1
uneven development, 35, 110, 160
unions, *see* trade unions
United Kingdom, 5, 10, 17, 31, 54, 183
United Nations, 23
United States of America (USA), 6, 8, 17, 23, 31–4,
    53–4, 56
    and globalisation, 22, 27, 29
user-pays principle, 9

'visioning', 201
Victoria, 5, 197, 198

water
    degradation, 144
    policy, 61–2
    see also irrigation
weeds *see* ecological issues
welfare, 43, 77, *see also* social – welfare
Western Australia, 5
women, *see* farmers – female, gender
Working Nation, 21, 56–7, 76, 92, 113, 169
World Trade Organization, 22–3, 28, 30, 147–8, 151,
    see also trade

young people, 65

For EU product safety concerns, contact us at Calle de José Abascal, 56–1°, 28003 Madrid, Spain or eugpsr@cambridge.org.